Tudor History and the Historians

Tudor History
and the Historians

F. SMITH FUSSNER

✠✠
✠✠

BASIC BOOKS, Inc., Publishers

New York / London

Preface

IT IS CHARACTERISTIC of books on contemporary historiography that they should be obsolescent on the day they are published. No one need regret the fact; it is evident that important new books do appear fairly regularly. Among the books and articles I should like to have discussed (had they been available before this manuscript was completed) are: W. K. Jordan's magisterial *Edward VI: The Young Prince* (1968); Wallace MacCaffrey's splendid narrative, *The Shaping of the Elizabethan Regime* (1968); J. J. Scarisbrick's reevaluation of the second Tudor, *Henry VIII* (1968); Theodore K. Rabb's *Enterprise and Empire*, with its methodological discussion of computer-based research; Patrick McGrath's *Papists and Puritans under Elizabeth I* (1968); Christopher Hill's social history, *Reformation to Industrial Revolution* (1967); and Sir Anthony Wagner's monumental *Heralds of England: A History of the Office and College of Arms* (1967). Eric Kerridge has advanced new and challenging arguments and evidence in *The Agricultural Revolution*. *The Cambridge Economic History of Europe*, Vol. IV, "The Economy of Expanding Europe in the Sixteenth and Seventeenth Centuries," edited by E. E. Rich and C. H. Wilson, contains new comparative interpretations. The importance of local historical studies in England in recent years is discussed in "The Place of the Victoria County Histories in the Revolution in Historical Method," *Times Literary Supplement* (Mar. 13, 1969, pp. 269–270), a review of the recently published volumes in Shropshire and Gloucester in the Victoria County History series. A volume of *The Journal of Contemporary History* (III, 2, 1968) is devoted to reappraisals of history, historiography, and the social sciences. A bibliographical work of great importance should be mentioned: *Writings on British History, 1901–1933*, 3 vols. (1968) which supplements *Writings on British History 1934–1945*, in seven volumes. The recently published study of Sir Walter Raleigh by Pierre Lefranc, *Sir Walter Raleigh: Ecrivain* (1968) is indispensable for an understanding of Raleigh's work and ideas, and is illuminating, if controversial, on his role as a historian. An article by

C. H. George, "Puritanism as History and Historiography," *Past and Present* (No. 41, Dec. 1968), pp. 77–104, argues vigorously against the temptation to make "Puritanism" into a single all-embracing methodological concept; George criticizes the "Weber-Woodhouse-Haller syndrome of analytical errors" (p. 98). An illuminating article by Arthur B. Ferguson, "Circumstances and the Sense of History in Tudor England: the Coming of the Historical Revolution," *Medieval and Renaissance Studies* (1968), pp. 170–205, contains important evidence and arguments on some of the subjects dealt with in Chapter V (which should be supplemented by Ferguson). Finally, the Spring 1968 issue of *Daedalus* is devoted entirely to a collection of essays on historical demography; and Volume 3 of *The New Cambridge Modern History*, *The Counter-Reformation and the Price Revolution 1559–1610*, edited by R. B. Wernham (Cambridge, 1968) is now available.

In the index the reader will find subject headings which should make this book easier to use.

It should be noted that Tudor writers have been classified on the basis of publication dates, not by dates of birth or death. To have included all the Tudor generations in a chapter on Tudor writers of history would have resulted in a mere catalogue of names. The greater Elizabethan historians who published under the early Stuarts will be discussed in a later volume in this series.

Some of my colleagues at Reed College read parts of this book in manuscript, and I benefitted from their criticisms and special knowledge. I am most grateful to Marvin Levich, Philosophy; Richard H. Jones, History; T. C. P. Zimmermann, History; and Carl Stevens, Economics. It is not their fault if my errors proved irremediable. Rebecca Pollock, the Reed Librarian, has, as always, provided books (often on short notice) and good counsel on a multitude of occasions. Edith Uunila, who typed the pencilled manuscript and performed innumerable necessary chores, earned my gratitude and that of the reader. It is a special pleasure to acknowledge the benefit I derived from conversations with my colleagues at the University College of Swansea, Wales, where I spent a pleasant and profitable year as a Fulbright Professor in 1964–1965. To many others whose names do not appear here I owe help of various kinds. My wife and children imagine that they have not contributed much to this book; in this, they are mistaken.

Reed College, October 1969   F. S. F.

Contents

Tudor History and the Historians

Tudor Histories and the Historian

1

Problems of Historiography

HISTORIOGRAPHY MEANS written history and the writing of history. Dr. Johnson varied the definition only slightly: "The art or employment of a historian." The essential meaning of the word is clear enough, but the ways in which it can be used are almost as varied as the historian's art. In its original meaning "history" was not the totality of past experience or a mere relation of incidents, but a learning or knowing by inquiry.[1] Among the Greeks the account of a systematic inquiry became identified with "historical" narrative and analysis. But Herodotus, unlike Thucydides, did not confine his inquiries to past politics; he also inquired into natural and social history, and he thus provided a concept of general history that embraced science, social science, and literary art. Deriving from the Greek idea of history as inquiry is the subsequent notion of history as "a systematic account (without reference to time) of a set of natural phenomena, as those connected with a country, some division of nature or group of natural objects, a species of animals or plants, etc."[2] Although now rare, except in the sense of Natural History, this usage was widespread in the sixteenth and seventeenth centuries, when a historiographer might be referred to as one who "set forth the Description of the Earth in Figure." John Caius wrote to Conrad Gesner concerning a "manyfolde historie contayning the divers formes and figures of Beastes, Byrdes, and Fyshes, the sundry shapes of plantes, and the fashions of Hearbes, &c."[3]

History shares with science, art, and religion a concern with the interpretation of past experience; and the arts, sciences, and religions of the Western world are thus all, in some measure, historical. History, however, is distinguished from other inquiries and from mere antiquarianism by its aims and methods. The aim of pure historical research is the discovery of truths about the past; the aim of pure historiography is the narration of truths about the past. Historical truth is established by methods or procedures of verification that have reference to documents, artifacts, or other traces of past events; historical method is secular in that it excludes appeals to unverifiable speculative suppositions such as providence. The historian aims to tell the truth about what has been, by means of a critical analysis of evidence, which he has methodically gathered and assessed, then coherently arranged to support chronological, descriptive, and explanatory statements or generalizations. Such a definition may be awkward, but it is essential to the argument of this book. In practice, most Tudor historical writers were historians only part of the time. The distinction between history as inquiry and other forms of "historical" writing, or merely fictional reference to the past, must be recalled whenever the words "history" or "historical" are used, since "historiography" has been defined broadly throughout to cover some works which were not primarily historical, or were historical in method but not in aims, or in details but not in name.

All societies may be said to have some concern with the past, but myths and traditions are not history. The Greeks (as M. I. Finley has argued) did not write history before Herodotus.[4] The invention of history was a unique event; historiography became intellectually distinct from all other forms of inquiry. Myths and traditions about the past may have been a necessary condition for the emergence of historiography, but they were not a sufficient condition. In the sixteenth century the situation was different: historiography was itself a tradition. Progress was the issue, not invention. All sorts of historical conditions, attitudes, and traditions combined to make possible historiographical progress. One purpose of this book is to inquire into conditions and causes that favored the progress of historical studies in Tudor England; another is to describe trends in modern Tudor historiography.

When the Greeks associated history with memory, art with imagination, and philosophy with reason, they drew attention to the fact that history was distinguished by reference to a faculty of the mind. Memory was what made possible experience and therefore history. It will not do, of course, to stand too long on this ice bridge over a philosophical crevasse, but one may step quickly over it to the safe ground of fact. Historiography is, in fact, an artificial extension of memory; without written histories, knowledge of ancestral experience would depend on each new generation's memorizing the experience of the race.

A modern computer is perhaps the ideal type or model of historical memory, for it re-creates the recorded data of a multitude of events. It is thus an exact extension of memory, whether or not it can also be considered an extension of reason or of imagination. But if historiography is an artificial memory, it is also a selective memory; and the conceiving mind, like the computer itself, must be programmed. In this sense, all collections of books, documents, observations, or artifacts are selections that tell something about the collector. A library, a record collection, a botanical notebook—these may be said to write the history of an intellectual development. For this reason, the word "historiography" has sometimes been extended to mean the books, manuscripts, and official papers that help to define the attitudes and assumptions of men or institutions. A clear example is "the historiography of the foreign office." In *Africa and the Victorians* the authors call attention to the role of official thinking as a cause of late Victorian imperialism, pointing out that "in the course of events, the great Departments of State and the Indian Service had compiled special historiographies of their own." [5] But in the end the dynasts lost their way in history; and when their historiography no longer offered solutions to their problems, it was consigned to the archives and thus to historians.

In the sense of a version of the past, historiography has helped to make history. Protestant historiography reinforced the Protestant ethic. Both Catholic and Protestant writers disputed the strategic ground of antiquity, attempting to claim Apostolic precedents for their respective Churches. Attack and counterattack led finally to technical surprises: the critical examination of sources, and later the synthesis of particulars into a narrative or argument that would stand the test of critical methods. In fields other than religion similar developments took place: ideas about the past helped to make history in law, political theory, medicine, physics, military tactics, botany, diplomacy, and astronomy. Advances, especially during the sixteenth century, were often conjoined with new versions of the history of each field of study.

The historical consciousness of the early modern world was not defined by antiquaries, chroniclers, and historians alone. Historical writers included all those who expressed ideas about the relevance of the past to the present, and their ideas contributed to historical consciousness no matter what titles they gave their books. John Foxe's *Book of Martyrs* was historical in its method and form of argument although not in its didactic purpose. History in the narrow sense—a true account of the past based on methodical investigation—stands at one end of a spectrum, and mere invention about the past stands at the other. In between is a whole range of "historical" attitudes. Works which contributed to or expressed the historical consciousness of the age were not necessarily "written" only on parchment or paper; the stonemason's, engraver's, and woodcarver's arts gave expression to the heraldic pride of noblemen and gentlemen. Conscious of ancestral dignity, and anxious to impress a public that expected the blazoning of family arms, the lesser and greater leaders of Tudor England helped to educate the nation to an awareness of historic tradition. The importance of a favorable context for the growth of historical studies cannot be stressed too strongly: historiography moved with the general intellectual environment. Henry Thomas Buckle was right in maintaining that "There will always be a connection between the way in which men contemplate the past and the way in which they contemplate the present." [6] Because history helped to make history, the final chapter of this book is largely devoted to the growth of historical consciousness.

The most comprehensive definition of historiography, covering not only written history derived from original authorities but also the sources of historical knowledge—even the methods and philosophies of history developed by writers in other fields—is the product of a twentieth-century concern with total historical contexts. It is important to remember, however, that this kind of historicism was quite foreign to the sixteenth century, when a formal distinction between history and antiquities was maintained, at least with reference to the classical world.[7] Although the nonclassical or postclassical historian might be indistinguishable from an antiquary, the idea of historiography was still dominated by classical precedents. The political implications of historiography were beginning to be appreciated, but Henrician intellectuals were still a long way from such a concise modern formula as "whoever controls the present controls the past; and who controls the past controls the future." What was obvious to the more able Tudor intellectuals and administrators was that both antiquarian precedents and humanist histories could serve the state. Exploring the propaganda value of history, some writers traced the royal genealogy from the Trojan Brute through King Arthur to Henry Tudor, whose coming fulfilled an ancient prophecy—a British king who would overcome the Saxon invaders. The source of this historical propaganda was Geoffrey of Monmouth's *Historia Regum Britanniae,* a work which created legends and called them fact. Henry VII was not the first king of England whose claims to the throne were supported by medieval symbolism (the Red Dragon of Wales was in fact Roman in origin, though long identified with the British cause), nor was he the first king to be greeted as the fulfiller of Merlin's prophecy. The political uses of legendary history had been perceived by many fifteenth-century historians. Still, Henry VII thought it worthwhile to encourage popular belief in the British history, and to make use of the supposed British descent of the Tudor dynasty, in order to emphasize his not unimpeachable title and regality.[8] More significant for the development of historiography, however, was the new humanist history, which could also be used for political purposes.

Polydore Vergil (1470–1555) wrote accurate, critical history in the best humanist tradition. His fine Italian contempt for medieval myths earned him undeserved obloquy, especially among later English writers, who preferred the comfort of prejudice to the pride of truth. Polydore knew how to flatter Henry VIII, whom he addressed in the preface to his *Anglica Historia:* "I thought that History was the one thing lacking to the glory of your kingdom of England." But what was original and probably most valuable to Henry VIII in Polydore's *History* was his information concerning the notion of *imperium:* "It was the humanist's use of the word *imperium,* probably, that sent him [Henry VIII] dreaming and speculating until he had elaborated his theory of the Imperial Crown which, in 1521, he disclosed to Thomas More."[9] The statutes of the sixteenth century bear witness to the continuing significance of the idea of an "imperial crown." The historical details of Polydore Vergil's argument might be tedious but the conclusions were not. Henry VIII did not at first envisage an attack on the papacy, but he had no difficulty in convincing himself by 1533 not only that the Roman Catholic Church had accepted the authority of the ancient Roman emperors to determine internal church affairs but that the imperial authority had devolved on the kings of England. Until the reign of Henry II kings had been well aware of their rights; Henry VIII was therefore merely taking back rights that were his own in the Act of Restraint of Appeals. England was "an empire, and so hath been accepted in the world, governed by one supreme head and king . . . with plenary, whole and entire power, preeminence, authority, prerogative and jurisdiction." This, the preamble read, was manifestly declared in "divers sundry old authentic histories and chronicles." [10] It mattered not that the constitutional position did not really sustain the arguments that history was asserted to prove—the significant fact is that history was invoked. The theory of papal usurpation was by its very nature historical and it was bound to stimulate interest in the first publication of Polydore Vergil's *History* in 1534.

"It is not the fact that a certain concept was paramount in a certain civilization that matters most," Leo Spitzer reminds us, "but the way in which it was present at various times: the way in which its influence made itself felt in details." [11] "Historiography" was a concept which was beginning to make itself felt in Tudor society in ways that were new, although not unprecedented. Increasingly, officials called up past precedents to support present policies and saw to it that even medieval writings were made available for propaganda. The publication, in 1535, of William Marshall's translation of parts of the *Defensor Pacis* by Marsilius of Padua must, in fact, be considered to be part of the historiography of the Reformation.[12] Other examples of the use of ancient and modern writings to establish a particular version of the past may easily be found. Perhaps the clearest analysis of the importance of different traditions of English political thinking in the years from approximately 1500 to 1700 comes from W. H. Greenleaf, who has contrasted the "political theory of order" with the "political theory of empiricism." Both theories might appeal to the past, but the latter was explicitly historical, "the result of the influence of the classical authorities used, of moderns like Machiavelli and of the medieval constitutional tradition." [13] The juxtaposition of these two world views provides, in Greenleaf's opinion, the best historical perspective of the age:

> They were crucial aspects of the so-called conflict of "ancients" and "moderns," of the process by which the idea of decay was replaced by that of progress, of the intellectual ferment surrounding the de-

velopment of the "new philosophy." They embodied for many men the growing antagonism between the traditional and the new in all spheres of thought and activity. They reflected the disharmonies which arose between an established style of explanation and discussion, and the widening range of human experience.[14]

In this broad perspective many of the accepted interpretations of sixteenth-century intellectual history might profitably be re-examined. One purpose of this book will be to suggest reasons why historical attitudes manifested themselves in such an ever-increasing number of details of Tudor life.

Only recently has historiography been recognized as a distinct branch of historical inquiry. Although there are historiographical studies dating from the sixteenth century they are for the most part commentaries on the classics rather than studies in the history and methods of historical writing. To a generation familiar with the historiography of the assassination of President Kennedy it is readily understandable that both the natural and the human history of tragedy may be analyzed in terms of the interaction of ideas and events. The Warren Report's fundamental importance lay in the fact that it raised basic questions in both history and technology. Like any document in a major research tradition it was subject to historical criticism, which took the form of questioning the evidence, the interpretation, the reasons why the report was issued at a certain time, and what bearing the circumstances of the time had on the findings of the commission. One of the few things that everyone could agree on was that the Warren Report was a politically important piece of historiography.

Ideas and events are not always so closely connected, but being accustomed to historicist ways of thinking we assume that connections must exist. This was not assumed in the sixteenth century. History under the Tudors was thought of as "philosophy teaching by examples," and although good historians surmounted their own philosophical clichés, they did not write intellectual history. There was, as yet, very little concern with the problem of relating an intellectual product to its historical environment. In comparison with the range of problems dealt with by modern intellectual or cultural historians, the work of the Tudor historians and chroniclers appears to be narrow and confined. Yet the growth of modern historical disciplines was greatly stimulated by the favorable environment of the Tudor age. Any student of Tudor historiography must ask why this was so.

Powerful concepts, theories, and methods are the basis for historiographical progress.[15] The *systematic* collection of information and its logical ordering are essential conditions of progress, no less than the availability of data and the historian's effective command of the technology and techniques to test his theories. In the twentieth century the historian's concepts, theories, and methods have been made explicit, and often they come from fields such as economics, sociology, psychology, or anthropology, all of which have established independent research traditions. It is instructive to compare the twentieth and the sixteenth centuries in this respect. Although Bodin and a few others proffered useful observations, especially on how to evaluate the works of historians, they showed little concern with the kind of questions discussed in the last few years in the pages of *History and Theory*. This does not mean that earlier historians had no theories, or that they were not quick to borrow from philologists and other scholars. The French prelude to modern historiography was of fundamental importance. Bodin summed up the chief subject matter of his *Methodus* (1566) by pointing out that "Indeed, in history the best part of universal law lies hidden; and what is of great weight and importance for the best appraisal of legislation—the custom of the peoples, and the beginnings, growth, conditions, changes, and decline of all states— are obtained from it." [16] However, the range of modern theories of the state and of historical change make even Bodin seem elementary; and most Tudor chroniclers perforce seem naïve.

It is commonly said that in judging sixteenth-century writers one must not apply twentieth-century standards. In most cases the opposite is true: one must apply twentieth-century standards in order to judge sixteenth-century accomplishments. Historical differences can be known only by comparison, which is the reason for including both contemporaries and later writers in a book on Tudor historiography. The development of new concepts and new methods was, however, a very slow process; the hard-won gains of the nineteenth and twentieth centuries owed much to sixteenth-century breakthroughs, but often the price of new truth was the spread of new error.

The modern concept of *culture history* shows how far historians and anthropologists have come from the random speculations of the Renaissance, and how very closely related historical and anthropological methods have become. Alfred L. Kroeber, whose work is of particular interest to historians, has put it simply: "Anthropology is not wholly a historical science, but large areas of it are historical in interest and intent." [17] A sense of history is not characteristic of the "savage mind"—there is, indeed, according to Lévi-Strauss, a fundamental antipathy between history and the classificatory concepts characteristic of primitive totemism. Historical consciousness stands clearly opposed to hereditary systems of classification:

> This perhaps explains what one is tempted to call the "totemic void," for in the bounds of the great civilizations of Europe and Asia there is a remarkable absence of anything which might have reference to totemism, even in the form of remains. The reason is surely that the latter have elected to explain themselves by history and that this undertaking is incompatible with that of classifying things and beings (natural and social) by means of finite groups.[18]

The fact is that we live and think in radically historical terms, and we tend to explain by historical constructions even those societies that are least like our own. Anthropology "provides the approaches by which time considerations are revealed and conceptualized in otherwise static data," but historiography provides "the means by which such findings are turned into valid and useful historical perspectives of the peoples concerned." [19] Culture history thus illustrates one of the ways in which historiography has been assimilated in other disciplines; its relevance to Tudor intellectual history will be argued later.

A self-conscious concern with theory has been one of the most remarkable features of recent historiography. The importance of quantification in history was recognized over a century ago by Henry Thomas Buckle, who was perhaps premature rather than deluded in his insistence on the need for more scientific methods in history.[20] Economic history has probably achieved the most substantial results from the application of theory, and from rigorous procedures of quantification, but even intellectual history (as Buckle again insisted) can profit from explicit theories or hypotheses of explanation, and from accurate counting. Although chronology has been the characteristic concern of the historian, it does not define history; and although new information is essential to new historical theory, it does not by itself create it. In discussion of the problems of innovation in historiography the zone of sharp focus will be on whatever theories, perceptions, or ideas the historian used to organize his information. This practical use of theory by historians has been called "colligation": the discovery of appropriate headings for the organization and presentation of research. Modern historians have been concerned with colligation as a method rather than as a philosophical problem.[21] Theories of historical knowledge—the coherence theory, the correspondence theory, covering law theory, and various theories of truth or empirical verification—have been of concern primarily to philosophers. The historian of history is usually more interested in the ways in which historiography represents "projected contemporary thought about past actuality, integrated and synthesized into contexts in terms of cultural and sequential time." [22]

The chronology of historiography since the Renaissance poses basic problems of continuity and change, of evolution and revolution, of imitation and innovation.[23] No single book on so broad a topic as Tudor historiography can do more than indicate the nature of these problems; and only detailed monographic studies may eventually provide the basis for a chronology acceptable to most specialists. Arguments in favor of a "historical revolution" in the late sixteenth century were advanced in an earlier book and need not be repeated here.[24] Criticism of these arguments centers largely on the question of whether or not Elizabethan and Jacobean historians originated new methods. That borrowing and imitation took place is undeniable, but that English historiography was greatly improved is equally undeniable. Few innovations are unprecedented; few precedents exactly cover new cases. The paradox is revealed in the history of law, in church history, and in historiography: innovation went masked as imitation, novelty wore precedents, change was justified in the name of continuity. To understand the patterns of change one must examine some of the conditions that made possible the revolutionary "take-off" in English historiography that occurred between about 1580 and 1640. The historical revolution of the nineteenth century can only be treated summarily, for its history has yet to be written.

In the early sixteenth century articulate citizens with humanistic interests were beginning to make different assumptions about change than were made by their medieval forbears. They were beginning to prefer experience to authority and "to study the problems of the national community in a relation to the co-ordinates of time and place which is as familiar to the modern mind as it would have been strange to the medieval." [25] Subtle changes are by definition hard to explain, and it is especially dangerous to assume that the connotations of such words as custom, antiquity, authority, degree, order, change, decay, history, etc. were the same in the sixteenth century as they are today. The nineteenth-century historical revolution was much more profound in its effects than earlier intellectual revolutions. Moreover, "since 1800, the discovery of unlimited time has fractured the foundations of earlier world-views even more irreparably than the earlier discovery of unbounded space." [26] The discovery of time in the nineteenth century embraced not only science and history but many other ranges of human thought as well. To explain changes in historiography, knowledge of chronological context is essential, but to explain the controversies that have divided historians requires rigorous selection and sharp definition of the central problems. The one requirement competes with the other, making compromise a necessity. In the discussion of sixteenth-century historians and historiography the primary emphasis will be on texts and contexts; in the chapters on nineteenth- and twentieth-century historical writing the emphasis will be on the nature of the controversies and on the analysis of historians' methods.

One of the notable features of Renaissance historiography is the lack of histories of the classical world. Arnaldo Momigliano has recently observed that "When ancient history was studied for its own sake, independently of antiquarian research and universal history, it was meant either to provide materials for moral and political reflections or to help the understanding of texts read primarily for stylistic reasons." [27] The radical distinction between classical antiquity on the one hand, and the antiquities and histories of particular countries on the other, was at least in part a reflection of the pervasive belief in the decay of nature, which had as its corollary a belief in the superiority of ancients over moderns. The Middle Ages bore the impress of many classical remains, but to most medieval writers the history of unbelievers was of no interest—sacred history overpowered secular.[28] The humanists, idealizing the achievements of classical antiquity, preferred to think that no one could improve on historians such as Plutarch, Livy, or Tacitus. Consequently, residual medieval attitudes reinforced a tendency on the part of Renaissance humanists to examine the histories of modern nations more critically than the histories of ancient authors: "While there was a canonical history of Greece and Rome, there was no canonical history of Britain, France, Germany or Spain." The absence of canonical national history opened the way for the new historiography—"Indeed, political and religious reasons, especially after the Reformation, impelled the radical rewriting of the various national and local histories outside (and usually later than) Greece and Rome with all the aids to study which research in libraries and archives could provide." [29]

The controversies that divided sixteenth-century historians were primarily those of religion and politics; the controversies that divide twentieth-century historians are primarily ideological and methodological.[30] Seldom are widely held views completely antithetical: Marxist and bourgeois, Catholic and Protestant, liberal and conservative, scientific and humanistic histories have common points of reference. Were this not so there would obviously be no basis for controversy about the meanings of the facts. Sociologically oriented historians using computers appear to have little in common with humanistically oriented historians who hold that history is a literary art; but in fact they do understand one another, and sometimes even learn from one another. Both are aware of the differences between past and present in ways that the Tudor chroniclers were not; both share a secular viewpoint that is as distinctive as the religious viewpoint of an earlier age; and both disagree more about the relevance of general theories than they do about specific facts. The problem of selecting the best or the most representative historical writing of an age is always difficult, but ever since the Renaissance time and print have compounded the problem. The sheer quantity of nineteenth- and twentieth-century historiography dealing with Tudor England stands like a mountain, defying all who would climb it. No one can pretend to familiarity with every feature of that looming terrain; and different historians will find different landmarks from which to take bearings. The main purpose of this book, aside from the discussion of historians' methods, will be to help the reader find his way along the trails of controversy and to recognize some of the historiographical landmarks. The book should be used as a guide to further exploration, not as a substitute for it.

Can history be objective? It is a test of endurance as well as of intellect to sort and grade the various answers. Much depends on whether or not history uses tests of objectivity comparable to those used in the natural sciences, in which there are regular procedures for settling issues and in which relevant general covering laws can be specified in experimental work. Like scientists, historians claim truth as an ideal, but they often disagree about what is relevant to the explanation of an event. It would, however, be very misleading to stress disagreement more than agreement, bias more than honest error, subjective interpretation more than objective criticism. A false perspective on historiography results from total concentration on the controversies that divide historians; the areas of agreement are evidence that history, like the "logico-experimental" sciences, yields cumulative knowledge. Unanimity, as J. A. Passmore has pointed out, is not to be found in any branch of human inquiry, and "if we press the criterion of objectivity too hard, it applies to no form of inquiry; slacken it slightly and history edges its way in with the rest." [31] Objectivity is sometimes an issue between historians—certainly it was an issue between Catholic and Protestant historians in the sixteenth century, and later—but lack of objectivity is not the only reason why historians disagree. That the best Catholic and Protestant historians are today equally dedicated to objectivity, that the best Marxists and liberal-conservative historians may try equally hard to tell the truth, and that, despite growing areas of agreement, they and other historians nevertheless disagree—that is the fact that must be explained.

Historical revision provides a good point of departure for the analysis of historians' quarrels. When Sir Thomas Smith offered a novel explanation of the problem of inflation in the sixteenth century, calling attention to the impersonal workings of a market economy, he was engaging in historical revision. "This is a mervelous dearthe," he noted, "that in such plentie cometh, contrary to his kynd." [32] The historical explanation of dearth (or high prices) was only a part of Smith's economic argument in the *Discourse of the Common Weal*, some of which was mistaken. But he did provide a new way of looking at an old problem. Like other humanists he was searching for a cause, and his book provided a theoretical framework which later writers could build upon—a theory "not of an organism governed by the universal principles of justice accepted and analyzed with typical subtlety by the medieval schoolmen, but of an economic mechanism impelled by particular, often variable forces, natural in origin and observable, impersonal and amoral, yet subject to the intelligent direction of human agencies." [33] It should be evident that this kind of revision constituted an intellectual mutation, one which made possible a new analysis of the historical forces at work in the Tudor economy. Sir Thomas Smith's theory lacked the refinements we expect in modern theoretical models; and Smith did not search the archives for confirming evidence. Nevertheless, his book is an example of how historical revision, based on a relatively simple causal explanation, might finally lead to disagreement, controversy, criticism, research, and ultimately to a whole series of new theories. Sir Thomas Smith was not the least important and interesting of the intellectual forbears of Adam Smith; *The Wealth of Nations* makes explicit some of the profoundly secular assumptions of the *Discourse*. Adam Smith rejected many of Thomas Smith's favorite arguments, but he would have agreed that the best way to encourage the use of the plow would be "to let them have more profitt by it then they haue, and libertie to sell it at all times, and to all places as frely as men maie doe theire other thinges." [34]

The greater the heuristic value of a new theory or idea of explanation the less likely it is to win immediate acceptance in all its details. It is the characteristic of new approaches to the subject matter of history that they should raise new problems. Scholars not only question the relevance of an explanation if applied in new ways, or to other times or places, but are skeptical and critical of the formulation of new ideas and demand verified supporting evidence. One of the salutary functions of debate is to uncover unexamined assumptions and methodological difficulties in an argument. The debates in *Past and Present* illustrate how historians differ on many large issues, such as the "general crisis of the seventeenth century," which involved complex problems of definition, of evidence, and of historical theory.[35] The continuing controversy about Marxist interpretations of history illustrates an even more general problem, that of the sociological assumptions of the historian.

Karl Marx was surely the most influential theorist of society in the modern era. His ideas of explanation emphasized (more perhaps than he intended, and certainly more than most historians would now be willing to concede) the economic necessities. The heuristic value of Marx's theory of history has been, if anything, more important than his contributions to socialist economics. It is impossible to avoid Marxist residues even in orthodox "bourgeois" historiography. The "storm over the gentry" is a case in point: the remote origins of that storm are to be sought in Marx's analysis of the so-called primitive accumulation of capital. What Marx and Engels did was to provide a whole series of new insights and strongly worded theories that have stimulated discussion, criticism, and debate for generations. Engels in 1890 admitted that "Marx and I are ourselves partly to blame for the fact that younger writers sometimes lay more stress on the economic side than is due to it." He went on to say that "We had to emphasize this main principle in opposition to our adversaries, who denied it, and we had not always the time, the place or the opportunity to allow the other elements involved in the interaction to come into their rights." [36] What he might truly have said was that no new theory can take account of the various criticisms, objections, and adverse evidence that may be brought to bear against it. The function of criticism is different from the function of imaginative creation—the critic must, like Mephistopheles, be a spirit that denies; the creator must, like Faust, attempt to give meaning to experience. It is perhaps unnecessary to add that since the two must travel together, there is little justification for displays of bad manners.

Near to Marx in importance as an original social thinker in the nineteenth century was Alexis de Tocqueville. The sociological tradition owes much to him, especially to his extraordinary insights into the roots of power. The conflict between political power and traditional authority was a preoccupation that led him to analyze American and French society, and to make comparisons that brilliantly illuminated historical and functional differences. Although his direct influence on Tudor historiography was slight, his indirect influence, through Max Weber, was surprisingly important. Max Weber not only took up some of his ideas, but engaged in a broad frontal attack on the whole problem of historical transition: "Contrast between traditional and modern society forms, for Weber as for Tocqueville and Marx, the essential background for his theory of power." [37] The problem of defining the nature of the transition from medieval to modern society was a critical one, especially for Weber and for Marx—even though Weber denied that he was writing history; and Marx left to the Marxists the task of explaining the feudal genesis of the bourgeoisie. From Weber's work on religion, especially *The Protestant Ethic and the Spirit of Capitalism*, have come some of the major historical revisions of the twentieth century. And from Weber's generalizations about the nature of political power (which stem in part from Tocqueville's particularist analyses of history) have come some of the important analytical concepts of recent historiography: "rationalization," "community," "status," "calling," etc. This is not to say that other scholars such as Durkheim, Sombart, and Simmel have not made notable contributions to the definition of these ideas, but Tudor historians have made the most use of Weber and Marx.

Nearly every writer discussed in this book contributed something to the revision of historical opinion. The difference between the explanations advanced by historians and those put forth by economists, sociologists, political scientists, psychologists, and anthropologists is essentially that historians have tended to regard hypotheses, whether borrowed or invented, as heuristic devices for investigating particular historical problems; the "social scientists" have tended to regard hypotheses as heuristic devices for investigating and revising particular theories or models. In the course of borrowing from one another and criticizing each other's methods, historians and social theorists have sometimes demonstrated that confusion is a powerful stimulant of controversy; but in nearly every case, genuine controversy has clarified issues and made historians more aware of their methodological mistakes. A case in point is again the controversy over the gentry, which extended far beyond the issues first raised by R. H. Tawney in "The Rise of the Gentry," published in the *Economic History Review* in 1941.[38] Subsequent writers criticized Tawney and each other on issues ranging from statistics and sampling techniques to problems of sociological classification and personal bias. In the course of the debate Lawrence Stone concluded that the question was badly posed, that "fertility of hypothesis was running far ahead of factual research," and that "what was needed was a massive assault upon the surviving records, economic and personal, of the landed classes of the period." [39] The results of his own brilliantly planned offensives are recorded in *The Crisis of the Aristocracy* (1965). Although the book did not settle every question, it put the whole controversy on a new plane, and proved that careful use of the methods of social science, governed by the historian's judgment, can result in better evidence and in a decided narrowing of areas of disagreement.[40]

The most salutary theories of history are those which have heuristic value in developing new evidence or in bringing out new meanings in available data. For the historian, facts are sovereign; for the social scientist, theories; for both, it is the interplay of fact and theory that forms the corpus of the discipline. Writers who have achieved fame primarily as theorists have been accorded a place in this book as theorists: Marx, Buckle, Weber, and others have influenced Tudor historiography not by virtue of control over specific sectors of evidence but because they wrote penetrating interpretations, or produced new theories, or advocated new methods that historians found useful. Max Weber's ideal type analysis, for example, postulates a model characterized by logical coherence. The Protestant ethic as an ideal type does not exist in historical time, but historians may define actual Protestant ethics—e.g., that of Geneva in the sixteenth century, or that of the Marian exiles—by reference to Weber's general model. In this sense the value of the ideal type is demonstrated by the factual deviations from it.

Most historians have been only indirectly influenced by large theories of society; they have, in effect, developed their own methods of investigating social structure. Many nineteenth- and twentieth-century historians produced original and influential books by asking novel questions that called for meticulous archival research. Wide knowledge of unpublished records, both public and private, became the recognition code of professional historians—appropriately represented by Sir Lewis Namier and Sir John Neale. The Namier approach has been criticized for being limited in its psychological assumptions, and for placing too much emphasis on structural analysis, but Namier's work is more than "Namierism." The *History of Parliament* that Namier began (and to the editing of which he devoted the last years of his life) will stand as a memorial to his research methods; and the fact that "Namier's telescope" was one which other historians were eager to use is significant—group research on a common topic has become one of the characteristic features of twentieth-century historiography.[41]

In his books on the Parliaments of Elizabeth's reign, Sir John Neale posed some of the questions that Namier had asked about the Parliaments of the eighteenth century. Who were the members? To what classes of society did they belong? How did they come to be elected? And how were elections conducted? The transformation of Parliament, as well as the changes in the political nation as a whole, become evident upon the reading of Neale and Namier. Neale did not simply imitate Namier; similar problems suggested similar methods. A. F. Pollard, Neale's predecessor at the University of London, began the revolutionary reinterpretation of Tudor parliamentary history; and his biographical studies may have been as suggestive to Namier as they were to Neale. The point, in any case, is not who influenced whom (there are good reasons for calling Bacon the first Namierite historian) but what methods historians found to be most useful, and how teaching made available the findings of research.[42]

Intellectual influences on Tudor writers will find no place in this book, except insofar as modern Tudor historians have written about such influences. The value of intellectual biography is not in question, but space is—some information about the times, and about the circumstances in which historians lived must suffice.

Henry Thomas Buckle was virtually insulated from contemporary society and from face-to-face criticism. His *Introduction to the History of Civilization in England* bears the marks of his loneliness, his precocity, and his self-educated conceit. He lived before there were graduate seminars in history at English and American universities; and one of his idiosyncrasies was that he detested library research—he bought most of the books he used. The contrast between Buckle and the modern academic professionals is instructive: Buckle shunned the kind of research and teaching that has come to distinguish twentieth-century scholarship. How influential the modern seminar has been in spreading new ideas about history is a subject that would repay further study. The twentieth-century historical seminar has been developed into a powerful tool of research; and Tudor historiography in particular has profited from the fact that scholars of the stature of Dickens, Elton, Jordan, Mattingly, Neale, Stone, Tawney, and others both living and dead have made teaching an integral part of research. The result has been a very rapid expansion and testing of new ideas, and a remarkably efficient system of information exchange. Scholarly generosity among historians has been every bit as noteworthy as scholastic quarrelsomeness. To stress only the cut and thrust of controversy and the savagery of reviewers is to miss an essential quality of historical work: communication.

The founding of the Institute of Historical Research in London in 1921 coincided roughly with the emergence, in England and the

United States, of university graduate schools of history, some of which have become the dissemination centers for a continuing historical revolution. The cooperative nature of the research for the *History of Parliament* (a project carried on at the institute, and financed, since 1951, by a British Treasury grant) makes it evident that an important part of modern historiography consists of "filling the gaps" in historical knowledge. Clearly not every historian can achieve originality; and of those who do, few go on to achieve greatness. "The great historian," as defined by Namier, "is like the great artist or doctor: after he has done his work, others should not be able to practice within its sphere in the terms of the preceding era." [43] Who some of the great Tudor historians are may be surmised from this definition, but the adjective "great" suggests invidious comparisons and may appropriately be omitted in a book about live historians. The fact is that historians come in all varieties, and their conclusions have various degrees of historical probability and usefulness. It would be simply pedantic to maintain that J. S. Brewer, the Victorian editor of *The Letters and Papers of Henry VIII*, was not a historian because he edited Tudor manuscripts, while Hallam was one because he wrote narrative constitutional history. Both deserve a place in any history of Tudor historiography. Orders of precedence among historians depend on merits not peculiar to their special fields of interest. A few general categories, which serve to classify the different kinds of historiography, will suffice to make useful distinctions. Readers may easily add refinements of their own.

The fundamental distinction between primary sources and secondary works has been maintained throughout this book. Primary sources are of two kinds: original and derived, the former being the manuscripts and artifacts that have come down to us in the form in which they were first made; the latter are those, or any other sources, that have been changed by editing, printing, or other means. A sixteenth-century manuscript of Stow's *Survey* is an original primary source; an Everyman edition of the same book is a derived primary source. A sixteenth-century church brass is an original primary source—a modern rubbing is derived; manuscripts are the original primary sources from which modern printed editions are derived; etc. Secondary works are those which attempt to explain some part of history, including contemporary history, or which are commentaries on events to which the writer was not an eye-witness. Obviously in the history of historiography, as in other histories, secondary works may be considered to be primary sources—Camden's *Britannia*, for example, becomes a primary source in Tudor historiography if it is thought of as a sixteenth-century document about which a history is to be written. Although the distinction between "sources" and "secondary works" has been maintained as a methodological postulate (and as a convenience in organizing some chapters), it has not been used as a basis for sectioning the chapters dealing with the Tudor historical writers. The use of sources by sixteenth-century chroniclers and humanist historians, the humanist editing of classical texts, and the publication of statutes, or of documents relating to church history—these aspects of Tudor historiography will be only very summarily discussed in connection with developments in historical method. A distinction between archival research and research based on printed sources was familiar to Tudor historiographers, but it was not until the nineteenth century that basic research in Tudor history could rely to a great extent on printed collections.

The availability of good printed sources has been a powerful force in shaping historiography ever since the Renaissance. In the early seventeenth century Selden complained that Englishmen were only just beginning to edit and publish their own historical records. Today it is possible for distinguished historians to carry on research in certain fields by using printed sources exclusively, although in most fields this is obviously not the case. In the course of the seventeenth and eighteenth centuries some of the classic collections of books and manuscripts were made, and publication of English historical documents on an extensive scale was begun. Augustan scholarship was, in general, more concerned with medieval than with Tudor history, partly because the state papers of the Tudors were not yet readily accessible.[44] Most of the nineteen volumes of John Strype's collected works, however, were devoted to Tudor biographies and editions of Tudor works; Rymer's *Foedera* (London, 1704–1735) remained the major source of information about treaties and other diplomatic documents, including those of the Tudors, until late in the nineteenth century; and the *Harleian Miscellany*, *Somers Tracts*, and other eighteenth-century collections contained valuable Tudor writings. But it is clear that the great age of Tudor scholarship, which we are still in, began in the nineteenth century.

The narrative histories written by nineteenth-century historians have perhaps obscured some less famous but no less significant developments. Froude's volumes on Tudor history from the death of Henry VII to the Armada were based on extensive research in original primary sources, but Froude's achievement was made humanly possible by the massive publication of edited documents. Indeed, both the narrative histories and biographies of the nineteenth century and the "problematic histories"—i.e., monographic studies of particular problems—rested on the supporting joists of published sources. The pace of historical revision quickened with each new series of historical record publications; and the normal historical practice of "gap filling" became more like normal scientific practice —a mopping-up operation. New theory is decisive in both scientific and historical revolutions, but it depends on a body of ascertained and available evidence. The accumulation of manuscripts in libraries and record offices, and their publication by various societies, official bodies, and individuals has been to history what the accumulation of accurate observations has been to astronomy or biology. Newton and Darwin both required a body of accurate available data to work with. During the latter half of the nineteenth century the trickle of record publications in Great Britain became a steady, broad, and powerful flow. Printed source materials freed historians to move into the archives, while the publication of edited calendars simplified and greatly expedited the task of original research.

Most of the great document-publishing societies founded during Queen Victoria's reign eponymously honored scholars and benefactors of the sixteenth and seventeenth centuries. The Parker Society devoted itself to the publication of religious documents; the Camden Society ranged broadly in historical sources of the Tudor period; the Selden Society specialized in legal literature; the Hakluyt Society published manuscripts of voyages and re-edited the *Principall Navigations*; the Chetham Society, specializing in local history, honored a seventeenth-century merchant of Manchester, who bequeathed £ 8,000 for educating poor boys and founding a public library. Various national and local historical societies were founded, including the Royal Historical Society; county record societies began to flourish, often with amateur backing; and the publication of the *Victoria County History* was begun in 1900.[45] Various specialized reviews and journals made their appearance, including *The*

English Historical Review (1880) and *The American Historical Review* (1895), in addition to general magazines which printed historical pieces (*Fraser's Magazine* and *The Saturday Review* were perhaps the most notable). Interest in the records of Catholic and Protestant churches and in the martyrdom consequent upon the Reformation led eventually to the founding of the Catholic Record Society and to other specialized church history societies. In addition to the *Calendars of State Papers*—Domestic, Foreign, Venetian, etc.—there were published various guides to the public records; reproductions of records using new technical methods were attempted; and the annual *Reports* of the Deputy Keeper of Public Records provided detailed inventories, indexes, and descriptive catalogues of some of the records, as well as current descriptions of cataloguing methods. The *Dictionary of National Biography* began publication in 1885, making it much easier for scholars to identify historical and literary figures. The *New Shakespeare Society* published many documents, including Harrison's *Description of Britain*, in addition to Shakespeare studies. *The Early English Text Society*, founded in 1864, derived from the German scholarly tradition and, like the other societies concerned with publishing pre-seventeenth-century material, it became indispensable to contemporary scholarship. The *Reports of the Historical Manuscripts Commission* began the task of listing and calendaring valuable material in private collections; and after 1899 important documents, and abstracts, or extracts from documents, were published independently instead of appearing as appendices to the *Reports*. Public museums and galleries such as the National Art Gallery (1824) added to the resources available to a history-minded public.[46]

It may easily be seen that the "print-made culture" of the twentieth century had its beginnings in the later fifteenth century and that few of the nineteenth-century departures were entirely new. Nevertheless, the recovery of past experience, and the capital accumulation of documents, proceeded slowly during the Tudor period, and then underwent a jolting acceleration in the nineteenth and twentieth centuries. The problem of scarcity, which had made historiography difficult in earlier centuries, was converted into the problem of overabundance—how to take arms against a sea of print. "All views of history," according to Elizabeth Eisenstein's useful hypothesis, "have been fundamentally shaped by the ways records are duplicated, knowledge transmitted, and information stored and retrieved." [47] The antiquaries, librarians, and archivists of the sixteenth century, many of whom were enthusiastic humanists, performed some of the functions that were later to be taken over by learned societies, quasi-public libraries such as the Library of Congress and the British Museum Library, and by the Public Record Office. Leland's antiquarian work in the mid-sixteenth century was influential because his manuscripts passed by purchase or gift to other scholars, notably Camden; the use of historical records in controversy was understood by Bale, Foxe, and their contemporaries; but transcriptions from the records were the rule, printed documents the exception. And men of integrity like Lambarde, who had custody of public records, did not foresee a time when no fees would be charged for the inspection of documents. Print was indeed revolutionary in the sixteenth century, allowing contemporaries to "see" much more of the past than ever before; and print preserved for posterity much that might otherwise have perished in Tudor conditions—especially the plays and the poetry for which few libraries found room. Tudor intellectuals were unquestionably print-conscious, but they lived in a society that was still profoundly influenced by oral and scribal traditions. The stress on rhetoric and the arts of memory in Tudor education, the oral traditions of the Inns of Court, the virtual absence of an attitude that defined as "public" all the records or archives of government departments, not just legal records—these are reminders that the Tudors inhabited a world that was still, in its habits, conventions, and legal attitudes, closer to the fifteenth century than to the seventeenth or later centuries.

To say that the role of the intellectuals has changed since the Reformation is to repeat a platitude; to say what the exact nature of the changes has been is to define a major historical problem. The amount of research devoted to a topic is not necessarily a measure of its importance, but in this case it is evident that intellectuals believe that it is important to investigate intellectual genealogies and ancestral reputations. Interest in general intellectual history is, however, relatively recent. Apart from literary history and biography, and special studies in legal history, philosophy, and theology, the history of ideas was little cultivated before the nineteenth century. Attempts to treat intellectual or, more properly, cultural history as a major branch of historical inquiry first began to appear in the eighteenth century.[48] Of special interest as an early example of the historiography of the intellect is Henry Hallam's *Introduction to the Literature of Europe in the Fifteenth, Sixteenth, and Seventeenth Centuries* (1837–1839), a reference work that is still useful. Not until 1940, however, was there a learned journal in the English language devoted to the problems of intellectual history—the *Journal of the History of Ideas*. Since World War II intellectual history has become fissiparous; research areas have been divided, and intellectual historians have developed new methods and new interests in the social sciences. The history of the intellectual classes, a topic proposed by Buckle, has been clarified by scholars writing on topics ranging from administrative history to Tudor patronage, and from the history of schools and universities to population growth. According to some historians, "alienated intellectuals" may be discovered at work in all revolutionary epochs. It has been argued that the "Forerunners of the Reformation" have their place in the history of the Reformation, the Radical Reformation, and the Counter Reformation, and that intellectual leadership was decisive for the success of attempts at reform.[49]

The question that must be asked at this point is: "Who are the intellectuals?" If the word "intellectual" is used narrowly to mean a member of a "small inner elite, or self-styled elite of writers and cultural dignitaries," then it is hard to make broad comparisons between historians, lawyers, theologians, and others who contributed to the growth of historical consciousness and to historiography. If the intellectuals are identified broadly with "the whole upper stratum of society"—as in the Russian use of the word "intelligentsia"—then the word "intellectual" describes anyone who was not a worker or a peasant.[50] Neither definition is particularly appropriate for dealing with historiographical problems in the sixteenth century; a third must therefore be invoked: writing and attitudes toward work defined the intellectual. An intellectual in Tudor society was not just anyone who had been educated in a university or at one of the Inns of Court. Members of established professions were often intellectuals, but many were simply "practicing" lawyers, doctors, clergymen, etc. Those who were "professionals" in another sense—politicians, administrators, practical-minded mariners, soldiers, or businessmen—might be intellectuals, although most were not, even though they displayed qualities of intellectual leadership. The distinguishing sign was their attitude toward work: intellectuals were concerned with the history or traditions of their work, or with the work of society at large. Intellectuals were writers (though not necessarily of published works) and they were concerned with theories, interpretations, and criticisms within particular disciplines, including politics. The historiography of a discipline (in the broad sense earlier described) was a matter of direct concern to them. They thus had some "idea of history," no matter how egregious. This definition in terms of a key characteristic is neither too broad to be meaningful nor so narrow that it would not allow comparisons to be made on the basis of articulate thought; what is excluded is thought that is merely technical or concerned primarily with day-to-day operations. Utopian thought, insofar as it stated or implied a theory of history, clearly was the product of intellectuals—even though they might be as diverse in background as Sir Thomas More and Robert Owen.

The sociology of value-oriented movements (Tudor Puritanism provides an example) has been analyzed by Neil J. Smelser in his *Theory of Collective Behavior*. Sequences involving the mobilization of opinion, the articulation of norms, and the definition of values imply that the role of intellectual leadership was crucial. While not specifically dealt with by Smelser, the problem of intellectual leadership is one that necessarily involves attitudes toward history; even the radically antihistorical theorists testify to the importance of historical traditions by opposing them, usually in the name of reason. The extent to which ideas of history contributed to the strength of Puritanism is still a moot question, but the tragedy of American Puritan historiography, as Peter Gay has shown, is that here, "much as the American Puritans enjoyed their history, they experienced the revolutionary developments in seventeenth- and eighteenth-century historiography as victims, not as actors, let alone as pioneers." Their loss of mastery was mirrored in their history, which they continued to write "as though nothing had changed." [51] The cultural significance of historical thought, especially since the sixteenth century, is sufficient reason to make "ideas of history" a defining trait of intellectual work.

Modern intellectuals are no longer a homogeneous group, and their differing attitudes toward superiors in rank and power depend to a large extent on inherited traditions. In a suggestive article the sociologist Edward Shils put forward the thesis that the legitimacy of authority is not the result of firsthand experience but of "traditions and teachings which are the gradually accumulated and attenuated product of the activities of intellectuals." [52] The traditions he suggested as having been especially important in forming the attitudes of intellectuals toward authority since the Reformation are: (1) scientism, or the denial of the validity of tradition as such; (2) a romantic tradition stressing spontaneity; (3) the apocalyptic tradition; (4) the populist tradition, with its worship of the common man, and (5) an "anti-intellectual" tradition of order. Historians may find that the five traditions specified by Shils are not identifiable through several centuries, but the force of his argument about tradition remains—intellectuals have defined legitimacy with reference to certain historically specifiable traditions. Whether they denied the importance of tradition, as in revolutionary scientism, or argued for the wisdom of prejudice, as in the anti-intellectual tradition of order, they concerned themselves with "traditions of use," as Selden called them, and they defined themselves as intellectuals by that very concern. Education may be said to characterize all intellectuals, but those who are educated technicians, those who merely perform work without reflecting on it, must be placed in an outer circle with others of their kind—those who ignore the past and tend to repeat old errors in making new ones.

It may well be asked why a definition of the intellectual is so important in a book on Tudor historiography. The answer is that it allows meaningful comparisons to be made across a variety of fields, and that it provides a unifying network of argument; the "uses of the past" in Tudor society will, it is hoped, suggest ways in which the study of historiography can contribute to an understanding of general intellectual history. Works such as Holdsworth's magisterial *History of English Law* (1903–09) contain a great deal of information about the development of different ideas of legal tradition and history. Joel Hurstfield in *The Queen's Wards* pointed out that when writers in the sixteenth and seventeenth centuries tried to explain—or explain away—feudal wardship and marriage (which they believed to have originated in a somewhat unhistoric division of society), they were often wrong, "but their opposition to—or defense of—feudal marriage was governed by this vision of the past." [53] The importance of Hakluyt's chronicling of England's maritime and naval exploits was not just that Hakluyt helped to establish an attitude favorable to colonial venture. "The book must always," according to the geographer Boies Penrose, "remain a great work of history, and a great sourcebook of geography, while the accounts themselves constitute a body of narrative literature which is of the highest value in understanding the spirit and the tendencies of the Tudor Age." [54]

There is no need to multiply examples of how Tudor attitudes toward the past can be inferred from a variety of modern histories, or to insist that some historians have been more concerned than others with describing intellectual traditions. It should be clearly understood that the present book is not a comprehensive survey of Tudor historiography but rather an attempt to select and interpret historical writing in relation to key problems. It is hoped that significant trends have not been ignored, and that historians whose works are discussed will not feel that injustice has been committed in the name of an interpretation. "History is in the beginning envy, in the continuation labour, and in the end hatred," Camden wrote, and his stoicism is more memorable than excuses.[55] Still, a few more remarks on what this book is about may prevent futile searches and unnecessary critical ire.

Only in recent years has the study of historiography come to be considered respectable in the sense in which the study of past politics was and is still considered respectable. Many historians have been reluctant to admit that discussions of methodology or philosophical attitudes could be a part of "hard" history. Indeed, some would argue that an apprenticeship in political or economic history alone qualifies one to advanced opinions about political or economic historiography. While it is true that specialists in particular fields can usually point out deficiencies of information or interpretation in general accounts, it is also the case that a general account of Tudor historiography is wanting. This book is meant to supply the want—in part, however, for the full history of Tudor historiography remains to be written. Like any book on historiography this one will have failed in its purpose if it does not move readers to re-examine specific historical works. Historiographical studies should be passports to histories and to the sources, and thus to the actual past. The importance of the "Heath series" of pamphlets on historiography (for that is what they are) is that they have served to acquaint readers with historiographical traditions. Students who take the selections for the whole, failing to read the original writings, inevitably have a very moth-eaten knowledge of history and how it is written. Historians of history can only demonstrate the value of studies in historiography by being themselves historians.

Every historian may be said to have a philosophy of history, although very few can be called philosophers of history. Practicing historians are concerned with problems of evidence and proof, interpretation and theory, analysis and conjecture—they are seldom directly concerned with "synthetic" philosophy of history in the manner of Augustine, Hegel, Spengler, or Toynbee. An example of the kind of philosophical problem that must, however, be of concern to the most empirical-minded historian is that of time and history, as illustrated in the recent Beiheft of *History and Theory*, devoted to "History and the Concept of Time." Two related aspects of the problem of time are defined, one historiographical, the other methodological. Chester G. Starr argued that "remarkable distortions have been introduced into historiography through the confusion of philosophical views with historical attitudes." He went on to point out that the historian and the philosopher have described very different concepts of time, and concluded that the modern historian should be concerned with the "variable speed and direction of the events of his story." [56] Momigliano disposed of the theory that the Hebrews either ignored time or had a different idea of time from the Greeks; and his methodological aphorism is apt: "philosophers must be compared with philosophers"—not with historians or saints, as some modern theologians have tried to do.[57] If it is true that among the ancient Greeks "the philosophers drew little or nothing from historical literature save *exempla* in later days" and that exchanges between historians and philosophers almost disappeared, then what happens to our notions of context and climate of opinion? This is the problem to which Siegfried Kracauer addressed himself:

> At a given historical moment, then, we are confronted with numbers of events which, because of their location in different areas, are simultaneous only in a formal sense. Indeed, the nature of each of these events cannot be properly defined unless we take the position into account which it occupies in its particular sequence. The shaped times of the diverse areas overshadow the uniform flow of time. Any historical period must therefore be imagined as a mixture of events which emerge at different moments of their own times. Thus the overstuffed interiors of the second half of the nineteenth century be-

longed to the same period as the thoughts born in them and yet were not their contemporaries. It is an incoherent mixture. This is nothing to wonder at. Are not our minds incoherent also? . . . The integrated personality is a prejudice of modern psychology.[58]

The meaning of this passage could be illustrated in a variety of ways. Art historians have long been used to basing periodization on artistic criteria; and the use of the word "baroque" to describe seventeenth-century politics is only a case of politics imitating art. The variety of meanings attached to the word "baroque" strongly suggests that the different "baroques" describe different things and evaluate them differently. Modern literary critics have been understandably reluctant to accept interpretations that make of literature a mere reflex of history. Literature has, perhaps rightly, been likened to an "early warning system," although the New Critics have tended to be synchronic, asserting that literature is concerned with universals, or with literary forms, not with social problems that are unique to a given society. Philosophers like Etienne Gilson have argued that philosophy studies itself, its problems being set by previous philosophical thought.[59] And scientists, and some historians of science, have urged the same thing about scientific work: the scientist starts from previous scientific work; his social environment is irrelevant. The extreme position denies that any meaningful connections can be made between what happens in one field and what happens in another. This, however, was not Kracauer's conclusion: "contemporaries commune with each other in various ways; so it is highly probable that their exchanges give rise to cross-linkage between the accomplishments and transactions of the moment." [60] The historian must recognize the danger of attributing too much importance to a temporal context, thus "overburdening chronology with significance," yet he must, like Burckhardt, search for and try to describe meaningful wholes—"The Renaissance must be thought of not as an incoherent conglomerate of events but as a whole with a meaning which pervades its every element." [61]

It should be evident that methodological problems of great difficulty are raised by these considerations. There is something which might be called the "contextualist fallacy" that has emerged from modern historicism. Historians have, therefore, every reason to ask why a period or an epoch is new, and whether or not it is proper to speak of revolutions "as marking true breaks when time becomes a swift sword, cleaving through old customs to a new world." [62] One reason for calling Tudor England a unity might be that print was still enough of a novelty to be efficient in propagating ideas, yet enough of a habit to make communication easy, and expensive enough to discourage really massive abuses. The question of a "Tudor age," however, cannot be disposed of simply by references to print, or to a chronology of kings and queens bearing Welsh surnames. The problem of transition is involved in any discussion of chronological unity. The second chapter of this book focuses on that problem, but an attempt has been made to explore attitudes toward time as well. There are many versions of these old lines which describe the varying senses of time:

> When as a child I laughed and wept, time crept.
> When as a youth I walked and talked, time walked.
> When I became a full-grown man, time ran.
> When elder still I daily grew, time flew.
> Soon I will find in passing on, time gone.

The sense of time as an even flow, implicit in historical annals, is very different from this subjective sense of time as accelerated movement. Historians have seldom talked about historical time as though it were capable of moving at different rates, but they have sometimes recognized that "linear time" is not an appropriate measure of great events. The Reformation in England may have been less of a shock than the continental Reformation was to contemporaries, but it was a distinct and in some respects sudden break from the present in the name of the past—an example, perhaps, of how people "often walk backward into the future." [63]

The sense of time as "even-flow" is perhaps characteristic of periods of stability, when the social structure appears to be legitimate to the intellectuals; the sense of time as a quickening of pace is characteristic of periods of instability or revolution, when the social structure seems to stand in need of a Godly Thorough Reformation. In the later Middle Ages, there began "a long period of transition, in which moments of rapid and explosive change alternated with moments of stalemate and frustration." Puritanism, in sixteenth-century England, provided an "ideology of transition"; and that is one of the best reasons for studying its history.[64]

A table of contents sets forth the main divisions of any book, but it does not explain why important topics have been ignored. Ideally a book on historiography should be a criticism of fact as well as of theory; in practice the factual details of a history book can seldom be assessed, if only because the critic's proficiency is limited. Time, effort, and research must precede historical revision. Whether or not a particular historical thesis is true is a question that has had to be consigned, along with other awkward questions, to the curiosity of the reader. Some histories have been dealt with as entities; others have been cited piecemeal in different chapters. The rationale behind this is convenience—some books lend themselves to one kind of treatment, others to another. Since it has been necessary to choose among a great many books, some principle of selection, beyond that of personal interest, was necessary. In general, historiography since 1945 has been dealt with in greater detail than earlier historiography. Works on the history of Tudor philosophy and science have been cursorily treated; works on literature, apart from the drama, have had to be omitted.

A national literature was the great achievement of Tudor society, and Tudor literary historiography constitutes a major subject in itself. Shakespeare's history plays, although written at the end of the Tudor age, are obviously central to any discussion of Tudor historical thought—therefore the discussion of Tudor literary historiography will be focused on the plays. Coleridge made the suggestive comment that "in the purely historical plays, the history *informs* the plot; in the mixt it *directs* it; in the rest, as *Macbeth, Hamlet, Cymbeline, Lear,* it subserves it." [65] A good deal of modern literary criticism of the history plays might be thought of as commentary on Coleridge. About 220 plays dealing with British history and historical legend were written during the Elizabethan period. There is no simple explanation for the popularity of the history play. English literary historians have, for the most part, simply ignored the whole question of accounting for the Tudor taste for history. The problem of a developing historical consciousness in the sixteenth century remains crucial, however, for an understanding of the dramatic and other literary conventions of the Tudor age.

The growth of the audience for history in the years since World War II has been extraordinary. In a single year, 1965, the history titles published in Great Britain increased by 15 per cent, and in the

United States by 24 per cent over the previous year—the largest increase in any category of books. "The past is strange, and the more rapidly and drastically it has been transformed, the greater its fascination"—E. J. Hobsbawm's words describe the sixteenth century as well as the twentieth.[66] In certain respects Tudor England and the United States might both be called ahistorical societies which, in very different ways, have attempted to build themselves an identity out of history. In both Tudor England and the United States the hypothetical "average man" has acquired opinions about history which have sanctioned action. The rebellion of the Northern Earls or the Pilgrimage of Grace were protests against the turns of history just as surely as the Negro revolt in the United States is directed against historic injustices in the name of a version of history. Those who were not writers and not intellectuals have "made history" no less than the intellectual leaders. The historian's problem is how to arrive at knowledge of the "average man" without seeing him as the intellectual sees the peasant. Intellectuals, and especially intellectual historians, are apt to ask about other intellectuals, not about the inarticulate. But it is the inarticulate readers and listeners who must ultimately be understood—unless we settle for the notion that the intellectuals alone determine history. A book about historiography may avoid the larger question of how history made history by concentrating on the scholarly ideas of professional historians and ignoring the reading public. Or, it may attempt to draw inferences from written history which tell something about the opinions of inarticulate men and women, and about attitudes toward history that were not the product of reasoned investigation. The purist usually prefers his history straight: tags of learning and scraps of popular history can so easily be dismissed. But history bears witness to the vanity of purists, as well as to the brute strength of slogan-minded multitudes. A pure history of ideas risks being sterile in order to be accurate; an essay on historical consciousness risks being inaccurate in order to take account of human contrarieties. In this book projections from known writings to unknown readings must be accepted for what they are—attempts to discover outlines of the historical consciousness of the age. Dr. Johnson's observation about the proof of historical facts was that "if a man could say nothing against a character but what he can prove, history could not be written." [67] Professional historians are persuaded that history can be written only if the facts can be proved—history is not fiction. But proof, like the other daughters of Time, cannot be hurried. To introduce problems, and "to let the matter have a fair chance by discussion" is the reason for a book such as this, intended not for specialists but for general readers with an interest in Tudor history and historiography.

The various purposes of the book have already been identified; different chapters deal with different problems. However, the bones of the book's argument give shape to its various parts. Recent problems in Tudor historiography are best understood in relation to some of the classical arguments defining the nature of the Tudor transition. The growth of historical consciousness is connected with the development of new historical methods; and it is therefore particularly instructive to compare nineteenth- and twentieth-century achievements with earlier efforts to write accurate history—the problems of continuity and change in history can scarcely be better illustrated. The views and controversies of modern social and economic historians must obviously be taken into account before one asks what attitudes and conditions made possible innovations in historiography in the late sixteenth century. The history of Tudor historiography is itself a part of general intellectual history; even the true innovators have had to think and write in the idioms of their own time. Every historian will see in his sources, and will recognize as his sources, what he has learned to see and recognize; he may add to his resources, but he cannot start from scratch. The time has come, however, to heed Nietzsche's admonition: "The author must keep his mouth shut when his work starts to speak."

NOTES

1. See M. I. Finley, "Myth, Memory, and History," *History and Theory*, IV, No. 3 (1965), 285–302, esp. 295–300.
2. See under "History," definition 5, *A New English Dictionary on Historical Principles*, ed. James A. H. Murray (Oxford, 1888 ff.).
3. Johannes Caius, *Of Englishe Dogges* (London, 1576), p. 1; see also "To the Reader" on Gesner's "huge heapes of histories."
4. Finley, *op. cit.*, pp. 299–300.
5. See Ronald Robinson, John Gallagher, and Alice Denny, *Africa and the Victorians* (New York, 1961), pp. 21, 287, 471.

6. Quoted by J. B. Black, *The Art of History* (London, 1926), p. 1; see Henry Thomas Buckle, *History of Civilization in England* (New York, 1910), I, 289.
7. See George Huppert, "The Renaissance Background of Historicism," *History and Theory*, V, No. 1 (1966), 48–60. For the distinction between classical and nonclassical historians see A. D. Momigliano, *Studies in Historiography* (London, 1966), pp. 7–8 and "Ancient History and the Antiquarian," *passim*.
8. This paragraph is largely based on Sydney Anglo, "The British History in Early Tudor Propaganda," *Bulletin of the John Rylands Library*, XLIV, No. 1 (1961), 17–48.
9. Richard Koebner, "The Imperial Crown of the Realm: Henry VIII, Constantine the Great, and Polydore Vergil," *Bulletin of the Institute of Historical Research*, XXVI (May 1953), 29–52; cf. G. R. Elton, *The Tudor Constitution* (Cambridge, 1960), pp. 329–336.
10. See Elton, *op. cit.*, pp. 344–345.
11. Leo Spitzer, *Classical and Christian Ideas of World Harmony: Prolegomena to an Interpretation of the Word "Stimmung"* (Baltimore, 1963), p. 9.
12. The best modern edition, with a useful introduction, is that by Alan Gewirth, *Marsilius of Padua, The Defender of the Peace* (New York, 1967).
13. W. H. Greenleaf, *Order, Empiricism and Politics: Two Traditions of English Political Thought 1500–1700* (Oxford, 1964), p. 9; see also pp. 1–57.
14. *Ibid.*, p. 10. Cf. Hiram Haydn, *The Counter-Renaissance* (New York, 1960), pp. 84 ff. Haydn's book is valuable, although the term "counter-renaissance" has not caught on.
15. See American Historical Association, *AHA Newsletter*, IV, No. 5 (June 1966), 14 and *passim*.
16. John Bodin, *Method for the Easy Comprehension of History*, trans. Beatrice Reynolds (New York, 1945), p. 9. The importance of French legal humanism in the development of modern historiography is dealt with by J. G. A. Pocock in *The Ancient Constitution and the Feudal Law* (Cambridge, 1957), pp. 1–29.
17. A. L. Kroeber, *An Anthropologist Looks at History* (Berkeley, 1963), pp. 152–156; also A. L. Kroeber and Clyde Kluckohn, *Culture: A Critical Review of Concepts and Definitions* (New York, 1963), *passim*.
18. Claude Lévi-Strauss, *The Savage Mind* (Chicago, 1966), p. 232 and *passim*; see also Claude Lévi-Strauss, *Totemism*, trans. Rodney Needham (Boston, 1963); cf. George Homans, *The Nature of Social Science* (New York, 1967), p. 1; and Margaret Mead, *Cultural Patterns and Technical Change* (New York, 1953), p. 28 and references there cited.
19. See Julius Gould and William L. Kolb (eds.), *A Dictionary of the Social Sciences* (London, 1964), p. 172 and under "culture history" *passim*.
20. See Buckle, *op. cit.*, I, 16 and *passim*; there is an excellent study of Buckle's thought by Giles St. Aubyn, *Victorian Eminence* (London, 1958).
21. For this definition of colligation see W. H. Walsh, *An Introduction to the Philosophy of History* (London, 1951), pp. 23, 59 ff., 150. Most modern historians have found relatively little in the debates of philosophers that is directly applicable to the problems of historiography—a point that was brought out in the symposium edited by Sidney Hook, *Philosophy and History* (New York, 1963), esp. Parts II and IV.
22. Gould and Kolb, *op. cit.*, p. 172, quoting W. W. Taylor, Jr.
23. On the chronology of historiography see Wallace K. Ferguson, *The Renaissance in Historical Thought* (New York, 1948); Ferguson's earlier essay, "Humanist Views of the Renaissance," *American Historical Review*, XLV, No. 1 (1939), 1–28, provides an essential introduction to contemporary views.

24. See F. Smith Fussner, *The Historical Revolution: English Historical Writing and Thought 1580–1640* (London, 1962).
25. Arthur B. Ferguson, *The Articulate Citizen and the English Renaissance* (Durham, 1965), p. 401.
26. Stephen Toulmin and June Goodfield, *The Discovery of Time* (London, 1965), p. 266; see also, by the same authors, *The Fabric of the Heavens* (1961) and *The Architecture of Matter* (1962).
27. Momigliano, *op. cit.*, p. 6.
28. See Marie Schulz, *Die Lehre von der historischen Methode bei den Geschichtschreibern des Mittelalters* (VI–XIII *Jahrhundert*), (Berlin and Leipzig, 1909), pp. 76 ff.
29. Momigliano, *op. cit.*, pp. 7–8.
30. By "ideological" something more is meant than the merely political connotations of the word. See Erik H. Erikson, *Young Man Luther* (New York, 1962), p. 22.
31. J. A. Passmore, "The Objectivity of History," in William H. Dray (ed.), *Philosophical Analysis and History* (New York, 1966), p. 91.
32. [Sir Thomas Smith], *A Discourse of the Common Weal of This Realm of England*, ed. Elizabeth Lamond (Cambridge, 1954), p. 37. Lamond identified the writer as Hales in the first edition of this book, published in 1893, but Mary Dewar has shown that Smith was the author. See Mary Dewar, *Sir Thomas Smith, A Tudor Intellectual in Office* (London, 1964).
33. A. B. Ferguson, *op. cit.*, p. 279.
34. [Sir Thomas Smith], *Discourse*, ed. Lamond, p. 59.
35. Most of these essays were collected and edited by Trevor Aston, *Crisis in Europe* (London, 1965); there is a short Introduction by Christopher Hill. Several of the essays make reference to sixteenth-century trends, and one, by John Bossy, discusses "The Character of Elizabethan Catholicism."
36. *Karl Marx and Friedrich Engels: Selected Correspondence 1846–1895*, trans. Dona Torr (New York, 1942), p. 477.
37. Robert A. Nisbet, *The Sociological Tradition* (New York, 1966), p. 141.
38. Reprinted with a Postscript by Tawney in E. M. Carus-Wilson (ed.), *Essays in Economic History* (London, 1954), pp. 173–214.
39. Lawrence Stone, *Social Change and Revolution in England 1540–1640* (London, 1965), p. xiii and *passim*.
40. Cf. *ibid.*, p. xiv; the Introduction by Stone is itself an excellent essay on recent historiography.
41. See John Brooke, "Namier and Namierism," *History and Theory*, III, No. 3 (1964), 331–347; 335 on Namier's telescope.
42. On Bacon as the intellectual ancestor of Namier see Menna Prestwich, *Cranfield: Politics and Profits under the Early Stuarts* (Oxford, 1966), pp. 139–140.
43. Quoted by Brooke, *op. cit.*, p. 331.
44. See Fussner, *op. cit.*, pp. 69–91 and the references there cited.
45. On the *Victoria County Histories* see R. B. Pugh, "The Structure and Aims of *The Victoria History of the Counties of England*," *Bulletin of the Institute of Historical Research*, XL, No. 101 (March 1967), 65–73.
46. See Richard A. E. Brooks, "The Development of the Historical Mind," in Joseph E. Baker (ed.), *The Reinterpretation of Victorian Literature* (Princeton, 1950), pp. 130–152. Space limitations forbid discussion of libraries, but the *Catalogues of the Manuscript Collections* and the *Catalogues of the Printed Books* of the British Museum should be consulted by all interested students.
47. Elizabeth L. Eisenstein, "Clio and Chronos, An Essay on the Making and Break-

ing of History-Book Time," *History and the Concept of Time*, Beiheft VI of *History and Theory* (1966), p. 40; the phrase "print-made culture" is also hers, p. 39.

48. Cf. Johan Huizinga, "The Task of Cultural History," in *Men and Ideas*, trans. James S. Holmes and Hans Van Marle (New York, 1959), pp. 17–76, esp. p. 60. D'Alembert and others in France opened the subject of intellectual history in the *Encyclopedia*.

49. See Heiko A. Oberman, *Forerunners of the Reformation: The Shape of Late Medieval Thought*, trans. Paul L. Nyhus (New York, 1966), esp. pp. 42 ff.

50. Gould and Kolb, *op. cit.*, under "Intelligentsia."

51. Peter Gay, *A Loss of Mastery, Puritan Historians in Colonial America* (Berkeley, 1966), p. 25.

52. Edward Shils, "The Intellectuals and the Powers," *Comparative Studies in Society and History*, I (1958–1959), 5–22.

53. Joel Hurstfield, *The Queen's Wards: Wardship and Marriage under Elizabeth I* (London, 1958), p. xix.

54. Boies Penrose, *Travel and Discovery in the Renaissance 1420–1620* (New York, 1962), p. 395.

55. Quoted by J. Collinson, *The Life of Thaunus* (London, 1807), p. 173.

56. Chester G. Starr, "Historical and Philosophical Time," in *History and the Concept of Time*, p. 25.

57. Arnaldo Momigliano, "Time in Ancient Historiography," *ibid.*, p. 8.

58. Siegfried Kracauer, "Time and History," *ibid.*, p. 68. See also the important argument in George Kubler, *The Shape of Time: Remarks on the History of Things* (New Haven, 1962).

59. See Etienne Gilson, *The Spirit of Medieval Philosophy*, trans. A. H. C. Downes (New York, 1940), p. 411 and *passim*. The early warning system analogy was suggested by Marshall McLuhan in *Understanding Media* (2nd ed; New York, 1964), p. xi.

60. Kracauer, *op. cit.*, p. 72.

61. *Ibid.*, p. 71.

62. Starr, *op. cit.*, p. 33.

63. *Ibid.*, p. 34.

64. See Michael Walzer, *The Revolution of the Saints: A Study in the Origins of Radical Politics* (Cambridge, Mass., 1965), pp. 311–312.

65. S. T. Coleridge, *Literary Remains*, ed. H. N. Coleridge (London, 1836), II, 160–161; quoted by Lily B. Campbell, *Shakespeare's "Histories," Mirrors of Elizabethan Policy* (San Marino, 1958), p. 9.

66. See E. J. Hobsbawm, "Growth of an Audience," *Times Literary Supplement* ("New Ways in History"), April 7, 1966, p. 283.

67. James Boswell, *The Life of Samuel Johnson*, ed. Arnold Glover (London, 1901), II, 233.

2

The Transition Question

To STUDY PERIODS is to study problems. It may be that the period called the Renaissance is a "pseudo-problem," created by the irresponsible use of language, but there are good reasons to deny this; and there are good reasons to believe that the self-interpretation of the period in the writings of Renaissance humanists profoundly affected modern historiography.[1] Paul Otto Kristeller modified his earlier skepticism about the Renaissance debate, acknowledging that it has been, in many ways, fruitful; and his admonition to dig for more facts remains salutary: "interpretations and theories of a past period, in the long run, will not be judged on their agreement with our preferences or with those of like-minded persons, but in their accordance with the available texts and documents of the period which we are trying to describe."[2] A theory that must be tested (for its cogency can only be asserted here) is that the writings of the humanists, especially the Erasmians, and of the early Protestants and their Catholic opponents, biased the ways in which English historians conceived of periodization in English history. The transition problem in Tudor historiography can also be seen as part of the more general, philosophical problem of continuity and change through time. It will be evident that contemporary interests nearly always did alter cases—Seebohm's *Oxford Reformers*, for example, may have come "somewhat closer to the latter-day Oxford Movement than to the age of Colet, More, and Erasmus."[3] Since the transition problem is a crucial one, in intellectual as well as in social, religious, or political history, a few clarifying distinctions should be made.

Much of the disagreement and controversy about the problem of the Renaissance can be shown to turn not upon factual disagreement and mere equivocation but upon the status of such phrases as "crucial turning point," and, more particularly, upon the respective merits of different types of explanations. Marvin Levich has called attention to the difference between anticipatory and causal explanations: one event anticipates another event in the career of a discipline "when it adumbrates the distinctive features of the second event and when it occurs before it," but a causal explanation "does not presume that the events resemble each other in any significant way."[4] Anticipations of modern scientific doctrines of motion may be found in the Middle Ages, but Buridan's theory of impetus was not necessarily a cause of the scientific revolution of the seventeenth century. Similarly anticipations of the historiographical doctrines of Tudor Despotism or the "New Monarchy" do not necessarily explain why such doctrines were advanced in the nineteenth century. In general the periodization of English history into "medieval" and "modern" corresponds to a break first suggested by Renaissance humanists, who may be said to have influenced sixteenth- and seventeenth-century historiographers and to have anticipated some of the doctrines of transition found in nineteenth- and twentieth-century historiography. The "Middle Ages" was not a current phrase until the seventeenth century.[5] The influence of the humanists on historians from the sixteenth to the eighteenth centuries was a causal influence insofar as historians accepted the general assertions first put forth by the humanists or, in other contexts, by Protestant or Catholic polemicists. Historians far removed in time from the humanists were less directly influenced by them. But the distinctive features of Hume's "revolutionary" theory of the revival of antiquity were foreshadowed by Vasari, Erasmus, and the martyrologist, John Foxe.

By concentrating on four main questions the Tudor transition problem can be related to the larger debate about the meaning of the Renaissance. The questions are: (1) When was the Renaissance? (2) What was the importance of antiquity in English thought and expression of the sixteenth century? (3) Were historical changes of the Italian Renaissance and its northern sequels revolutionary or evolutionary? (4) Are crucial turning points comparable in different areas of history? The first question the humanists answered directly or by implication: The Renaissance began when antiquity was revived and scholasticism rejected. Who should be honored as the first humanist was a question variously answered in the *cinquecento*—Dante, Boccaccio, Petrarch, and Giotto were suggested, among others. But should all of these men be considered humanists? And was the most important feature of the Renaissance the "revival" of antiquity in the arts and in humane letters? Among recent interpreters of the Renaissance different answers have been given. The medievalism of the Renaissance has been stressed by such scholars as Paul Otto Kristeller and others, who in no way reject the term Renaissance; and Huizinga's epigram exposes an important truth: "as long as the Renaissance lasted, the Middle Ages actually continued." [6] What was characteristic of one field was not necessarily so of others. The importance of antiquity for science may have been less than it was for philology or art. It has indeed been argued that "The humanism and the scholasticism of the Renaissance arose in medieval Italy about the same time . . . [and] co-existed and developed all the way through and beyond the Renaissance period as different branches of learning . . . [and] all kinds of adjustments and combinations between humanism and scholasticism were possible and were successfully accomplished." [7]

The purpose of such a brief commentary on the main questions is to underline what should be obvious, that ambiguities have multiplied; the humanists did not adumbrate the complexities of modern scholarship. What they did do was to insist on periodization—on the idea, if not the name, of the Dark Ages. Erasmus, who was possibly the most influential humanist in England, was adept at making invidious comparisons between the times of Duns Scotus (hence the word "dunce") and the period of the revival of letters by the humanists. In the *Colloquies* he compared Scotus's fountain to a frog pond, and wrote that "I would much rather let all of Scotus and others of his sort perish than the books of a single Cicero or Plutarch." [8] Although he favored, on the whole, academic caution ("Not that I condemn the former [Scotus] entirely . . ."), he nevertheless drummed home the humanist lesson: the period of scholasticism was inferior both to the present and to antiquity. [9] Others developed the idea of the Renaissance still further during the course of the sixteenth century. In fact, the Renaissance was "divided into periods by Vasari; applied to music by Galilei; and to medicine by Vesalius; and extended to include printing, gunpowder, and voyages of discovery by Rabelais and Fernel." [10]

What the Erasmian humanists found in pagan antiquity was not unlike what they found in Christian antiquity: a model of life, a moral and a stylistic ideal worthy of imitation. Conscious historical ideals of life were not unknown, even in the twelfth century, as Huizinga has pointed out: "a classical renascence was harbored not only in Scholasticism and the study of Roman law: there were important classical elements even in the chivalric forms of life which to our way of thinking were so typically medieval." [11] Nevertheless, the fifteenth- and sixteenth-century humanists sought and found a much richer historical context in antiquity than medieval writers had found—"it was the enrichment that mattered, not the imitation." And Huizinga's conclusion about the significance of antiquity deserves to be quoted at length:

> Engrossed in antiquity as the result of an admiration for it and a desire to resurrect it, people became more and more aware of its *historical* character: seeking for what could unite, they found what divided. Via antiquity and from antiquity, man learned to think historically, and once he had learned to do so he had to give up historical ideals of life with a general human significance. . . . Hence it is history itself that has banished historical ideals of life as tenuous shadows.[12]

The humanist writers, in short, were bearers of new historical thought, and this was no less true in England than in Italy.

Questions about the chronology of the Renaissance, like those about the unity of the period, or about analogous earlier "renascent" movements, may be put aside—scholarship on these subjects has been prolific and even a glance at some book spines will reveal the differences of chronological and philosophical opinion.[13] The crucial point is the relation of the Renaissance to the Middle Ages, not its relation to modern civilization which, as Wallace K. Ferguson has argued, "is a subsidiary problem dependent on the historian's notion of the extent to which Renaissance culture differed from that of the Middle Ages and the direction in which the deviation occurred." [14] In *The Renaissance in Historical Thought* Ferguson noted that it was largely the Italian humanists of the fifteenth and sixteenth centuries who set the standards for secular state histories for two hundred years, and that they established the fundamental theses about the revival of learning and the arts that were to prevail until the romantic movement.[15] But the new humanist concept of history emerged most clearly in the writings (and, more particularly, in the reform programs) of Erasmus, whose most influential historical thought "was that implicit in his whole program for the reform of religion and good letters." The central conception of this Erasmian program was the humanist belief in the necessity "of returning to the original sources of pure Christianity and Classical culture." [16] Given this fact, it is not surprising that Erasmian humanists should have been sought as allies by Protestant reformers. Erasmians and reformers shared a conviction that the sources of Christianity were more important than mere traditions, though they differed on what should be done. But the reformers adopted from the Erasmians "two historical conceptions that were to help shape the orthodox Protestant view of the Middle Ages and the Renaissance, not to mention that of later generations whose thought was less consciously oriented by the Reformation. The first of these was that classical literature and evangelical Christianity revived together; the second, that it was the monks and schoolmen who were largely responsible for the intervening darkness." [17]

In England this aspect of humanist thought was perhaps most conspicuous in the historiography of Puritanism, but it was almost as evident in the writings of Anglican apologists. It must be clearly understood, of course, that this did not mean that people lost interest in medieval history (which was, in the sixteenth century, still recent, not "medieval"). If anything, interest in the medieval past increased, and most of the great works of sixteenth- and seventeenth-century scholarship were concerned with medieval history. Periodization, however, had become a subject of controversy during the sixteenth century between Protestants and Catholics; and Enlightenment historians revived this controversy in secular form. The word "Renaissance" remained uncommon in English historiography; and even today most English historians tend to think of the English Renaissance as simply one aspect of the Tudor age. But if the "Renaissance" was never thoroughly domesticated in British usage, the period was characterized as a turning point by many historians, including Hume, who based his periodization of political history in part on his understanding of the importance of a revival of the arts, letters, and sciences.

When Hume's history of the house of Tudor was first published in 1759, it caused a clamor almost equal to that against his earlier volumes on the first two Stuarts. His discussion of Tudor changes is interesting not only for what it reveals about his Enlightenment and Tory preferences, but because it re-creates and adds to earlier humanist interpretations. The discovery of the Renaissance by the Enlightenment was not as important an event in intellectual history as the discovery of the Renaissance by Burckhardt in the nineteenth century, but the Humean-humanistic interpretation continued to exert its influence in England even after Lingard and Froude had written their histories.

For Hume, the reason for studying periods that were "horrid and deformed" was that thereby men might learn to cherish science and civility. The death of Richard III (whom Hume condemned as a tyrant and murderer) prompted him to remark that "we have pursued the history of England through a series of many barbarous ages, till we have at last reached the dawn of civility and science, and have the prospect, both of greater certainty in our historical narrations, and of being able to present to the reader a spectacle more worthy of his attention." [18] Hume attributed the introduction and progress of freedom to the introduction and progress of the arts. Although he wrote primarily about past politics he was mindful of the importance of the economic as well as the fine arts: "the art of printing . . . extremely facilitated the progress of all these improvements: the invention of gunpowder changed the whole art of war: mighty innovations were soon after made in religion . . . and thus a general revolution was made in human affairs." [19] Here Hume appears to be using the word "revolution" to mean a drastic change, but earlier he had spoken of revolutions in society as though these were returns, or periods in a natural cyclical pattern:

> Those who cast their eye on the general revolutions of society, will find that, as almost all improvements of the human mind had reached to their state of perfection about the age of Augustus, there was a sensible decline from that point or period; and men thenceforth relapsed gradually into ignorance and barbarism. . . . But there is a point of depression as well as of exaltation, from which human affairs naturally return in a contrary direction, and beyond which they will seldom pass, either in their advancement or decline.[20]

The lowest period of ignorance, Hume believed, occurred in the eleventh century; under the Tudors a spirit of innovation, aided by the power of print, was detectable despite the backwardness of the age—a backwardness manifest in More's unfortunate decision to burn Bainham as a heretic. In any case, the reign of Henry VII "was a kind of epoch in the English constitution," especially since the power of the kings of England had scarcely ever been "so absolute during any former reign." [21] The Tudor policy of law enforcement Hume thought was necessary, but he attributed the "great revolution" in the constitution more to changes in general "manners of the age" than to changes in the laws, and concluded that a new respect for history was instrumental in changing men's convictions. Printing helped to disseminate heresy, and although philosophy did not profit for a long time, there was nevertheless an increasing tendency to question established authority:

> The minds of men, somewhat awakened from a profound sleep of many centuries [by the Reformation], were prepared for every novelty, and scrupled less to tread in any unusual path which was opened to them. And as copies of the scriptures and other ancient monuments of the Christian faith became more common, men perceived the innovations which were introduced after the first centuries; and though argument and reasoning could not give conviction, an historical fact, well supported, was able to make impression on their understandings.[22]

It should be evident that Hume's analysis had been anticipated in many ways by the humanists and the Protestant reformers of the sixteenth century. The "radical break" thesis was probably more congenial to the Enlightenment historian than any continuity thesis could have been; and Hume was more radical in stating it than most earlier writers. However, for all his tendency to undervalue the Middle Ages and to discover in the Tudors, and especially Elizabeth, the strong-willed creators of a new benevolent despotism, Hume did not dismiss medieval achievements, especially in the arts; nor did he, like the Whigs, bestow "unbounded panegyrics on the virtue and wisdom of Elizabeth." [23] Although incapable of the deep sympathy with twelfth-century humanist attitudes displayed by Dom David Knowles, Hume at least noted that the monkish writers were "full of allusions to the Latin classics, especially the poets." [24] Hume, in short, was a Tory historian who contributed to the Whig interpretations of history, but he was a better historian than has sometimes been supposed.[25]

Hume's contemporary and fellow Scotsman, William Robertson, also believed that the sixteenth century was a crucial turning point, not only in the history of England but of Europe.[26] The Reformation, he wrote in his *History of Scotland*, was one of the greatest events in the history of mankind, and "the revival of learning in the fifteenth and sixteenth centuries roused the world from that lethargy in which it had been sunk for many ages."[27] Like Hume, Robertson attributed a great deal of importance to the rise of reason and the new spirit of inquiry of the sixteenth century; the study of the ancients was largely responsible for "enlightening the human mind with liberal and sound knowledge."[28] From the mid-eighteenth century perspective the crucial turning point in English history was the sixteenth century. Robertson was perhaps more willing than Hume to acknowledge medieval precedents, but both historians held to an essentially revolutionary theory of historical change, finding in the Renaissance both the causes and the precedents of the Enlightenment.

Looking backward from the mid-eighteenth century, one may perceive that there was a relatively quiet period in the history of the idea of the Renaissance from the 1580s to the 1750s. The reasons for this were many, including the fact that, in England at least, many of the greatest scholars were medievalists either of necessity (the records of the Tudors were unavailable except in private collections) or from choice—the relevance of medieval history to contemporary problems was one of the great themes of Augustan, and especially Jacobite, scholarship.[29] The concept of a crucial turning point in the sixteenth century was most staunchly maintained, as one might expect, by those who were most thoroughly Protestant, and later Whig, in their opinions. The cautious Camden had avoided the issue and, like Stow, deprecated the loss of historical monuments during the course of the Reformation.[30] John Selden was too much concerned with the subtleties of his own historical arguments in the *Historie of Tithes* to pay much attention to the subtleties of chronology, although he obviously had little sympathy with the pre-Reformation "lazy clergy" whom he casti- along with all those who attempted to maintain the "declining Empire" of ignorance.[31] Selden, however, shared with most of the English scholars and lawyers of the seventeenth century an immense admiration for the secular achievements of medieval Englishmen. Harrington, in *Oceana*, pursued his political theory through ancient and English history; he believed that Henry VII had begun the fatal attack on the baronage, and that Henry VIII had thoroughly upset the balance of the Commonwealth.[32] Hobbes, whose political theory could also be stated as history, argued that the Reformation witnessed a loss of priestly control over the reading habits of the public, and that the universities, despite their long traditions of Aristotelian scholarship, were largely responsible for the new disruptive thought. England broke out of the net of Catholic Aristotelianism in the time of Henry VIII; although the king was right to challenge Rome, the universities were at fault because they became the core of the rebellion.[33] Bishop Burnet, after the Restoration, enlarged upon earlier Protestant views of the importance of the Reformation, which he saw as a great change, revolutionary in its consequences; he approved of the activity of the "restorers of learning, such as Erasmus, Vives, and others" who helped to expose monkish ignorance and ill-manners to the world.[34]

Thomas Warton's *History of English Poetry*, published between 1774 and 1781, represented the revival of classical learning during the fourteenth and fifteenth centuries as "a revolution, the most fortunate and important in most other respects, and the most interesting that occurs in the history of the migration of letters. . . . After many imperfect and interrupted efforts this mighty deliverance, in which the mouldering Gothic fabrics of false religion and false philosophy fell together, was not effectually completed until the end of the fifteenth century." Warton wrote one of the first histories of a literary genre, and his point of view was, perhaps understandably, colored by his admiration for the Italian humanists, especially Petrarch who "had in an eminent degree contributed to reclaim, at least for a time, the public taste, from a love of Gothic manners and romantic imagery." [35]

Until the twentieth century, "revolutionary" theories of transition were probably more in evidence than "evolutionary" ones. The Catholic thesis regarding the Reformation was essentially like the Protestant in dwelling on sudden change; and if Catholics were less inclined than Protestants to trace the beginnings of liberty to the breach with Rome this did not necessarily imply a superior theory of history, only a negative vote. In *The Whig Interpretation of History*, Herbert Butterfield said many true and important things about the tendency of modern historians "to write on the side of Protestants and Whigs, to praise revolutions provided they have been successful, to emphasize certain principles of progress in the past and to produce a story which is the ratification if not the glorification of the present." [36] His book is worth perusing for the sake of what it says about the historical process, and about the need for viewing with suspicion the "Whig historian's quest for origins." The *Whig Interpretation* was a manifesto, however, not a history. The Whig historians were not necessarily only Whigs or Protestants, and the quest for origins was not necessarily an illegitimate enterprise. The Whig interpretation to which Butterfield referred was simply bad history; and bad history could be written by those who had no taste for revolutionary explanations, or crucial turning points, or secular theories of progress.

The nineteenth-century contribution to the transition problem took many forms, and must be understood in terms of contemporary historicism and evolutionary ideas, as well as in terms of older patterns of historical thought. To trace the vastly complex intellectual history of nineteenth-century historiography is not yet possible. Precedents for revolutionary views, including those of Marx and the Marxists, may be found as far back as the sixteenth century; this is not to deny originality to Marx. Precedents for the medievalist's thesis of continuity (as distinct from radical change) may be found even earlier; the likeness of past to present was an unquestioned assumption of most medieval chroniclers and historians. Modern medievalists, however, do not dispute differences between past and present but the particular differences that separate medieval from modern history. Continuity, in their view, is simply not broken by the Renaissance. Probably the most significant historiographical activity of the nineteenth century was that which involved source collecting and editing. The groundwork for scientific history was laid by scholars who devoted themselves to perfecting the philological instruments of the early humanists. The sharp edge of the revolutionary thesis was first blunted by medievalists who drew attention to the complexities of the transition, and to medieval precedents for Tudor achievements. The work of Stubbs and Tout in particular opened the way for the "revolt of the medievalists" in this century. In different areas of history new questions were asked about the relationship of Renaissance to Middle Ages and in the twentieth century the whole concept of a Tudor transition was challenged—the great divide was perhaps 1945, but not 1485.[37]

The medievalists of the sixteenth and seventeenth centuries were the forerunners of those who have disputed most effectively the revolutionary view. The political implications of the ancient constitution and the feudal law have been illuminated by J. G. A. Pocock, who described how the scholars of the seventeenth century tended to assume that precedents from a much earlier age had direct relevance to their own.[38] Robert Brady, who dedicated his history to James II, sought to demonstrate by authentic records and search into "the originals of things" that all the "Liberties and Priviledges the People can pretend to, were the Grants and Concessions of the Kings of this Nation, and were Derived from the Crown." [39] The assumption Brady made was that history was a continuum; his medieval historical argument was politically compelling only if there had been no significant breaks or crucial turning points in constitutional history. Change was recognized in the sense that *plus ça change, plus c'est la même chose.*

During the eighteenth century the public records of England were much more difficult of access than they had been in the seventeenth century. In the course of the nineteenth century, as record publishing increased, "record-mindedness" again became a virtue. C. R. Cheney dated the new attitude toward the study of English medieval history from the last quarter of the nineteenth century. V. H. Galbraith was not inclined to put a high value on medieval scholarship in nineteenth-century England, having had to correct the anachronisms and Gladstonian views of some of his Victorian predecessors,[40] but he would presumably have agreed that "the increase of accessible records and the accumulated scholarship of a century have altogether changed the content of history." [41] The new record-mindedness of the nineteenth century differed from the older seventeenth-century concern with records in important respects. The Public Record Office Acts and other measures affecting the public records, passed between 1838 and 1898, provided the machinery for the custody, superintendence, care, and identification of the public records, which were placed under the jurisdiction of the Master of the Rolls. The conservation of the records was the primary duty of the Record Office, but making the records available to students was a second and no less important duty.

Means of reference, a system of public search rooms, and plans for extensive publication of records, in addition to purely organizational matters, were provided for by a series of Parliamentary acts and administrative orders. Calendars, catalogues, and indexes to the records were published, as well as selections from the records themselves. During the nineteenth century the Public Record Office was responsible for the editing and publication of over 250 volumes in the Rolls Series (of which not more than a dozen were actually drawn from the public records). In addition to this official activity various private and local bodies and individuals were concerned with records and other historical sources; indeed, since 1838 over sixty record-publishing societies have come into existence in Great Britain alone. The recently founded *List and Index Society* aims to make available the various lists and indexes to materials in the Public Record Office. Various foreign archives were gradually explored for material relating to English history, and in 1862 the Record Office inaugurated a new policy of publishing "Letters and Papers Relating to English Affairs."

At present, some seventy volumes drawn from the archives of Brussels, Milan, Rome, Simancas, Venice, and Vienna, as well as from medieval archives in France (for one volume), have been published. Although a great many of the publications of the Record Office and of other, private organizations were documents of medieval history, there was no slighting of Tudor material. The *State Papers of the Reign of Henry VIII* in eleven volumes was published by the old State Paper Commission of 1825 (the commission was renewed in 1830). Then the Record Commission of 1800–1837 published, in over sixty folio volumes (and some twenty octavo), the *Statutes of the Realm,* in addition to Rymer's *Foedera* (in an incomplete, badly edited text), five volumes of *Privy Council Proceedings,* and *Parliamentary Writs and Returns,* as well as other material. The *Calendars of State Papers, Foreign* were begun in 1861, and in 1864 the *Letters and Papers of Henry VIII* initiated an experiment by which not only state papers but documents from other classes (not necessarily from the public records) were included. Between 1864 and 1932 thirty-seven volumes were produced; a similar method was employed in the *State Papers Relating to Ireland* and in the *Carew Papers.*[42] The *Calendars of State Papers, Domestic* were also begun in the nineteenth century. In general the editing and calendaring of the mid-nineteenth century was inferior to that of Stubbs, J. H. Round, and other later editors. Only a sample of record publications can be discussed here, but students may consult the *British National Archives*

(Sectional List No. 24) for fuller information with dates of publication.

It should be evident even from this brief survey that printed records of one sort or another were being made available to students in quantity, and that a far better basis for accurate history and historical comparison existed in 1900 than had existed in 1800. Yet it is also true that before World War I relatively few historians actually spent much time working their way through the bundles of parchment and paper in the Public Record Office. The foundation of the London School of Economics in 1896 and of the Institute of Historical Research in 1921, as well as changes in the graduate school curricula in England and America, and the continuing research for the *Victoria County History* from about 1900 onward, were more directly responsible for the record-searching habits of twentieth-century historians. But medieval and Tudor historians could not have written new history to higher standards without building upon nineteenth-century work. Clearly the recognition of growing complexity was not just the result of medieval scholarship; Tudor historians were also responsible for the revision of opinion. The continuity thesis remained for the most part implicit rather than explicit in nineteenth-century historiography, and the crucial turning points favored by most historians continued to be those earlier described. But as the issues began to be more clearly defined, the transitions were seen to be different in different areas of research. Broader knowledge of the European Renaissance led to comparisons and to the realization that the English Renaissance was uniquely shaped by the English Reformation. A survey of nineteenth-century opinion reveals that the opening up of new archives and the development of new techniques, especially in economic history, led to a far greater variety of opinion than had existed earlier.

The foremost English historians of the early nineteenth century, Henry Hallam and John Lingard, had little in common except a devotion to history and to the ideal of impartiality. The "judicious Hallam," as Macaulay called him, counted among his friends the influential Whigs who gathered at Holland House and Bowood.[43] Lingard was a north country Catholic priest, educated at Douai, who combined a lifelong scholarly career with his parish duties. He published the first three volumes of his *History of England* in

1819; these brought the story down to the time of Henry VIII.[44] The remaining volumes were published at intervals between 1820 and 1830, and were revised by Lingard as new material became available. Lingard very soon discovered how difficult record research could be at this time. The faults of the original Record Commission were notorious by 1830, when Harris Nicolas wrote a series of pamphlets complaining about the conditions of work in the records and urged that further reforms were necessary: "The Government prefers that the Records should perish rather than that they should be allowed to illustrate British history." [45] This was an exaggeration, but the conditions governing use of the public records were, indeed, still deplorable. Anyone who reads the early Deputy Keeper's reports will quickly realize that the repositories were not only many in number and scattered, but that they were insecure, in danger of fire, "liable to damp" and consultable only at the greatest inconvenience.[46] Valuable documents were still apt to be carried about and damaged by clerks; catalogues were still scarce, often inaccurate or unintelligible, and fees were still high. Despite these handicaps, Lingard made good use of State Paper Office documents in 1806 and later; and in 1817 he went to Europe to explore the archives in Paris, Milan, and Rome.

In the "Preliminary Notice" to the 1849 edition of *The History of England*, Lingard described in detail the new sources that had become available to him and explained what his history owed to these and other recently published works. It was fitting that his final words as a historian should have been about the sources:

> In disposing of the new matter derived from these several sources, I have strictly adhered to the same rules to which I subjected myself in the former editions; to admit no statement merely upon trust, to weigh with care the value of the authorities on which I rely, and to watch with jealousy the secret workings of my own personal feelings and prepossessions. Such vigilance is a matter of necessity to every writer of history, if he aspire to the praise of truthfulness and impartiality.[47]

It was to Lingard's credit that he retained much of his impartiality even while writing "a book which the Protestants would read." Conscious of the "stately and dignified tread of the historic muse," Lingard believed that the Catholic case must be built on ascertained facts, not on assertions by Counter Reformation historians.[48] He was "the first Englishman to have attempted to use material from the Simancas archives in the interests of English history," [49] and his revisions of earlier Protestant views have withstood remarkably well the test of time.

The difficulties of using the Simancas archives were even more formidable than those faced by historians wanting to consult records in England. Lingard nevertheless managed, with the help of Catholic friends, to get information (though not transcripts) which enabled him to revise accepted views, including the conventional picture of the Spanish marriage of Henry VIII and the "black legend" of Philip II. As one might expect, Lingard saw the Reformation as a "religious revolution," which "produced the most important innovations in our religious polity," [50] but he was very cautious about discussing this as a crucial turning point in English history. He listed among the causes of the spread of Lutheranism the recent invention of printing and the "numerous body of scholars called Humanists," but in general his narrative took little account of the transition problem. Time, for Lingard, flowed evenly and smoothly, like a broad river; every fact or event was equally important, and was carried by the same steady current. Lingard was well aware of the political nature of his narrative but he sought to explain each event as it occurred, without writing essays of general interpretation. He implicitly adopted the continuity thesis.

Whig history has been described as a "story of fortunate development achieved by steps that were intrinsically correct." [51] Whig constitutional historians were most Whig when they dealt with the seventeenth-century revolutions, but they did not necessarily believe that the transition from medieval to modern England occurred in the seventeenth century. Although Hallam was convinced that Henry VII's reign had not "formed a great epoch in our constitution," and that the King's policies were somewhat overrated, he was quite certain that the end of the Plantagenets marked a turning point. The reign of the first Tudor was undoubtedly a new era in English history:

> It began in revolution and a change in the line of descent. It nearly coincides, which is more material, with the commencement of what is termed modern history, as distinguished from the middle ages, and with the memorable events that have led us to make that lead-

ing distinction, especially the consolidation of the great European monarchies, among which England took a conspicuous station.[52]

Hallam went on to provide an outline of the classical Whig interpretation of the Tudor age. Henry VIII appeared as a tyrant, whose sins were forgiven because he was responsible for the Reformation.[53] There was a reason why Henry's machinations had failed to subvert English liberties: "The courage and love of freedom natural to the English commons, speaking in the hoarse voice of tumult, though very ill supported by their superiors, preserved us in so great a peril." [54] Nothing seemed "more to have sustained the arbitrary rule of Henry VIII than the jealousy of the two religious parties formed in his time . . ." [55] The Reformation was, however, more than a difference of opinion. It was a true revolution, brought about not by theological controversy but "on a persuasion that fraud and corruption pervaded the established Church." [56]

In explaining the general European Reformation, Hallam argued (anticipating the Marxist myth of the substitute Napoleons) that the leaders were merely instruments of change: "No revolution has ever been more gradually prepared than that which separated almost one half of Europe from the communion of the Roman see; nor were Luther and Zwingli any more than occasional instruments of that change, which, had they never existed, would at no great distance of time have been effected under the names of some other reformers." [57] The revolutionary thesis was here stated in its pure form. Yet behind the whole Whig interpretation of the transition there lay a curious notion of continuity, which was evident in Hallam's idea that the constitution, once it had been perfected, never really changed. It was just a matter of filling up the outline —the constitution was already complete in outline in Plantagenet times; the boundaries of the prerogative had been set, and although the Tudors might overstep boundaries they did not attempt to become absolute by destroying the constitution. Liberty had been "the slow fruit of ages." Under Henry VII it was "still waiting a happier season for its perfect ripeness, but already giving proof of the vigor and industry which had been employed in its culture." The "general privileges of the nation were far more secure than those of private men," thanks to the persistence through time of the ancient constitution.[58] The origin of the Whig interpretation was to be found in Coke; Hallam differed from Coke primarily in allowing for a previous process of development. But, once developed, the constitution provided continuity and stability in the face of change; even in 1641 "scarce any material change" was made in the ancient constitution.[59]

Hallam's *Constitutional History* appeared in 1827; it was the first full-scale history of the English Constitution. Hallam had little to say about the history of administration, and his idea of the constitution was at once too narrow, in that he thought the constitution was somehow embodied in fundamental laws which arbitrary power could not change, and too broad, in that he thought of Whigs and Tories as spokesmen for different ideas of the political role of government: "the Whig had a natural tendency to political improvement, the Tory an aversion to it." [60] Hallam admitted that it was not easy to distinguish Whig from Tory "because those denominations, being sometimes applied to factions in the State intent on their own aggrandizement, sometimes to the principles they entertained or professed, have become equivocal and do by no means, at all periods and in all occasions, present the same sense." Still, the clash of principles echoed throughout English history. Hallam perceived change in the government, but his history was incapable of explaining the relationship between politics, government, and constitution. Hallam's scholarship, although not quite as firmly based in the sources as Lingard's, was still outstanding; and Hallam established the major outlines of English constitutional history for almost two generations. His historical duel with Hume, especially over the issue of the "mixed constitution," was to be revived much later by McIlwain and others. Macaulay called the *Constitutional History* "the most impartial book that we have ever read." [61] Impartiality was not the least of Hallam's virtues, and from Hallam to Stubbs and Gardiner there is a clear line of descent.

More than any other nineteenth-century English historian James Anthony Froude set the nineteenth-century version of Tudor history. A brilliant stylist, he saw history as a dramatic narrative based on facts ascertained by careful research. He was criticized unmercifully by Freeman ("Froude is certainly the vilest brute that ever wrote a book"), but Pollard in 1904 urged that Froude's mistakes "were no greater than those of other historians, and there are not half-a-dozen histories in the English language which have been based on so exhaustive a survey of original materials." [62] Froude's twelve volumes on the Tudors appeared at intervals between 1856 and 1870; they illustrated some of the philosophical and methodological assumptions that Froude discussed in his lecture on "The Science of History," delivered in 1864.[63] Froude had no faith in Buckle's ideal of historical general laws and theories. He maintained that the historian should not theorize, should not tell his readers what to think of the facts, and should not write *about* this man or that: "Let us hear the man himself speak, let us see him act, and let us be left to form our own opinions about him." [64] Froude, however, did not hesitate to state his own opinions about important issues; after all, history itself was "a voice forever sounding across the centuries the laws of right and wrong." [65] There might be revolutions and reformations but the moral law endured; so, in fact, did the law of reason of state, which Froude invoked to explain the Reformation. A consistent thinker Froude was not, but he provided the first full-scale "political" interpretation of the Reformation, which he regarded as the most important turning point in English history.

Froude began work on the Tudors after he came to Plas Gwynant in Wales in the spring of 1850:

> Two years out of the three during which we lived at Plas Gwynant, I had been reading diligently into the times of the Tudor Princes with a view to the life of Elizabeth. More and more I had become interested in the political aspect of the Reformation as distinct from the doctrinal. If it was a revolt against idolatry and superstition, it seemed to me still more of the laity against the clergy, and of the English nation against the Papal supremacy. It became, therefore, essential to understand what the laity and clergy of England were like, what were their respective characters, what the causes were which had created such a burst of indignation and a revolution at once so violent and so restricted within the control of the law. An enquiry so considerable became difficult if not impossible in my Welsh hermitage.[66]

The Reformation Froude regarded as "the grandest achievement in English history, yet it could never have been brought about constitutionally by modern methods." [67] The great work of reform was carried out by Henry VIII and Elizabeth, supported by the strongest and bravest of their subjects (including the Puritans); Froude thought, perhaps rightly, that universal manhood suffrage, had it been in effect before the Armada, would have brought back the pope.

The drama of history was so strongly sensed by Froude that he even argued that history should be written "like a drama." This meant that there should be no moralizing or theorizing about this or that period of history. Yet by the very choice of his image Froude implied that there were crucial turning points in the plot, and that history, like Shakespearean tragedy, demonstrated tragic necessities. Unlike most earlier historians, Froude tried to suggest the different awareness of time that prevailed in periods of stability as contrasted with periods of storm and change.[68] An image that recurs often in his *History of the Reign of Henry VIII* is that of a storm, building up from the early spattering thunder showers of Lollardry to the full force of the Henrician gale.[69] Wycliffe and the Lollards, however, were "no proper part of the history of the Reformation," but rather a prelude, a "separate phenomenon." This much was consistent with Froude's view that, despite religious and constitutional precedents (which he discussed at some length), the Reformation under Henry and Elizabeth was unique. In the twelfth century the clergy had won the battle "because they deserved to win it," but subsequently they forfeited their right to prevent reform. The nation was ready for sweeping remedies by the sixteenth century, and for secularization. But this did not mean that Englishmen lost their religion; rather, they were able, through Protestantism, to enjoy the fulfillment of it. Froude remained true to his Whig preferences, and to his early dislike of Catholic versions of history, including Lingard's. The Catholics saw in Henry and Elizabeth only "monsters of iniquity," Froude believed, but he himself would explain their greatness both as Englishmen and as reformers.[70] Froude ended by praising Henry for his statesmanship and chastising Elizabeth for her want of understanding, but he admired both as the instruments of "the greatest achievement in English history, the 'breaking of the bonds of Rome' and the establishment of spiritual independence." [71]

In truth, Froude thought of the whole period from the accession of Henry VIII to the defeat of the Armada as transitional in English history. The medieval state he attempted to describe, but he found the task both uncongenial and difficult: "Between us and the old English there lies a gulf of mystery which the prose of the historian will never adequately bridge." Medieval England was foreign—"the transition out of this old state is what in this book I have undertaken to relate." [72] Froude's explanation of the transition was largely in terms of individual actions and motives. His general argument was clear: the Reformation was an act of state, necessary but not inevitable. The Act in Restraint of Appeals was revolutionary: "The state of the law could not have been clear, or the statute of appeals would not have been required." [73] The extremity of the case was what justified the ex post facto nature of the act. "The alternative," Froude repeatedly said, "was an all but inevitable civil war, on the death of the king; and practically, when statesmen are entrusted with the fortunes of an empire, the responsibility is too heavy to allow them to consider other interests. *Salus populi suprema lex*, ever has been and ever will be the substantial canon of policy with public men, and morality is bound to hesitate before it censures them." [74] In retrospect, the king had been sensible and responsible, leading the nation but not outrunning it. What were the long-term results? "Beyond and besides the Reformation," Froude concluded, "the constitution of these islands now rests in large measure on foundations laid in this reign." [75]

The English Reformation was part of a larger European movement, which Froude discussed at greater length in his volumes on Elizabeth. The Catholic age was passing; Europe was no longer to be unified by a common faith. The contest was ultimately one between freedom and authority, between a progressive Protestant England and a decadent Catholic Spain: "Singing its own dirge, the doomed Armada went upon its way, to encounter the arms and the genius of the new era, unequally matched with unbelievers." [76] Before he died Henry VIII had done "whatever man could do to ensure the rational progress of the revolution"; and Elizabeth, thanks to fortune and the good advice of her ministers, had secured the gains of her father. [77] Froude believed that it was the business of the reader to draw the conclusions, and that it had been his own "to search for the facts among statutes and state papers misinterpreted through natural prejudice and imperfect knowledge, and among neglected manuscripts fast perishing of decay." [78] His faith was that of the nineteenth century; but as A. L. Rowse has observed, Froude has more affinities with the twentieth century than with the nineteenth. [79]

After Macaulay and perhaps Froude, the most widely read English historian of the nineteenth century was John Richard Green.

His *Short History of the English People,* published in 1874, was an immediate popular hit; Green eschewed "drum and trumpet history" to concentrate on the "figures little heeded in common history—the figures of the missionary, the poet, the printer, the merchant or the philosopher." [80] Although he was an able scholar and well read in the records, according to Stubbs, Green depended to a large extent on printed sources; he was not an innovator in his *Short History* so much as a popularizer—that is, he was a spreader of current ideas. His version of Tudor history was dominated by three theses: the "New Monarchy" thesis; the "New Learning" thesis; and the idea that the "Renascence" (the spelling was advocated by Matthew Arnold) was a significant part of English history. These terms became part of the historical vocabulary of Englishmen, thanks in large part to Green's skill at clear exposition. The New Monarchy had emerged from the ruin produced by the Wars of the Roses, which "if they did not utterly destroy English freedom . . . arrested its progress for more than one hundred years." [81] Green's overestimate of war damage fitted with his underestimate of the constitutionality of Tudor rule. Edward IV was the first of the New Monarchs and, beginning about 1471, parliamentary life was almost suspended: "if we seek a reason for so sudden and complete a revolution, we find it in the disappearance of feudalism." [82] Freedom had been won by the baronage and protected by the Church; the barons were reduced to a mere wreck by civil war, while the Church was struck down by Cromwell. It is worth quoting at some length Green's explanation of the New Monarchy, since it is one that has persisted, in various revisions, right down to the present:

> If we use the name of the New Monarchy to express the character of the English sovereignty from the time of Edward the Fourth to the time of Elizabeth, it is because the character of the Monarchy during this period was something wholly new in our history. There is no kind of similarity between the Kingship of the Old English, of the Norman, of the Angevin, or the Plantagenet sovereigns, and the Kingship of the Tudors. The difference between them was the result, not of any gradual development, but of a simple revolution; and it was only by a revolution that the despotism of the New Monarchy was again done away. . . . But revolutionary as the change was, we have already seen in their gradual growth the causes which brought about the revolution. The social organization from which

our political constitution had hitherto sprung and on which it
rested had been silently sapped by the progress of industry, by the
growth of spiritual and intellectual enlightenment, and by changes
in the art of war.[83]

Here was the theory of the New Monarchy (which Green
identified with "The Tudor despotism"), expressed with force, almost with violence. Again and again Green stressed the revolutionary character of this transition, arguing that the strength of the
New Monarchy rested on the revolution in the art of war—"The
introduction of gunpowder had ruined feudalism." [84]

The New Learning thesis was, understandably, also couched in
revolutionary terms. Quoting the picturesque if silly phrase of Taine
—"For the first time men opened their eyes and saw"—Green
went on to argue that "Experimental science, the science of philology, the science of politics, the critical investigation of religious
truth, all took their origin from this Renascence—this 'New Birth'
of the world." [85] The high hopes of the early sixteenth century humanists were foiled, yet the New Learning persisted—especially,
in England, in alliance with religion: and even Henry VIII "remained the steady friend of the New Learning." [86] The picture of
Henry VIII as the masterful despot was never drawn in bolder
strokes than by Green: the work of slavery "was quietly wrought
through the Law"; the New Monarchy at last realized its power,
for the Church "became a mere instrument of the central despotism"; and a "reign of terror, organized with consummate and mer-
ciless skill, held England panic-stricken at Henry's feet." [87] This
picture of revolutionary despotism in the early English Renascence
persisted, despite the best efforts of more than one generation of
Tudor scholars. The New Monarchy thesis was later elaborated
by Pollard, and, in its various forms, it has become a stock argument
of historians who see the Tudor age as above all one of revolutionary transition. The Renaissance, the Reformation, and the Recep-
tion of Roman Law formed the tripod of a new orthodoxy of
change; the survival of medieval limiting agencies was only gradually appreciated. The problem of the nature of Tudor despotism,
or absolutism, was not discussed by Green. Recent historians have
probably argued more about the defining characteristics of the early
sixteenth-century monarchies than they have about the medieval-
modern antithesis, or about the constitutionalism-absolutism antith-

esis; yet the old vocabulary remains, and "the business of working toward an adequate historical language with which to describe the balance of continuity and change looms as one of the great methodological challenges facing the next generation of historians." [88]

The contrasts between Green and Stubbs are striking. Green was a young historian and topographer, who published his greatest book when he was thirty-seven; he died at forty-six without having made his way into the academic estate. William Stubbs owed his bishopric to his *Constitutional History* (1874–1878); and, as Regius Professor of Modern History at Oxford, he "became the paragon of the establishment in the academic world for the following hundred years." [89] Stubbs' interpretation of medieval constitutional history was not directly relevant to his ideas about the transition, which reflected Whig convictions. No amount of careful scholarship could mask the moral. Stubbs shared the nineteenth-century faith in progress, although he doubted that any historian had yet arisen who could account "on the principles of progress, or of reaction, or of alternation, for the tides in the affairs of men." [90] He had the scholar's distrust of any bias toward a priori theories that might substitute for mastery of the facts; and he was skeptical, as well, of efforts to make too much of the problem of periodization. He accepted the conventional notion that the Middle Ages ended with the coming of the Tudors. They might give no promise of light, but "it was 'as the morning spread upon the mountains,' darkest before dawn." [91] Believing as he did that "the power of good is more progressive and more prolific" than that of evil, Stubbs thought that he recognized a law of progress—all things worked for the best, despite appearances:

> The failure of the house of Lancaster, the tyranny of the house of York, the statecraft of Henry VII, the political resurrection under Elizabeth, were all needed to prepare and equip England to cope successfully with the principles of Richard II, masked under legal, religious, philosophical embellishments in the theory of the Stewarts.[92]

Here, implicit in the Whig notion of progress, was a medievalist's doctrine of continuity; the transitions of history were leading somewhere; mere succession was belied by the fact that Englishmen somehow drew upon their history in every crisis.

In his *Seventeen Lectures on the Study of Medieval and Modern History,* delivered yearly between 1867 and 1884, Stubbs outlined his theories of how history should be studied, praising the methods of the German universities, noticing the recent spread of interest in history, and connecting this with the extension of the work of learned societies, work in local history and genealogy, and in records. After calling for greater efforts and a broader view of European history, Stubbs proceeded to discuss in some detail his views on continuity and change. These lectures will repay study, if only because they refute the notion that he was unaware of the problems of defining the complex relationship between these polar opposites of history. He argued that medieval history was a useful study precisely because it cast light on modern history. In the great drama of human history as a whole it was important to select "The history of those nations and institutions in which the real growth of humanity is to be traced: in which we follow the developments, the retardations and perturbations, the ebb and flow of human progress, the education of the world, the leading on by the divine light from the simplicity of early forms and ideas where good and evil are distinctly marked, to the complications of modern life . . ." [93] In this broad context the reign of Henry VII appeared (albeit in a later lecture) as a "critical transitional age," which would have been very much what it was no matter who was on the throne of England.[94] The invention of printing, no less than new factors in the European balance of power, constituted the "starting point of a new stage in History." [95] The really important matters, such as the influence of the printed book on society, were apt, Stubbs noted, to be ignored by contemporaries; critical change was often embodied in new ideas or techniques that "did not come easily into historical contemporaneous exposition." [96] Stubbs was arguing in much the same way that Green had argued; nor did he see any reason to call the early Tudors anything but despots. But Stubbs had a much more subtle grasp of the nature of the relationship between medieval and modern history than might be supposed merely from his remarks on the Tudors.

In his lecture of 1880 "On the Characteristic Differences between Medieval and Modern History," he summed up his thinking on the subject as follows:

Medieval History is a history of rights and wrongs; modern History as contrasted with medieval divides itself into two portions; the first a history of powers, forces and dynasties; the second, a history in which ideas take the place of both rights and forces. The point of time at which we should mark the separation in the latter is the French Revolution. There is a continuity of life through all three; the fundamental principle, which still holds its ground in the struggle of ideas, is distinctly traceable in the primitive struggle of rights and wrongs; and far more and more distinctly in the modern struggle of the balance of power; but in the first and second period, ideas have little weight compared with rights and forces; in the first rights are more potent than forces, in the second forces are more potent than rights; and now rights, forces and ideas are matched in the arena of modern politics in such a way as to make right and force themselves ideas.[97]

Although Maitland was unimpressed by this passage and believed that Stubbs was not happy among abstractions of such a high order, it is at least evident that Stubbs was working toward an original formulation.[98] The statement was no mere generalization for the sake of effect. Stubbs was trying to "colligate," to bring under appropriate headings a mass of evidence, and to make verifiable sense of the differences between medieval and modern history. His success is another matter. The clear point of Stubbs' argument was that continuity, especially continuity of historic right, was a proper object of historical knowledge. The notion of freedom broadening down from precedent to precedent was not inherently silly, and Stubbs suffered more from stylistic incontinence than from historical simplicity. In England "the rights struggled for are historical rights and the liberties secured are historical liberties." [99] Stubbs was arguing a legitimate point; as a medievalist he had come to believe that in the area of rights there was no abrupt transition but rather a slow growth. From Stubbs' urging of this point much modern criticism of the transitions has proceeded. Stubbs owed his vast reputation to the *Constitutional History*, to his *Select Charters*, and to his work as an editor of volumes in the Rolls Series; in all these and in his lectures he showed himself capable of producing ideas. The recent strictures of Richardson and Sayles testify, in fact, to the effectiveness of Stubbs' teaching; in the *Governance of Medieval England* (1963) the authors felt obliged to attack Stubbs as someone who "failed to view medieval men and medieval institutions operating in a medieval setting." His conclusions were to be regarded "as hypotheses rather than facts" —Stubbs said this much himself to Sir Charles Firth—but the warning was forgotten by his admirers, who failed to see that the *Constitutional History* was "a hasty textbook" which contained "a mountain of chaff." [100] The wrath of two distinguished medievalists, bestowed on one who had lain for over fifty years in the grave, is perhaps as telling a tribute as any paid by Stubbs' admirers. The obvious charge against Stubbs was that he imported into history ideas about contemporary life. True, he was influenced, especially in his lectures, by contemporary talk about Imperialism and the Balance of Power; and, like other historians, he sometimes used Darwinian metaphors. But that in his *Constitutional History* he merely purveyed High Church prejudice and Victorianism is an exaggeration. He tried to use general ideas to characterize events and periods. So do most historians, and, in retrospect, their ideas sometimes have an old-fashioned look. But without generalizations history would be reduced to mere chronicles and editorial business. The importance of Stubbs for Tudor historiography is that, as a medievalist, he saw the Tudor transition as a problem to be investigated, not as a *fait*:

> With the battle of Bosworth the medieval history of England is understood to end. It is not, however, the distinct end of an old period, so much as the distinct beginning of a new one. The old dividing influences subsist for half a century longer, but the newer and more lasting consolidating influences come from this time to the front of the stage. The student of constitutional history need not twice go over the same ground; he may be content to wait for the complete wearing out of the old forms, whilst he takes up the quest of the new, and dwells more steadily on the more permanent and vital elements that underlie them both.[101]

Stubbs was, in effect, calling for a new view of Tudor history, enlightened by medieval studies.

One of the ablest pupils of Stubbs was Thomas Frederick Tout, whose *Chapters in the Administrative History of Medieval England* appeared in six volumes between 1920 and 1931. Criticizing Stubbs for neglect of the administrative history of the later Middle Ages, Tout argued that "administration is more important than legislation" and that medieval history should be studied in its own terms and on the basis of comparisons, especially between French and English institutions.[102] Tout stressed form and function, and the idea of "evolutionary continuity." Carrying on with the New Monarchy thesis, Tout saw in "the powerful chamber of the late 15th century and in the passing of administration from the hands of the chancellor to those of the king's secretary . . . one of the explanations by which the 'new monarchy' of the Yorkist and Tudor kings carried out its will." [103] Later on he pointed out how the growth of material civilization, wealth, prosperity, and comfort "cried aloud for a more orderly state of society than that bequeathed by the Middle Ages." [104] With the strengthening of the crown under Edward IV and the Tudors a new England began to emerge, but, Tout argued, the New Monarchy "involved no startling new departures." Tout's contribution to the transition question was not just a further stress on continuity, but, more important, a highly specialized attack on the problem of administrative history. G. R. Elton, W. C. Richardson, and S. B. Chrimes may, in important respects, be said to have taken up the problem of administrative history where Tout had left it.[105] Tudor administration was a subject that both medievalists and Tudor scholars needed to know more about. The history of the Exchequer had been established on solid foundations by Thomas Madox in 1711, but Tout complained that the history of the Chancery and the Wardrobe "had not had their history written at all." [106]

The grand masters of nineteenth-century historiography wrote narrative and analytical surveys of large historical periods. Their views were broad, and their scholarship looked thorough; even that impossible goal, "coverage," appeared to be within reach. But what had occurred was an optical, or rather historical illusion; the things men knew least about, they seldom asked about. The illusion of completeness was made possible by ignorance. Stubbs, Froude, Macaulay, and Ranke (not to mention other Europeans, or Americans) apparently had invaded their areas so successfully that only mopping-up operations would afterwards be called for. But one after another the syntheses of the nineteenth century were attacked. Illusions were uncovered; special studies cut down the unsupported generalizations; and if the main body of nineteenth-century scholarship was not destroyed, it was shown to be exposed and vulnerable. From historians such as Maitland, T. F. Tout, and other specialists came studies that cast doubt on some of the views of their own masters. The transition generalizations, which had seemed relatively safe to earlier nineteenth-century historians, began to seem ever more dubious in the light of specialized research.

Two movements of significance are evident in late nineteenth- and twentieth-century historiography: specialization, and a growing concern with economic and general social history and theory. Specialization involved not only a narrowing of the fields of inquiry but the application of special techniques of analysis to special fields. Economic history became a separate discipline, but even in established fields, such as the history of law, significant revisions were made. The growth of specialization followed the rising curve of university enrollments; and whereas a little social or economic theory had sufficed for most historians early in the nineteenth century, a working knowledge of Marx, Weber, and other theorists less famous began to be considered important for well-educated historians in the twentieth century.

In most fields these changes were beginning in the closing decades of the nineteenth century. Sir John Seeley, no less than the Webbs, advocated the virtues of "practical" history, which would have a direct bearing on current affairs. Like Robinson in America (who advocated a "New History" based on current politics and social science), Seeley believed that the problems of British policy were ones that history could help to clarify. In *The Growth of British Policy* (1895), Seeley attempted to trace the origins of modern British policy and of the "Britannic idea." Modern policy, he thought, had its origins during the reign of Elizabeth and grew to maturity in the late seventeenth century. The diplomatic revolution of the sixteenth century he described in fact, if not in name, for he had an enviable capacity to generalize usefully and intelligently. He saw the Reformation and Counter Reformation as important factors in the balance of power; but the crucial change in English history was brought about by Elizabeth, not by her father: "all the modern life and greatness of England can be traced to those forty-four years." [107]

In fields other than foreign policy and diplomacy new ideas of periodization were also put forward. After the turn of the century A. F. Pollard was establishing a reputation as the foremost Tudor specialist since Froude, but he became best known for two books that dealt with more general topics: *Factors in Modern History*

(1907) and *The Evolution of Parliament* (1920). The latter was the outcome of studies begun in 1903 at the suggestion of F. W. Maitland. The history of Parliament attracted able scholars in both England and America at this time. C. H. McIlwain and F. J. Baldwin wrote on the subject and helped to establish an American tradition of English historiography. The starting point of all these studies of Parliament was Maitland's introduction to the *Memoranda De Parliamento*, which he edited for the Rolls Series in 1893.[108] Pollard called it "the most original and suggestive essay that had ever been written on the medieval English parliament." [109] In the *Evolution of Parliament*, Pollard argued that the Tudor despots achieved national liberty by emancipating England from its medieval liberties: "By centralizing power the Tudors expanded English liberties and converted local privileges into a common national right." [110] This procedure was "revolutionary." With regard to the papacy Pollard argued that the Reformation did mark a distinct break. Quoting Maitland's jest about the Anglo-Catholics (they believed that the English Church was Protestant before the Reformation and has been Catholic ever since), Pollard went on to urge that medieval precedents did not cover Tudor cases:

> The arguments for English ecclesiastical independence generally fall very wide of the mark. Nothing, for instance, could be more misleading than the contention that Henry VIII did no more than William I had done when he claimed to determine which pope should be recognized in his dominions. Henry eradicated the jurisdiction altogether: William merely asserted a voice in the determination of who should wield it. . . . The middle ages were, like other times, a period of change; and what is true of one century is false of another.[111]

The argument, as Pollard developed it, was that the medieval church and state were institutions that differed completely in law, language, ritual, and organization. Divided loyalty early became a major problem. As the secular power became more national, the ecclesiastical clung more and more to its own international character. The conflict of ideals produced a practical conflict of jurisdiction. Every manifestation of nationalism opened a fresh breach with the Catholic Church.[112] The continuity of history was, in this sense, a continuity of change and crisis—the repudiation of the

Roman imperial and papal tradition was implicit in the conflicts of the later Middle Ages. Following the then current debate about sovereignty Pollard argued that "without the Reformation there could have been no such thing as modern sovereignty," but he thought that it was "an error to regard sovereignty as the creation of the age of Luther and Machiavelli." [113] It was an even greater error, however, "to regard the English constitution as complete in the reign of Edward I." Change was dialectical, the result of interacting "factors."

Pollard's views on the evolution of Parliament were those of a man who saw revolutionary and evolutionary developments as compatible; it was very much a question of definition. The Tudors created a revolution in the form of government, but they did not make unprecedented demands on Parliament and the nation. The word "revolution" was an accommodating one—it had been used to characterize many kinds of change; Pollard saw that what really mattered was the comparison between specific medieval and Tudor cases. "Evolution" might suggest slow change and the idea of precedents broadening down from generation to generation, but Pollard did not mean quite this when he used the word in his title, *The Evolution of Parliament*. For him, evolution definitely included sudden changes—revolutions, if not actual mutations. He denied, in *Factors in Modern History*, that there were sudden vanishings or surprises in history—like nature, history did nothing by leaps.[114] Yet the steady drift of his argument, especially in his later books, was that there were critical or "revolutionary" turns in history, when the pace of change rapidly shifted. The Tudor age was a clear example; time had collected its forces for a swift surprise. Henry VIII, Pollard argued, "directed the storm of revolution which was doomed to come, which was certain to break those who refused to bend, and which may be explained by natural causes, but cannot be judged by moral considerations." [115]

The reputation of *Factors in Modern History* was so great that it partially obscured Pollard's contributions to Tudor studies. J. H. Hexter attacked the Whiggish assumptions of Pollard's *Factors* and suggested ways in which modern research has rendered some of the "factors" obsolete. If Hexter's essay dwells too much on Pollard's Darwinian language and neglects Pollard's "revolutionary" arguments, that is perhaps because Hexter zeroed in on one book. Pollard did write about "emerging nationalism" and the "rising middle class" in ways that suggested evolutionary gradualism. But no historian escapes inconsistency; and Pollard's arguments were more subtle, less obviously straight-line projections of ascending trends, than one might expect from reading only his first course of lectures. Readable and interesting Pollard certainly was, and still is —perhaps his misfortune was to be too often reprinted. The merit of Hexter's critique is not entirely that it disposes of fallacies, cites omissions, and condemns a possibly outmoded vocabulary, but that it specifies the new directions in which historiography has moved during the last fifty years:

> The study of sixteenth-century history during the past fifty years, then, has not sustained Pollard's decision to assimilate Protestant-ism and the defection of universalism to each other, and to reduce them to epiphenomena thrown up by the rise of the middle class and of nationalism. . . . Moreover . . . historians of various as-pects of the sixteenth century, as we have noted, have felt impelled to deal with other polarities besides Catholic-Protestant and Church-State. Among them are town-hinterland, lay-clerical, secu-lar-religious, *Realpolitik*-legitimacy, realm-province, dynasty-region, *gubernaculum-jurisdictio*, court-country. No more than the Catho-lic-Protestant polarity will these others fit the patterning of history that makes the sixteenth century the great divide between feudal universal-medieval on the one hand and middle-class-national-modern on the other.[116]

In the last sentence Hexter takes his stand with those who ques-tion the whole thesis of a Tudor transition. In his essay on "A New Framework for Social History" he stresses the importance of social continuity: "In the history of the English aristocracy from 1066 on, there are bends; but there is no break in the continuity of its existence." [117] The "revolutionary" thesis, which originated with the humanists, was first questioned by antiquaries, later on by medievalists, and finally by sixteenth-century experts who, like Hexter, dismissed the transition question as irrelevant: "Today, doubts about the wisdom of selecting this particular line of divi-sion merge with yet graver doubts about the actuality, and even the convenience, of the very concepts, medieval and modern." [118]

From general histories to special studies, from theory implicit to theory explicit, from the amateur to the professional. This would seem to sum up the history of modern historiography—progress resulted from the appropriate division of labor. Hexter's skepticism is peculiar to the twentieth century; he describes a lack of confidence that comes from too much information rather than too little. The historiography of the twentieth century has been dominated by professionals to an extent unheard of in the nineteenth century. The virtues of twentieth-century professional historiography derive from training, organization, expert knowledge, information exchange, and intensive research. The man who helped to found the Institute of Historical Research and the Historical Association, who recognized the need for professional training and foresaw a great history school at the University of London, A. F. Pollard, began his career before professionalism was established in English history schools and lived to see its results. The historical revolution of the twentieth century (according to Hexter) seems to consist of piecemeal advances, as historians examine particular times and places and try to find a new vocabulary of conceptions better suited to bringing out their true character.[119] If the seventeenth century was the heroic age in historical scholarship, and the nineteenth century the age of individualism, the twentieth century has become the age of the graduate school and of corporate professionalism. The popularity of general histories has not declined, but the best general histories can and do rest on solid monographic research. To pursue the history of the transition question in twentieth-century historiography, concentrating on a few major writers, might be misleading. Individual historians stand for methods, specialties, and concepts that are part of professional technique. In the following chapter some of the lines of recent research will be discussed as they bear on arguments about the historical content and meaning of the Tudor transition. It is too early to discard and bury old terms such as "medieval" and "modern," around which controversy still flames. The ideological divisions of the twentieth century operate like a bellows to keep old controversies burning; to understand some modern trends in Tudor historiography it is necessary to go back to the first volume of Marx's *Capital* (1867).

Marx's contribution to the transition question took the form of an argument about historical theory, which could be related to any future forms of transition. England was not unique; Marx believed strongly in general covering laws. The bourgeois revolution would everywhere obey laws of historical development. Marx set the precedent for speculating in historical futures; his successors assumed that the right formula would enable them to make a killing. Long before 1917 Russian Marxists were split over the issue of what kinds of conditions and tactics would be necessary for the success of a bourgeois revolution. Making predictions on the basis of different interpretations of Marx, and a very limited knowledge of history, the Russian factions might never have made a revolution but for the hard-headedness of Lenin. The problem of interpreting the transition from feudal to bourgeois society, from medieval to modern history, was difficult enough; choosing the right formula for action called for skills other than those of the historian. One of the few books that deals with the tactical issues of the transition problem is Stanley Moore's *Three Tactics* (1963). Marx on the question of tactics was by no means unequivocal; there are reasons why minority revolution, majority revolution, or reformist formulas are plausible. And each tactic can be justified on the basis of Marxist history and theory. What lends particular importance to the Marxist interpretation of English history is that it was in England that the first major bourgeois revolution occurred. In one obvious sense the transition from medieval to modern society took place in the decades from 1640 to 1660, but in another the crucial transition occurred earlier—the "capitalist era dates from the 16th century." [120] The problem that Marx bequeathed to the Marxists was how to account for the transition from feudal to bourgeois modes of production and social relations before the actual revolution of the seventeenth century put power in the hands of the bourgeoisie.

Marxist historical theory is too dense a thicket to penetrate in a few paragraphs. It will be instructive, however, to notice some of Marx's arguments about the causes of the transition in England. "The prelude of the revolution that laid the foundation of the capitalist mode of production," Marx wrote, "was played in the last third of the 15th and the first decade of the 16th century. A mass of free proletarians was hurled on the labour market by the breaking up of the bands of feudal retainers . . ." [121] This was scarcely a convincing statement of the source of free labor, and Marx perforce sought other explanations: "The process of forcible expropriation of the people received in the 16th century a new and frightful impulse from the Reformation, and from the consequent colossal spoliation of the church property." [122] Marx had already spoken of a "revolution in the conditions of production" in the sixteenth century; now he went on to discuss the origins of the proletariat and of the "primitive" accumulation of capital. The details of Marx's arguments need not be repeated, but it is worth noting that he applied the term "revolution" rather freely to the Tudor period, even speaking of an "agricultural revolution which commenced in the last third of the 15th century, and continued during almost the whole of the 16th . . ." [123] It was the expropriation and eviction of the agricultural population that not only freed industrial capital, labor, and materials, but also created the home market. The royal power itself was "the product of bourgeois development." [124] The immanent laws of capitalist development, operating with the inexorability of laws of nature, hastened on the whole transition. History moved like a convoy along a road, its elements sometimes lagging behind and sometimes speeding up to keep the rendezvous at Naseby.

To the extent that "the landowners and workers, the feudal lords and the common people, fell, so the capitalist class, the bourgeoisie, rose." [125] Revolution depended on conditions; conditions were created by revolution. The significance of all this for historiography is apparent. Marx set problems for later economic historians and he provided a new vocabulary for historical discussion. The lack of economic statistics and of monographs devoted to economic history made it easier for Marx to be wrong; the accumulation of such monographs and statistics has made it harder for devout Marxists to be right. Thorold Rogers' pioneering work, *A History of Agriculture and Prices*, was published between 1866 and 1887 and it was the first full-scale study. A Victorian Liberal, who deplored revolutionary ways, Rogers complained in his lectures on *The Economic Interpretation of History* that economic history had been habitually neglected. He maintained that the "revolutions in English history, the depositions of princes, the change in the succession, the control of Parliament over the executive, may have been brought about by a plurality of causes, but the fiscal or economic cause dominates the whole." [126] This was not Marxism, but it was easily misconstrued as Marxism. The later history of controversy between the pro- and anti-Marxists has often revealed both parties wearing the sad expressions of the misunderstood. But quarrels were not confined to those who accepted and those who rejected the words of Marx. In the early 1950s a discussion was begun in the pages of *Science and Society* between Marxists who did, and others who did not, accept the view that England was still predominantly feudal in the sixteenth century. The bourgeois revolution had occurred either under the Tudors (or perhaps earlier) or else under Oliver Cromwell. A third position of gradualism (the bourgeois revolution was piecemeal) was alluded to by Maurice Dodd in his introduction to the symposium collection, *The Transition from Feudalism to Capitalism.* Christopher Hill's summary comment was that "The absolute monarchy was a different form of feudal monarchy from the feudal-estates monarchy which preceded it; but the ruling class remained the same . . ." [127] The real transition therefore did not occur until the bourgeoisie took power in the seventeenth century. However, the problem that had precipitated the argument remained—how to treat the economic system in the transitional period between the decline of feudalism and the beginning of the capitalist period in the later sixteenth century. Was there, in this complex transition, a distinct mode of production, neither feudal nor capitalist? And if so, how was it to be described? Socialist semantics became entangled in historical semantics. [128]

To call attention to Marxist problems of definition is also to call attention to the wider question of definitions in historical writing, Some anti-Marxist historians have been Marxists in spite of themselves, lacking any clear alternative framework of interpretation. Most historians have had to reckon with Marxist meanings: *classes,* which rise or decline; *ideologies* of law and religion; *feudal* attitudes and ways of life as opposed to *bourgeois;* the *economic basis* of transitions and revolutions; and distinct periods, marked out by actions that might have been performed by history's substitute players—*if*'s followed by *then*'s. Marxist definitions have been attacked repeatedly by professional historians. The definition of feudalism, for example, is certainly no simple matter, especially if evidence from different times and places is allowed to count; and the Marxist tendency to conflate feudalism and manorialism is unacceptable to most medievalists. But the problem of defining terms has certainly been sharpened by debate. Every Tudor historian must be prepared to deal with non-dictionary definitions of feudalism, the gentry, the middle class, and countless other terms. To know the alternatives, and how each can be criticized, is part of the Tudor historian's job. In this sense, surely, Marxist thought must be studied, and not simply dismissed as perverse. Those who know nothing of Marx should be resigned to repeating his errors.

The historiography of the Tudor transition may be summarized, up to the twentieth century, by saying that most of the major historians believed in some form of a Tudor revolution. Contrary to popular belief, the Victorians were not so enchanted by evolutionary gradualism and the unbroken continuities of history that they failed to see anything else. The significance of Tudor "revolutionary change" in Victorian historiography was not that this merely represented overdramatization, or the Whig quest for origins; an attempt was being made to describe the shift away from medieval ideas and social organization toward something quite different. Most historians believed that "different" could be equated with "better"; and too many historians traced the origins of modern liberty straight to the Reformation. But the success of Butterfield's attack on the Whig interpretation of history has perhaps resulted in a new orthodoxy, no less dangerous than the Whig. The danger was perceived by Butterfield himself: "The watershed is broken down if we place the Reformation in its historical context and if we adopt the point of view which regards Protestantism itself as the product of history. But here greater dangers lurk . . . for we may fall into the opposite fallacy and say that the Reformation did nothing at all." [129] Some historians have indeed gone so far as to deny that significant long-term changes took place in sixteenth-century England. Their arguments will be discussed in the next chapter. The general view of the Tudor period taken by nineteenth-century historians was that it was a watershed. The revolutions of the seventeenth century were named, "Puritan" and "Glorious"; those of the sixteenth century were usually described in terms of other movements. Earlier writers had drawn attention to the revolutionary importance of the printing press, but perhaps it was not the least of Stubbs' contributions to English historiography to assert that not everything of importance was recorded in the state papers and chronicles. There were quiet revolutions to be considered.

The general chronology of Tudor history was firmly established by about 1920. Major changes in historical interpretation between World War I and II resulted from the continuing pursuit of special studies (monographic history); from the application of social science techniques to the available evidence; from the continued serial publication of calendars of state papers and other documents; and from the steady increase in numbers of professionally trained teachers and research workers, many of whom were conspicuously "record-minded." Since 1945 the major shifts of emphasis seem to have been in the direction of local and comparative studies, and toward a more consistent professionalism which has seen fit to borrow ideas from French demographers and from various social theorists. An article written in 1956 by G. R. Elton on "Fifty Years of Tudor Studies at London University" makes the essential point: "The fifty years dominated by Pollard, Tawney and Neale have produced a professional attitude and professional training among Tudor scholars, with the result that the history of sixteenth century England has been completely rewritten—in quite a real sense for the first time." [130]

The piecemeal character of the change in Tudor historical interpretation since 1900 should not distract attention from the fact that improved techniques played a vital role. Most nineteenth-century historians were accustomed to using words like "revolution" in a rather loose sense, just as Acton could speak, rather loosely, of "the law of continuity and the operation of constant forces." [131] It was not until after 1920 or thereabouts that really intensive work on unpublished local and national records began to be undertaken. Neale and others, following a biographical approach, discovered more and more about the hitherto unknown lives of members of Parliament. Knowledge, when properly fused with the right questions, could easily destroy old generalizations. The technique of piecing together many scattered references called for a far wider acquaintance with unpublished papers, both private and public, than earlier historians could command. And men such as Tawney brought to bear on Tudor history the insights of Marx, Weber, and Troeltsch. Gradually, as the older versions of Tudor history were dismantled, the monolithic nature of the Tudor transition came to be doubted. Economics and politics, literature and population, religion and science, did not necessarily move at the same pace. Indeed, some historians suggested that retrogression in religious thought had been just as characteristic as progress; others held that the continuity of medieval culture persisted, so that even the American Revolution relied on medieval doctrines; still others urged the need for a much more careful application of counting techniques and a much more exact definition of terms. Those who wielded the axe and the flail with the greatest effect sometimes attacked even the potentially useful baggage train of the enemy: "The only way you can fit history into what is roughly described as the economic or class interpretation is to leave out half or three quarters of what happened and not to ask any very bright questions about the remnant." [132] One may appreciate the wit, yet question the truth of the saying. Economic historians have proceeded by asking bright questions about countable things. The modern reinterpretations, of Tudor history and of the Tudor transition in particular have been brought about by historians who became dissatisfied with the interpretations they started with. Any interpretation is foolish if it inhibits a historian from refining his techniques for finding out what happened; and every interpretation must be judged on the basis of how much it contributes to the understanding of particular historical facts. History cannot be reduced to a set of theoretical general laws, but neither can history be written without any theory at all. The revisions of Tudor history produced in the twentieth century must be considered in the light of new approaches and new sources.

NOTES

1. See Wallace K. Ferguson, *The Renaissance in Historical Thought* (Boston, 1948), p. 29 and *passim;* and Herbert Weisinger, "The Renaissance Theory of the Reaction against the Middle Ages as a Cause of the Renaissance," *Speculum,* XX (October 1945), pp. 461–467.
2. Paul Otto Kristeller, "Changing Views of the Intellectual History of the Renaissance since Jacob Burckhardt," in *The Renaissance: A Reconsideration of the Theories and Interpretations of the Middle Age,* ed. Tinsley Helton (Madison, 1961), p. 46.
3. Harry Levin, "English Literature of the Renaissance," in Helton, *op. cit.,* p. 125.
4. Marvin Levich, "Disagreement and Controversy in History," in *Studies in the Philosophy of History,* ed. George H. Nadel (New York, 1965), p. 41.
5. See Ferguson, *op. cit.,* p. 74.
6. Johan Huizinga, "Historical Ideals of Life," in *Men and Ideas* (New York, 1959), p. 91.
7. Paul Otto Kristeller, *Renaissance Thought* (New York, 1961), I, 116; see also Kristeller, "Changing Views," p. 42.
8. *The Colloquies of Erasmus,* trans. Craig R. Thompson (Chicago, 1965), p. 65.
9. *Ibid.,* pp. 65, 225; see Ferguson, *op. cit.,* pp. 40–41, for other instances.

10. Peter Burke, *The Renaissance* (London, 1964), p. 4.
11. Huizinga, *op. cit.*, p. 90.
12. *Ibid.*, p. 91.
13. The bibliographical material collected by Ferguson alone in *The Renaissance in Historical Thought* gives some idea of the range of controversy.
14. Wallace K. Ferguson, "The Reinterpretation of the Renaissance," in William Henry Werkmeister, ed., *Facets of the Renaissance* (New York, 1963), pp. 1–18, from p. 2; and Ferguson, "The Interpretation of the Renaissance: Suggestions for a Synthesis," *Journal of the History of Ideas*, XI (1951), 483–495.
15. Ferguson, *Renaissance in Historical Thought*, p. 29.
16. *Ibid.*, pp. 40 ff.
17. *Ibid.*, p. 46; on Erasmus's influence see H. R. Trevor-Roper, *Men and Events* (New York, 1957), pp. 35–60.
18. David Hume, *The History of England* (Boston, 1858), I, 18; II, 507; see also III, 77. Cf. Laurence L. Bongie, *David Hume, Prophet of the Counter-Revolution* (Oxford, 1966).
19. Hume, *op. cit.*, III, 76–77.
20. *Ibid.*, II, 508.
21. *Ibid.*, III, 68–69.
22. *Ibid.*, p. 134.
23. *Ibid.*, IV, Appendix 3, esp. p. 358.
24. *Ibid.*, II, 526, note V. Cf. Dom David Knowles, *The Historian and Character and Other Essays* (Cambridge, 1963), esp. pp. 19 ff.
25. Cf. Hume, *op. cit.*, II, 324, on feudalism and "perpetual revolution."
26. William Robertson, *The History of the Reign of the Emperor Charles V* (Philadelphia, 1876), pp. 12–14.
27. William Robertson, *History of Scotland* (New York, n.d.), pp. 58–62.
28. Robertson, *Charles V*, pp. 502–503.
29. See J. G. A. Pocock, *The Ancient Constitution and the Feudal Law* (Cambridge, 1957); and David Douglas, *English Scholars 1660–1730* (London, 1951).
30. Weisinger, *op. cit.*, p. 467 and the writings there cited. Camden's distaste for the destruction of religious monuments may be seen in the Introduction to his *Annals*. See [White Kennett (ed.)], *A Complete History of England* (London, 1706), II, 365; Stow was rather less direct, but his dislike of change and his contempt for defacers of ancient monuments are apparent throughout the *Survey*. See Charles Lethbridge Kingsford (ed.), *A Survey of London by John Stow* (Oxford, 1908), I, 220 and *passim*.
31. John Selden, *The Historie of Tithes* (London, 1618), p. xvi.
32. James Harrington, *Oceana* (Heidelberg, 1924), pp. 48–55.
33. Thomas Hobbes, *Behemoth*, ed. William Molesworth (New York, 1963), p. 74 and *passim*. Cf. *Leviathan*, Chap. 29, "Of Those Things That Weaken, or Tend to the Dissolution of a Commonwealth," which points to reading of ancient histories (Greek and Roman) as a cause of rebellion.
34. Gilbert Burnet, *The History of the Reformation of the Church of England* (London, 1837), VI, 35; and VI, xxxi.
35. See Thomas Warton, *History of English Poetry from the Eleventh to the Seventeenth Century* (London, 1870), pp. 590–593. Quoted in Denys Hay (ed.), *The Renaissance Debate* (New York, 1965), p. 18.
36. Herbert Butterfield, *The Whig Interpretation of History* (London, 1950), p. v.
37. See Garrett Mattingly, "Some Revisions of the Political History of the Renaissance," in Helton, *op. cit.*, pp. 1–23.

38. Pocock, *op. cit., passim.*
39. Robert Brady, *The Complete History of England* (London, 1685), "To the Reader."
40. V. H. Galbraith, *Studies in the Public Records* (London, 1948), p. 104. See also his *Historical Research in Medieval England* (London, 1951), pp. 45–46.
41. C. R. Cheney, *The Records of Medieval England, An Inaugural Lecture* (Cambridge, 1955), pp. 4–5.
42. See *Guide to the Contents of the Public Record Office* (London, H.M. Stationary Office, 1963); this is a revised edition of Giuseppi's *Guide* of 1923–1924. There is a complete listing of Government Publications in *British National Archives*, Sectional List No. 24, Revised to 1st March, 1968 (H.M.S.O., London, 1968); see also Sectional List No. 17, *Publications of the Royal Commission on Historical Manuscripts.* The illustrations in the text are just that—illustrations.
43. See Leslie Stephen, *Hours in a Library* (London, 1920), II, 223–249; Lloyd Sanders, *The Holland House Circle* (n.p., 1908); and the *Dictionary of National Biography.*
44. In the 1849 edition the first three volumes only brought the story down to Henry VI. See John Lingard, *The History of England* (London, 1883).
45. Quoted by C. P. Gooch, *History and Historians in the Nineteenth Century* (New York, 1952), p. 268.
46. See E. L. Erickson, *British Sessional Papers* (New York, n.d.) for discussion of the Deputy Keeper's reports. The "First Report" of the Deputy Keeper of Records appeared in 1840. See p. 191 for reference.
47. Lingard, *op. cit.*, I, xiii.
48. *Ibid.*, xix. It is worth noting that Lingard's publisher was a Protestant.
49. Edwin Jones, "John Lingard and the Simancas Archives," *The Historical Journal*, X, No. 1 (1967), 76.
50. Lingard, *op. cit.*, IV, 449, 452.
51. See R. W. K. Hinton, "History Yesterday, Five Points about Whig History," *History Today*, IX, No. 11 (November 1959), 720.
52. Henry Hallam, *The Constitutional History of England from the Accession of Henry VII to the Death of George II* (New York, 1874), I, 25.
53. *Ibid.*, pp. 43, 50.
54. *Ibid.*, p. 36; cf. 60.
55. *Ibid.*, p. 69.
56. *Ibid.*, pp. 95; 70, 79.
57. *Ibid.*, p. 70.
58. *Ibid.*, pp. 18, and 18–22 *passim.*
59. *Ibid.*, II, 102.
60. *Ibid.*, III, 194–195.
61. Quoted by Corinne Comstock Weston, "Henry Hallam (1777–1859)," in *Some Modern Historians of Britain*, ed. Herman Ausubel *et al.* (New York, 1951), p. 29.
62. See A. F. Pollard, *Thomas Cranmer and the English Reformation 1489–1556* (London, 1927), p. viii; Freeman's intemperate marginalia are discussed in Herbert Paul, *Life of Froude* (New York, 1906), pp. 160–161. Cf. Waldo Hilary Dunn, *James Anthony Froude, A Biography 1818–1856* (Oxford, 1961), pp. 1–11, 242–243.
63. See James Anthony Froude, *Short Studies on Great Subjects* (New York, 1877), I, 7–36. Much of the lecture was taken up with a refutation of Buckle's theories.
64. *Ibid.*, p. 34.

65. *Ibid.*, p. 28.
66. Quoted by Dunn, *op. cit.*, p. 174.
67. Quoted in *ibid.*, p. 202, from Froude's autobiographical notes.
68. See James Anthony Froude, *History of the Reign of Henry VIII* (London, 1909), I, 1.
69. *Ibid.*, pp. 123, 296.
70. Quoted by Dunn, *op. cit.*, p. 170, from an autobiographical fragment.
71. James Anthony Froude, *The Reign of Elizabeth* (London, 1912), V, 478. Froude's original title implied that he would cover the whole reign; he stopped with the Armada. The American, E. P. Cheyney, completed the work in *A History of England, From the Defeat of the Armada to the Death of Elizabeth* (New York, 1914–1926).
72. Froude, *Henry VIII*, I, 39.
73. *Ibid.*, p. 268.
74. *Ibid.*, pp. 268–269.
75. *Ibid.*, III, 424, 425.
76. Quoted by Beatrice Reynolds, "James Anthony Froude," in Ausubel *et al.*, *op. cit.*, p. 54, citing Froude's *The Spanish Story of the Armada and Other Essays* (New York, 1892), p. 29.
77. Froude, *Henry VIII*, III, 421.
78. *Ibid.*, p. 422.
79. Quoted by Reynolds, *op. cit.*, p. 60.
80. John Richard Green, *A Short History of the English People* (London, 1915), I, xi.
81. *Ibid.*, p. 272.
82. *Ibid.*, p. 273.
83. *Ibid.*, p. 274.
84. *Ibid.*, p. 285.
85. *Ibid.*, p. 293.
86. *Ibid.*, p. 293.
87. *Ibid.*, p. 313.
88. Arthur J. Slavin, *The "New Monarchies" and Representative Assemblies* (Boston, 1964), p. xv.
89. Norman F. Cantor (ed.), *William Stubbs on the English Constitution* (New York, 1966), p. 2. Cantor's recent textbook, *The English: A History of Politics and Society to 1760* (New York, 1967), is particularly valuable for its historiographical comments, not only on Stubbs but on many other historians; see especially pp. 278–294.
90. William Stubbs, *The Constitutional History of England in Its Origin and Development* (5th ed.; Oxford, 1926), II, 656; see also III, 518–519.
91. *Ibid.*, III, 632; see also 629–636 *passim*.
92. *Ibid.*, p. 632; II, 653.
93. William Stubbs, *Seventeen Lectures on the Study of Medieval and Modern History* (Oxford, 1900), p. 95, from "On the Purposes and Methods of Historical Study."
94. *Ibid.*, p. 389, from "The Reign of Henry VII."
95. *Ibid.*, p. 390.
96. *Ibid.*, p. 391.
97. *Ibid.*, p. 239.
98. Maitland's essay, "William Stubbs, Bishop of Oxford," is reprinted in *Selected Historical Essays of F. W. Maitland*, ed. Helen M. Cam (Cambridge, 1957); see p. 275.
99. See Stubbs, *Seventeen Lectures*, pp. 255–256.

100. H. G. Richardson and G. O. Sayles, *The Governance of Medieval England from the Conquest to Magna Carta* (Edinburgh, 1963), pp. 7–8 on continuity, 20–21, and Chap. 1 *passim.*
101. Stubbs, *Constitutional History*, III, 240.
102. T. F. Tout, *Chapters in the Administrative History of Medieval England* (Manchester, 1920–1931), I, 5, 2–8.
103. *Ibid.*, p. 28.
104. *Ibid.*, IV, 67.
105. Cf. G. R. Elton, *The Tudor Revolution in Government* (Cambridge, 1962), pp. 10–13.
106. Tout, *op. cit.*, I, 13.
107. Sir J. R. Seeley, *The Growth of British Policy* (Cambridge, 1895), I, 250.
108. Maitland, *Selected Historical Essays*, pp. 52–96; see Helen Cam's Introduction, pp. xv–xx.
109. A. F. Pollard, *The Evolution of Parliament* (London, 1964), p. v.
110. *Ibid.*, p. 175; see also pp. 173–175, 214–215.
111. *Ibid.*, pp. 191–192.
112. *Ibid.*, pp. 190–195.
113. *Ibid.*, pp. 216–217.
114. A. F. Pollard, *Factors in Modern History* (3rd ed.; London, 1932), pp. 37–38; cf. J. H. Hexter, *Reappraisals in History* (London, 1961), pp. 38, 26–44 *passim.*
115. A. F. Pollard, *Henry VIII*, with an Introduction by A. G. Dickens (New York, 1966), p. 352.
116. Hexter, *op. cit.*, p. 34.
117. *Ibid.*, p. 19.
118. *Ibid.*, p. 32.
119. *Ibid.*, p. xi; see the Foreword by Peter Laslett.
120. Karl Marx, *Capital, A Critique of Political Economy*, ed. Friedrich Engels, Vol. I, *The Process of Capitalist Production*, trans. S. Moore and Edward Aveling (Chicago, London, 1909), p. 787.
121. *Ibid.*, p. 789.
122. *Ibid.*, p. 792.
123. *Ibid.*, p. 815.
124. *Ibid.*, p. 789.
125. Karl Marx, *Selected Writings in Sociology and Social Philosophy*, ed. T. B. Bottomore and Maximillien Rubel (London, 1963), p. 138.
126. James E. Thorold Rogers, *The Economic Interpretation of History* (London, 1918), p. 432.
127. Paul Sweezy *et al.*, *The Transition from Feudalism to Capitalism, A Symposium* (essays from *Science and Society* [New York, n.d.]), p. 75.
128. See *ibid.*, p. 25 and *passim.*
129. Butterfield, *op. cit.*, pp. 56–57; see also pp. 47 ff.
130. *Times Literary Supplement*, "Historical Writing" Supplement, Jan. 6, 1956, p. viii.
131. Lord Acton, *Essays in the Liberal Interpretation of History*, ed. and with an Introduction by William H. McNeil (Chicago, 1967), p. 361.
132. Hexter, *op. cit.*, p. 187.

3

New Approaches to Tudor History

LORD ACTON COMBINED the highest virtues of the nineteenth-century scholar-aristocrat with the insights and instincts of a twentieth-century comparative historian. Since his death in 1902 his reputation has suffered not eclipse but enhancement. The latest republication of his essays (in 1967) inaugurates a series of volumes titled "Classic European Historians." Acton knew very much more than he wrote, and he thought very much more about what needed to be done than he actually did. His importance for Tudor historiography lies in the fact that he treated England as a part of the continent, a part of the main of European history. It was the common whole, he believed, that was the proper unit of historical study; the advice to study problems, not periods, was elementary —his insight into the international nature of modern historical study was fundamental. Tudor historians have to reckon with Acton's professional influence, not because he wrote Tudor history (which of course he did not), but because he understood why insular history was inadequate.

Among historians whose ideas have stimulated further discussion and research Acton must be accorded a prominent place. Over against his Liberal confidence in "the advance of moral over material influence" and his evangelical readiness to act the part of a hanging judge of historical crimes, one must set his still fresh generalizations about liberty, power, and history. He ended his Inaugural Lecture with the statement that "whatever a man's notions of these later centuries are, such, in the main, the man himself will be. Under the name of History, they cover the articles of his philosophic, his religious and his political creed." [1] The idea that a man defines himself by the kind of history he believes in has only in recent years begun to be fully appreciated. Acton insisted on the idea of progress and argued that history's line of march was on the whole "from force and cruelty to consent and association," but he believed equally that power was what had corrupted the modern world—"therefore the method of modern progress was revolution." [2] It was a law of modern history that power tended to expand indefinitely until checked by superior force; neither race, nor religion, nor ideology had been so great a cause of universal enmity and national strife. The nature of modern power forced upon the historian the method of comparison. And if liberty had been preserved, secured, extended, and finally understood, as Acton maintained, reflecting on four hundred years of "rapid change but slow progress," then the historians of liberty would have to compare causes and account for differences.[3]

Acton brought to the study of history in Great Britain a close knowledge of German professional techniques and a determination to make specialization serve the wider purposes of universal history.[4] In a letter to the contributors to the *Cambridge Modern History*, Acton (who was the first editor) expressed his hopes that impartiality, expertise, and an appropriate division of labor would result in universal history transcending particular national histories. The gap between expectation and performance was inevitably greater than Acton anticipated. The value of the Cambridge undertaking, however, was proved by the use made of it, and by the sense of perspective it provided. The *New Cambridge Modern History* bears witness to the importance of the old. Some of Acton's hopes could not be fulfilled; others have been fulfilled in part by historians in the twentieth century who have looked across national boundaries to see common problems, with often different solutions. Acton's cosmopolitan and catholic viewpoint helped to make possible some reconciliation of divergent views; his ideal was a Reformation acceptable to Catholics and Protestants alike. "Contributors will understand," he wrote, "that we are established, not under the Meridian of Greenwich, but in Long. 30° W."—that is, somewhere on the high Atlantic, far from the green meadows and fine towns of England; Acton knew that the historian's preferences betray him more than his aversions.[5]

This chapter will attempt to describe some of the ways in which the shape of Tudor history has been changed by new methods, new questions, and new information. The transition problem remains central, if only because different investigations have revealed the need for different chronologies. Comparative studies in economic and social history have produced a better awareness of what was and was not typically Tudor, yet a great deal remains to be done; every man must still expect to be his own comparative historian. Intellectual history by its very nature overruns boundaries. Tudor intellectual historians have had to take into account not only the peripatetic and cosmopolitan humanists, especially Erasmus, but churchmen whose attitudes were shaped by French Calvinism or Roman Catholicism, as well as a veritable array of other writers who owed heavy debts to the ancients, to medieval authors, and to their own contemporaries. Statistical studies of one kind or another have proved enormously helpful, if controversial, in describing or explaining changes in the economy, in the population, and in the social structure. An orderly survey of these and other approaches to Tudor history may begin with general problems and comparative studies, then proceed to more specialized histories.

Different histories require different chronologies. This is perhaps most evident in demography and in the history of technology. The demographer looks for trends in the data. These may be explained by events in social or political or economic history, but the chronology is determined by the trend. The emergence of a European marriage pattern (late marriages and relatively large numbers of unmarried people in the population) was a unique and profoundly important event in world history. The beginnings of this trend have been located in the sixteenth century; on the basis of comparative studies of local and national data a whole new set of questions has been raised which no Tudor historian can ignore.[6] Demography, as LeRoy Ladurie has pointed out, is a new discipline which can trace through the centuries "the shifting balance between life and death, and propose a long term chronology, still based on the relationship between population and production. From this point of view it links up directly with economic history, based on the centurial *trend.*"[7] That much more evidence is needed before large-scale syntheses can be offered, demographic historians have been the first to insist. But E. A. Wrigley has pointed out, in *An Introduction to English Historical Demography*, that "The dark ages of population history ended in 1538, not in 1837. . . . The year 1538 when parish registers were first kept in England provides a clear-cut beginning to the period." [8]

Technological history may also provide a new chronology, important for both economic and social history. A. R. Hall has argued that turning points in economic history must be related to technological changes in methods of production, and that as the history of science becomes more professional the probability is that the artificial frontiers between it and economic history will be traversed:

> Through the history of technology historians may be induced to examine more carefully the correlations between scientific and economic and social history: correlations that are commonly taken as axiomatic, but have rarely been worked out in detail. Very different techniques and types of knowledge will have to be brought together to make this possible, to yield a kind of universal history of man in his natural environment. . . . For it is more apparent now than it was even half a century ago that if the history of science is something more than a history of scientific ideas and theories, if it is to be in fact a history of human attitudes to and knowledge of the rest of the natural world, then for the greater part of history the attitudes of the farmer and craftsman must be studied alongside those of the philosopher and mathematician.[9]

The extent to which these and related problems have emerged in the writing of general history since about 1945 may be studied in four special supplements on historical writing which appeared in 1956 and 1966 in the *Times Literary Supplement*.

"Future historians of English historical writing are likely to reveal the first half of the twentieth century as a time when most historians temporarily lost their bearings." [10] So surmised Keith Thomas, and many historians have agreed with him. The Victorians were fairly certain that constitutional and political history moved along main roads; history could be regarded as past politics. Since 1900 historians have tended to regard history more as a cross-country hunt—over hedgerows, across fenced fields, and through towns. The problem was how to keep track of one's bearings while moving about in often unfamiliar terrain. Less metaphorically stated, the problem was simply that of how to utilize rapid increases in historical knowledge. Tudor historians in the twentieth century have had to try to integrate newly specialized histories and monographs into some kind of meaningful general account. No longer could they feel certain that the old Whig or Liberal concepts of historical order were adequate. The appeal of Marxism to historians during the thirties was in part that it seemed to provide an overall integrating theory that was at least adaptable to the new needs of historical explanation. Conceptual rigidity was preferable to licentious doubt. More recently the need for greater conceptual precision has been revealed in debates on topics ranging from the rise of the middle class to the rise of the gentry, and from the price revolution to the Tudor revolution in government. Economic models and sociological theories have proved useful as tools of analysis; but when historians must integrate specialized monographs into narrative history, then what counts is personal judgment, originality, and a capacity for making illuminating comparisons and accurate generalizations. These are the qualities that distinguish historical narrative from outlines and mere chronicles; therefore a brief discussion of Tudor general histories will be found at the end of this chapter.

In 1927 the French medievalist, Marc Bloch, pointed out that the comparative method was already well tried and had long since proved its value. The reasons for studying "differences in environment" were evident, but the difficulties of the task were formidable. National historical vocabularies did not correspond with one another, as Bloch knew, and only intensive local investigations could provide a true basis for comparison between, for example, France and England with regard to the all-important enclosure movements. These striking transformations, which led in England to "the disappearance of communal obligations and the growth of individualism in agriculture," were not visible in French economic history.[11] The point Bloch made was that a variety of comparative studies should be undertaken, especially with a view to defining the differences between societies which shared common origins and were subject to the same general influences. Point-for-point comparative studies have been disappointingly few, but the bases for comparison have been steadily widened, especially as English-speaking historians have moved, along with Europeans, to investigate histories other than their own. Urban history in its most recent forms has become explicitly comparative, as is evident in the recent volume by H. C. Koenigsberger and George L. Mosse, *Europe in the Sixteenth Century*, which forms part of a new General History of Europe. The Renaissance and Reformation obviously can not be studied in isolation; the international historiography of each is therefore of central concern to the Tudor historian. Modern printing and color reproduction techniques have in themselves made possible new insights into the common ideas, the art forms, and the literature of Europe in the Renaissance. André Chastels' *The Age of Humanism, Europe 1480–1530* (1963) is but one instance of a type—books designed around a series of representative plates. In this case the international character of the undertaking is evident, the volume having been published under the auspices of the Council of Cultural Cooperation following the first Art Exhibition of the Council of Europe in 1954.

Comparison is obviously not new in historiography, as readers of Herodotus are aware, but there is a distinct sense in which the twentieth century has transformed an old virtue into a new method. The founding of the journal, *Comparative Studies in Society and History*, in 1958, was a recognition of this fact. On the other hand, monographs on local or particular topics often invite comparisons but do not make them; this is not necessarily a fault, for differences of scale impose differences of approach. It is evident that the volumes in the *New Cambridge Modern History* on the Renaissance and the Reformation can be more explicitly comparative and synthetic than, for example, Hans Baron could be in *The Crisis of the Early Italian Renaissance*, or Roberto Weiss could be in *Humanism in England during the Fifteenth Century*. Significant generalizations, inviting a comparison of conditions, nevertheless made Baron's book of special interest to Tudor historians. In the first years of the *quattrocento*, Baron argued, the cultural atmosphere of Florence was transformed. The influence of Florentine ideas and interests spread outward through Italy and thence to the wider world; a new historical outlook arose, and a new ethical attitude that opposed the scholars' withdrawal from civic life. The period of transition around 1400 in Florence was short; the contrast with the *trecento* was correspondingly sharp. The applicability of Baron's analysis to other periods and countries remains to be worked out, for Baron himself aimed at clarity and precision in a limited field. The broader issues were, however, apparent: "At the end of our analysis, therefore, we should ask to what extent the answers found to the problems of the political and cultural transition about 1400 can serve as keys to more inclusive historical phenomena—other and wider aspects of Florentine history, as well as the later growth of Renaissance Humanism outside Florence and Italy." [12] How far the paradigms of civic humanism apply to England is a question that has only begun to be explored. Arthur Ferguson's *The Articulate Citizen and the English Renaissance* defined a sharp transition in Tudor political and social thought, which was part of a larger Renaissance pattern. The civic humanism of Florence, according to Ferguson, pointed more toward the realistic analysis of princely statecraft in Machiavelli than toward the Commonwealth of Tudor thought, but the divergence between Italian and English patterns was perhaps less significant than the similarities.[13]

The *New Cambridge Modern History* has been criticized for being old-fashioned in its assumptions and uneven in execution.[14] The sixteenth-century volumes are, however, among the best. Large-scale comparisons and syntheses were not among the aims of the new series, which was "planned neither as a stepping stone to definitive history, nor as an abstract or a scale reduction of all our knowledge of the period, but as a coherent body of judgments true to the facts." [15] The scale of the work, however, made it possible to deal effectively with some national differences, and to treat certain international movements as units. There is much to be gained from reading the introductions of Denys Hay and G. R. Elton to, respectively, *The Renaissance, 1493–1520* and *The Reformation, 1520–1559*. Whether or not the Renaissance was a turning point, and whether or not the Reformation constituted a definable period in European history are questions that can only be answered on the basis of European-wide investigations. It is perhaps worth noting that Denys Hay also wrote *Europe, The Emergence of an Idea*, and that G. R. Elton wrote *Reformation Europe 1517–1559*, the best survey of this period in English. The transition of the sixteenth century, when viewed from a European perspective, may not have marked the beginning of "modern times" (a sufficiently vague phrase, as Elton pointed out) but it did mark the beginning of the ascendancy of Europe.[16] The dominant role of Europe in the world from the sixteenth to the twentieth century is a fact; the sixteenth century, in this sense, constituted a beginning in many national histories.

Philippe Ariès approached the transition from medieval to modern history from an entirely different viewpoint, that of family life, especially in France between the fifteenth and the nineteenth centuries. Although not specifically a comparative study, but rather one dealing with European attitudes and mores, *Centuries of Childhood* deals with the transition question in a significantly original way. "The appearance of the portrait of the dead child in the sixteenth century," Ariès writes, "accordingly marked a very important moment in the history of our feelings." [17] By 1600 toys had become an infantile specialty; expurgated editions of the classics began to be published by the end of the sixteenth century; the evolution of schools toward an authoritarian master-pupil relation corresponded to the general tendency of the sixteenth century toward absolutism; and starting in the fifteenth century the idea of the family underwent a "slow and profound revolution." [18] In the end, according to Ariès, it was not individualism that triumphed but the family. Using a wide variety of evidence (paintings and diaries, games, children's books, costumes, curricular regulations, and student rules, as well as architectural and iconographical sources), Ariès explained the gradual emergence of modern ideas of the child and the family. A great deal of social history may be seen reflected in the mirror of childhood. The concept of innocence in children was foreign to the Middle Ages; expurgated classics were a tribute to the new importance of childhood. Privacy became a matter of concern to families and therefore to architects. It has been suggested, by W. G. Hoskins, that in England the taste for privacy, light, and air was not only moving from the upper classes downward but that the Great Rebuilding of the sixteenth century helped to stimulate population growth.[19] The sense of privacy did not develop suddenly, but the new architecture may well have been a corollary of the changing idea of the family. In any case, the value of Ariès' sociological-intellectual history must be sought in how well it integrates the facts of social history, and in how useful it proves to be as a model for research.

During the past decade or so another form of "conceptual history" has been developed, particularly by English-speaking historians who have sought to go beyond the rather narrow History of Ideas approach.[20] The work of Lovejoy in intellectual history was certainly fruitful, but to trace a unit idea through time is not necessarily to understand how the idea itself functioned in a given society or what its social connotations were. Eugene Rice's *The Renaissance Idea of Wisdom* (1958) was, by contrast, a history of the intellectual process of secularization in different countries, including England, in the fifteenth and sixteenth centuries. The medieval notion of the wise man was essentially static; perfection came as a gift of grace. The humanists found in Prometheus their symbol. "Paralleling the extension of the content of wisdom to include the facts of human history is an extension of its sources to include the experience distilled from these facts"; and, as Rice went on to observe, "it is characteristic that both Elyot and Celtis identify experience with history and travel." [21] The wisdom of the Reformation was "unashamedly revelational," but wisdom gradually came to be identified with prudence during the sixteenth century. Moral solvency had its attractions for serious burghers. Secularization and innovation were evident, but Rice stressed the fact that in the sixteenth century old and new ideas coexisted: "This coexistence, in time and in individuals, of tradition and innovation reflects the ideological confusion of a period of transition." [22]

Ideas of childhood or of wisdom can be shown to have had different sociological significance at different times. The idea of history can also be seen in its sociological context, in which case historical thought becomes a part of what has been called "the self-conceptualization of societies in time." Linking together political theory and historiography, intellectual history and social history, images of the past and styles of legitimization of the present and future, this approach to the history of thought studies the conceptual languages of societies in time. George H. Sabine's A *History of Political Theory* and J. W. Allen's A *History of Political Thought in the Sixteenth Century* both represented the classical approach to political theory by way of analysis. "The sixteenth century," according to Allen, "was a period of relatively rapid and of formally revolutionary change," but it was also true that "essential psychological change preceded the formal revolution." [23] The value of Allen's book is not in question, even though he did not describe psychological change; like Sabine, he understood by the history of political thought a sequence of important books requiring commentary and analysis. Many true and important things were said by Allen about Calvin and Hooker and other writers, and about the nature of Protestantism; but the changing content, function, and application of political ideas was not Allen's primary concern. His book was published in 1928, Sabine's in 1937; since then historians have become more concerned with the functional significance of political and historical thought.

The historian who has contributed most significantly to the analysis of methodological problems in the history of political thought is J. G. A. Pocock. He has described the revisionist trend in the historiography of political thought as follows:

> Increasingly, then, the history of political thought is becoming the study of a nation's legitimating concepts under stress, and of the consequent changes in ideas concerning the philosophy of political knowledge, the history of the self-legitimating community, and sometimes—to link the two—the philosophy of historical knowledge. As regards early modern Europe, this work has been vigorously carried on by Italian scholars, employing the Crocean concept that all social thought is ultimately a matter of society's historical self-knowledge; but American, British and Antipodean writers, working from very different premises, have also been applying to Renaissance political literature—Florentine, French and English—the perception that political thought consists of modes of legitimation and their criticism, and includes both images of society's continuity in time and ideas concerning the problems of knowledge and action in the flow of secular events.[24]

A variety of books could be used to illustrate this point. J. G. A. Pocock's *The Ancient Constitution and the Feudal Law* (1957) was a pioneering study, which was based in part on a comparative analysis of French and English historiography in the sixteenth century. Greenleaf's *Order, Empiricism, Politics* (1964) described the uses of history; and Robert Jay Lifton, in two articles dealing with the attitudes of modern Japanese youth toward history, provided a new conceptual model for the analysis of historical ideologies.

The sense of historical dislocation accompanying rapid social change was described by Lifton in terms of Weber's ideal-type analysis. The extent to which Japanese patterns are analogous to Tudor patterns is obviously a matter for debate, but the points made by Lifton are fundamental for an understanding of the uses of the past. There are "common patterns—shared images and styles of imagery—which men call forth in their efforts to deal with the threat and promise of a changing outer and inner world." [25] The Japanese modes of transformation, restoration, and accommodation are ideal types, arrived at in part by means of psychiatric research, but similar patterns can probably be discovered in "any society in a state of marked transition." [26] Tudor analogues need to be investigated.

The extent to which twentieth-century psychiatry has contributed to an understanding of history must be judged on the basis of the best books and articles, not the worst. The Freudian fad of the twenties and thirties has passed; serious psychological investigation of historical characters has been conceded to be no job for the amateur. In *Psychoanalysis and History* (1963), Bruce Mazlich argued the need for better psychological interpretation and provided examples of psychoanalytic history. An article by Philip Rieff on "The Meaning of History and Religion in Freud's Thought" set forth some of the more general psychological patterns that are of interest to historians. For the historian of historiography the article is essential reading, since it makes the case for the psychological importance of historical consciousness and tradition. "The first thing to say about history," Rieff maintains, "is that it is never, properly, past." History lives in the mind. Tradition Rieff defines as "the transformation of history into personality," and, quoting Freud, as "the historical content of the mass unconscious." [27] Other general books dealing with the relationship of psychology and psychoanalysis to history include Muzafer Sherif, *The Psychology of Social Norms* (1965); H. Stuart Hughes, *Consciousness and Society* (1958); Lancelot Law Whyte, *The Unconscious before Freud* (1960); and Abram Kardiner *et al.*, *The Psychological Frontiers of Society* (1945). The suggestive study of the psychoanalytical meaning of history by Norman O. Brown, *Life against Death* (1959), argues that "a reinterpretation of human history is not an appendage to psychoanalysis but an integral part of it" and that "a theory of history must embrace a theory of neurosis." [28] His discussion of the Protestant era has relevance for Tudor history, yet Brown's criticisms of Troeltsch, Weber, Tawney, and Fromm on the Protestant ethic are vitiated by his own failure to take into account recent work in demography and economic history. If under Protestantism "the death instinct becomes the master of the house," this psychic event should mark a major transition, but Brown's analysis of the psychology of Martin Luther is suggestive rather than historically persuasive.[29] Moreover, the absence of Calvin's name in the index is not reassuring to historians.

The biographical approach would seem to be one most congenial to those wishing to make psychoanalysis serve history. An early attempt at psychological analysis of Tudor character was made by J. C. Flügel in 1920, "On the Character and Married Life of Henry VIII." Most historians have remained skeptical of Flügel's methods of argument; Henry's "desire for incest" has not been, and perhaps cannot be, established, even if one accepts the entire Freudian psychoanalytical vocabulary. On the other hand, Erik H. Erikson's *Young Man Luther* (1958) indicates what can be accomplished by a trained psychoanalyst who is aware of historical influences. Professional historians have been inclined to ignore psychoanalysis; they have often, therefore, been deceived by the rationalizations of their historical heroes. Professional psychoanalysts (with a very few notable exceptions, such as Erikson) have been inclined to ignore historical contexts and to misconstrue historical evidence; they have often, therefore, been deceived by their own theories. The fact is, of course, that historians in the twentieth century can still write excellent history without taking into account psychological theories. "Political biography" need not deal with subconscious motives in order to be true, stimulating, and useful. Biographies of Queen Elizabeth such as those by Mandell Creighton and Sir John Neale, and short lives such as those by Milton Waldman and Joel Hurstfield, have been essentially political. A. L. Rowse expressed a common, if curious, opinion when he praised Waldman for getting complex personalities straight "without intensive psychological probing." The vacillations of Elizabeth, however, have not been explained satisfactorily by the theory that she was always politically motivated; the need for a better understanding of psychological patterns is evident in this case and in countless others. Although in Tudor history the general influence of psychological theory has perhaps been mostly negative—historians have reacted against crude attempts to write psycho-history, such as Francis Hackett's *Henry VIII*—the response of the profession to William L. Langer's call for more psychology, made in 1957, has been on the whole sympathetic.[31] The demand for more sophisticated techniques of analysis has as yet, however, not created its own supply. From the point of view of the Tudor transition question, Erich Fromm's *Escape from Freedom* (1941) and Zevedai Barbu's *Problems in Historical Psychology* (1960) still provide the most suggestive commentary. Finally, from a medical viewpoint, Gregory Zilboorg's *A History of Medical Psychology* (1941) remains perhaps the best general account. Zilboorg argued that the first psychiatric revolutions occurred in the sixteenth century, primarily as a result of the work of Vives, Paracelsus, Weyer, and others, including Bodin.[32]

The history of science as a separate discipline is almost entirely a creation of the late nineteenth and twentieth centuries. From the early work of Pierre Duhem attacking Burckhardt's view of the Renaissance (Duhem in 1925 argued that in the field of science there was no Renaissance, only continuity from medieval ideas) to the latest books on sixteenth-century science, there has been a steady advance in the learning that has been marshaled in debate. Edward Rosen's article on "Renaissance Science" (1961) described the general line of development.[33] Because there were few outstanding Tudor scientists, the best works of modern scholarship have dealt with the scientific Renaissance as a European movement. At the end of the nineteenth century A. D. White, in *A History of the Warfare of Science with Theology* (1896), reflected a contemporary preoccupation with "letting the light of historical truth into that decaying mass of outworn thought which attaches the modern world to mediaeval conceptions of Christianity . . . a menace to the whole normal evolution of society." [34] White's book, biased though it was, opened the way for the great histories of science that were to come later—histories that examined the transition question on the basis of fresh evidence and from independent viewpoints. The history of science makes demands on the general historian, who must somehow master the complexities of epicycles, the vagaries of unfamiliar taxonomy, and the mathematical shorthand of scientific explanation. Fortunately during the last twenty-five years a number of excellent, readable texts for laymen have appeared: Herbert Butterfield's *The Origins of Modern Science* (1957); A. C. Crombie's *Medieval and Early Modern Science* (1959); Charles Singer's *A Short History of Scientific Ideas* (1959); George Sarton's *The Appreciation of Ancient and Medieval Science During the Renaissance* (1953), and *Six Wings* (1957); A. Wolf's *A History of Science, Technology and Philosophy in the 16th and 17th Centuries* (1950); Alexander Koyré's *From the Closed World to the Infinite Universe* (1957); Marie Boas's *The Scientific Renaissance* (1962); Arthur Koestler's *The Sleepwalkers* (1959); and three books by Toulmin and Goodfield, *The Fabric of the Heavens* (1961), *The Architecture of Matter* (1962), and *The Discovery of Time* (1965). The list is by no means exhaustive, but the dates are significant. Most of the best general surveys have been written since 1945.

Controversies in the historiography of science have centered around four major problems: (1) the chronology of science; (2) the importance of the sociological context; (3) the nature of the intellectual correlations between science and religion, and science and the arts; and (4) the methods of approach appropriate to the history of science. The scientific "medievalists" have tended to deemphasize the importance of the Renaissance in the history of science, stressing the contributions of medieval scholasticism and of Greek philosophy in the development of scientific ideas. They would agree with "Renaissancists," however, that the scientific revolution of the seventeenth century was characterized by the extensive use of mathematics. The problem, however, is how to account for Copernican and Galilean discoveries. Why did these occur at a particular time, and why (given the fact that the old-world picture was not modeled on mathematics) did these discoveries win acceptance among the best minds of western Europe? The "pure" historians of science, like the "pure" historians of philosophy have tended to ignore historical contexts and to assume that the history of science or philosophy was a history of problems, solutions, and further problems. Insofar as the history of science was regarded as pure problem-solving, it was an intellectual history of ideas, with only limited significance for the general historian. Tudor scientists of the first rank were scarce—the most important was William Gilbert, whose *De Magnete, Magneticisque Corporibus* (1600) was in fact the first great scientific work published in England. But the career of Gilbert, who was Queen Elizabeth's physician, illustrates the problem of how to assess the importance of sociological contexts, as well as the problem of intellectual correlations, in the history of science; and any discussion of Gilbert's scientific achievement raises fundamental questions about the methods appropriate to the history of science. Of necessity, Tudor scientists are here defined by publication dates, not by birth dates.

1. In *The Scientific Renaissance 1450–1630* (1962) Marie Boas maintained that the period marked a definite stage in the scientific revolution:

> It was an era of profound change; but the change was curiously consistent. Equally, this era marks a break with the past. I do not wish to deny the importance or validity of the medieval contribution to science, especially to mathematical physics; but however much sixteenth-century scientists drew from the science of the fourteenth

century, they were separated from it by three generations' passionate attempt to revive Graeco-Roman antiquity in fifteenth century Europe. . . . The revolutionary theories and methods of the 1540's were fully realized by 1630.[35]

The thesis of progress has been asserted again and again in the history of science. Yet progress was not necessarily vectorial. Koestler, in *The Sleepwalkers,* noted that "The progress of Science is generally regarded as a kind of clean, rational advance along a straight ascending line; in fact it has followed a zig-zag course, at times almost more bewildering than the evolution of political thought." [36] Gilbert, like Copernicus, illustrates the fact that the posture of the age was Janus-like: the remote past was viewed as having a literal magic, yet the future could be seen as being rational, experimental, and scientific. Gilbert's treatise was the first outstanding Tudor work in experimental science, but "it is also, and more certainly, the last important work in natural magic, for Gilbert's work is closer to Dee's archemastry than any other sixteenth-century attempt to study the hidden forces of nature." [37] Gilbert was within the traditions of his time—more, perhaps, a natural magician than a seventeenth-century experimental scientist.

2. The history of mathematics in the sixteenth century shows not only that Platonic influences were still very strong, but also that practical utility counted for much—Dee hoped to "stir the imagination mathematical: and to inform the practiser mechanical." [38] The relationship between various intellectual traditions in the sixteenth century occupied Henry Osborne Taylor in his pioneering survey, *Thought and Expression in the Sixteenth Century* (1920). Thereafter, during the twenties and thirties, a number of attempts were made to account for the scientific revolution in England in socioeconomic terms.[39] More recently, in older journals such as *Isis* (founded by George Sarton in 1912) and in newer ones such as the *History of Science* and *The Journal of World History,* debates have been continued. The history of science linked up at many points with the history of technology, which was becoming a separate but closely related discipline—Abbot Payson Usher, in 1929, published his *History of Mechanical Inventions;* and in 1957, the third volume of *A History of Technology,* covering the period from 1500 to about 1750, was published by Singer, Holmyard, Hall, and Williams. Both were general surveys,

which provided excellent introductions to the specialized literature on Tudor technological history. The craftsmen who contributed to sixteenth-century advances in military technology, land drainage, cartography, ship design, navigation instruments, and printing (to name only a few areas in which craftsmen were innovators) were obviously not scholars or scientists in today's sense; but Francis Bacon recognized that craftsmen and scientists alike were essential to progress, and that each could aid the other. In recent historiography debate about the relative importance of craftsmen as opposed to scholar-scientists in the sixteenth century has increased. Craftsmen did not contribute much to the Elizabethan world picture, or to Elizabethan knowledge of astronomy and cosmography; but for reasons which will become apparent, the history of Tudor technology and of craftsmen's innovations cannot be separated from the history of science or, indeed, from the history of religion and economic history.

3. In *Astronomical Thought in Renaissance England* (1937), Francis R. Johnson presented the first detailed study of Tudor astronomical thought, following important earlier articles on Thomas Digges and Robert Recorde.[40] In *Ancients and Moderns* (1936), R. F. Jones discussed the rise of the scientific movement in seventeenth-century England in relation to cultural traditions, beginning with a chapter on Elizabethan attitudes. It was not only in relation to general intellectual history that Tudor scientific thought attracted the attention of scholars. The crucial problem of how science was related to society became an extension of the debate about the relationship between religion and capitalism. The original thesis of Max Weber, put forward in 1905 in *The Protestant Ethic*, stressed the idea that Protestantism, especially in its Calvinist form, contributed to the emergence of worldly asceticism, which promoted industry, thrift, and labor. The variations on this theme, and criticisms of it, from Tawney to Robertson and, most recently, Kurt Samuelsson, need not be considered here. The importance of Weber's thesis was that it asserted correlations between religion and economics that could be verified only by intensive research in special fields. In 1936 R. K. Merton expanded the by then familiar argument that in the seventeenth century science and technology in England owed much to Puritanism.[41] Although most of the evidence for a connection between religion and science came from seventeenth-century sources, clearly the direction of develop-

ment in the sixteenth century was crucial. The growth of Puritanism correlated quite closely in time with the growth of experimental science; the question was whether or not the correlation was accidental and fortuitous, or causal, or merely influential—a parameter in the complex religious and cultural history of England from the mid-sixteenth to the mid-seventeenth century.

Max Weber himself contributed to the confusion of terms when he wrote that his study was intended to be "a contribution to the understanding of the manner in which ideas become effective forces in history." [42] He also maintained that he wanted to investigate the "points at which certain correlations between forms of religious belief and practical ethics can be worked out," and that he would, as far as possible, seek to clarify "the manner and the general *direction* in which, by virtue of those relationships, the religious movements have influenced the development of material culture." [43] This passage makes it clear why some historians were moved to investigate the correlations between Puritanism and science. During the 1930s Renaissance scholars, notably Erwin Panofsky, had analyzed the contribution of art to science and had suggested the importance of the artistic craftsman as a technological innovator. In 1959, in a collection called *Critical Problems in the History of Science,* edited by Marshall Clagett, revisionist arguments were put forward by Giorgio de Santillana and Rupert Hall, challenging the view that the scientific Renaissance could be accounted for either on the basis of scholarly interests in mathematics or on the craftsmanship thesis of innovation, which had already won support from Marxist historians. Hall argued that the scientific scholar of the sixteenth and seventeenth centuries was a man "learned not merely in recent scientific activities and methods, but in the thought of the past. It seems superfluous to argue that the majority of the scientists of the time were of this type, neither technicians nor ignorant empiricists." [44] Science diverged from other branches of scholarship without ever severing its academic affiliations. The Baconian thesis, along with its modern variations, asserted that scientists had to learn from craftsmen. The technological empiricists were, in this view, emphatically necessary for the scientific revolution. Hall argued, however, that scientific empiricism was itself a philosophical artifact, created by learned men— "it stands in about the same relation to craftsmanship as the theory of evolution does to the practices of pigeon fanciers." [45] Hall's main point was that "there is no straightforward answer to any question about the whole nature of the scientific revolution." [46] In the final analysis, the roles of the scholar and the craftsman were complementary. But this still begged the question of the sociological relationship between religion and science.

4. The major works of R. K. Merton, especially his lengthy monograph in *Osiris* in 1938 and his "Studies in the Sociology of Science" in *Social Theory and Social Structure* (revised edition, 1957), asserted a sophisticated version of Weber's thesis, that Puritanism was especially favorable to the development of science—indeed, Puritan utilitarianism and Puritan rationalism and empiricism formed the essence of the spirit of modern science. "It may very well be that the Puritan ethos did not directly influence the method of science, and that this was simply a parallel development in the internal history of science," Merton argued, "but it is evident that through the psychological compulsion toward certain modes of thought and conduct this value-complex made an empirically founded science commendable rather than, as in the medieval period, reprehensible or at best acceptable as sufferance." [47] This was to push the question of origins back to the sixteenth century and beyond. Neither Merton (who reviewed most of the historiographical controversy in the revised edition of "Puritanism, Pietism and Science") nor T. K. Rabb, in his essay on "Puritanism and the Rise of Science" in the *Journal of World History* (1962), addressed himself primarily to the question of how Tudor science was related to Tudor Puritanism. Rabb, however, challenged the Weber-Merton orthodoxy, urging the need for strong qualifications and more careful definitions. The problem of the relationship between craftsmen and scholars in the history of science was largely a question of who were Puritans and who were traditionalists. The Marxists had maintained that the scholarly conservatives of the sixteenth and seventeenth centuries were traditionalists in both religion and science, whereas the craftsmen were innovators in their attitudes toward religion and science. The Weberians were inclined to stress ideas and religious attitudes more than social roles, but they were at least sympathetic to the view that Puritanism (especially left-wing Puritanism) was more congenial to craftsmen than to scholars. Three important works that questioned details of the Weber thesis appeared between 1939 and 1959: M. M. Knappen's *Tudor Puritanism* (1939), P. H. Kocher's *Science and*

Religion in Elizabethan England (1953), and M. H. Curtis's *Oxford and Cambridge in Transition, 1558–1642.* None of these books, however, explicitly challenged Weber's thesis as a whole (which was, however, being vigorously debated by Reformation scholars such as R. Hooykaas and François Russo in the pages of the *Journal of World History*).[48] A new controversy about the sociology of science in Tudor and early Stuart England was set off by Christopher Hill's *Intellectual Origins of the English Revolution* (1965), a book which developed ideas already suggested in *The Century of Revolution* (1961).

The main lines of Hill's argument converged on the English revolution of the mid-seventeenth century. Hill's argument stressed the correlation between Puritanism and science but reversed the Merton priorities. Instead of Puritanism being the prior commitment that helped to make possible the development of science, Hill argued, among other things, that experimental philosophy had helped to make men equal; thus the scientific radicals "used the Protestant doctrine of the priesthood of all believers to justify preaching by laymen, and not merely by university-trained specialists." [49] The attack on authority and the appeal to experience were manifested equally in religion and science. Most of Hill's book was devoted to studies of Bacon, Ralegh, and Coke— Elizabethans by training, although most of their works were published in the seventeenth century. Crucial to Hill's argument, however, was his discussion of London science and medicine, and in particular his discussion of Gresham College, founded in 1596 by the most astute financial agent and advisor to the Tudor monarchy. Hill's point was that "before Bacon began to write an intellectual revolution was under way," and that Gresham College was the locus of new intellectual and social attitudes.[50]

Criticism of Hill's argument has somewhat obscured the fact that his book was almost the first to thrust the Scientific Revolution into the purview of general English history; the sociological conditions for the rise of science were explicitly stated and the conclusion drawn that the intellectual conflicts in history, science, law, and religion were not only related to the social and political conflicts of the age but that all were aspects of a single revolution.[51] This monistic view of history was precisely what was challenged by Hill's critics. H F. Kearney, in a review in *Past and Present* (1964), touched off a long debate when he arrived at two negative conclusions: there was no simple connection between Puritanism and science, and there was no direct connection between economic and scientific development. The review was an attack not on sociological arguments as such but rather on the particular arguments and evidence used by Hill; in his conclusion Kearney urged the need for a more critical vocabulary to escape from the pseudo-problems that had grown up around terms such as Puritanism, merchant classes, gentry, etc.[52] The debate continued for some time in the pages of *Past and Present,* involving other scholars and further arguments and evidence. Theodore K. Rabb, who also rejected Hill's conclusions, urged that newer theories, such as those of Stephen Toulmin and T. S. Kuhn, might offer more promising avenues of approach toward an understanding of the nature and causes of the scientific revolution.[53] Methodology became the central issue at this point: the history of science was asserted to be a special kind of history requiring special methods.

The unique importance of Toulmin and Goodfield's *Discovery of Time* (1965) lay in the fact that it considered both nonhistorical and historical sciences (the spectrum running from physics to psychology, sociology, and history) in relation to common problems of method and time perspective. The historical factor in science had usually been dismissed as either irrelevant or conceptually misleading; the authors argued that there had been a close likeness in the growth of historical consciousness in many widely separated disciplines, and that recurrent patterns of theory in the "historical sciences"—whether of man or of nature—showed that similar problems usually were resolved by similar strategies. The human discovery of time, in the sense of a discovery of compelling reasons for accepting an immensely long time scale, could only be understood by studying the whole temporal development of "historical" attitudes. "As one field after another has been opened up," the authors wrote, "there has been a striking continuity of problems and methods. Where questions of motivation are not crucially involved, the historical inferences by which we reconstruct the past show a common form both in different centuries and in different historical sciences." [54] As in their earlier books, Toulmin and Goodfield asserted the importance of a kind of comparative approach to problems in the history of science. The intellectual genealogy of science, and common intellectual patterns were emphasized rather than sociological conditions.

A very different approach was employed by Thomas S. Kuhn in *The Structure of Scientific Revolutions* (1963), a methodological study that generalized some of the ideas put forth in his earlier book, *The Copernican Revolution* (1957). The historical orientation of *The Structure of Scientific Revolutions* was evident in the opening pages, which criticized traditional "textbook" views of the history of science. The traditional stereotype was development-by-accumulation, but Kuhn challenged this view. Out-of-date science was not necessarily unscientific simply because it had been discarded. Stressing the integrity of science in its own time, Kuhn argued that scientific progress depended on a series of "revolutions," which were resolved by the scientific community itself: "the net result of a sequence of such revolutionary selections, separated by periods of normal research, is the wonderfully adapted set of instruments we call modern scientific knowledge." [55] Crises are the necessary preconditions for the emergence of novel theories, according to Kuhn, who used Copernicus as one illustration of his thesis. To describe the book as an extended essay on the problem of defining revolution in science would be unfair to the complexity of the argument, but Kuhn's awareness of the problem is evident in every chapter. To the Tudor historian his discussion of the parallelism between political and scientific revolutions is bound to be stimulating, especially in view of the historiographical theories outlined in the last chapter. In science, as in politics, Kuhn argued, when polarization occurs, *"political recourse fails."* [56] There is no way to resolve a revolutionary crisis in the paradigm structure of normal science: "the premises and values shared by the two parties to a debate over paradigms are not sufficiently extensive for that. As in political revolutions, so in paradigm choice—there is no standard higher than the assent of the relevant community." [57]

Two further books which have relevance for the historiography of revolution and of science are: *Revolution*, edited in 1966 by Carl J. Friedrich as Volume VIII of *Nomos*, a study devoted to the many meanings of the word "revolution"; and *The Scientific Intellectual* (1963) by Lewis S. Feuer, a study of the psychological and sociological origins of modern science; the latter was explicitly concerned to refute the Weber thesis. Problems in the history of science linked up inevitably with problems in economic history.

Economic history has flourished in the twentieth century. Capitalists and Communists agree about its importance. In commenting on new trends in the subject, M. Postan called attention in 1956 to the number of new chairs in economic history in British universities, to the number of specialized journals devoted to the history of transport, agriculture, and technology, and to the output of print dealing with various aspects of economic history.[58] The causes of such rapid growth in a modern industrial society are not hard to hunt. Everyone from local antiquaries to left-wing undergraduates finds reason to be interested in ancient enterprise. Collectors of Indian weapons and of craftsmen's hand tools, of Tudor tankards and of American barbed wire, have in common an interest (no matter how rudimentary) in some aspect of economic history. The English economic history debates of the late nineteenth century centered on the work of Archdeacon Cunningham and Sir William Ashley, who echoed imperialist politics and, more faintly, earlier German academicians. The great Tudor economic historians of the next generation were George Unwin and R. H. Tawney, who moved by different routes to the left in politics. In the 1930s economic historians tended to view economic history in terms of crises and commercial fluctuations. Marxist explanations became more common, yet English economic history remained traditional in its methods. John Maynard Keynes "rediscovered" the economic theory of the early Mercantilists, but he was not writing economic history. The economic history of Tudor England was written almost exclusively by historians with some knowledge of economics, not by theoretical economists with an interest in history. Any intelligent student with a layman's knowledge of elementary economics could read and understand most of the essays in the *Economic History Review*. By 1956 the situation was beginning to change as medievalists and modernists applied new techniques of quantification to the data:

> The relation between aggregate output of agriculture and the productivity of new land, the "terms of trade" between agriculture and industry, the effects of supply of bullion and of population trends on the movements of prices, the part which technical change played in the evolution of industry—these are a fair sample of the topics which now [1956] occupy the medieval economic historians. What agitates the modernists are problems like relative contributions of birth rates and death rates to long-term trends of population, the validity of the Marxian hypothesis of expropriation of peasant landholders as a prerequisite of the Industrial Revolution, the influence

of the rate of interest on the supply of capital, the behavior of businessmen in different phases of industrial development, the responsiveness of labour to the economic stimuli of wages.[59]

Clearly these topics have not all received the same amount of attention from Tudor historians; but insofar as the Tudor age is regarded as the period in which medieval and modern trends intersect, the strategic importance of Tudor economic and social history has had to be recognized. Since 1956 the use of economic theory in historical writing has increased, although the "new" economic history has not yet altered the approaches to Tudor history.

The "new" economic history has been called "econometrics" and, with less regard for the sensibilities of the muse, "Cliometrics." Although the terminology is ambiguous, the general meaning is clear: theoretically structured, quantitative economic history, or, more narrowly, "model building." The treacherous shoals beneath the surface of this definition may cause all but the most theoretical-minded of Tudor economic historians to steer clear. However, the methodological problems charted by the "new" economic historians are pertinent to many aspects of Tudor economic history. Current debates about the relationship of economic history to the study of comparative economic systems, or about the interdependence of "new" and traditional approaches to economic history, have raised questions about the underlying assumptions of economic historiography. The historical utility of models, the relationship of economic "values" to price indices, the differences between verification in history and in economics, the role of hypotheses and figments, and the differences between typification and idealization have become subjects of controversy among economists and economic historians.[60] As the "household accounts" approach has been supplemented by model building, contrary-to-fact predictions, and other operations dependent upon economic theory, the need for at least some acquaintance with current controversy has become evident. The purpose of this brief introduction is to call attention to a few of the theoretical issues, not to resolve technical problems.

According to R. W. Fogel, one of the best known American econometric historians, the traditional outlook must be revised:

Some historians have held that there is no point in applying powerful statistical methods to economic history because the available data are too poor. In actual practice, the correlation often runs the other way. When the data are very good, simple statistical procedures will usually suffice. The poorer the data, the more powerful are the methods which have to be applied.[61]

Economic theory, according to Fogel, can be employed to circumvent the data problem. Models, estimates, and mathematical manipulations can be used to "bring out," or substitute for, inadequate data. In sum, "The fundamental methodological feature of the new economic history is its attempt to cast all explanations of past economic development in the form of valid hypothetico-deductive models." [62] According to Fogel's critics, notably Fritz Redlich, historical economic models are dubious devices, and the production of such models is, at best, "quasi-history," which cannot be verified.[63] The problem of verification is crucial, for by verification the historian has traditionally meant going directly to the sources. Max Weber was perhaps the first writer to deal explicitly with the nature of historical models, and he would presumably have agreed that their refinement by mathematical means does not alter the fact that they are distortions of historical reality. The function of the model or ideal type is to permit comparisons and to sort out the "essential" features of historical constructs. A model, such as Weber's ideal Protestant ethic, or Walzer's "model of radical politics," is useful if it allows the historian to see something he would not otherwise have recognized in his data; the historian's test, however, is *empirical* reference, not mere coherence, and not prediction in a logical manner from postulates. To the economist as such, verification takes place if logical deductions can be made from postulates, or if "the assumptions of the model are empirically valid," which usually means acceptable to the profession.[64] The theoretical economist is not concerned with accounting for changes in economic taste or cultural values. "To the extent that traditional economic history stresses institutions, noneconomic factors and imponderables," Fritz Redlich writes, "it might draw for theoretical support on sociology and anthropology rather than economics; whereas the 'new' economic historians rely exclusively on the latter." [65]

The idea that it is empirically possible to draw a distinction between the economic and the noneconomic data has been accepted by some economic historians and rejected by others. "This division into two categories of data has the unavoidable effect of separating the actual economy from the pure economy of theory," according to Arthur Schweitzer, "and of purifying the strictly economic data to such an extent that they fit the requirements of Theory." [66] The intricacies of this debate may be pursued in the learned journals. The basic criticism of the use of economic models in history is simply that they represent abstractions which cannot show how everyday economic life depended on the total cultural-historical environment. They may be "approximations" or "ideal types," but to the extent that they are *particular* ideal types, representing particular historical periods and people, they become less useful to the economic theorist (who wants a more general theoretical framework); and, at the same time, they become more and more like the historian's merely descriptive categories. The great economic historians developed broad frames of historical reference—the industry, the city, the economic region, feudalism, capitalism, business cycles —but how they arrived at these frameworks is often overlooked; and it is perhaps too easy to make the mistake of assuming that ideal types can be verified and made to substitute for historical facts.

Perhaps the true importance of the "new" economic history is that it has tried to make things more explicit:

> History may be a "good story," but its credibility often depends on implicit assumptions. By making these assumptions explicit, the new economic historians are attempting to increase the area within which reasonable men can agree. The use of explicit theoretical models provides the reader with the opportunity to understand thoroughly what the investigator is doing and therefore to make a reasoned decision as to whether he agrees with the way the questions have been posed. In addition, the application of explicit quantitative techniques in conjunction with these models provides the same kind of opportunity with reference to the historical data involved. When an estimate of an historical magnitude is used within an explicit theoretical framework, the reader knows what the estimate is supposed to represent. He can then bring his skill as an historian to bear on the question of its appropriateness and authenticity. [67]

What is said here of economic models applies also to "model building" in general. To the extent that the "new" economic history aims at making explicit the underlying assumptions of statistical measurement, however, it links up with traditional economic history. If there has been one consistent trend in Tudor economic history during the past twenty years or more it has been the increasing use of quantitative tools and the increasing insistence on the part of historians that the underlying assumptions of measurement should be made explicit. The storm over the gentry has resolved itself largely into a debate over the statistical tables in Lawrence Stone's *The Crisis of the Aristocracy*. The problem of how to make allowance for the sixteenth-century inflation has become the center of a controversy about the statistics in W. K. Jordan's books on English philanthropy in the decades from 1480 to 1660. The problem of determining the nature and magnitude of population changes in pre-censal periods has occupied the Cambridge Group for the History of Population and Social Structure. Criticism of *An Introduction to English Historical Demography* (edited by E. A. Wrigley and published in 1966) and of Glass and Eversley, *Population in History* (1965), has centered on the techniques of measurement advocated by demographers to piece out the limited supply of statistical data. Methodological problems in demography are directly related to economic questions, if only because, as D. E. C. Eversley pointed out, "when we begin to consider the interrelatedness of food supplies and their effect on survival and procreation on the one hand and the inability of a starving population to spend money on consumer goods on the other, we realize that we are here faced with one of the fundamental relationships between populations and economy." [68] It is unnecessary to insist that measurement, whether of manors or of marriages, requires a high degree of cooperation between historians, statisticians, and social scientists. The Polish Marxist, J. Kabk, has suggested that mathematics is the basic tool and that the "mathematization" of learning is a process common to all the disciplines.[69]

In this overview of recent trends, the transition question may serve as an index of comparison for the different ways in which economic and social historians have assessed the significance of new special studies. The long Mississippi of history has cut many channels over the centuries, and the delta islands change in number and shape every decade as new knowledge builds up at the spits. The main contours of social and economic history are easily recognized, but the lesser islands—incipient specialties—have no agreed-upon designations. Tudor economic history has grown up around certain main problems: agrarian, monetary, industrial, commercial, household, governmental, demographic. Conceptual problems create currents that tend to join economic with social, intellectual, or other kinds of history—the history of mercantilism, the history of wages and prices, the history of capitalism in relation to religion, etc. It will be appropriate to begin with William Cunningham's *The Growth of English Industry and Commerce in Modern Times* and then proceed to the more specialized works of Tawney and others; from each island a glimpse of those nearest it (and of some downstream from it) may be had.

The Growth of English Industry and Commerce was published in 1882 and was frequently revised by Cunningham. He set the basic arguments about mercantilism and about the importance of capitalistic attitudes that were to dominate the thinking of two generations of English historians. According to him, modern times really began with the reign of Elizabeth, when Englishmen attained a sense of national unity. The acquisition of money for reasons of state was noticeably modern; and Cecil's mercantilist policies, along with the recoinage and the beginnings of English banking, helped to strengthen the state. Nevertheless, other events, notably the fall in the price of silver, and changing attitudes toward usury (which amounted to a "revolution in public opinion"), conspired to bring about an economic crisis. "It is practically certain," Cunningham wrote, "that the constitutional crisis of the seventeenth century, and the parliamentary disputes which led to the Civil War, were greatly embittered by the fall in the value of silver and the consequent poverty of the Crown." [70] In short, the economic crisis of the sixteenth century aggravated, and helped to bring about, the political crisis of the seventeenth century.

After Cunningham's general account came a whole series of studies of particular industries and commercial enterprises, as well as investigations of the gilds and companies of London, of apprenticeship, of governmental efforts at economic regulation, and, of course, fuller histories of mercantilism and of the Tudor economy as a whole. [71] Some of these books will be discussed in a later chapter; here the trend of interpretation is important. The first edition of E. Lipson's *The Economic History of England*, largely concerned with the Middle Ages, appeared in 1915; two further volumes on "The Age of Mercantilism" appeared in 1931. In the third, revised edition of the entire work, first published in 1943,

Lipson incorporated a long Introduction (to Vol. II) "designed to provide a synthesis and an interpretation of the various aspects of England's economic development from the close of the Middle Ages to the 'Industrial Revolution.' " [72] This essay, incorporating the findings of then recent specialized research, provides a useful context for studying twentieth-century revisions of Tudor economic history. Although Lipson divided the "Middle Ages" from the "Age of Mercantilism" in the sixteenth century, he stressed continuity rather than change. Having lived through the depression decade and the early years of the war, he was very much concerned with the problems of a planned economy and thought of his introduction as setting England's first planned economy in a historical light:

> In the age of Mercantilism the issue was fought out whether individualism should be allowed a free hand or kept vigorously under control, whether the dissolving forces of commercialism should ruthlessly destroy the medieval fabric of society or remain subject to the traditional checks and balances . . . The ideal of the old order was stability: that of the new order was progress. For a century (1558–1660) England was distracted by the conflict between these rival concepts. [73]

A few of the books that significantly shaped or modified the views of Lipson included Lipson's own work on *The History of the Woolen and Worsted Industries* (1921); volumes of *The Victoria County History*; R. H. Tawney's *The Agrarian Problem in the Sixteenth Century* (1912); E. F. Heckscher's *Mercantilism* (English edition, 1935); *Prices and Wages in England,* edited by Sir William Beveridge and others (Vol. I, *Price Tables. Mercantile Era,* 1939); J. U. Nef, *The Rise of the British Coal Industry* (1932); and R. E. Prothero, *English Farming Past and Present* (1912; revised edition, 1936).

The close connection between local history and economic history has become a platitude if not a postulate. Without question, some of the most significant revisions in Tudor historiography in recent years have come about as the result of a closer look at history on the local and regional levels. [74] Pioneering interpretations, however, have often been the reason for more detailed studies of local sources. A glance through G. E. Fussell's Introduction to Lord Ernle's classic (Prothero was created baron in 1919) will reveal the extent to which local studies modified earlier views of the enclosure movement and other features of Tudor agrarian history.[75] The historiographical essay by Joan Thirsk in the *Agricultural History Review* (1955) reinforces the point and adds greatly to an appreciation of the landmarks in agrarian history.[76] Lord Ernle brought practical knowledge of farming to the writing of agrarian history, but the broad outlines of his interpretation of Tudor agrarian history did not differ markedly from those of Cunningham. The reign of Elizabeth marked a definite stage in English history, when the "medieval organization of society, together with its trade guilds and manorial system of farming had broken down." [77] Farming shared in the general prosperity under Elizabeth; enclosures, unfortunate though they were for the dispossessed, were necessary for progress in farming methods. The failure of some agriculturists to adapt themselves was the price paid for progress.

It was R. H. Tawney, in *The Agrarian Problem in the Sixteenth Century*, who delved deeper into the Tudor evidence, following the work of I. S. Leadam, E. F. Gay, and A. N. Savine, and provided what might be called the classical interpretation of the "agrarian revolution." [78] Tawney was far more interested in the social consequences of the agrarian revolution of the sixteenth century, than in the extent to which it fostered technical progress. His own socialistic sympathies were engaged on the side of the dispossessed. Although he denied, in his Introduction, that he had answered the question of what place ought to be given to the agricultural revolution in the transition from medieval to modern conditions of agriculture, he stated in his conclusion that "what made the new methods of agriculture not simply an important technical advance in the utilization of the soil, but the beginning of a social revolution, was the insecurity of the tenure of large numbers of the peasantry . . ." [79] Tawney saw that the statistical evidence about enclosures was inconclusive, but his major argument was not statistical but moral and intellectual: "In the infinite complexity of human relationships, with their interplay of law with economics, and of economics with politics, and all with the shifting hopes and fears, baseless anticipations and futile regrets, of countless individuals, a change which to the statistician concerned with quantities seems insignificant, may turn a wheel whose motion sets a world of unseen forces grinding painfully around to a new equilibrium." [80] By 1642 the channels of economic history had been carved deep and sure. Tawney's position in the debate over the rise of the gentry was implicit in his early study of agrarian problems; and the contrast between "statistics" and "the meaning of statistics" is still a live issue.

Lawrence Stone, in his Introduction to the Harper Torchbook edition (1967) of *The Agrarian Problem*, pointed out some of the influences that shaped Tawney's thought, and the extent to which Tawney's conclusions have been either altered or substantiated by recent research. The two factors that were least understood by Tawney were demographic pressure and regional variations. Improvements in statistical measurement and in the amount of data altered many of Tawney's conclusions:

> Today we are beginning to be aware of the critical importance of demographic growth as a destabilizing factor. It was the demographic growth which stimulated the change to a market economy by increasing the number of townspeople dependent on the countryside for food supplies. It was relentless demographic growth which multiplied the number of villagers until the pressure on the land became acute. It was this rather than the enclosing activities of monopolistic landlords which caused the struggle over the common lands and the encroachments on the waste. . . . Population pressure has replaced the wicked enclosing or rackrenting landlord as the *diabolus ex machina*; and it now seems unlikely that eviction due to enclosure for pasture was responsible for more than a very small proportion of the vagrants of sixteenth century England.[81]

In short, the weakness of the custom of the manor, and the ineffectiveness of government attempts at intervention and regulation are understandable; we no longer assume that governments can eliminate the problems that rising populations create. "If the last twenty years will appear in retrospect as the heroic age in the study of the agrarian history in England," Lawrence Stone concluded, "Tawney will stand out as the pioneer, blazing a trail thirty years before the first settlers arrived." [82]

The book which best sums up recent trends in agrarian economic history is *The Agrarian History of England and Wales*, Vol. IV, *1500–1640* edited by Joan Thirsk (1967). A collection of essays by specialists (including the editor), this massive volume of over 900 pages explores the ramifications of agrarian history in detail. Both as a synthesis of local and national studies, and as an attempt to open up fresh approaches based on new research, the book is a major achievement. The significance of agrarian activity in the Tudor period, when land and farming dominated the economy, made inevitable a number of excursions into fields of general social history. The importance of the statistical tables required some discussion of the problems of compiling and using statistics. In the Tudor period, when a long series of observations from the same source were lacking, when regional variations were extreme, and when the relative importance of products could not be accurately measured, there seemed to be little reason to apply sophisticated economic techniques: "The nature of the material is such that the use of refined techniques is obviously out of the question." [83] What stands out perhaps most clearly here and elsewhere in the book is the caution which frames the generalizations. Although older views of the "New Monarchy" were rejected out of hand by Gordon Batho—"The nature of early Tudor kingship is now recognized to have been not a 'new monarchy' but fundamentally medieval"—he was careful to explain that in economic matters the lack of any numerous body of estate papers, coupled with the rudimentary accounting techniques of Tudor landlords, limited debate.[84] The gentry controversy was reappraised by more than one writer; and it is instructive to notice how recent research modified earlier positions. Peter Bowden sums up:

> The inflation of Tudor and early Stuart times is generally believed to have confronted English landowners with serious problems: problems which derived from the inelasticity of tenures, and which, so it is argued, could only be overcome by the adoption of rational techniques of estate management, or—according to another school of thought—by an injection of income from the proceeds of office or business. Under the influence of these conceptions, historians have envisaged major shifts in the balance of economic, social, and political power in the century preceding the Civil War. If such theories carry great scholarship behind them, they also seem in the light of present evidence to be built on very uncertain foundations. . . . In most districts, pressure of population created a constant need for additions to the cultivated area, while on demesne lands, if not on customary holdings, tenancies could be periodically renewed at greatly enhanced rents in money or in kind. . . . Whatever doubts may linger about the landowner's position in the years before 1580, few can remain in connection with the succeeding period up to 1620,

which saw a massive redistribution of income in favour of the landed class: a redistribution which, in the final analysis, was as much at the expense of the agricultural wage-earner and consumer as of the tenant farmer . . . In general, given the level of personal expenditure, the prosperity of the landowner in Tudor and early Stuart times must have depended much less upon his social origins than upon the nature of the land which constituted his estate and its sensitivity to economic change.[85]

Seen from the point of view of the landlords, the transition of the sixteenth century was one from relatively hard times to a progressive, if uncertain, prosperity. If the fifteenth century was "the golden age of the English labourer," in the phrase of Thorold Rogers, the late sixteenth century was the beginning of an iron age for labor and the beginning of landlord domination.[86]

The importance of local history was stressed by Joan Thirsk in her essay on enclosing and engrossing. The lack of a convenient river system for exporting grain, and the presence of heavy clay soils in the Midlands, for example, were technical reasons for the early conversion of arable to pasture. In the long run, however, the transition in English agriculture that had the most revolutionary consequences was one that went unnoticed by contemporaries:

> Common fields and pastures kept alive a vigorous co-operative spirit in the community; enclosures starved it. . . . After enclosure, when every man could fence his own piece of territory and warn his neighbours off, the discipline of sharing things fairly with one's neighbours was relaxed and each household became an island unto itself. This was the great revolution in men's lives, greater than all the economic changes following enclosure.[87]

It is hard even to imagine that communal way of life that is now lost. Only the local historian, living with the visual evidence of the past, can paint the portrait of such a conservative yet changing society, as A. L. Rowse did in *Tudor Cornwall*.

Agrarian history may be considered a particular illustration of Tudor social and economic history. Its methods of statistical measurement, especially with regard to monetary trends, its comparative approach to local and regional data, its use of demographic research, and its concern with the broader problems of Tudor society —all these are characteristic of the best modern work in Tudor economic and social history. Monographs and special studies have worn away the sharp outlines of earlier interpretation, making most agrarian historians wary; Welsh society was unlike English society, and generalizations about either must take account of newly documented differences. If there are fewer epigrammatic statements about the nature of the Tudor transition this is in part because the essential facts—about the sixteenth-century inflation or about the disposition of monastic lands—are not currently in dispute; primarily, however, it is because there is much less certainty about "general" trends. Soil cultivation methods, for example, changed much less drastically than methods of land use; the rise in sheep and wool prices, once thought to be a dominant factor in explaining enclosures, is now seen to be much less important; all agricultural prices rose, and in the long run cattle and grains exceeded sheep and wool. Still, there were obviously significant changes: the secularization of monastic lands; the increase in the scale of marketing operations, with accompanying problems for the government; and the emergence, in a century of complex change, of the "new man," the private trader who was far removed, spiritually and intellectually, from communal ways and from the paternal hierarchies of church and state.[88]

Finally, from the point of view of new methods which have forced the revision of older opinion, few books on agrarian history have had greater impact than Maurice Beresford's *The Lost Villages of England* (1954). Making use of a wide variety of evidence, including aerial surveys, family archives, old maps, public records, and private fieldwork, Beresford was able to show how inaccurate the conventional picture of depopulation was, and how misleading the literary evidence alone could be; and yet also how perceptive some contemporary observers were: "If there was very little total depopulation in the second half of the sixteenth century, and if the depopulation reported in 1517 seems to have been the end rather than the beginning of a flood, then we are very near to the sentiment expressed by John Hales in 1549." [89] Archaeologists may investigate more "lost" villages because historians have become curious about old maps, historical geography, and the possibilities of research in libraries of aerial photographs.

Secularization of the land as a consequence of the English Reformation did not mean that the new state Church ceased to be a landlord, but the process of secularization contributed to the

Church's economic problems. The tithes controversy of the seventeenth century was the response of intellectuals to the hard bargaining of laymen and churchmen over land rights through the centuries. Church history uncovers its own problems of land, labor, and capital.

The continuity of church history sets it apart; unlike agrarian history, which was a creation of the nineteenth century, the history of the Church has been written in a continuing form since the time of St. Augustine. Church history in the broadest sense is the history of religion. The methods of religious history today are those of secular history—there is no privileged status for revelation. Yet there is a sense in which the traditional distinctions—common at the beginning of the seventeenth century—between sacred and secular history, linger on. Ancient controversies, mixed with anxieties about the present and a few odd facts about the past, have sometimes resulted not in history but in a speculative philosophy of history. Arguments about grace abounding, or about the role of providence in the history of church or state, must be dismissed. It should be noted, however, that a few books, such as Father M. C. D'Arcy's *The Sense of History, Secular and Sacred* (1959) or Herbert Butterfield's *Christianity and History* (1950), have helped to make Christian beliefs plausible to men of a secular-minded generation, who no longer respond to religious passion and polemics. The traditions of religious historiography, touched upon by Father D'Arcy, have grown up around the interests of churchmen. Only in this century has the sociological interpretation of church history begun to develop a tradition of its own. Six main categories of religious history may be distinguished: (1) institutional history, deriving from St. Augustine's concern with the continuity of the Church in *The City of God*; (2) biographical history, originating in the medieval Lives of the Saints; (3) intellectual history, which might, so far as it concerns doctrine, be traced to the Church Fathers; (4) economic history, largely a nineteenth-century innovation; (5) local history which, in England at least, goes back to White Kennett's *Parochial Antiquities* (1695); and (6) sociological history, Germanic in origin and still greatly influenced by the ideas of Karl Marx, Max Weber, and Ernst Troeltsch.

Institutional histories of the Church of England have followed fairly conventional patterns. R. W. Dixon's *A History of the Church of England* was published in six volumes between 1887 and 1902;

it presented an Anglican apologia for the years 1529–1570. *The Constitutional History and Constitution of the Church of England* by F. Markower appeared in translation in 1895, without the blessing of a marriage between style and information. In 1904 W. H. Frere published *A History of the English Church in The Reigns of Elizabeth and James I*; and James Gairdner published *A History of the English Church in the Sixteenth Century from Henry VIII to Mary*. In 1910 R. G. Usher brought out, in two volumes, *The Reconstruction of the English Church, 1583–1610*. These became the "standard works," often consulted if not often read. Institutional historiography, at least of the Tudor state Church, has not flourished in recent years. Except for articles published in historical journals most of the significant work on institutional problems has dealt with aspects of the Reformation, or with the Church before the Reformation.[90] Recusants and Puritans have attracted the attention of those historians who share the twentieth-century interest in alienation, sacrifice, and the causes of capitalism's malaise. Of books on the Reformation itself there is no end in sight. Perhaps it could be said that the best recent work has been accomplished by those who, whatever their private creeds, believe in the humanistic Reformation doctrine of *adiaphora*—"things indifferent," which should not occasion strife. Certainly the best modern survey, *The English Reformation* (1964) by A. G. Dickens, stresses the importance of *adiaphorism* in the institutional policies of the English Church. Dickens further argued that the significance of the Cromwellian revolution was not just that it cleared the decks, but that the fourth decade of the sixteenth century should be seen "in relation to the Anglican future as much as to the medieval past." A Reformation of compromise and detachment resulted from Henrician efforts to found a new state Church; the traditional view which dated the beginning of Anglicanism from the publication of Cranmer's first prayer book, or from the accession of Elizabeth, remained imperceptive.

Some of the best recent work on the English Reformation has come from Catholic scholars. The English translation of *The Reformation in England*, by G. Constant, appeared in 1934 and set a precedent; Constant was readable and he provided shrewd commentary on many issues, including Henry's divorce.[91] His bibliographical knowledge was impressive, and as a Frenchman he could take a detached, albeit sometimes dogmatic, view: "Englishmen are not lovers of abstract ideas. Not being logical like the French, nor mystics, like the Germans, they do not enter into theological quarrels; they are more for questions of a practical nature. . . . The Reformation in this country was brought about solely by a grievance of a practical order intimately bound up with a question of money." [92] The work of Dom David Knowles on *The Religious Orders in England,* in three volumes (1948–1959), established itself almost at once as one of the major classics of English historiography. Having pointed out the lack of distinguished men in the monasteries during the seventy years between the death of Henry V and the adolescence of More and Wolsey, the Regius Professor of Modern History at Cambridge began his third volume, covering the Tudor dissolution, with the observation that "The advent of the first Tudor sovereign marked no epoch in the history of the religious orders in England." [93] Making much fuller use of unpublished materials, both local and national, and, in the narrative of the dissolution, working with the unprinted reports of the commissioners of 1536, Knowles provided an account unmatched by any earlier writer; the idealized monasteries of Cardinal Gasquet, portrayed in *Henry VIII and the English Monasteries* (1888–1889), were turned to myth by the researches of a fellow Benedictine. The work of A. Savine, *English Monasteries on the Eve of the Dissolution* (1909), and S. B. Liljgren, *The Fall of the Monasteries and the Social Changes in England Leading up to the Great Revolution* (1924), both dealing mainly with economic matters, still contain useful information, but their interpretations of the evidence no longer seem so persuasive. A. G. Baskerville's *English Monks and the Suppression of the Monasteries* (1937) retains its value as an important interpretation based on original research. In his epilogue Knowles posed with great candor the most difficult questions, and his historiographical conclusions are especially noteworthy:

> There was a time when apologists of the Middle Ages attributed to the Dissolution almost every ill which they deplored in the sixteenth and later centuries: the secular and servile state, the upstart nobility, the parliamentarian gentry, the later oligarchy, pauperism, capitalism, avarice, and atheism. More recently still, there has been a tendency to minimize the extent of the revolution. It has been said that the religious were so earthbound that their disappearance left no spiritual void, while at the same time the existing landowners had already such a footing within the monastic estates either as

leaseholders or administrators that the Dissolution had little social or economic effect. It would seem true that it is very difficult to distinguish any save the most superficial results in these spheres from those of other disturbing influences of the time, religious, social, and economic, but a summary review may not be out of place.[94]

In concluding his review, Knowles made the point that when once a religious house or a religious order sinks to the level of a purely human institution, then "Whatever its works may be, they are the works of time and not of eternity." [95] Medieval monasticism was an integral part of medieval society and declined with it, yet in some respects the monastic orders brought upon themselves the dissolution orders of the state.

The three-volume work of Father Philip Hughes, *The Reformation in England* (1951–1954), has become the standard Catholic history of the Reformation to the death of Elizabeth, the last volume of which is virtually a history of Catholic resistance movements during Elizabeth's reign. Making use of printed authorities and calendars, Hughes wrote a general religious history, not the detailed history of an institution. His work is significant not because of new methods or new manuscripts but because it reflects the extent to which Catholic historians of Protestantism have accepted the premises of Lingard's scholarship and have developed greater understanding and charity. Yet it remains true that the Reformation is a formidable massif, which appears very different to scholars who see it from different Christian viewpoints. To Hughes the Reformation was symptomatic of "A world in Revolution." Much as he admired the unique achievements of Englishmen in law and government, and much as he deplored the monks who were "more interested in their hunting dogs than in their sacred studies," he could not treat the events of the Reformation without passing moral, intellectual, and ultimately religious judgments.[96] If it is the case, as Croce maintained, that no one can discover "what Plato thought" without inquiring "whether it is true," then Hughes's approach to Jewel's *Apologia* is perhaps appropriate.[97] The *Apologia* was certainly a work of propaganda which can be criticized on historical grounds. But some of Hughes's questions about this *Apologia* were only doubtfully appropriate in a work of history: "Who shall say the minds and souls it damaged" or how many it "robbed of the remnants of their Catholic faith?" [98] Such questions may be answered by rhetoric, but not, given the evidence, by the methods of secular history. Another kind of problem is that of the nature and popularity of the "religious revolution" under Edward VI. Hughes concluded emphatically that "The reformation in the reign of Edward VI was, in actual fact, as little loved, or longed for, as the governments that brought it to pass." [99] The evidence that weighs for the statement was given, but not that which weighs against it. The passage of four centuries has not, in Tudor religious history at least, transformed the old explosive powders into mere harmless dust.

The writing of Tudor lives has a distinguished tradition, going back to the Tudor classics: Roper's *Life of More*, Cavendish's *Wolsey*, and Foxe's *Book of Martyrs*. These convey a sense of immediacy and personal conviction that is seldom achieved except in firsthand accounts. Even though Foxe was influenced by medieval literary tradition (especially by the martyrology of the *Golden Legend*), he was too passionate a Protestant and too good a historian to want to confuse fact with fiction. [100] The sense of "presence" in biography is the product of many skills, but a necessary condition is intimate knowledge. Important work was done by Strype in the eighteenth century, and by Pocock in the nineteenth century, to make available the letters and other records of the Reformation. Not until the twentieth century, however, was it possible to write thoroughly documented, modern biographies of early Tudor prelates and politicians. The concluding volumes of the *Letters and Papers of Henry VIII* became available to historians around 1910; and these printed sources and summaries still form the basis of historiography for the period 1509–1547. [101] Moreover, the *Dictionary of National Biography* (1885–1900) made possible a new kind of historiography, which could take account of the lesser personalities of the Tudor period; intellectuals in particular received attention. In an age in which religious books predominated, it was possible to trace the activities of a number of relatively obscure men who had written on religious topics. The *D.N.B.* for the Tudor period has been therefore of the utmost importance in religious historiography.

Among the earliest and best of the full-scale modern biographies were those by A. F. Pollard: *Henry VIII* (1902), *Cranmer* (1904), and his masterpiece, *Wolsey* (1929). The limitations of Pollard's approach, his relative neglect of cultural history, his misjudgments of contemporary religious life, his neglect of the archives (in favor of the printed *Letters and Papers*), his overestimate of Wolsey's legal and administrative reforms and his underestimate of Cromwell's importance—all these faults have been pointed out, yet it remains true that Pollard's *Wolsey* is a great achievement. Reinterpretations of Wolsey and of other sixteenth-century figures have been based largely on a more thorough exploitation of Pollard's methods. Having personally written five hundred biographies for the *D.N.B.*, Pollard was perhaps entitled to make use of printed sources. The fact is that sound biographies of some individuals can be written without benefit of transcriptions from the manuscript sources, as is evident from a list of titles: R. W. Chambers' *Thomas More* (1935), W. Schenk's *Reginald Pole* (1950), J. F. Mozley's biographies of *Tyndale* (1937), *Foxe* (1940), and *Coverdale* (1953), and V. J. K. Brook's *A Life of Archbishop Parker* (1962). Other biographers, while still depending on printed sources, have made more or less extensive use of manuscripts in their work: Edward Sturtz in *The Works and Days of John Fisher* (1967), Jasper Ridley in *Thomas Cranmer* (1962), Lacey Baldwin Smith in *Tudor Prelates and Politics* (1953), and H. F. M. Prescott in *Mary Tudor* (1952). Yet whether working with manuscripts or with printed sources historians have tended to employ the same biographical methods. Some recent biographies of Tudor religious and political leaders have provided new interpretations, thanks partly to general advances in historiography and partly to diligent research in private papers; but biography remains, in Namier's phase, "the ritualist form of English historiography." [102] Behemoth biography, exemplified in Spedding's *Bacon* or Masson's *Milton*, can seldom be written unless there are masses of surviving letters or other documents; and Tudor biographies have therefore not tended to be overweight.[103] In general it might be said that the resources for new full-scale Tudor lives are strictly limited; new psychological approaches may succeed in revising some current opinions; but probably group studies, such as those provided by William Clebsch in *England's Earliest Protestants* (1964), or by Pearl Hogrefe in *The Sir Thomas More Circle* (1959)—both specialized studies in intellectual history—will henceforth preponderate.

Intellectual history in the broadest sense includes the history of theology, education, and preaching. In all these fields far-reaching revisions have been made during the last half century. The growth of intellectual history as a discipline has benefited Tudor religious historiography in at least three ways: more studies of Tudor religious writings have been made by trained historians instead of by enthusiastic or contentious amateurs; the complex of relays and connections between religious and secular thought has slowly been traced, not only in short monographs, but also in extensive surveys; and the history of education has been virtually rewritten. Some biographies, such as Sturtz's biography of Fisher, deal to a large extent with intellectual history; and numerous books on the Reformation provide information about Tudor intellectual development. Protestant and Counter Reformation currents have received the most attention, but in *The Radical Reformation* (1962) George H. Williams made the case for viewing the Anabaptists, Spiritualists, and Evangelical Rationalists as a kind of "third force"—Radicals who incurred the enmity of Protestants and Catholics alike. How the historical attitudes of Protestants contributed to the modern idea of progress has been the subject of many books, one of the more recent being Ernest Lee Tuveson's *Millennium and Utopia* (1949). Tuveson stressed the continuity of historical thought, arguing that it was the coming together of the New Philosophy and the old millenarianism that produced the modern idea of progress.[104] A rather different view of historical change was taken by William Haller in *Foxe's Book of Martyrs and the Elect Nation* (1963), which stressed the revolutionary importance of emerging Protestant nationalism. William Haller's earlier study, *The Rise of Puritanism* (1938), although it dealt mainly with seventeenth-century Puritanism, set forth major arguments about the nature of Puritan ideas and attitudes, to which most subsequent work has made explicit reference.

The prevailing view in the 1930s of the relationship between Anglicanism and Puritanism was that the basis of conflict was economic or political, not theological or psychological. Haller thought otherwise. Taking seriously the arguments of Puritan intellectuals, Haller considered predestination to be "The central dogma of Puritanism." [105] In this he followed the lead of Weber and Tawney; but like W. H. Frere in *The English Church in the Reigns of Elizabeth and James I, 1558–1625* (1904), Haller stressed the importance of doctrine itself and of religious doubts about salvation, rather than Weber's "worldly asceticism" or Tawney's idea that Puritanism was "the religion of trade." The controversy over the importance of predestination in Protestant and especially Puritan thought became part of a wider debate in the 1940s over the importance of ideas in history. As the reader will see, controversy about the definition of Puritanism and about the importance of ideas as opposed to interests has become chronic in Tudor religious historiography.

Intellectual historians, until recently, very often failed to discuss issues of historical theory in any detail, although the importance of such issues was obvious. Peter Munz in *The Place of Hooker in the History of Thought* (1952) argued that movements or periods in thought hardly ever follow each other in chronological order, but rather seem to exist side by side; economic and intellectual forces may emphasize one trait rather than another at any given historical moment. Historians must therefore be prepared to deal with traditions of thought, all of which are in some sense "contemporary." [106] The idea of the Church was the subject of constant controversy in the sixteenth century. Support for the opposed Anglican and Puritan positions could readily be found in the writings of St. Augustine. The visible Church could be regarded as part of the mystical body of Christ, or as something indifferent; the holiness of the Church might depend on the divine calling, or it could be argued that only the predestinated Saints were holy and therefore only they belonged to the Church. In *The Doctrine of the Church in Anglican Theology, 1547–1603* (1955), H. F. Woodhouse explored this problem (from the point of view of twentieth-century ideas of reunion) and his book points up the difficulty of discussing doctrine apart from differences of opinion.

In *Anglican and Puritan, The Basis of Their Opposition, 1558–1640* (1964), John F. New flatly denied that predestination was characteristic of Calvinism or Puritanism. He attempted to show that the fundamental differences between Anglicans and Puritans were indeed intellectual and theological, but he maintained that these differences had been misunderstood. The importance of predestination in the writings of Troeltsch and Weber, Tawney and Haller, was a misrepresentation of religious history. The Puritan was not, as Usher and many other twentieth-century historians had argued, tortured by suspense because he did not know if he would be saved; he knew, and his assurance gave him strength. Anglicans and Puritans in the sixteenth century shared many beliefs, but the best approach to their differences was through theology rather than church government or economics.

The trouble with most modern interpretations was that they "looked at the Church from a predominantly political standpoint— a reflex of modern secularism." [107] New either modified or rejected many of the historical generalizations that had become historically orthodox earlier in the century. Puritanism was not characterized by predestination, was not kept active by anxiety, was not liberalistic, was not tolerant of usury, or of the ways of the world in its doctrine of calling, and was not devoted to the idea of contract or a mutual covenant between God and man. The last point modified the fundamental and classic argument of Perry Miller about the nature of Puritan theology, set forth in 1939 in *The New England Mind, The Seventeenth Century*. Clearly this was revisionism with a vengeance; and in his conclusion New took the trouble to define explicitly the nature of his disagreement with the views of Charles H. and Catherine George expressed in *The Protestant Mind of the English Reformation, 1570–1640* (1961).[108]

The argument of the Georges was that the differences between Puritans and Anglicans were minimal, that both were in general agreement about the *via media*, and that the essential cleavage was between Protestant and Catholic; only briefly, during the years of the Marprelate Tracts and when Cartwright and Travers fought the church authorities, was there anything like an identifiable and distinct Puritanism. The "Puritan Revolution" thesis was thus rejected—there was no specific Puritan dynamic, because the term Puritan itself was "tentative, vague and inconclusive." The Georges concluded that in their efforts to find a distinguishing line between Puritans and Anglicans they had found "no issue, doctrinal or ecclesiastical, of which we can speak in other than relative terms." [109] Their book was iconoclastic in that it denied that there was any causal connection between Puritanism and revolution. But it was also explicitly "historiographical," in that it rejected point by point the arguments that Max Weber had developed in *The Protestant Ethic*. In describing their own general viewpoint about the linkage between Protestant thought and the surrounding climate of social attitudes and practices, the Georges assumed a mildly Marxist stance:

> The orientation and purpose of placation, worship, and sacrifice, and the uses to which this power is applied, whether social or antisocial, widely ethical or narrowly opportunistic, confirming or under-

mining of institutional stabilities, depend upon time, place and specific circumstances. We choose therefore to see religion in any social or historical situation as simply one among many conditioning factors and itself conditioned far more than it conditions.[110]

What made the Georges' book important, however, was not their philosophy of history but their positive arguments aimed at showing how and where Max Weber went wrong in his analysis of the relationship between religion and capitalism.

The importance of Max Weber as a catalyst is apparent—whether from the point of view of religion and intellectual history, or of capitalism and economic history, Weber's ideas have stimulated controversy and revision. The Georges' conclusions can be summarized briefly:

> Where then is the "spirit of capitalism" in its Protestant guise? It simply does not exist in England before 1640. There is a spirit of work, of frugality, of rationality in opposing waste and the misuse of economic resources, but any push toward a society of individual profit-seeking, competition for economic rewards, and social mobility scaled to the economic pursuit of wealth comes not from the ideology of Protestantism, but from the lay and secular world *sui generis*. Above all, it is impossible to argue that Protestantism in any way encouraged a profit system when the massive, uniform bulk of sermon and tractate literature equated any desire for profit (as opposed to service) with covetousness . . .[111]

The association of capitalism with Protestantism, they concluded, was nevertheless an important and unique historical fact. What happened in sixteenth- and seventeenth-century England was nothing less than the triggering of the whole series of revolutionary social and economic explosions of the modern world. An economic revolution was linked to a religious revolution in the sixteenth century by time and circumstance, not by causal connection. Protestantism and capitalism shared common enemies: the Roman Catholic Church and feudalism. Even though "The ambitions of capitalist entrepreneurs and the ideals of Protestant religiosity often made common cause against the institutional and ideological bias of the past, reinforcing one another in their independent struggles, they could not share the future." [112] The reason was simple—in the modern, secular world of business and science, religion would no longer constitute a third force.

If one recent trend in intellectual history has been the renewed attempt to understand religious thought in its own terms ("Protestantism made the last great effort to identify the moral goals and to direct the moral actions of the ruling classes in the west," according to the Georges), another has been the effort to discover more about the emergence of secularism and to trace the connections between religious and secular ideas.[113] The problem of toleration in this context was crucial, and W. K. Jordan's pioneering work, *The Development of Religious Toleration in England* (4 vols.; Vol I, 1932), dwelt upon the complex interplay of secular and religious forces which helped to promote the idea of toleration in Tudor England. Another kind of investigation, aimed at describing the nature of publishing in sixteenth-century England, has illuminated intellectual history in a different sector. H. S. Bennett, in *English Books and Readers 1475–1557* and *1558–1603* (1952 and 1965), showed how the conditions of the book trade affected the intellectual life of the age, and to what extent the preponderance of religious and devotional books—approximately half the printer's output before 1557—gave way, during Elizabeth's reign, to the claims of various kinds of secular literature. Recent books and articles on the history of Tudor education have demonstrated that secular influences were slowly gaining ascendancy. The intellectual revolution of the Renaissance was fundamentally at odds with traditional educational ideas and practices which had for so long served the chivalric culture of the nobility and the scholastic culture of the clergy.[114] Finally, since preaching must be considered a part of education in Tudor times, it will be appropriate at least to take note of two important books on the subject: *Preaching in England* (1964) by J. W. Blench, and *The Godly Preachers of the Elizabethan Church* (1965) by Irvonwy Morgan.

Recent books and articles on the history of Tudor education have significantly altered earlier views of the subject, although the work of W. H. Woodward and Foster Watson remains important. H. C. Porter in *Reformation and Reaction in Tudor Cambridge* (1958) pointed out how important academic politics were in spreading new ideas—universities were the nurseries of the Church—and how academic intellectuals, angrily disputing about the nature of grace, were in fact acting out parables of continuity and change in history. Seen from within the college precincts, disputes between Puritans and Anglicans appear to be quarrels be-

tween living, irritable, fallible men, not dialectical encounters between resounding abstract nouns. In *Oxford and Cambridge in
Transition 1558–1642* (1959), Mark H. Curtis drew upon a number of studies by American scholars (especially those of Franklin Le
Van Baumer, J. H. Hexter, and Fritz Caspari), supplemented them
by his own researches, and produced a controversial study of the
transition problem as it manifested itself in the universities.[115] Arguing that the Tudors transformed the universities from ecclesiastical to civil institutions, Curtis concluded that the governing classes
gained a far greater number of places, and took far more interest in
the universities in the sixteenth century than they ever had pre-
viously. Moreover, the Tudors had applied a consistent policy of
building up the importance of the colleges (and the heads of colleges) at the expense of the older university structure. The result
was a new emphasis on undergraduate education. With the influx
of young aristocrats and other well-born scholars, many of whom
became virtuosi, the older curricular requirements began to be
dropped, or at least supplemented by newer scientific and humanistic learning. It was also the case, Curtis argued in a later article,
that there was an oversupply of "alienated intellectuals" in Stuart
society because of the increased demands of the Elizabethan church
for educated clergy.

Rather more iconoclastic was Kenneth Charlton's book, *Education in Renaissance England* (1965), which attacked the argument
that the gentry and aristocracy came to the universities to be educated: "The gentry sent their sons to university primarily for social
rather than educational reasons, as a useful, indeed necessary form
of conspicuous consumption." [116] Charlton published the first general survey of English education in the Renaissance, and he took
pains to make clear the basis of his disagreement with other scholars. His historiographical criticisms of Sir John Neale's thesis of a
"cultural revolution" resulting from increased university attendance
are consistent with his criticisms of W. K. Jordan's views about the
importance of philanthropy in furthering education: there was no
revolution. In both the upper and lower levels of formal education,
changes were not as significant as the persistence of "traditional
learning." [117] In this sense Charlton was a "medievalist" who
stressed institutional continuities and agreed with Bacon's criticism of the universities. There was one educational change, however, that conformed to the pattern traced in other fields by Jordan,

Neale, and other scholars—education was becoming secularized. The really significant changes occurred outside the formal establishment; it was the practical, secular, business-minded printers and booksellers, not the university clerics, who promoted new educational ideas. Knowledge came to be regarded as something to be shared, as reading became a habit. It was this that transformed society: "If anything about the gentry 'rose' it was their standard of education, and this was as true of their literary and cultural interests as it was of that part of their education which fitted them for public life." [118] But the new books, including the new histories and the new treatises on science, were not being assigned in the schools, Inns of Court, or universities. Progress depended on informal education.

A work which complemented Charlton's appeared in the following year—Joan Simon's *Education and Society in Tudor England* (1966). Her book was designed to correct the misconceptions that had grown up during the previous half century with regard to the grammar schools and the role of the state in English education. The generally accepted view had been that the Reformation was a period of destruction, "that grammar schools were crippled or swept away and elementary schooling obliterated during the reign of Edward VI." [119] The source of the case against the early Tudor monarchs was A. F. Leach's *English Schools at the Reformation* (1896), a book which upheld the view that the excellent English medieval schools had been sacrificed during the sixteenth century in a sudden, dramatic reversal of policy. What Joan Simon stressed was the complex interaction between the schools and universities and the surrounding society. The "revolutionary change" thesis was scrapped; continuity, however, was everywhere dappled by change. The Reformation did not destroy Renaissance trends, but gave them new direction. The needs of the state and the gentry came to predominate over those of the Church and the clergy. A critical turning point did indeed occur under Edward VI, but the dissolution of the chantries was more than the end of a medieval tradition; it was the beginning of a national system of Protestant education, the culmination of earlier Protestant, humanist, and nationalist trends. Educational change could not be explained merely by invoking abstractions such as "the Renaissance," or by referring to the efforts of gentlemen to acquire an education for the sake of status, opportunity, or in order to conform to a set pattern.[120] The prototypes of the gentleman kept changing, like everything else; only by setting educational policies in the whole context of social history could they be understood.

In historiography, as in war, the importance of any sector along a broad front must be determined by relating it to the overall problem of the deployment of forces. Just as it is possible for a small tactical breakthrough to alter the line, so is it possible for well-planned local offensives to peter out unless reinforced—local breakthroughs can be exploited only by general commanders. The importance of this principle has been recognized by historians in nearly all fields in recent years: attack along a narrow front, whether it be in intellectual, or economic, or local history, demands careful planning, and recognition of the relationship between particular objectives and broad tactical and strategic aims. The significance of local research in the history of prices and agricultural methods has already been noted. In the economic history of the Church the bond between general and particular studies has been no less close. The national scene was the focus of Christopher Hill's *The Economic Problems of the Church* (1956), while W. K. Jordan's studies of English charities were based on a massive study of county and national sources. The argument of Christopher Hill was that behind the Puritan attack on the church "lurked economic considerations, appealing especially to the interests of land-hungry magnates and of business men great and small." [121] The economic dilemma of the Church was decisive in preventing reform; and Laud's efforts to reverse history came too late. Jordan's topic was nothing less than the changing patterns of social aspirations between 1480 and 1660. His work will be discussed in more detail in a later chapter; here all that need be said is that the decline in charitable bequests to the Church marked a real turning point in both the economic and the intellectual history of the Church. Although much of Jordan's evidence was drawn from an intensive study of ten counties, he was primarily concerned with strategic generalizations—that is, with secular trends based on the accumulation of statistical data. The importance of local history as such for an understanding of church history in the sixteenth century may be seen most clearly, perhaps, in the writings of A. G. Dickens, who has written about the Reformation on the local, national, and international levels.[122]

In *Lollards and Protestants in the Diocese of York, 1509–1558*

(1959), Dickens embarked on a regional survey which demonstrated in detail how far from the old Tudor saga of Divorce, Parliament, Dissolution, and Prayer Books were the findings of modern scholarship. The creative role of the state had been much exaggerated by Powicke and others. Powicke had begun his essay on *The Reformation in England* (1941) with the statement that "the one definite thing which can be said about the Reformation in England is that it was an act of State." [123] While this might be true in some important respects it was far from true as a categorical generalization about Church history. In his inaugural lecture, "Heresy and the Origins of English Protestantism," Dickens almost reversed the argument: "At no stage was the English Reformation an isolated act of state." [124] The detailed evidence for this revisionist view had been presented in *Lollards and Protestants*. The argument concerning Lollard tradition—a tradition that had greatly contributed to Reformation changes—could be summed up as follows:

> So far as this evidence goes, the Lollard tradition had become diffused and sometimes even manifested itself in skepticism rather than in affirmation by the time it began to meet with Tyndale. Its historical importance may lie in the fact that it united with the more worldly types of anti-clericalism to form an extensive platform of critical dissent upon which various newer movements could build. The discovery that even the society of a northern and conservative shire was to some extent still permeated by a diluted Lollardry seems to provide an important missing link in the history of the English Reformation. It helps to show that the latter did not originate as a mere foreign doctrine imported by a handful of intellectuals and mysteriously imposed by the monarchy against the almost unanimous wishes of a Catholic nation. The foreign seed fell upon a ground well-prepared for its reception, and prepared by something more than anti-clericalism or royal propaganda.[125]

This thesis of the continuity of Lollard influence was explored further by Margaret Aston in two articles which discussed the ways in which Tudor writers, especially Foxe and other historical writers, made use of Lollard precedents in their work. In "Lollardry and the Reformation: Survival or Revival" (*History*, 1964), Aston argued that Lollardry was, at least in intellectual history, more of a revival than a survival; in "John Wycliffe's Reformation Reputation" (*Past and Present*, 1965), she concluded that misconceptions about Wycliffe, the father figure of English Protestantism, were greatly if unintentionally enlarged by writers intent on making a new historical tradition.

Historical continuities in the sixteenth century might or might not be interrupted, or misconceived; local history might or might not reflect national history. In Caernarvonshire the masses remained unmoved by the Reformation until, in Elizabeth's reign, the Bible and Prayer Book were translated into Welsh. Only then was there a radical break with tradition.[126] Local conditions could determine to a very large extent the success or failure of Reformation policies.

Finally, there is what may be called the sociological approach to religious history. To some historians "sociological" is a synonym for pretentious, abstruse, and silly; to others the adjective almost consecrates the noun it modifies. Here "sociological history" means simply history with the emphasis on social questions or, more narrowly, history which makes use of sociological theory. During the last two or three decades interest in religious history has increased, and most studies of Protestantism, Puritanism, and Catholicism have been more or less explicitly concerned with sociological problems, if not with the sociological theory of religion. In *The Catholic Laity in Elizabethan England, 1558–1603* (1964), William R. Trimble addressed himself to the perplexing sociological question: why did the Church of Rome, still legally established in England at the beginning of 1558, shrink to a small minority of Englishmen by the beginning of 1603? Intensive work in the public records provided information about the declining social and economic status of Catholics, and about the efforts of seminary priests to revivify Catholicism. In retrospect it appeared that there were several reasons for the contrast between the Catholic and the Puritan laity. One important cause of frustration and defeat was the long secular decline of the Church as a religious institution. Effective leadership was in the hands of the Elizabethan government, along with effective force. The government, in effect, could afford measured toleration. From the point of view of the Catholic Church the transition under Elizabeth marked a point of no return.

In *The Elizabethan Puritan Movement* (1967), Patrick Collinson showed how the Puritan underground operated, and how, with sympathizers in high places, it became for a time a threat to the state. He wrote:

> This is a study of church puritanism as a movement, and as a political and ecclesiastical organism; of its membership, structures and internal contradictions; and of the effort to redeem what Elizabethans understood by the "outward face" of religion, the institutions, discipline and worship of the Church. For the most part events have been allowed to speak for themselves according to what may be thought a rather old-fashioned plan.[127]

The plan may have been old-fashioned; the questions and the evidence were not. The importance of tracing the overgrown trails of patronage had been recognized much earlier by Sir John Neale and by other political and social historians; Collinson used well-tried methods on new material. Puritans constituted in some sense a church within the Church; elements of the "church type" and the "sect type" (as differentiated by Ernst Troeltsch) were combined in the Puritan movement. The success of the Puritan conversions stood in marked contrast to the failure of the Catholics to maintain power and influence. The history of the process by which Tudor England became fervently Protestant, a process which left lasting marks as the result of the seventeenth-century triumph of Puritanism, had never before been so fully revealed.

The Puritan movement was chronically subject to internal strains and spasms. The moderates, with a talent for compromise and survival, accepted the Church and were usually willing to conform to its usages. The extremists, more concerned with "discipline," repudiated episcopacy and sometimes all human government in words that often ruled out compromise ("the bishop's authority is Antichristian, *ergo* not to be obeyed"); they were dangerous both to the established Church and to their own moderate allies. The spiritual grandchildren of the opposing factions of 1584 would, as Collinson put it, "find themselves in opposed armies and their great-grandchildren on either side of the great divide separating the established Church from Dissent." [128] Distinguishing between the moderate and the subversive extremists, Whitgift pressed his attack only against the latter. After 1584 this policy helped to assure the eventual victory of the Church of England.[129] The tactics of the Puritan extremists were particularly difficult to combat, however, because private religious observances were encouraged.

It was in the household communities, which included servants and other retainers, that the Puritan "church within the Church had its tangible local expression." [130] The failure of Puritan morale after 1588 was largely owing to the deaths of important patrons, notably the earl of Leicester, but if the movement began to lose its cohesion it did not fall apart. The decline of the Puritan movement in the 1590s coincided with the beginnings of the great age of Puritan religious experience; Puritanism as a religious reawakening would in time work a quiet revolution as profound as any dreamed of by the Presbyterians. At the Hampton Court Conference the Puritan movement, having profited from earlier failures, was prepared to accept a moderate Protestant settlement based on episcopacy; the chance for a statesman-like solution was lost by James I. What Collinson's work helped to establish was "that surrender to the drastic prescriptions of the presbyterians on the one hand, and exclusion from an interest in the national Church of the great and growing body of religious experience which we know as puritanism on the other, were never in this period the simple alternatives open to the government of the Church of England." [131]

In striking methodological contrast to Collinson's account, *The Revolution of the Saints* (1965) by Michael Walzer dealt with the Puritan movement in relation to sociological theories, especially those of Marx and Weber. Walzer saw Puritanism as the paradigm of later revolutionary movements. Whereas Collinson stressed political tactics, and the actual networks of patronage and propaganda developed by the Elizabethan Puritan movement, Walzer stressed ideology and political psychology, arguing that the appeal of Puritanism to the intelligentsia and the gentry was that it provided an ideology appropriate to the transition from traditional to modern society. The Calvinist saint was only "the first of those self-disciplined agents of social and political reconstruction who have appeared so frequently in modern history." [132] Puritans, Jacobins, and Bolsheviks behaved in similar ways because they all belonged to times of historical crisis and transition. The end product of Walzer's analysis was a "model of radical politics." His book was analytical rather than narrative in approach, and its Weberian "ideal type" argument virtually ignored the interplay of personalities and differences of opinion within the Puritan movement. The gain in clarity and coherence was at the expense of subtle shading—it was line drawing as opposed to chiaroscuro. If the saints were "sociologically competent" men, who embraced Puritanism because they felt confident they *had* been called, they were at the same time stern Calvinists who accepted the state as a necessary, indeed desirable instrument of repression. Although the leadership of the Puritan movement came from the intellectuals, with support from the gentry, ultimately Puritanism was a choice, not a mere reflex of "social disorder and personal anxiety." [133] Historical Puritanism, as Walzer acknowledged, was more than a sociological type, but he was much less concerned with Puritanism's changing ideas and attitudes than he was with its enduring functional characteristics. The psychological effect of Puritanism, with its emphasis on Godly warfare and conflict, was to make revolution available to the minds of seventeenth-century Englishmen.[134] Walzer rejected or greatly modified the conclusions of Marx, Weber, Tawney, and other scholars, including Christopher Hill, but he owed more to the methods of Max Weber than to those of Sir John Neale. "The outcome of Puritan activity," Walzer concluded, "was Godly watchfulness, magistracy, and revolution." [135] The political effects of Puritanism were more immediate and significant than the economic effects described by Weber and Tawney. As an example of what has been loosely called "sociological" history, *The Revolution of the Saints* is not entirely typical, precisely because it makes a point of explicit sociological generalization, and because it draws heavily on sociological theory.[136]

From the foregoing discussion of religious historiography it is evident that, as in other fields of Tudor history, "established views, hallowed for years by an apostolic succession of clichés, have been deprived of orthodoxy." [137] The problems dealt with by political and constitutional historians of Tudor England are not unique, even with respect to subject matter; with respect to methods and styles of argument, religious and secular historiography have much in common. In a later chapter some of the problems peculiar to the state, society, and the individual will be discussed. Here a summing up of recent views will be in order. Revisions in the history of religion may stand for revisionist trends in other areas of Tudor history. The bibliographical surveys in *Changing Views on British History* (1966) provide a ready means of identifying important contributions from different fields in recent decades, and the problems that these present for a Tudor synthesis. The age of the great multivolumed narratives by individual historians has passed; Froude, Macaulay, Stubbs, and Gardiner were nineteenth-century giants, on whose shoulders pygmies might stand, but not a younger race of giants. In the twentieth century historical analysis has shaped our understanding of Tudor history far more than narrative synthesis. Single-volume texts emphasizing interpretation have replaced the great narratives because professional historians have recognized the need for progress reports on their own efforts to rebuild historical foundations.

The transition problem still provides a valuable clue to the differences between nineteenth- and twentieth-century trends in Tudor historiography. What is perhaps most obvious is the variety of opinions and interpretations now available, each offering an explanation of part of the whole, none offering a full synthesis of special histories. Least obvious, perhaps is the implicit assumption that sustains twentieth-century historiography: acceptance of the multiform shapes of historical time. The quest for a meaningful formula to explain literary, scientific, and religious events, either as reflexes or as determinants of the social order, has not been entirely abandoned, but it is obvious that few historians, even Marxists, believe that a "solution" is in sight. Most historians would now argue that different techniques—functional or structural analysis, as opposed to dialectical analysis, for example—are appropriate to different questions or subject matters. The point has been made succinctly by M. M. Postan, who adds that "an historian must concern himself with change, because change illuminates as nothing else can the nature of social problems; but light thus shed comes not only from the direct current running through the unbroken continuum of history, but also from those alternating impulses by means of which ideas or institutions adjust themselves to the shifting historical environments." [138]

To make lateral connections between ideas or institutions and the surrounding society is to stress one kind of interpretation; to connect the ideas and institutions of one period with those of an earlier period may be equally important, but the resulting interpretation will be different, and will satisfy different criteria of relevance. In general it could be said that twentieth-century historiography has developed around four or five methodological nodes. Structural analysis emphasizes the structure of politics, patronage, Puritanism, etc. in a particular, historical setting; functional analysis emphasizes the functions served by ideas or institutions in a given setting; structural-functional differences provide the most common index of change; dialectical analysis emphasizes change through time, either as a result of some logic of intellectual development or as a result of necessities imposed by history, and defined by Marxist or general economic theory; "sociological" analysis may combine these elements, or make use of explicit sociological theory, in an attempt to correlate ideas and events in different historical sectors, especially by statistical means; and finally, psychological analysis emphasizes human purpose as it changes in response to circumstance.[139] Each of these general types of analysis, illustrated in the foregoing chapters, reveals a different relationship between continuity and change. Each is sometimes inappropriately used, and each may be combined with others in appropriate or inappropriate ways. Small wonder, then, that historians often appear to be at odds with one another, especially with regard to what constitutes "transition."

In the light of current knowledge the Tudor century was a period characterized by many different kinds of historical change. In religious history some changes were obviously revolutionary, others not; in political history there were few structural innovations, but there were changes of function—the role of the intellectuals was rapidly changing; and the functions of the royal household were being replaced, according to Elton, by national bureaucratic methods and instruments; the history of education showed remarkable formal continuities, but equally remarkable informal changes, especially under the revolutionary impact of the printing press; the continuity of medieval scientific ideas has been established in some fields, while in others, such as astronomy and anatomy, sixteenth-century changes were profoundly important for the future; in short, no single formula can express the varying rates of historical change. Historians who have espoused an extreme "continuity" position, as Peter Laslett did in *The World We Have Lost* (1965), have usually been obliged to argue that some one aspect of history was so basic that changes in other areas could safely be ignored. Thus Laslett argued that prior to the industrial revolution of the late eighteenth century England was a "one-class" society—continuity was the dominant fact about medieval and early modern history; the only "sociological" change that mattered was demographic change.[140] Similarly, on the basis of single aspects of history it has often been argued that revolutionary change was the dominant characteristic of the Tudor period. Still another position was recently described by H. R. Trevor-Roper, in an essay on "Witches and Witchcraft" (*Encounter*, 1967), in which he argued convincingly against the idea that intellectual history since the Renaissance could be understood in terms of linear progress. If any overarching generalization were permissible it would be that retrogressions took place in the midst of progress, and that, as L. Fèbvre put it, "in its innermost structure the mentality of the most enlightened men living at the end of the sixteenth and the beginning of the seventeenth century was radically different from the mentality of the most enlightened men of our time." [141] The responsibility of the Protestant clergy for the revival of the witch craze in the sixteenth century was undeniable, but so was the responsibility of the Dominicans earlier and the Jesuits later. The real cause of the sixteenth-century revival, especially after about 1550, was the conflict of religions brought about by the Reformation. Only an appreciation of historical irony could "save the appearances" of older views of Church history. The Reformation and Counter Reformation, for all their achievements, represented intellectual regression.[142]

What then can be said for generalizations about the Tudor transition, or rather, transitions? Some of the best recent textbooks on Tudor history are those by S. T. Bindoff, *Tudor England* (1950); J. D. Mackie, *The Earlier Tudors* (1952); James A. Williamson, *The Tudor Age* (1953); G. R. Elton, *England under the Tudors* (1955); Christopher Morris, *The Tudors* (1955); J. B. Black, *The Reign of Elizabeth* (2nd ed., 1959); G. W. O. Woodward, *Reformation and Resurgence* (1963); and Roger Lockyear, *Tudor and Stuart Britain* (1964). Each of these books provides stimulating generalizations, emphasizing different aspects of the Tudor age. Terms such as the "price revolution," the "agrarian revolution," or the "diplomatic revolution" occur in several texts, and are perhaps best understood as conventional labels. One of the most unequivocal statements of the revolutionary nature of the Tudor transition came from G. R. Elton:

> The Tudor revolution thus not only created national sovereignty; it also acknowledged the supremacy of statute on which the modern English state rests. That means that it established the sovereignty of the king in parliament, otherwise known as constitutional or limited monarchy. Whatever may have been the case before Crom-

well's work—whatever Wolsey may have stood for—there was no
Tudor despotism after it.[143]

The thesis of a "Tudor revolution in government" has not gone un-
challenged, but what is more noteworthy is the fact that the controversy pivoted on issues of politics and adminstration. To go beyond this, to ask why Shakespeare should have flourished in the
Elizabethan environment, or why poetry and history should have
captured the imagination of the age, might seem to many historians
meaningless. The answers to such questions certainly will not be
found ready-made in the state papers or other archives. To separate
history from literature, art from economics, and diplomacy from administration has become a modern convention based on the frag-
mentation of "original research." Clearly it is much easier to make
chronological divisions on the basis of limited subject matter than it
is to attempt to specify how and why different transitions occurred when they did.

The *Oxford History of England*, in which the volumes by Black
and Mackie cover the Tudor period, divides in order to rule; the
chapters on intellectual developments are set apart from those on
politics. Nothing is more characteristic than the landscape-painting
metaphor of foreground and background in modern historiography:
to political historians it is the "intellectual background," and to literary historians it is the "political background" that can safely be
discussed in pithy generalizations. The Tudor revolution in government occurred under Henry VIII, the diplomatic revolution under
Elizabeth, the price revolution under all the Tudors except Henry
VII, who retains, however, the distinction of being the first, and
the wiliest Tudor of them all. The problem of organizing large
masses of information is admittedly prodigious, but more and still
more information clearly will not simplify that problem, or make
any easier the task of general interpretation. The final point to be
made about recent trends in Tudor historiography is simply that the
best historians have come to recognize the problems of print—that
is, that some of the most interesting questions about Tudor history
are those which call for fresh ideas. The errors of many nineteenth-century and earlier historians have been corrected, but their
books continue to be read because they still have the power to suggest new ideas and connections.

It is not necessary to worry the sociological vocabulary in order to make use of sociological insights, nor to become a disciple in order to appreciate the insights of Marx. Christopher Morris in *The Tudors* outlined his reasons for considering the Tudor century a century of revolution, in which each of the great changes meant more work to the government. There was, he believed, a demonstrable connection between Culture, Politics, and the Tudors.[144] Lawrence Stone, describing the crisis of the aristocracy, fitted innumerable facts about changes in the way of life of the English aristocracy into a coherent whole. A good beginning has already been made on the next assignment, which is to build connections between the special fields of research. The relations between Society, the State, and the Individual may eventually be understood as sets of configurations; the conditions under which changes in one set effect changes in several others may eventually be known. At present the historiography of the recent past is the best omen for the future.

NOTES

1. Lord Acton, *Essays in the Liberal Interpretation of History*, ed. and with an Introduction by William H. McNeil (Chicago, 1967), p. 358; see also pp. 401–402. There are important discussions of Acton in Gertrude Himmelfarb, *Lord Acton, A Study in Conscience and Politics* (Chicago, 1952); and Lionel Kochan, *Acton on History* (London, 1954).
2. Acton, *op. cit.*, pp. 401–402.
3. *Ibid.*, p. 419.
4. For German and French views see Fritz Stern, *The Varieties of History* (New York, 1956).
5. Acton, *op. cit.*, p. 399; cf. p. 358.
6. See J. Hajnal, "European Marriage Patterns in Perspective," in D. V. Glass and D. E. C. Eversley (eds.), *Population in History: Essays in Historical Demography* (London, 1965), pp. 101–143.
7. Emmanuel LeRoy Ladurie, "From Waterloo to Colyton," *Times Literary Supplement*, Sept. 8, 1966, p. 792. Cf. Glass and Eversley, *op. cit.*, Chap. 1.
8. E. A. Wrigley (ed.), *An Introduction to English Historical Demography: From the Sixteenth to the Nineteenth Century* (Cambridge Group for the History of Population and Social Structure, Publication No. 1 [New York, 1966]), p. xi. See also Peter Laslett's Introduction, pp. 1–13.
9. A. R. Hall, "Technology and Science," *Times Literary Supplement*, Jan. 6, 1956, p. xxiii.
10. Keith Thomas, "The Tools and the Job," *Times Literary Supplement*, April 7, 1966, p. 275. Cf. G. R. Elton, *The Practice of History* (New York, 1967), pp. 7 ff.

11. Marc Bloch, *Land and Work in Medieval Europe*, trans. J. E. Anderson (Berkeley, 1967), p. 49.
12. Hans Baron, *The Crisis of the Early Italian Renaissance: Civic Humanism and Republican Liberty in an Age of Classicism and Tyranny* (Princeton, 1966), p. 457; see Chap. 1 *passim*.
13. Arthur B. Ferguson, *The Articulate Citizen and the English Renaissance* (Durham, 1965), p. 201; cf. J. G. A. Pocock, " 'The Onely Politician': Machiavelli, Harrington and Felix Raab," *Historical Studies Australia and New Zealand*, XII, No. 46, 265–296.
14. See the review by Christopher Morris, *History*, XLVII, No. 159 (February 1962), 64–66.
15. Sir George Clark, "General Introduction: History and the Modern Historian," in *The New Cambridge Modern History*, Vol. I: *The Renaissance 1493–1520*, ed. G. R. Potter (Cambridge, 1957), p. xxiv.
16. See Introduction to *The New Cambridge Modern History*, Vol. II: *The Reformation 1520–1559*, ed. G. R. Elton (Cambridge, 1958), pp. 14–22.
17. Philippe Ariès, *Centuries of Childhood: A Social History of Family Life*, trans. Robert Baldick (New York, 1965), p. 40.
18. *Ibid.*, p. 369.
19. W. G. Hoskins, "The Rebuilding of Tudor England 1570–1640," in *Provincial England: Essays in Social and Economic History* (London, 1963), pp. 144 ff.
20. For criticisms see in particular Arthur O. Lovejoy, *Essays in the History of Ideas* (New York, 1960), pp. 1–13; and Lovejoy's "Reflections on the History of Ideas," *Journal of the History of Ideas*, I, No. 1 (January 1940), 3–23; Rush Welter, "The History of Ideas in America: An Essay in Redefinition," *Journal of American History*, LI, No. 4 (March 1965), 599–614; and John Higham "Intellectual History and Its Neighbors," *Journal of the History of Ideas*, XV, No. 3 (June 1954), 339–347; also Maurice Mandelbaum, "The History of Ideas, Intellectual History, and the History of Philosophy," Beiheft 5 (1965) of *History and Theory*, "The Historiography of the History of Philosophy," pp. 33–66.
21. Eugene F. Rice, Jr., *The Renaissance Idea of Wisdom* (Cambridge, Mass., 1958), pp. 99–100, 106.
22. *Ibid.*, p. 213.
23. J. W. Allen, *A History of Political Thought in the Sixteenth Century* (2nd ed.; London, 1941), p. xiii.
24. See Pocock, *op. cit.*, pp. 268–269; see pp. 265–296 and references cited, *passim*.
25. Robert Jay Lifton, "Individual Patterns in Historical Change: Imagery of Japanese Youth," *Comparative Studies in Society and History*, VI (1963–1964), 369–383, from p. 369; see also Frederick Wyatt, "In Quest of Change," *ibid.*, pp. 384–392; and Kenneth Kenniston, "Accounting for Change," *ibid.*, VII (1965), 117–126; Lifton's further comment is at *ibid.*, VII, 127–132.
26. Wyatt, *op. cit.*, p. 388.
27. Philip Rieff, "The Meaning of History and Religion in Freud's Thought," in *Psychoanalysis and History*, ed. Bruce Mazlich (Englewood Cliffs, 1963), pp. 25, 29, 30.
28. Norman O. Brown, *Life against Death: The Psychoanalytical Meaning of History* (New York, 1959), pp. 12–13.
29. *Ibid.*, p. 232.
30. In Mazlich, *op. cit.*, pp. 124–149.
31. See William L. Langer, "The Next Assignment," *American Historical Review*, LXIII, No. 2 (January 1958), 283–304; and Bruce Mazlich, "Inside the Whales," in *Times Literary Supplement*, July 28, 1966, pp. 667–669.

32. Gregory Zilboorg, *A History of Medical Psychology* (New York, 1941, 1967), pp. 175–244 *passim*. This is not the place to list the various histories of medicine and of psychiatry which contain useful interpretations of sixteenth-century psychological doctrines and medical attitudes. The *Journal of the History of Medicine and Allied Sciences* (1946–   ) should be consulted.

33. See Edward Rosen, "Renaissance Science as Seen by Burckhardt and His Successors," in *The Renaissance*, ed. Tinsley Helton (Madison, 1961), pp. 77–104; see also *History of Science, An Annual Review of Literature, Research and Teaching*, I (1962). Eric H. Boehm and Lalit Adolphus (eds.), *Historical Periodicals* (Santa Barbara, 1961), list international journals.

34. A. D. White, *A History of the Warfare of Science with Theology* (reprinted New York, 1960), from the Introduction, p. vi.

35. Marie Boas, *The Scientific Renaissance* (New York, 1962), p. xi. This view is probably not typical of most writing on the history of science in this period. Cf. A. C. Crombie, *Medieval and Early Modern Science* (New York, 1959).

36. Arthur Koestler, *The Sleepwalkers* (London, 1959), p. 15.

37. Boas, *op. cit.*, p. 190. It is perhaps misleading to suggest that Gilbert was the first outstanding Tudor scientist. Some of the Tudor naturalists made important contributions. See Charles E. Raven, *English Naturalists from Neckam to Ray* (Cambridge, 1947).

38. Quoted in *ibid.*, p. 197.

39. See A. Rupert Hall, "Merton Revisited," *History of Science*, II (1963), 1–16.

40. See Francis R. Johnson and Sanford V. Larkey, "Thomas Digges, The Copernican System, and the Idea of the Infinity of the Universe in 1576," *Huntington Library Bulletin*, No. 5 (April 1934), pp. 69–117; Francis R. Johnson, "The Influence of Thomas Digges on the Progress of Modern Astronomy in Sixteenth-Century England," *Osiris*, I (January 1936), 390–410; and Johnson and Larkey, "Robert Recorde's Mathematical Teaching and the Anti-Aristotelian Movement," *Huntington Library Bulletin*, No. 7 (April 1935), pp. 59–87.

41. R. K. Merton, "Science, Technology, and Society in Seventeenth Century England," *Osiris*, IV (1938). See also T. K. Rabb, "Puritanism and the Rise of Experimental Science in England," *Journal of World History*, VII, No. 1 (1962).

42. Max Weber, *The Protestant Ethic and the Spirit of Capitalism*, trans. Talcott Parsons, with a Foreword by R. H. Tawney (New York, 1948), p. 90. On the controversy over this book see S. N. Eisenstadt, *The Protestant Ethic and Modernization: A Comparative View* (New York, 1968).

43. Weber, *op. cit.*, pp. 91–92.

44. See Marshall Clagett (ed.), *Critical Problems in the History of Science* (Madison, 1959), esp. Rupert Hall, "The Scholar and the Craftsman in the Scientific Revolution," pp. 3–23; and Giorgio de Santillana, "The Role of Art in the Scientific Renaissance," pp. 33–65; and the accompanying commentaries on both articles. The quotation from Hall is on p. 10.

45. Hall, *op. cit.*, p. 18.

46. *Ibid.*

47. See Robert K. Merton, "Puritanism, Pietism, and Science," in *Social Theory and Social Structure* (Glencoe, 1957), pp. 574–606, esp. p. 579; also Merton's entertaining classic, *On the Shoulders of Giants: A Shandean Postscript* (New York, 1965).

48. See the collection edited by Guy S. Metraux and François Crouzet, *The Evolution of Science* (New York, 1963).

49. Christopher Hill, *Intellectual Origins of the English Revolution* (Oxford, 1965),

p. 11a; cf. Hill's argument in *Past and Present*, No. 29 (December 1964), pp. 88–97, esp. p. 89—both science and Protestantism were characteristic of a value shift.

50. Hill, *Intellectual Origins*, p. 69.
51. The review of Hill's book by Trevor-Roper in *History and Theory*, V, No. 1 (1966), 61–81, concentrates on historiographical issues, rather than on issues in the history of science. Other reviewers have questioned Hill's arguments about the relationship between science and religion. Trevor-Roper criticized Hill's factual details and concluded that his thesis about Puritanism and modernity was wrong; a "catalogue of errors" sought to invalidate a general interpretation. Controversies are apt to produce bruises, as well as surprises; in the long run, all historians may profit from careful sifting of the evidence in footnotes on both sides.
52. See H. F. Kearney, "Puritanism, Capitalism and the Scientific Revolution," *Past and Present*, No. 28 (July 1964), pp. 81–101, esp. 100.
53. Theodore K. Rabb, "Religion and the Rise of Modern Science," *Past and Present*, No. 31 (July 1965), pp. 111–126, esp. 126.
54. Stephen Toulmin and June Goodfield, *The Discovery of Time* (New York, 1965), p. 268.
55. Thomas S. Kuhn, *The Structure of Scientific Revolutions* (Chicago, 1962), p. 171.
56. *Ibid.*, p. 92; Kuhn's italics.
57. *Ibid.*, p. 93; cf. Ariès, *op. cit.*, pp. 19–20.
58. M. Postan, "Economic Social History," *Times Literary Supplement*, Jan. 6, 1956, p. vi.
59. *Ibid.*, p. vi.
60. See in particular the essays by Redlich, Fogel, and Schweitzer listed in the following notes.
61. R. W. Fogel, "The 'New Economic History,'" *Economic History Review*, XIX, No. 3 (December 1966), 652.
62. *Ibid.*, p. 656.
63. Fritz Redlich, "'New' and Traditional Approaches to Economic History and Their Interdependence," *Journal of Economic History*, XXV, No. 4 (December 1965), 480–495, esp. 486 ff.
64. Fogel, *op. cit.*, p. 656; see also Lionel Robbins, *An Essay on the Nature and Significance of Economic Science* (London, 1952), Chap. 5 *passim.*
65. Redlich, *op. cit.*, p. 492.
66. Arthur Schweitzer, "Economic Systems and Economic History," *Journal of Economic History*, XXV, No. 4 (December 1965), 664.
67. Peter Tenin, "In Pursuit of the Exact," *Times Literary Supplement* ("New Ways in History, No. 2"), July 28, 1966, p. 653.
68. D. V. Glass and D. E. C. Eversley, *op. cit.*, p. 36; see the reviews of this in the *Economic History Review*, and in the *Times Literary Supplement*, Jan. 6, 1966.
69. J. Kabk, "Mathematics and Complexity," *Times Literary Supplement* ("New Ways in History, No. 3"), Sept. 8, 1966, p. 803; cf. also the recent handbook by W. J. Reichmann, *Use and Abuse of Statistics* (London, 1964).
70. William Cunningham, *The Growth of English Industry and Commerce* (Cambridge, 1912), p. 170; see also pp. 180–181.
71. The reader is referred to the excellent new bibliographical handbook compiled for the Conference on British Studies by Mortimer Levine, *Tudor England 1485–1603* (Cambridge, 1968).

72. E. Lipson, *The Economic History of England* (10th ed.; London, 1948), II, Preface, v.
73. *Ibid.*, Introduction, pp. cxv–cxvi; see also p. i of the Introduction, and the Preface.
74. See A. G. Dickens, "The Writers of Tudor Yorkshire," *Transactions of the Royal Historical Society*, 5th ser., XIII (1963), 49–76.
75. See Lord Ernle, *English Farming Past and Present*, 6th ed., with an Introduction by G. E. Fussell and D. R. McGregor (London, 1961), pp. lvii–lxv.
76. See Joan Thirsk, "The Content and Sources of English Agrarian History after 1500," *Agricultural History Review*, VIII (1955), 66–121.
77. Ernle, *op. cit.*, p. 78; see also pp. 64 ff. and 103 for remarks on enclosures.
78. Eric Kerridge used the idea, though not the exact phrase, as the title of his recent book, *The Agricultural Revolution* (London, 1967). Unfortunately this book arrived in this country too late to be included in this discussion of agricultural historiography. Kerridge challenges the whole conventional chronology of English agricultural history as outlined by Lord Ernle, by T. S. Ashton in *The Industrial Revolution* (London, 1948), and, most recently, reaffirmed in a book—with almost the same title as Kerridge's—by J. D. Chambers and G. E. Mingay, *The Agricultural Revolution, 1750–1880* (New York, 1966).
79. R. H. Tawney, *The Agrarian Problem in the Sixteenth Century* (New York, 1967), p. 406; cf. pp. 4–5 and *passim*. See also Tawney's *The Acquisitive Society* (London, 1920). Tawney's socialism stressed social controls, such as the Webbs advocated.
80. Tawney, *The Agrarian Problem*, p. 402.
81. Lawrence Stone, Introduction to *ibid.*, pp. vi–vii.
82. *Ibid.*, p. xviii.
83. See H. P. R. Finburg (ed.), *The Agrarian History of England and Wales*, Vol. IV: *1500–1640*, ed. Joan Thirsk (Cambridge, 1967), p. 870; see also the statistical appendices, pp. 814–870, *passim*. For a highly critical estimate of this volume see the review by Eric Kerridge in *The Historical Journal*, II, 3 (1968), 583–586. But cf. the review by James E. Farnell, *Journal of Modern History*, IV, No. 1 (1969), 94–98, especially on the use of statistics.
84. See Gordon Batho, "The Crown," *ibid.*, p. 256.
85. See Peter Bowden, "Agricultural Prices, Farm Profits, and Rents," *ibid.*, pp. 694–695.
86. *Ibid.*, p. 594; see pp. 593–594.
87. See Joan Thirsk, "Enclosing and Engrossing," *ibid.*, p. 255. Modern farming techniques are becoming more and more "rationalized," with business methods applied to ever larger units, especially in the United States. Nevertheless, some of the older practices and attitudes remain; a number of small farmers still depend on each other's help in harvesting and in many other areas.
88. See Alan Everitt, "The Marketing of Agricultural Produce," *ibid.*, pp. 466–592, esp. p. 588.
89. Maurice Beresford, *The Lost Villages of England* (London, 1954), p. 148.
90. See esp. Glanmor Williams, *The Welsh Church from Conquest to Reformation* (Cardiff, 1962); A. Hamilton Thompson, *The English Clergy and Their Organization in the Later Middle Ages* (London, 1947); Irene Churchill, *Canterbury Administration* (London, 1933); E. T. Davies, *Episcopacy and the Royal Supremacy in England in the Sixteenth Century* (Oxford, 1950).
91. See G. Constant, *The Reformation in England: The English Schism and Henry VIII, 1509–1547*, trans. R. E. Scantlebury (New York, 1966), Appendix II; also T. C. Price Zimmermann, "A Note on Clement VII and the Divorce of

Henry VIII," *English Historical Review*, LXXXII, No. 324 (July 1967), 548–552.

92. G. Constant, *op. cit.*, p. 31.

93. Dom David Knowles, *The Religious Orders in England* (Cambridge, 1948–1959), III, 3; cf. II, 361–364.

94. *Ibid.*, III, 466.

95. *Ibid.*, 468.

96. Philip Hughes, *The Reformation in England* (New York, 1951–1954), I, 51; see Chap. 1 *passim*.

97. See R. G. Collingwood, *The Idea of History* (Oxford, 1946), p. 300.

98. Hughes, *op. cit.*, III, 101.

99. *Ibid.*, II, 147; the same sentence occurs on p. 138, but preceded by a clause: "All the evidence we possess goes to show that . . ."

100. See Helen C. White, *Tudor Book of Saints and Martyrs* (Madison, 1963), pp. 3–95, and 132–195 *passim*.

101. See the Introduction by A. G. Dickens to A. F. Pollard, *Henry VIII* (New York, 1966), p. xi, and Dickens' Introduction to Pollard's *Wolsey* (New York, 1966).

102. L. B. Namier, *Avenues of History* (London, 1952), p. 9.

103. See Paul Murray Kendall, *The Art of Biography* (New York, 1965), pp. 113–153, on contemporary biography; I have borrowed the phrase "Behemoth biography." See also John A. Garraty, *The Nature of Biography* (New York, 1964); and Donald A. Stauffer, *English Biography before 1700* (Cambridge, Mass., 1930).

104. Ernest Lee Tuveson, *Millennium and Utopia* (New York, 1964); cf. Ernst Troeltsch, *Protestantism and Progress* (Boston, 1958; first published 1912).

105. William Haller, *The Rise of Puritanism* (New York, 1938), pp. 83–85; cf. M. M. Knappen, *Tudor Puritanism: A Chapter in the History of Idealism* (Chicago, 1939), pp. 368–370. Haller's Appendix III discusses "The Historiography of Puritanism." Haller discusses the anxiety caused by the doctrine of predestination on pp. 83–91, where he follows Tawney.

106. Peter Munz, *The Place of Hooker in the History of Thought* (London, 1952), pp. 19–20.

107. John F. New, *Anglican and Puritan, The Basis of Their Opposition, 1558–1640* (Stanford, 1964), pp. 3–4; see also pp. 104, 107.

108. Cf. Perry Miller, *The New England Mind* (Boston, 1954), Chap. 3, in which he argues that Puritan thought derives from sixteenth-century Protestantism. For New's differences with the Georges, see New, *op. cit.*, pp. 104–111.

109. Charles H. George and Catherine George, *The Protestant Mind of the English Reformation, 1570–1640* (Princeton, 1961), pp. 398–405.

110. *Ibid.*, p. 74 note.

111. *Ibid.*, p. 172.

112. *Ibid.*, p. 173.

113. *Ibid.*, p. 121.

114. Kenneth Charlton, *Education in Renaissance England* (London, 1965), p. x.

115. Mark H. Curtis, *Oxford and Cambridge in Transition 1558–1642: An Essay on Changing Relations Between the English Universities and English Society* (Oxford, 1959), pp. ii, 13–15, 59–65, 231, for example. See also Curtis, "The Alienated Intellectuals of Early Stuart England," *Past and Present*, No. 23 (November 1962), pp. 25–43; and cf. Joan Simon, "The Social Origins of Cambridge Students, 1603–1640," *Past and Present*, No. 26 (November 1963), pp. 58–67.

116. Carlton, *op. cit.*, pp. 149–150.
117. *Ibid.*, pp. 128–130, 136–140, 149 ff.
118. *Ibid.*, p. 299.
119. Joan Simon, *Education and Society in Tudor England* (Cambridge, 1966), p. vi, and Preface *passim*.
120. *Ibid.*, p. 401; see pp. 299–403.
121. Christopher Hill, *Economic Problems of the Church* (Oxford, 1956), p. 43.
122. A. G. Dickens, *Lollards and Protestants in the Diocese of York, 1509–1558* (Oxford, 1959); *The English Reformation* (London, 1964), *Reformation and Society in Sixteenth Century Europe* (London, 1966).
123. F. M. Powicke, *The Reformation in England* (Oxford, 1941), p. 1.
124. A. G. Dickens, "Heresy and the Origins of English Protestantism," Inaugural Lecture, King's College, London, March 12, 1963 (n.p., n.d.), p. 22.
125. Dickens, *Lollards and Protestants*, p. 245.
126. Glanmor Williams, "The Reformation in Sixteenth Century Caernarvonshire," *Caernarvonshire Historical Society Transactions*, 1966, pp. 37–72. See also the same author's "Wales and the Reformation," Hartwell Jones Memorial Lecture, printed in *The Transactions of the Honourable Society of Cymmrodorion*, Session 1966, Part I, pp. 108–133.
127. Patrick Collinson, *The Elizabethan Puritan Movement* (Berkeley, 1967), p. 13; cf. Patrick McGrath, *Papists and Puritans under Elizabeth I* (London, 1967), a book which arrived in this country too late to be included—McGrath discusses the similarities between Papists and Puritans, in addition to other problems.
128. Collinson, *op. cit.*, p. 262.
129. *Ibid.*, p. 272.
130. *Ibid.*, p. 375.
131. *Ibid.*, p. 167.
132. Michael Walzer, *The Revolution of the Saints: A Study in Radical Politics* (Cambridge, Mass., 1965), p. vii.
133. *Ibid.*, p. 309.
134. *Ibid.*, pp. 290 ff.
135. *Ibid.*, p. 306.
136. See esp. *ibid.*, Chap. 5, "The Attack upon the Traditional Political World," with its analysis of Puritan symbolism.
137. See Perez Zagorin, "English History 1558–1640: A Bibliographical Survey," in *Changing Views of British History*, ed. Elizabeth Chapin Furber (Cambridge, Mass., 1966), p. 119. See also the other articles in this collection, esp. Lacey Baldwin Smith, "The 'Taste for Tudors'"; and Margaret Hastings' essay on the later Middle Ages.
138. M. M. Postan, "Function and Dialectic in Economic History," *Economic History Review*, 2nd ser., XIV, No. 3 (1962), 405.
139. Obviously these terms are all subject to controversy and question. On functional explanations, for example, see George C. Homans, *The Nature of Social Science* (New York, 1967), pp. 61–70.
140. Peter Laslett, *The World We Have Lost* (London, 1965), pp. 22–52, 150–151, 219–227; also pp. 18–21 attacking Marx.
141. L. Fèbvre, "Sorcellerie: Sottise ou Revolution mentale?" *Annales Economies —Societés—Civilization* (1948), p. 14; quoted by H. R. Trevor-Roper, "Witches and Witchcraft," *Encounter*, May 1967, p. 8. My translation of: "dans sa structure profonde, la mentalité des hommes le plus éclairés de la

fin du XVIe siècle, du debut an XVIIe siècle, ait différé, et radicalement, de la mentalité des hommes les plus éclairés de notre temps."

142. Trevor-Roper, "Witches and Witchcraft," pp. 32–33. This essay on witchcraft should be read in conjunction with Trevor-Roper's "The General Crisis of the Seventeenth Century," reprinted in Trevor Aston, ed., *Crisis in Europe: 1560–1660* (New York, 1967), pp. 63–102; and see also Trevor-Roper's argument about "structural" changes. *Ibid.*, pp. 117–123.

143. G. R. Elton, *England under the Tudors* (London, 1955), p. 168.

144. See Christopher Morris, *The Tudors* (London, 1955), pp. 22 ff.

4

Society, the State,
and the Individual

THE PARADOX OF PROVIDENCE is that it accounts for everything and
therefore explains nothing. To write about Tudor historiography
in terms of society, the state, and the individual may seem to account for everything and therefore to leave nothing to be explained
in other terms. No sharp boundaries separate social, institutional,
and biographical history from the history of ideas and economic history. None of the histories dealt with in this chapter should be
considered in isolation; they both explain and are explained by intellectual and economic histories. Theories about the relationship between ideology and the social relations of production have advanced beyond the layer-like formulations of Marx; and theories
about the relationship between religious and economic changes are
no longer merely variations on themes by Weber.[1] Still, both Weber
and Marx are indispensable for an understanding of modern controversies. This chapter will therefore open with general theories,
proceed to social and political histories, and end with biographical
studies. Its purpose will be to describe some of the principal features of modern Tudor historiography. Individuals, controversies,
and problems will take precedence over trends, methods, and revisions.

The publication in 1932 of Marx's early economic and philosophical manuscripts and of a complete text of *The German Ideology*
opened up a rich new vein of Marxist historical theory. The early
economic and philosophical manuscripts dealt primarily with the
problem of alienation in society; they revealed Marx as a humanist,

whose criticism of society was based on original insights into the psychological as well as the social problems of alienation. What distinguishes these writings, and so much else written by Marx himself, is historical awareness—the awareness of how every society is conditioned and determined by its own past, which lives on in various forms.[2] The problem of how human consciousness was related to the material mode of production was stated by Marx in various ways in the course of his life, and critics ever since have belabored Marx for making every conceivable error. It would be pointless to recapitulate these controversies which have produced whole shelves of books, a few of which are still worth reading. Some quotations from the economic and philosophical manuscripts may serve to make the point that Marx was considerably in advance of his time in understanding the psychological problems of history:

> Every self-alienation of man, from himself and from nature, appears in the relation which he postulates between other men and himself and nature. Thus religious self-alienation is necessarily exemplified in the relation between laity and priest, or, since it is here a question of the spiritual world, between the laity and a mediator. In the real world of practice this self-alienation can only be expressed in the real, practical relation of man to his fellow-men. The medium through which alienation occurs is itself a *practical* one. Through alienated labor, therefore, man not only produces his relation to the object and to the process of production as to alien and hostile men; he also produces the relation of other men to his production and his product, and the relation between himself and other men.[3]

Phrased succinctly and shockingly in *Theorien über den Mehrwert* was the principle that material production conditioned social relations and intellectual production:

> A philosopher produces ideas, a poet verses, a parson sermons, a professor text-books, etc. A criminal produces crime. . . . The criminal produces not only crime but the criminal law. . . . Further, the criminal produces the whole apparatus of the police and criminal justice, detectives, judges, executioners, juries, etc., and all these different professions, which constitute so many categories of the social division of labour, develop diverse abilities of the human spirit, create new needs and new ways of satisfying them.[4]

This passage may help to clarify some of the more abstract formulations in Marx's other writings; and it illuminates the oft-quoted phrase from *The German Ideology*: "Life is not determined by consciousness, but consciousness by life." [5] Marx had a hatred of abstractions divorced from real life. Surely this much of his argument was "salutary and medicinal, melting apparent surfaces away." Consciousness was from the very beginning a social product, according to Marx. It was a mistake for the historian to take at face value the statements of contemporaries: "while in ordinary life every shopkeeper is very well able to distinguish between what somebody professes to be and what really is, our historians have not yet won even this trivial insight. They take every epoch at its word and believe that everything it says and imagines about itself is true." [6] Such Marxist assertions can probably best be construed as "orienting statements" rather than propositions having predictive or explanatory value in history and social science, but they do direct attention to the kinds of questions that historians must ask themselves in weighing evidence. [7]

Leonard Kreiger, in "The Uses of Marx for History" (1960), called attention to the positive approaches of Marx. [8] Much of the commentary on, and controversy about, the relationship of Protestantism to capitalism reveals that the protagonists have defined their positions, consciously or unconsciously, with respect to one or another of Marx's orienting statements. Max Weber paid tribute to Marx's genius and never repudiated the contention that the materialistic method was of great importance in history and social science. It is no longer necessary to belabor the point that Marx criticized the unhistorical abstractions of the classical economists, just as the members of the German "historical school" did, and that Weber was the heir of both Marx and Schmoller. Weber's most uncompromising critic, Kurt Samuelsson, explained the popularity of Weber's theories on the ground that they were thought to be rebuttals of the materialistic interpretation of history. [9] Ephraim Fischoff, in discussing the history of the controversy over *The Protestant Ethic*, took pains to stress the Marxist residues in Weber's thought, and to argue that much of the criticism of Weber has been based on misunderstanding of his aims and methods. [10] Obviously Weber did believe that ideas could have an independent influence on events, but the real contrast between Weber and Marx was that between the historical pluralist and the historical monist.

In *The German Ideology* Marx and Engels argued that those historians who see a particular historical epoch only in its own terms, have to share the *"illusion of that epoch."* [11] If Tudor Englishmen thought of themselves as being primarily actuated by religious motives, that was their illusion; it was no reason for the historian to be deceived. Although this proposition was not original with Marx, he made it into a methodological postulate. The question he raised is one that still divides historians, although few would now explain events only by what men said and not at all by impersonal causes. The problem of consciousness assumed crucial importance in Weber's discussion of the Protestant ethic, particularly in his arguments about the growth of rationalism and worldly asceticism. And it is evident that nearly all modern discussions of the growth of secularism assume that unconscious changes of attitude can be historically verified. That Marx himself did not escape the illusion of his epoch has, of course, also been argued. Like Buckle, and many other nineteenth-century writers, Marx sought general covering laws which would somehow satisfy the norms of contemporary natural science. In his early essay on "Private Property and Communism," Marx summed up his hopes: "History itself is a *real* part of *natural history*, of the development of nature into man. Natural science will one day incorporate the science of man, just as the science of man will incorporate natural science; there will be a *single* science." [12] From a very different set of assumptions Buckle also formulated a "scientific" ideal. The business of the historian was to show "that the movements of nature were perfectly regular, and that, like all other movements, they are solely determined by their antecedents." This was not just radical historicism—Buckle believed that the true historian was a man "imbued with that spirit of science which teaches, as an article of faith, the doctrine of uniform sequence; in other words the doctrine that certain events having already happened, certain other events corresponding to them will also happen." [13] Of course, the laws of Buckle were not the laws of Marx. Buckle spoke of statistical and social laws of progress and of history, but he concerned himself largely with mental laws—"the progress Europe has made from barbarism to civilization is entirely due to its intellectual activity." [14] Consciousness determined life; modern history was the march of mind.

Although most of the "laws" Buckle thought he had discovered were preposterous, some of his historical generalizations were admirably discerning and original.[15] Believing that kings, statesmen, and legislators were more likely to retard than to hasten intellectual development, Buckle was disposed to look for and examine the correlations between different areas of intellectual activity.[16] His comments on the development of religious toleration infuriated some of his contemporaries, yet much of what he said about the growth of secularism has since been accepted. Even more important was his chapter on the origins of history, since it was one of the earliest attempts to relate historiography to general intellectual trends; and Buckle was perhaps the first English historian to recognize the importance of the French prelude to modern historiography.[17] Although he castigated medieval historians and wrote of the Middle Ages with even less sympathy than Gibbon, he nevertheless understood how important it was "to observe the way in which, during successive ages, historians have shifted their ground; since we shall find that such changes have in the long-run always pointed to the same quarter." [18] He went on to assert, with nineteenth-century English confidence, that this was "in reality, only part of that vast movement by which the human intellect, with infinite difficulty, has vindicated its own rights, and slowly emancipated itself from those inveterate prejudices which long impeded its action." [19] But if historiography was thus a symptom of the age, so was religion.

Looking at things on a large scale, Buckle believed that religion was the effect of improvement, not the cause of it. This was an important principle, which Buckle never lost sight of, even in his chapters on the condition of Scotland and on "the Scotch Intellect." When Max Weber cited Buckle as someone who had perceived a correlation between Calvinism and the spirit of capitalism he was mistaken.[20] Buckle had argued that "one of the causes of the triumph of the Baconian philosophy, is the growth of the industrious classes, whose businesslike and methodical habits are eminently favourable to empirical observations of the uniformities of sequence, since, indeed, on the accuracy of such observations the success of all practical affairs depends." [21] The connection between business methods and Calvinist theology was the reverse of what Weber believed it to be. Buckle had compared the Scottish Kirk to the Spanish Inquisition, and he attributed the eighteenth-century renaissance to a reaction against the theological spirit which had predominated in Scotland in the sixteenth and seventeenth centuries.[22] What Weber's mistake perhaps shows (aside from mere carelessness) is that he remembered Buckle as someone who had skillfully emphasized the influence of ideas on history. Buckle's reference to the importance of the "Theological Spirit," which issued in "ascetic and self-tormenting observances," was only superficially similar to Weber's—the real similarity was one of method: Buckle, like Weber, stressed the "spirit" of historical movements.[23] Unlike Weber, Buckle saw the spirit of secularism as the leading cause of the growth of an ethic favorable to capitalism. And unlike Weber, Buckle ignored Marx. There is a notable contrast between the historical materialism of Marx and the *geist* theories of Buckle, but it is not an entire antithesis. Buckle widened the scope of historical thought by insisting that intellectual influences could become effective forces in history only at a late stage in the connected evolution of intellectual, social, and economic life; intellectual accumulation took place on the basis of previous capital accumulation: "the history of the human mind can only be understood by connecting it with the history and the aspects of the material universe." [24]

It is unfortunate that Max Weber's general reputation rests on the narrow footing of *The Protestant Ethic*, which has been severely weakened by sixty years of historical criticism. The controversy over *The Protestant Ethic* (conveniently summarized by Samuelsson in *Religion and Economic Action*) has tended to overshadow Weber's other contributions to sociology and historical theory.[25] Tudor historians cannot escape the influence of Weber's best known thesis, but they can more easily judge it, and Weber, by becoming acquainted with some of Weber's comparative studies, and with the *General Economic History*. The extent to which Weber took account of the peculiarities of English developments in his discussion of the city, of mercantilism, or of capitalism, may come as a surprise to anyone accustomed only to the clichés of *The Protestant Ethic*. Weber's importance for Tudor historiography lies in the fact that he attempted to give conceptual clarity to the dynamics of Protestantism and capitalism, and thus to explain the transition from medieval to modern history. Like Marx, he showed by precept and example new ways in which historians could analyze their materials. Like Wilhelm Dilthey, he was a pioneer in the study of conceptual problems relating to the historicity of human existence and the historical character of knowledge.[26] He was mistaken in his interpretation of the history of Protestantism, and he left out of account important facts in the growth of modern capitalism; but his worst failure was simply the failure to solve the problem of *how* ideas and interests are related, which was exactly the point of his criticism of Marx. In *The Protestant Ethic* he clearly stated the problem: "It is, of course, not my aim to substitute for a one-sided materialistic an equally one-sided spiritualistic causal interpretation of culture and history. Each is equally possible, but each, if it does not serve as the preparation, but as the conclusion of an investigation, accomplishes equally little in the interest of historical truth." [27] Clearly Weber wanted to see both lines of inquiry meet, but as Reinhard Bendix has observed, "nowhere in his work is this view of the relative independence and intricate interdependence of ideas and economic interest fully stated beyond the cryptic remark that 'not ideas, but material and ideal interests, directly govern men's conduct.' " [28]

What then can be said for Weber as a historical theorist? The way in which he posed the question of the relationship between Protestantism and capitalism led directly to a wide-ranging controversy. This, in turn, resulted in a much more thorough investigation of the sources. Weber, along with other German sociologists, directed attention to the need for making explicit the methodological presuppositions of historiography. In *On the Methodology of the Social Sciences* he stated his reason for employing an ideal-type analysis:

> The construction of abstract ideal-types recommends itself not as an end but as a *means*. Every conscientious examination of the conceptual elements of historical exposition shows however that the historian as soon as he attempts to go beyond the bare establishment of concrete relationships and to determine the *cultural* significance of even the simplest individual event in order to "characterize" it, *must* use concepts which are precisely and unambiguously definable only in the form of ideal types. Or are concepts such as "individualism," "imperialism," "feudalism," "mercantilism," "conventional," etc. and innumerable concepts of like character by means of which we seek analytically and empathetically to understand reality constructed substantively by the "presuppositionless" *description* of some concrete phenomenon or through the abstract synthesis of those traits which are *common* to numerous concrete phenomena? Hundreds of words in the historian's vocabulary are ambiguous con-

structs created to meet the unconsciously felt need for adequate expression and the meaning of which is only concretely felt but not clearly thought out.[29]

This was a challenge to historians when he wrote; it remains a challenge today. Weber himself was not consistent in treating the Protestant ethic as an ideal type, nor was he consistent in his arguments about correlation as opposed to causation. *The Protestant Ethic* was to be "a contribution to the understanding of the manner in which ideas become effective forces in history" and was to show how "religious movements have influenced the development of material culture." [30] At the same time, however, Weber spoke of establishing "correlations"; he denied that the spirit of capitalism "could only have arisen as the result of the Reformation, or even that capitalism as an economic system is a creation of the Reformation."

In his *General Economic History* and *Law in Economy and Society*, Weber tended to stress factors other than the Protestant Ethic in the development of capitalism: "In the last resort the factor which produced Capitalism is the rational permanent enterprise, rational accounting, rational technology and rational law, but again not those alone. Necessary complementary factors were the rational spirit, the rationalization of the conduct of life in general and a rationalistic economic ethic." [31] Marx had viewed the modern capitalistic economic order as essentially irrational, leading to conflict and alienation; Weber saw the modern economy of capitalism as eminently "rational." Weber did not, however, believe that the rationalization of social life would liberate the individual; on the contrary, he had a profoundly tragic vision of a world in which technology and bureaucracy would spread like a cancer through historical organisms. Socialism was not the antithesis of capitalism but its caricature. The theory of rationalism or rationalization only gradually made its way into social science, and historians have perhaps been loath to employ a term which has acquired many meanings. Still, the concept of rational planning and behavior, as developed by Weber, provides a broad context in which particular historical activities can be placed. The administrative revolution carried out by Thomas Cromwell falls into place as an example of rational planning—"every reorganization that took place was in the direction of greater definition, of specialization, of bureaucratic order." [32]

The exact title of Weber's classic, *The Protestant Ethic and the Spirit of Capitalism*, reminds the reader that the book is about an ethical abstraction and the "spirit" of an economic abstraction. Weber illustrated the "spirit of capitalism" by quoting from Benjamin Franklin. This was the beginning of that chronological confusion from which sprang so much angry controversy. Weber did not always police the terms of his argument. The spirit of modern capitalism was one thing; the origins of that spirit something very different; and capitalism as an economic system was something still different. As a way of life among groups of men, capitalism had to originate somewhere. Weber dismissed the explanations of historical materialism as naïve, while admitting that "this origin is what really needs explanation." [33] The importance of origins was precisely the reason why Tudor historians, such as Tawney, were to take up the question. Weber maintained that "the most important opponent with which the spirit of capitalism, in the sense of a definite standard of life claiming ethical sanction, has had to struggle, was that type of attitude and reaction to new situations which we may designate as traditionalism." [34] Traditionalism was identified with Catholic attitudes; Protestant attitudes sanctioned change.

The *spirit* of capitalism (not capital sums, or entrepreneurial interests) was the motive force in the development and rationalization of capitalism. The conception of labor as a "calling" was necessary to the "spirit" of capitalism; and the chances of overcoming traditionalism were greatest in individuals with a Protestant religious upbringing.[35] Weber, in *The Protestant Ethic*, had rejected the notion that the development of the spirit of capitalism could be understood "as part of the development of rationalism as a whole." The reason was that "the history of rationalism shows a development which by no means follows parallel lines in the various departments of life." [36] The rationalization of law, in the sense of a logical simplification and rearrangement of the content of law, was achieved in late Roman law codes. English law, however, was a glaring example of backwardness during the sixteenth century, even though England had already attained a degree of economic rationalization. It is against this background that Weber's theses about the

Protestant ethic must be seen. Luther's concept of calling, the utilitarian character of Calvinist ethics, Puritan contributions to worldly asceticism, the importance of predestination, the debate over usury—these, and their connections with capitalist worldly activity, formed the bones of Weber's argument. Later discussions and investigations destroyed many of Weber's generalizations about the nature of sixteenth-century Protestantism and capitalism, but his methods remained; and the terms of his argument (although not his definitions of the terms) are still in widespread use. A brief survey of Weber's successors will serve to illustrate Weber's influence.[37]

The most important twentieth-century social theorist of the Christian churches was Ernst Troeltsch, who knew Weber and who pursued in detail several of the ideas that Weber had sketched in *The Protestant Ethic*. Troeltsch's great thousand-page study, *The Social Teaching of the Christian Churches* (1911; translated into English, 1931), was an example of sociological history, in which some Marxian and many Weberian strains came together; but its real importance lay in the fact that it provided the fundamental definitions of church and sect which have become part of the historian's vocabulary.[38] Although Troeltsch acknowledged the importance of Marx as a theorist, he denied emphatically that Marxist theory could account for Luther's religious ideas or for the Reformation world of thought—"the whole of this survey has shown," Troeltsch concluded, "that all that is specifically religious, and, above all, the great central points of religious development, are an independent expression of the religious life." [39] Christian ethical and religious aspirations were conditioned but not determined by the historical environment, although Troeltsch contended that "the social position and relations of the sects reveal the hidden reasons for sudden changes of religious thought, which could not have been explained from their merely intellectual dialectic." [40] Troeltsch borrowed from Weber the conception of worldly asceticism, and developed several of Weber's ideas about the relationship between Calvinism and capitalism.

The basic definitions of church and sect appeared in Troeltsch's discussion of medieval Catholicism. This was appropriate, for church-type and sect-type tendencies could be traced as far back as the primitive Church.[41] Although the main stream of Christian development followed the church type, the sect type, with its emphasis on the ideal of the holy community, on radicalism, and on literal obedience of the Gospel, had emerged in the medieval heresies and even in some elements of the religious orders, notably in the Franciscan movement.[42] The general characteristics of the sect type were the following: "lay Christianity, personal achievement in ethics and in religion, the radical fellowship of love, religious equality and brotherly love, indifference toward the authority of the State and the ruling classes, dislike of technical law and of the oath, the separation of the religious life from the economic struggle by means of the ideal of poverty and frugality, or occasionally in a charity which becomes communism, the directness of the personal religious relationship, criticism of official spiritual guides and theologians, the appeal to the New Testament and to the Primitive Church." [43] Thus the sect (conceived as an ideal type) was obliged to consider the Church as degenerate. In terms of sociological pattern variables, the sect was "particularistic" rather than "universalistic" in its orientation.[44]

The essence of the Church was its institutional character. The individual was born into the Church, with all that this meant in terms of tradition, hierarchy, sacramental grace, and ecclesiastical jurisdiction. The Church compromised with the world, yet remained holy and divine; its compromise was the basis of its universalism. To the Church, personal effort and service were only secondary; essential to the idea of the Church was the Church's objective possession of grace. The life of the sect lay in fellowship, in the unity of the group, which one entered on the basis of conscious conversion; the sect was thus opposed to the ways of the world, and tended to develop a more "ascetic" attitude toward life and thought. The one vitally important thing about the Church was that "every member should come within the range of influence of those saving energies of Grace; hence the Church is forced to dominate Society, compelling all the members of Society to come under its sphere and influence. . . . The Church is the great educator of the nations, and like all educators she knows how to allow for various degrees of capacity and maturity, and how to attain her end only by a process of adaptation and compromise." [45] A third sociological type defined by Troeltsch was mysticism, which stressed purely personal and inward experience. Groups founded on the basis of mysticism were personal, impermanent, lacking in forms of worship, and "unhistorical" in nature. But, as Troeltsch emphasized in his Conclusion, these three forms appeared alongside one another all through the centuries, "while among themselves they are strangely and variously interwoven and inter-connected." [46]

The usefulness of Troeltsch's typology to the Tudor historian is evident. Tudor Puritanism, as has been pointed out, consisted of an interweaving of church-type and sect-type attitudes, with the radicals inclining toward the particularism of the sect. Troeltsch's own discussion of the Protestant movement of the sixteenth century brought out some of the anomalies. He argued that English Calvinism was founded in the reign of Edward VI, and that during the reign of Elizabeth it drew closer to the Genevan ideal, as it came into contact with Scottish Calvinism. "It then gradually divided," Troeltsch wrote, "into three main currents, Presbyterianism, Congregationalism, and Puritanism which often merged into one another." [47] The later history of these three movements is perhaps the real justification for Troeltsch's decision to make clear-cut distinctions between them. Not all historians of Tudor Puritanism would agree with Troeltsch's Weberian characterization of the Puritan movement. Troeltsch spoke of Puritanism in general as "the moral school of the English middle classes." [48] That phrase has all too obviously passed into the folklore of the English-speaking world. There is no reason to pursue Troeltsch's arguments about seventeenth-century Puritanism, or to try to summarize his discussion of the later Free Church movement. What is essential in his argument pertains to the origins and nature of the English Free Churches. Were these the logical result of Calvinism or the result of special circumstances? Did the Baptists, Brownists, and Barrowists of the sixteenth century question the state church system and try to replace it with a voluntary Church based on the "holy community" because of their Calvinism or because of political and social circumstances? [49] Troeltsch gave cautious answers, but his main point was clear: the Free Church movement, represented in the seventeenth century by Congregationalists and Baptists in particular, was based on voluntaristic principles, was opposed to uniform state-church controls, was committed more and more to democratic procedures, to the separation of Church and state; and "above all, the Free Churches approximate more and more to the Sect-type, even when the idea of the Church is preserved, with all its dogmatic and ethical consequences." [50] Troeltsch brought together most of the arguments about Protestant, and especially Puritan and Free Church contributions to modern ideas of democracy, toleration, progress, etc.; the influence of Troeltsch's theories may readily be traced, both in general surveys such as Horton Davies, *The English Free Churches* (1952),[51] and in special studies.

Troeltsch was most vulnerable to critical attack on the historical flank. This was most evident in his discussion of Calvinism and capitalism. Like Weber he failed to make sufficient allowance for the changes that time wrought in these movements. Troeltsch was more cautious than Weber, but he defended the same argument:

> No one has ever asserted that Capitalism is the direct product of Calvinism. We can, however, say that both possessed a certain affinity for each other, that [the] Calvinistic ethic of the "calling" and of work, which declares that the earning of money with certain precautions is allowable, was able to give it an intellectual and ethical backbone, and that, therefore, thus organized and inwardly supported it vigorously developed, even though within the limits of anti-mammon.[52]

It is easy to see that such a statement is inherently vague—so, unfortunately, was the argument which explained the "affinity," and the nature of the development. Historians who reject Weber's arguments about Calvinism and capitalism must necessarily reject Troeltsch's dependent arguments, although it is well to recall that Troeltsch's aim was to make clear the significance of "Capitalism in the development of Calvinism," not the reverse.[53] In *Protestantism and Progress*, originally a series of lectures based on his scholarly work, Troeltsch said he believed that Weber had completely proved his case, but he also urged that the really revolutionary effects of Protestantism were to be found in the religious sphere.[54] Despite the importance of Protestantism for law, science, history, and economic development its influence was exerted indirectly and involuntarily. What were the psychological conditions that made possible capitalist civilization remained a question—one which R. H. Tawney recognized as fundamental. In his Foreword to the English translation of *The Protestant Ethic*, Tawney pointed out that there were many solvents of the attitude Weber had called traditionalism.[55]

In *Religion and the Rise of Capitalism* (1926), Tawney acknowledged his debts to English scholars but observed that "it is no reflection on their work to say that the most important contributions of recent years have come from continental students, in particular Troeltsch, Choisy, Sombart, Brentano, Levy, and, above all, Max Weber." [56] In the Preface to the 1937 edition of this work, Tawney went further in acknowledging his indebtedness to Weber, but he also pointed out the lacunae in Weber's argument and criticized him for not emphasizing sufficiently "the profound changes through which Calvinism passed in the century following the death of Calvin." [57] Like other writers on great historical themes, Tawney did not confine his arguments to a single century —even his own. What has been called "Tawney's century" is the period which separates the Dissolution of the Monasteries from the Great Rebellion.[58] Much of Tawney's historical argument in *Religion and the Rise of Capitalism* was directed at Stuart problems, which cannot be discussed at length here. In his persistent stressing of the revolutionary character of the sixteenth century, and in his vision of Reformation Europe as the outgrowth of expanding economic energies, Tawney proclaimed the importance of many factors, material as well as religious, in the development of new attitudes favorable to capitalism. "The religious revolution of the age came upon a world heaving with the vastest economic crisis that Europe had experienced since the fall of Rome," Tawney wrote, although he was equally insistent on the importance of medieval intellectual legacies—the idea of religion as embracing all aspects of human life, the functional view of class organization, and the religious doctrine of economic ethics.[59]

Tawney's thesis was directed as much against partisan misuse of Weber's "Protestant ethic" argument by Belloc and other Catholic historians, as it was against the chronological inaccuracies of the thesis itself.[60] Like Troeltsch, Tawney emphasized the continuity of Catholic and Protestant attitudes toward the unrestricted pursuit of gain, and argued that Protestant opinion in the sixteenth century was not prepared to sanction a "spirit of capitalism." Tawney's revision of the Weber thesis could almost be summed up in a sentence: "To think of the abdication of religion from its theoretical primacy over the economic activity and social institutions as synchronizing with the revolt from Rome, is to antedate a movement which was not finally accomplished for another century and a half, and which owed as much to changes in economic and political organization, as it did to developments in the sphere of religious thought.[61] The subtlety and complexity of Tawney's arguments were perhaps most notable in his discussion of the problems associated with the Church of England and the Puritan movement.

The land question, which had occupied Tawney earlier, provided the point of departure for his discussion of the changes in attitude toward pecuniary advantage that began in the sixteenth century. A revolution in the psychology of landowning was not the least important solvent of traditionalism.[62] Tawney's identification of this new attitude toward land-ownership, based on businesslike and impersonal forms of exploitation, formed the core of his later thesis on the "Rise of the Gentry." The characteristic of the period 1540 to 1640 was the collision between prevalent practice and the shrill diatribes of the Church against economic individualism.[63] The practical ineffectiveness of prohibitions against usury led to their theoretical abandonment; and secularism reinforced Puritanism in undermining the authority of the state Church. Puritanism, not the Tudor secession from Rome, was for Tawney the true English Reformation. Tawney's epigram—"Puritanism was the schoolmaster of the English middle classes"— was not original, but in many ways it sums up the gist of his historical argument.[64] It was not Weber but Tawney who established a new orthodoxy in English-speaking universities. Tawney contributed to the debate over the ties between religion and capitalism not just by adding more history, though this was important, but by a wise and quiet recognition of the contradictions which live "in vigorous incompatibility together" in the human soul. "There was in Puritanism an element which was conservative and traditionalist," he wrote, "and an element which was revolutionary; a collectivism which grasped at an iron discipline, and an individualism which spurned the savourless mess of human ordinances; a sober prudence which would garner the fruits of this world, and a divine recklessness which would make all things new." [65] How anticipatory of new problems and interpretations that statement was! The rest of Tawney's argument, tracing the effects of Puritanism (especially the ideal of a godly discipline versus the religion of trade) is not directly relevant to Tudor history. The continuing influence of Tawney's ideas on both Tudor and Stuart historiography is, however, beyond dispute—he survives intellectually, not because his ideas were for a time academically orthodox, but because he suggested the kinds of questions that were most worth exploring.

The essays collected by F. J. Fisher in honor of R. H. Tawney on the occasion of his eightieth birthday are some indication of the extent of Tawney's influence. The Tawney variant of the Weber thesis is far from dead, as may be seen in Christopher Hill's essay, "Protestantism and Capitalism." And in the tightly woven themes of Fisher's essay, "Tawney's Century," are many of the conclusions reached by historians who followed leads they found, or might have found, in Tawney's work. Hill's essay, published in 1961, hints at some of the arguments he later developed in *Intellectual Origins of the English Revolution*. The process by which historiography renews itself, taking from past atmospheres the wild yeast that will leaven new work, is by no means simple and well understood. In some cases a single idea can be traced through many books, but more often than not only intellectual resemblances can be proved. To try to account for the general influence of Marx or Weber or Tawney is a difficult, though useful task; to make one writer responsible for another's subsequent but similar ideas is to reduce history to the level of a paternity suit. General approaches and attitudes toward social and economic historiography can best be studied in the works of individuals. Marx, Buckle, Weber, Troeltsch, and Tawney represent different theoretical positions— —not all positions, and not the only important positions, but some which appear to have been influential. In the remainder of this chapter, and in the following one, a somewhat more cursory survey will be made of works which answer directly important questions in Tudor history.

It would not be too much to say that in order to understand the best social and economic histories written in the twentieth century some knowledge of historiographical positions and traditions is essential. There is no special vocabulary that historians use to convey the results of their studies; historians do, however, use arguments and phrases that have a resonance—the "Protestant ethic" activates a much fuller response if the principal arguments about it are known. One of the most significant general studies of Tudor and Stuart social history undertaken in recent decades, W. K. Jordan's multivolumed work on English philanthropy, carries on some of the lines of inquiry opened up by, among other writers,

Weber and Tawney. The fresh questions asked by Jordan had to do with the shift in men's aspirations and interests within the frame of charitable causes. His opening statement concerning the conception of the work indicates its range:

> This study is concerned with men's aspirations for their own age and for generations yet to come; with their heroic effort to shape the course of history by creating enduring social institutions which would contribute significantly, often decisively, in determining the structure and nature of the society just coming into being. It has been our purpose to record every gift and bequest made to charities, quite broadly defined, during the period 1480–1660 in a selected, and, it is hoped, representative group of ten English counties, which probably included about one third of the population and somewhat more than one half of the disposable wealth of the entire realm.[66]

The questions asked by Jordan dictated to a large extent the choice of methods; and his methodological innovations are of no less interest than his conclusions. Having counted in the course of his period 34,963 private donors who gave for charitable uses the sum of £3,102,696 9s., he was in a position to make statistical observations that carry great weight. The sweep of the evidence indicated that a profound secularization of society took place in the 180-year period, that despite differing degrees of velocity of change among the different classes of men, "a most powerful and significant cultural revolution was underway which came to include all classes of the society as private charity first redefined and then remade the social institutions of the realm." [67] The need for private charity had grown rapidly as the result of demographic and agricultural changes, urbanization, monastic expropriations, price inflation and epidemics; and an increasing sensitivity to suffering and want was evident, especially in the accusatory literature of the age.

For statistical purposes Jordan divided his period into ten-year intervals, but broader chronological divisions were also important— the "Pre-Reformation Era" lasted from 1480 to 1540; the years from 1541 to 1560 became the "Age of the Reformation"; the "Age of Elizabeth" spanned the decades from 1561 to 1600; and Jordan went on to discuss the "Early Stuart Period," lasting until 1640, and finally the "Revolutionary Era." His chronology was based on significant turning points as revealed in the evidence, but he rightly

insisted that in many respects the Elizabethan age reached fulfillment only in the next generation.

Out of the need to organize and present the findings of his entire
study came the concise, clear analysis of Tudor social structure in
Philanthropy in England. Discussions of degree have had a long history, especially in England, and Tudor writers including Shakespeare drew the characters of the different classes of men. Only in
comparatively recent years, however, have impressions been revised
by new historical facts. The changing structure of class aspirations
formed one of the main themes of Jordan's large-scale study. How
to estimate the wealth of the nobility and the upper and lower
gentry was a problem tangled in controversy, and much dull hard
work still lies ahead. Jordan did not have available to him in 1959
the results of Lawrence Stone's researches published in 1965 in
The Crisis of the Aristocracy, but the value of Jordan's class estimates is very great.[68] The aspirations of the gentry, and particularly
of the London merchants, were different from those of other
classes, the merchants especially being more farsighted, more secular, and more concerned with the needs of the poor and with
education.[69] The motives for charitable giving were mixed, as Jordan recognized, but the impulses of nonconformity were greater
than those of conformity. The metamorphosis from the needs of a
religious society to the requirements of a secular society demanded
explanation: "Just why did it occur that the customary bequests
from husbandmen in Somerset of a few pence for the needs of
their Parish church give way at about 1580 to equally customary
legacies of a few pence for the parish poor?" [70] This was to pose
the complex question of motives in its simplest, and ultimately perhaps most important form. The secular aspirations of husbandmen
followed by a generation or more those of the London merchants,
but there could be no doubt that a massive, revolutionary shift did
take place. Private charity, in Jordan's view, saved England from
social disaster and became an essential concomitant of public policy. Changes in the law accommodated the new attitudes, making
it possible for charitable trusts to be founded on the basis of capital
endowments.[71]

The concern of the Tudor governments with the problem of
poverty was largely, but not exclusively, an aspect of its concern
with the problem of maintaining public order. The motives of private donors were much more complex. Although the making of a

will was a particularly solemn occasion, when a man's true attitudes might be expected to come out, no one was more aware
than Jordan of the frailties of the method: "The historian mixes in
his method the rigorous disciplines of the scientist with the almost
intuitive skill of the artist, but his conclusions remain tentative,
suggestive, and humble, since he has at least learned that the image
of truth in any age is indistinct, inexact, and all too often fractured." [72]

Among the great moving impulses to charity was the emerging
Protestant ethic. "Though the great preachers lent their aid and animated it with their zeal, the Protestant social ethic which was
forged in the course of the sixteenth century was none the less profoundly secular in its spiritual concerns," Jordan wrote.[73] The stew-
ardship theory of wealth, according to which men were ac-
countable to God for the use they made of their fortunes, was
etched in the English conscience by a host of Calvinist divines. It
might be said that this was part of the Protestant "doctrine of
works." [74] In any case, the charitable responsibilities of men of
substance were well established within a generation after the
coming of the Reformation, and private responsibility for public
welfare was widely accepted by the close of the sixteenth century.
Here the importance of tradition becomes evident—imitation and
emulation added greatly to the original bequests of merchants
and gentry, as habits of responsibility spread among other classes
and across geographical boundaries. Puritan preachers were especially effective in promoting the new doctrines, hewing out of
Scripture and historical experience a broadly Protestant but specifically Puritan ethic.[75] In stressing the role of ideas, and changes in
the climate of opinion, Jordan aligned himself on the side of those
who have argued in favor of independent intellectual traditions.
That the growth of historical consciousness owed something to
the exhortations of divines, and to the desire of ordinary Protestants
to put Rome to shame, is one of the well-grounded hypotheses
that this study suggests. The taunts of Catholic controversialists
that justification by faith meant justification of stinginess invited
historical comparisons, which the Protestants themselves were
eager to make. The remains of the Catholic past not only reminded
Protestants of the good works of Catholic ancestors, but also of
their own presumed shortcomings.[76] The past was being enlisted
on the side of powerful emotions, guilt feelings, and ideas; ideolog-

ical comparison would lead eventually to genuine historical comparison.

The critical controversy that followed the publication of *Philanthropy in England* (1959), *The Charities of London* (1960), *The Charities of Rural England* (1961), and other parts of Jordan's study, centered on the statistical methods employed.[77] Jordan decided to present his statistical data in static form—that is, he did not attempt to adjust his curves to any index of price movements. The inflation of the sixteenth century was obviously a matter of great importance, but the problem was how to make the proper allowance for it. Reviewers who argued that the static nature of the statistical presentation cast doubt on the conclusions insisted that statistical adjustments should have been made on the basis of available price indices. Jordan denied that a true curve of the purchasing power of money could be constructed during this era of almost two centuries: "our own research has taught us that there were more complex variables of price in the England of our period than the economic historians have recognized, for price was above all affected by costs of transportation . . ."[78] Moreover he observed that different commodities rose in price at different rates, that wages in general lagged behind prices, that local prices were no measure of national prices, and that sixteenth-century tastes, aspirations, and expectations were radically different from our own.[79] His own statistical information regarding local prices, collected in the course of research, might be expected to alter some of the currently held estimates of the price level in Tudor England. The real point at issue, however, was not just statistical but historical. The use of multipliers might change the shape of certain curves, and thereby perhaps suggest that the magnitude of merchant giving was less impressive than it appeared to be, but ultimately the decision to rely on a specific statistical method has to be made by the historian on the basis of his understanding of the whole body of the evidence. The historian's judgment, not the statistician's, is sovereign. As in the counting of manors, it is necessary to examine the assumptions as well as the addition. What a wealthy "reasonable man" (in the lawyer's sense) might decide to do with his money in 1603 would depend on many factors, including his own estimate of the effects of inflation, and his own understanding of what could be accomplished by money invested in a charitable trust—the "men of this age wrought mightily with instruments which seem puny indeed to us." [80]

The Crisis of the Aristocracy 1558–1641 by Lawrence Stone represents social history of a different type. Stone was no less resolute than Jordan in his pursuit of historical statistics, but he presented a close-up view of the behavior of a single class—the rich and the titled—rather than a sweeping view of society from a single vantage point. Although he differed from Tawney in his conclusions, Stone acknowledged that his greatest intellectual debt was to Tawney. The long neglect of the history of the aristocracy could be explained by the character of research in social history during the previous fifty years, which had concentrated on the history of the exploited classes—the peasantry—and on the capitalist solvents of feudalism, the progressive gentry and urban merchants.[81] The main reason for the neglect of the aristocracy was that the sources were not available; only after World War II was it possible to make a serious study of the aristocracy, since the evidence in the national archives could only supplement that which "lay unsorted, uncatalogued, unknown, and inaccessible in the muniment rooms, cellars, attics, and stables of the great private houses of England." [82] Furthermore, the nature of the surviving records ruled out any large-scale study of the aristocracy before the middle of the sixteenth century, when the growth of literacy among the landed classes brought about an explosive increase in the number of surviving personal letters and documents. The methodological importance of contemporary French historiography was noted by Stone but he did not attempt to copy French historical methods, preferring to give due weight to "the imponderables of ideology and aspiration, prejudice and custom." [83] Statistical measurement was, however, the backbone of the book, for this was "the only means of extracting a coherent pattern from the chaos of personal behaviour and of discovering which is a typical specimen and which a sport." [84] Like Namier, Stone relied on biographical studies, but he criticized the tacit assumption that lay behind the "Namierite approach," namely, that human beings were motivated only by family connections and business interests. Simply because these were the interests most likely to have survived in the records was no reason to accept them as being decisive. Stone went even further, criticizing Jordan's argument that the aristocrats were lacking in the charitable ideals and aspirations of the gentry; aristocratic charity took the form of casual gifts rather than charitable trusts and therefore tended to pass unrecorded. And if the merchants were the largest givers to charity, this was, in Stone's opinion, because their circumstances were different, not because they showed a greater sense of social responsibility.[85]

Stone described clearly both his thesis and the preconceptions upon which it rested. The political and social crisis of the seventeenth century in England had hitherto been misconceived as the product of a changing social structure. The social *structure* did not change; the role of the various social classes changed, within a relatively stable structure. Changes of function could not be explained by changes in the means of production, or by other economic changes, although these remained the bedrock of history. Equally significant were role changes and changes of attitude—"changes in the nature and distribution of power, in the role of the state in society, in ethical values and in attitudes of mind: attitudes to God and Church, King and Commonwealth, to rank and title, to town and countryside, to spending and frugality, to charity and the poor, to education and the arts, to wives and children, to sex and marriage." [86] The shift from an economic to a sociological interpretation of history was part of a migration in historiography that had begun in the 1930s: "Today, somewhat belatedly, the problems of historical causation are beginning to be attacked with the powerful tools provided by Freud and Malinowsky, Weber and Veblen, in addition to the useful but clumsy old Marxist bulldozer." [87]

Between the fifteenth and the eighteenth centuries the English aristocracy was transformed from a group of territorial warlords into an oligarchy of cultivated, capitalistic parliamentarians. The decisive changes occurred in the period from about 1580 to 1620, which was, according to Stone, the real watershed between medieval and modern England.[88] The first half of the seventeenth century became, however, a period of real crisis for the aristocracy —they lost the influence they had gained over elections during Elizabeth's reign, and allowed the initiative to pass temporarily into the hands of the squirearchy. The "rise of the gentry" had been used to explain the decline of the aristocracy, but Stone argued persuasively that this explanation would not do—nor would the still earlier stereotype which asserted that mercantile and industrial capitalists were swept into power by a nascent industrial revolution. Having rejected the explanations of Froude, Tawney, Trevor-Roper, Nef, and others, Stone went on to build up his own— namely, that the crisis of the aristocracy was a crisis of adaptation on the part of the aristocracy to the compelling new forces in Elizabethan and early Stuart society.

In the eyes of the sixteenth century the peerage constituted a distinct group of "major nobility," as distinct from gentry. Enjoying very significant privileges, as well as exceptional wealth, the peers were an enormously influential group. The power they exercised in the House of Lords was especially important in the Tudor period.[89] The real inflation of honors began under James, but the demand had begun earlier: "the insatiable demand for status and honour between 1558 and 1641 is proof of the truth of what has been called 'Tawney's Law': that the greater the wealth and the more even its distribution in a given society, the emptier become titles of personal distinction but the more they multiply and are striven for." [90] In discussing economic changes as a cause of the crisis, Stone explained his statistical methods, how he set about counting manors, and why. The final word on the ups and downs of the gentry has probably not yet been written, but Stone's contribution to the debate added new and essential arguments based on fresh evidence. The key to his position was that "since one manor may be up to 100 times more valuable than another, the use of manorial counts as indicators of real wealth is only possible, if at all, *provided that the comparisons relate to large numbers of representative manors*—representative in the sense that they are statistically random samples." [91] The evidence thus calculated showed "that the holdings of the surviving peers of 1558 had fallen by about a quarter by 1602 and by a further fifth by 1641." [92] Relative to the gentry the peers were severely weakened, especially during the years from about 1580 to 1606. There was a crisis of money and land under Elizabeth, and a crisis of confidence under Charles I. The causes of decay were as complex as the causes of growth; and Stone's argument took both decay and revival into account. The subtle interweaving of these themes illustrated the thesis: "The rise of the gentry is to some extent—though certainly not entirely—an optical illusion, resulting from the temporary weakness of the aristocracy." [93]

Among the sociological causes of the decline of the peerage were ideas of conspicuous consumption, habits of litigation, the influence of Puritanism, traditionalism in the face of economic inflation, and increasing dependence on the crown. Stone could be witty as well as exact in his comments:

> Sixteenth century litigation combined the qualities of tedium, hardship, brutality, and injustice that tested character and endurance,

with the element of pure chance that appealed to the gambler, the fear of defeat and ruin, and the hope of victory and the humiliation of the enemy. It had everything that war can offer save the delight of shedding blood. It gave shape and purpose to many otherwise empty lives.[94]

The educational revolution that took place between 1540 and 1640 marked one of the decisive changes in English history, when the propertied classes "exploited and expanded the educational resources of the country." [95] The gentry and aristocracy began their drive for better education in the sixteenth century under the influence of humanism. As the technical requirements of office holding became more "intellectual," with a premium being placed on knowledge of ancient and modern history, competition between the nobility and gentry increased. In the early sixteenth century few gentlemen attended the universities; by 1600 it was the rule. By 1630, as Stone had pointed out elsewhere in an important article, there were more people being educated in universities in England than at any time before the 1930s.[96] The changes in taste and attitude that allowed the Ninth Earl of Northumberland to acquire twenty-four pictures of Roman emperors in 1586 could justly be described as revolutionary. Before the mid-sixteenth century the lack of surviving letters, along with other evidence, indicated that most aristocrats simply did not feel the need to write, much less to acquire intellectual habits. The growth of historical consciousness must be seen as part of this change in educational patterns and in the patterns of patronage. The nobility became patrons of the arts and of scholarship under Elizabeth, and the flowering of the Elizabethan age owed something to the active patronage of these educated men.[97] If in the short run the gentry were able to compete on more favorable terms, in the long run education insured the survival of the aristocracy as a ruling élite—"few revolutions of a revolutionary age were of greater importance." [98]

In *The Crisis of the Aristocracy*, Stone made use of many previous studies, drew upon a variety of theories, and grounded his conclusions on original research. Many of the crucial arguments of the book were directed toward the seventeenth-century crisis; but as in the case of Jordan's charity studies and other works spanning both Tudor and Stuart history, the reader must be expected to follow through and assess for himself the arguments and the critical objections. The stress here on sixteenth-century developments is not without justification, but inevitably the historical perspective has been foreshortened. Works of synthesis conceived on a large scale are rare, and around them may be grouped the more conventional books which form the historiographical traditions of the age.

General theorists such as Marx or Weber were innovators whose ideas were applicable to Tudor history without being derived from an intensive study of it. Innovative historians, immersed in the historiographical traditions of Tudor history, have been distinguished by the ability to ask new questions and exploit new kinds of sources using new techniques in addition to established methods. Jordan and Stone, innovative historians whose work in social history illustrates many historiographical traditions, opened up new areas of research—their innovations in method will be exploited and technically extended in the future. Modern computers can be expected to facilitate statistical studies and provide an even more efficient means of sorting, counting, and correlating than business machines using punched cards. Computerized research in history and humanities has in fact moved ahead very rapidly during the past few years. Thomas G. Barnes has been engaged in a computer-assisted study of cases brought before the Star Chamber from 1596 to 1641. Another Tudor research project based on the use of a computer is Theodore Rabb's analysis of some 8,000 investors in overseas enterprises in England between 1550 and 1630. Such studies, either not yet completed or, like Rabb's, only recently published, suggest what some of the new directions in Tudor scholarship will be.[99] Many quantitative questions cannot be answered by the methods of traditional historiography simply because the technical means are lacking; the kinds of questions that historians feed into computers, however, derive from the traditions of the historian's craft. It will be useful, therefore, to review briefly some of the more traditional approaches to Tudor social history.

Discussions of the class structure of Tudor England have until recently been based largely on conjecture, albeit on conjecture informed by literary evidence plus a "sampling" of family financial histories. The structural relationships between the classes is gradually beginning to be understood, as more information is brought together in the form of local studies and works based on family records. The inarticulate and submerged—poor peasants and poor townsmen—cannot be understood as fully as the aristocracy, the gentry, the merchants, and the intellectuals. Much has been done, however, to explore the ways of life of particular groups in Tudor society. Certain classes of local documents have become available only since World War II—for example, Quarter-Sessions records, which in some counties were virtually closed to students before about 1945. A new generation of local historians with professional training has grown up, and under the leadership of scholars such as W. G. Hoskins and H. P. R. Finberg, they have virtually rewritten local history in England. *The Midland Peasant* (1957) and *Provincial England* (1963) by Hoskins indicate what has been achieved.[100] Especially important pioneering studies of the housing revolution and of deserted village sites make the latter no less important than the former to the student of Tudor society. The role of the provinces in Tudor history has been consistently underrated until very recently. Partly under the influence of French historians such as Marc Bloch, whose ground-breaking study, *French Rural History*, came out in 1931 and was translated into English in 1966, the way of life of the rural classes in England began to be studied in depth and detail. Mildred Campbell's *The English Yeoman* (1942) has been reprinted in England and remains the most useful study of the yeomanry, those "40 shilling freeholders" who were one rank below the gentry but whose status, as Campbell pointed out, was not really defined legally but by reference to the groups above and below them in the social scale.[101]

The social structure of the towns, and especially of London, has been the subject of a great deal of specialized research. John Stow's *Survey of London* (1601) remains an indispensable book. In addition to the *Victoria County Histories*, mention should be made of the highly revealing study by Sylvia L. Thrupp, *The Merchant Class of Medieval London, 1300–1500* (1948), which destroys the notion that social mobility was somehow an invention of the sixteenth century. Despite the stability of the merchant class in medieval times, there was a great deal of movement in and out of it; and there were no sharp lines of social demarcation separating merchants from all others. Indeed, one lesson of the book is that there were widespread cultural similarities among all sections of the "middle strata." [102] Provincial towns have been studied in relation to the London administrative complex, and in terms of their own social structure, which was in many ways different from that of London. Wallace MacCaffrey's *Exeter* (1958) and J. W. F. Hill's *Tudor and Stuart Lincoln* (1956) are models of the type. Perhaps the best known and most successful attempt to describe the structure and character of a county in Tudor times was A. L. Rowse's *Tudor Cornwall* (1941). Cornwall was an integral part of the kingdom, but it was also a distinct and homogeneous society, with its own language and traditions. In the long series of county histories coming down from the Elizabethan age not the least distinguished was Carew's *Survey of Cornwall*, which described Cornwall at the end of the Tudor period; Rowse added to this tradition of county historiography, describing in lively detail the unique features and the economy of Tudor Cornwall, the counterpoint between local and national history, and the various ways in which the Reformation was felt in the everyday lives of Cornishmen. Conceived on a much broader chronological scale, the *Victoria County Histories* are the best guides to county history in general, but Rowse's volume remains a beacon for the Tudor historian.

Family histories, as distinct from individual lives or biographies, have usually dealt with the responses of a single family and its branches to changing political and social circumstances. One of the best nineteenth-century examples of the type was Augustus Jessopp's *One Generation of a Norfolk House* (1878), the work of an Anglican clergyman who wrote about the Walpoles of Norfolk. Sir Robert Walpole's Tudor ancestors were perhaps most remarkable for that one generation of young men who risked and lost their lives for the Catholic faith they had deliberately embraced—"These men were of the same stuff that Latimer and Rowland Taylor were made of; they were animated by the same enthusiasm, supported by the same intense earnestness, hurried along by the same fiery zeal, as free from vulgar worldliness, and as sincere." [103] Here, perhaps, was the beginning of the reveille for recusants that has made the Elizabethan Catholic martyrs almost as well known to the twentieth century as the Marian Protestant victims. For the most part family histories have been based on the discovery of letters and other papers, but there are regettably few century-long accumulations, such as the *Paston Letters*; and most historians have preferred to exploit family archives for biography. One of the most unusual and historically valuable collections of Tudor letters was the vast correspondence preserved by John Johnson, Merchant of the Staple, whose bankruptcy in 1553 led, through the vagaries of the law, to the preservation of his "writings and books." The surviving letters, approximately a thousand in number, form the basis of Barbara Winchester's *Tudor Family Portrait* (1955), which provides one of the few first-hand pictures of the everyday life of a Tudor merchant family. The Johnsons left no mark on posterity, but they lived and loved, celebrated birth and death, suffered the rise and the fall of fortune's wheel, like other men and women, indeed like ourselves.

For the gentry, more information is at hand, and books such as F. G. Emmison's *Tudor Secretary: Sir William Petre at Court and Home* (1961) are full of information on gentry customs and pastimes.[104] Alan Simpson's *The Wealth of the Gentry 1540–1660* (1961) explored the economics of family history, concentrating on the varying fortunes of Sir Nicholas Bacon and Sir Thomas Cornwallis and their families. The domestic life of the Elizabethans has been dealt with most fully by Lu Emily Pearson in *Elizabethans at Home* (1957), although an earlier survey by M. St. Clare Byrne, *Elizabethan Life in Town and Country* (1925), remains useful in its revisions. Certainly every student of Elizabethan attitudes must be grateful to Louis B. Wright for *Middle Class Culture in Elizabethan England* (1935). The role of women in Elizabethan society has been treated by Carol Camden in *The Elizabethan Woman* (1952). While the social history of the period before Elizabeth has attracted somewhat less attention, the brief survey by Penry Williams, *Life in Tudor England* (1964), which focuses on the half century from 1520 to 1570, contains much useful information distilled for the general reader. For a somewhat earlier period Paul Murray Kendall's *The Yorkist Age* (1962) contains a good deal of well-chosen material on manners and customs; and the *Paston Letters*, now available in several editions, remain sources of the utmost importance. The significance of these and other original and derived sources was admirably elucidated by C. L. Kingsford in *English Historical Literature in the Fifteenth Century* (1913).

To prolong a listing of important books on Tudor social history would require nothing more than bibliographical diligence. The significant fact is that special studies blanket nearly every field of social and economic history. In some areas series publications attempt to synthesize and sum up current knowledge. *The Agrarian History of England and Wales*, projected by Tawney, has been mentioned; the Oxford *History of English Art*, edited by T. S. R. Boase, is expected to be completed in eleven volumes; the *Buildings of*

England series, to which Nicholas Pevsner has contributed so much, has special significance for local history; the *Cambridge Modern History of English Literature* is well known, as is the more recent *Oxford History of English Literature*; and the *Oxford History of English Music* is recognized as a standard. The relevant volumes in each of these series discuss Tudor achievements. Aspects of Tudor life which are of special importance for urban historians are included in the histories of the various gilds, in the history of technology and of crafts—especially brewing, baking, and candle-making—and in histories of the regulated companies engaged in overseas trade, as well as in other works on economic history. The importance of heraldry and genealogy in the sixteenth century warrants special mention; these subjects were of great interest then, and are of great use to historians now. The work of Anthony Richard Wagner, Richmond Herald, provides the best introduction to English ancestry. The herald's visitations, which began sporadically in the fifteenth century, provide important clues to family history and are sometimes of use in identifying individuals. Visitations did not necessarily prevent bribery, collusion, and other forms of fraud, but among the Elizabethan heralds were many men of integrity and knowledge; Camden and Glover were outstanding scholars, by no means mere institutional ornaments. The reprinting of some of the visitations has been undertaken by local record societies.[105] The highly critical accounts of Tudor heraldry and genealogy by J. H. Round have been modified by Wagner, whose *English Genealogy* provides not only a comprehensive picture of genealogy in relation to history but an excellent survey of the various records which are of use to the genealogist and historian, plus a useful brief account of the College of Heralds. For the earlier history of the office Wagner's *Heralds and Heraldry in the Middle Ages* (2nd edition, 1956) remains the standard text, while G. D. Squibb's *The High Court of Chivalry* (1959) traces the vicissitudes of the Court of Chivalry from its origins in the fourteenth century and describes social and institutional history from the point of view of the civil law. Finally, there is the history of arms and armor, the history of costume, and histories of sundry relics—the tapestries, the furniture, the silver, jewels, and ornaments—without which it is difficult to reconstruct a vanished age.[106] At this point one moves from useful books to indispensable exhibitions; in the museums and portrait galleries lie the original sources of social history that can, with an ounce of imagination, clothe and revivify the abstract dead.

The history of Wales under the Tudors is at once a part of the main development of English society and the history of a separate mountainous, remote region with its own language, its own unruly traditions, its medieval British and ancient Celtic legends, its unique contrasts between coast, mountain, and valley, between marches and principality, and between English enclaves and the Welsh shires where Fluellen's pride and fighting prowess were alike nourished.[107] Welsh historical consciousness was kept alive by Welsh bards; and Welsh antiquaries such as Humphrey Llwyd in the sixteenth century recalled native historical greatness.[108] The success of Henry Tudor in 1485 appeared, indeed, to many Welshmen to be the belated triumph of Owen Glendower—"valiant as a lion and wondrous affable"—the ablest and most worthy of Welsh rebels, who has continued to be a folk hero to the present day.[109] To interested students the *Bibliography of the History of Wales* (2nd edition, 1962) will prove particularly useful, even to those who know no Welsh. The *Welsh History Review*, only very recently founded, is a tribute to the renaissance in Welsh Studies, which might be said to have begun with the publication of the *Transactions of the Honourable Society of Cymmrodorion* in 1877. *Elizabethan Wales: The Social Scene* by Geraint Dyfnallt Owen provides a survey of recent research, and Penry Williams' *The Council in the Marches of Wales under Elizabeth I* (1958) contributes importantly to administrative history. Glanmor Williams, in *The Welsh Church from Conquest to Reformation* (1962), traces in detail the origins of the Reformation in Wales, in a book which surveys the economic and social position of the clergy and is much broader and more original than the title alone might indicate. A good general survey of Welsh history is probably a necessity for the student and D. Williams, *A History of Modern Wales* (1950), provides a convenient narrative.

To sail from a Welsh port across St. George's channel to Ireland in the sixteenth century was to travel, in effect, to a foreign country. The English hold on Ireland was tightened under the Tudors, and "order" was established at the price of Irish revolts, but Ireland beyond the Pale was not Anglicized or converted to Protestantism. The Welsh were considered corrigible by the English; the Irish, by and large, were not. The history of Ireland under the Tudors remains separate, a matter more of foreign policy than of national administration. In the present context the view across the Irish Sea from England is what matters; the most useful description of English attitudes is to be found in *The Elizabethans and the Irish* (1966) by David Beers Quinn, a book which is particularly revealing of historical attitudes in the making.[110] For the detailed narrative one must still consult Richard Bagwell's *Ireland under the Tudors* (3 vols., 1885–1890), a standard, rigid, unimaginative Victorian history.

Tudor economic history has been virtually rewritten during the last thirty years in the pages of the *Economic History Review* and other journals. Some of the controversies that have shaped interpretation have already been mentioned; others, no less interesting, may be found by inspection. As in other fields of historiography debates have tended to cluster around certain books and problems, but the journal literature in economic history is at least as important as anything to be found within the covers of books. Among the most controversial and significant interpretations put forward by economic historians in the twentieth century are those which attempted to account for the "price revolution," the "industrial revolution," and what might, with reason, have been called the "mercantilist revolution" of the sixteenth century. According to many observers, the problems of industrial organization and capital formation in Tudor times are relevant to the problems faced by underdeveloped countries today—hence the fresh importance of George Unwin's *Industrial Organization in the 16th and 17th Centuries* (1904, reprinted 1957) and the recent critical appraisals of the process of capital formation by Alexander Gerschenkron, Ragnar Nurske, Simon Kuznets, and other economists. Taken together, these problems will form the basis for the following discussion of Tudor economic historiography. That each of the "revolutionary" theses has been challenged is not surprising, yet in each case the evidence points to an economic and social phenomenon that demands explanation. Something like a three- to fourfold rise in prices spread over a period of ninety years, from 1510 to 1600, does not seem much by twentieth-century standards, especially when the German inflation of the early twenties is considered, but it was enough to create suffering among contemporaries and disagreements among later historians. The difficulty of constructing adequate wage and price indexes is exceeded only by the difficulty of constructing a standard-of-living formula for the sixteenth century.

The assumptions made by John Maynard Keynes in his *Treatise on Money* (1930) were criticized by J. U. Nef, who made use of historical comparison in his critique of Keynes and of E. J. Hamilton, whose original argument that price and profit inflation stimulated the growth of capitalism was adopted with modifications by Keynes. It might with some truth be said that Hamilton's books and articles provided the starting point for modern arguments about the price revolution; that Nef's books and articles were the cause of controversies about the industrial revolution of the sixteenth century; and that Eli Heckscher's *Mercantilism* provided the basis for modern debates about the mercantilist transition. Journal articles and books followed in the wake of these major interpretations.

When Earl J. Hamilton published *American Treasure and the Price Revolution in Spain, 1501–1650* in 1934 he was primarily interested in Spanish prices and Spanish policies, but he made it quite clear in the Preface that Spain was simply the foremost example of a European power caught in the price revolution. Hamilton's highly technical arguments buttressed a relatively simple thesis:

> Pouring into Europe in a mammoth stream, American gold and silver precipitated the Price Revolution, which in turn played a significant rôle in the transformation of social and economic institutions in the first two centuries of the modern era. Thoroughly imbued with mercantilist principles, the rulers of Castile spared no pains to attract the largest possible flow of specie to the motherland, and to obstruct its outward passage. . . . Presumably the price revolution was more abrupt and transcendent in Spain than in any other European country, and *a priori* one would suppose that the phenomenon spread over Spain in concentric waves from Seville, the fountainhead.[111]

The close correlation between advancing commodity prices and the volume of treasure imports demonstrated beyond a doubt, Hamilton concluded, that from about 1535 until the end of the century, the "abundant mines of America" were the principal cause of the price revolution in Spain—and, albeit indirectly, of price rises in England and France as well. Hamilton invoked the mercantilist policies of the state to account for the pursuit of treasure, but in an earlier article he had attempted to show that American bullion was also responsible for the rise of capitalism between 1500 and 1700.[112] His thesis was that profit inflation, caused by the price inflation and the influx of precious metals, was the primary cause of the development of capitalism throughout Europe in the sixteenth century. Keynes drew from Hamilton's earlier statistical articles the conclusion that "the wealth of nations is enriched, not during Price inflations but during Profit inflations—at times, that is to say, when prices are running away from costs." [113] Capitalism was loosely defined by Hamilton, who enumerated several factors conducive to its growth, including the existence of nation states engaged in trade with one another, enclosure movements, better agricultural methods, and the Protestant ethic. Nevertheless, the primary cause was the discovery of the New World (this was only one of Marx's causes and not necessarily the most important).[114] For a variety of reasons the influx of precious metals brought about a situation in which wages lagged behind prices, to give entrepreneurs higher profits, while rents proved to be "sticky" upwards, indicating that capital accumulation did not come primarily from rent. The economic technicalities of this argument cannot be assessed here; the essential point is that Hamilton provided a statistically supported thesis which apparently explained the sixteenth-century inflation and its consequences. Keynes surmised that new purchasing power came to France and England as the result of private commerce.[115] The question was whether or not Hamilton's argument could in fact be considered a true explanation of the behavior of prices, and of the rise of capitalism elsewhere in Europe. At this point the genesis of industrial capitalism was of crucial importance.

John U. Nef published his classic, *The Rise of the British Coal Industry*, in 1932; it described a basic industry under capitalistic management, its relationship to other industries, and its influence on invention, the ownership of natural resources, industrial and financial organization, political power, and state policy in the period from about 1550 to 1700. The importance of coal in the medieval period, or before about 1550 in Britain, was not great according to Nef—there was little to distinguish the industrial organization of mining from other forms of early manorial and gild economy. The population increase alone could not explain the growth in the output of coal after 1550, nor could the exhaustion of timber supplies explain the rapid changes in the organization of the coal industry and the improved techniques which increased production. The right explanation, according to Nef, was an early industrial revolution.[116] The coal industry expanded as part of a general expansion and reorganization of British industry, especially of those enterprises engaged in the production of glass, metalwork, ships, salt, textiles, soap, gunpowder, alum, beer, etc. Instead of producing luxuries, Britain was turning to necessities as the basis of her new economy; the industrial revolution of the sixteenth century was made possible by British coal, and by the capitalistic exploitation of coal.[117] Not only did coal mining provide an opportunity for investment, it also drew capital from the merchants and from landed families:

> Until the sixteenth century, except for the financing of wars, or for the equipment of trading expeditions to bring back rich spices and jewels from the East, there had been little occasion in any part of western Europe to assemble such considerable sums of capital as were now required to start even one of the smaller collieries. The appearance of large business units in the British coal industry, and in other industries which depended for their progress upon supplies of cheap fuel, is a fact of the first importance in the history of modern capitalism, because of the resulting extension of a capitalistic financial organization over a wider field of economic life, over the production and manufacture of commodities, as well as their exchange.[118]

In "The Progress of Technology and the Growth of Large-Scale Industry in Great Britain, 1540–1640" (*Economic History Review*, 1934), Nef developed his general thesis, listing new manufactures that were introduced into England during the last sixty years of the sixteenth century, and describing the progress of technical methods. It was an exploratory article, not based on quantitative research, but it set the main line of argument—Britain took the lead in heavy industry during Elizabeth's reign, when the progress of technology resulted in a concentration of industrial capital.

The general thesis of an early industrial revolution was one that Nef never abandoned in his later works. In his article on "Prices and Industrial Capitalism in France and England, 1540–1640" (*Economic History Review*, 1937), he attacked directly the Hamilton-Keynes argument about the causes and consequences of the "price revolution," insisting that if the price revolution was the primary cause of the rise of capitalism, then one might expect similar effects in both France and England. Similarities, however, were not evident: large-scale industry developed only in England, despite the fact that in France labor was hardly less cheap than in England after 1550. Conditions for economic growth had been, if anything, more favorable in France than in England; and Keynes's epigram was false—periods of profit inflation not only coincided with periods of industrial expansion but with periods of depression. Nef's conclusion was that the effects of the price revolution were much more complex than Hamilton had thought. The expansion of Elizabethan industry was brought about to some extent by the growth of the home market. The earlier rise in prices was simply the result of the debasement of the coinage. Sharply rising timber prices in the later sixteenth century provided a stimulus to industrial improvement in England, but in France there was an industrial depression in the last quarter of the sixteenth century. Further comparisons between France and England, aimed at revealing the conditions of progress, were made by Nef in later books and articles.[119] He first published *Industry and Government in France and England, 1540–1640* in 1940, as the war was getting started, and although he resisted the temptation to discover in English constitutional history the principal cause of England's first industrial revolution, he argued that "the difference in the direction of national economic policies in France and England; and the much more important difference in the effectiveness of royal interference in the two countries, helps to account for the more rapid progress of heavy industry in England during the hundred years preceding the civil war . . ." [120] In *War and Human Progress* (1950) and in *Cultural Foundations of Industrial Civilization* (1958) he explored different but related questions of historical influence.

The criticisms of Nef's thesis took the form of questioning the extent, and therefore the significance, of industrialization in the sixteenth century. It is not possible to follow the details of this controversy, which is clearly still alive. Some of the main criticism appeared in an article by D. C. Coleman, "Industrial Growth and Industrial Revolution" (*Economica*, 1956). Peter Ramsey, who followed rather closely the line of Nef's critics in his text, *Tudor Economic Problems* (1963), was criticized in turn by Eric Kerridge, who pointed out that "innovation, not invention, is the stuff that industrial revolutions are made of." [121] This was true enough, and most historians would probably grant that innovation took place, but quantitative and qualitative questions remained: How many capitalists took part in the Tudor industrialization? What were their roles? During the 1930s it was rather fashionable to attribute to the mercantile and industrial capitalists a *progressive* role (comparable to the "progressive gentry") in the development of opposition to the Crown. It is no longer possible to accept this thesis in its entirety, for as Lawrence Stone observed, "The so-called industrial revolution of the period 1540–1640 has been cut down to size, and is now seen as a relatively minor development in terms of money invested or men employed." [122] As in other problems of historical change, however, it is necessary to distinguish between qualitative and quantitative questions, between innovations in technique, method, and even scale, and innovations which could be considered decisive determinants of the future. Military history provides a simple illustration of the difference: the tank was a genuine innovation in World War I, but its use was not on a sufficiently large scale, nor were the tactics of tank warfare sufficiently well understood to make the innovation decisive in ending the war. The Tudor industrial revolution was not "decisive" in this sense.

A third major thesis of the 1930s was that put forward by Eli Heckscher in *Mercantilism* (1931, English translation 1934). The phrase "mercantile system" had been used by Adam Smith to describe a trading, as opposed to an agricultural economy. The errors of mercantilism were many, according to Smith, but the most notable was the confusion of wealth with money; and the worst consequence of pursuing a mercantilist "balance of trade" policy was that, in practice, consumer interests were sacrificed to producer interests. The long history of the debate over mercantilist policies and theories was briefly summarized by Heckscher, who called attention to the importance of Schmoller, Cunningham, and others who had emphasized the elements of state building and the pursuit of relative power in early mercantilism. The significance of Heckscher's book was that it drew together various strands of earlier argument and presented a coherent case for regarding mercantilism as an "instrumental concept" which would enable one to understand the historical period between the end of the Middle Ages and the coming of *laissez faire*. Heckscher included in his analysis not only economic history but intellectual, social, and legal history, and he ranged widely across western Europe for his examples. He drew heavily on secondary works, including W. R. Scott's *The Constitution and Finance of English, Scottish and Irish Joint Stock*

Companies to 1720 (1912) and Lipson's *The Economic History of England*, which had its fifth edition in 1929. The transition from medieval to mercantilist policies was gradual, and medieval forms persisted into the nineteenth century in England; but Heckscher stressed also the "revolutionary" effects of the mercantilist emphasis on power, and the revolutionary characteristics of mercantilist thought. If England was the greatest innovator in economic history, the reason had something to do with the fact that Englishmen had achieved mercantilistic unification without any planning on the part of the state. In England, at least, the executor of mercantilism was liberalism with its doctrine of *laissez faire*.[123]

The doctrines and practices characteristic of mercantilism in Europe were grouped by Heckscher under five main headings: (1) Unification, (2) the Pursuit of Relative Power, (3) Protection, (4) Monetary Policy characterized by the pursuit of treasure and a favorable "balance of trade," (5) a Conception of Society.[124] Of these, the first and the last were of most concern to the Tudor historian. If mercantilism was "simply a convenient term for summarizing a phase of economic policy and economic ideas," as Heckscher wrote in a restatement for the *Economic History Review*, it was nevertheless the case that mercantilism described very different things in the course of three centuries.[125] The pursuit of power, to which Heckscher attached great importance in his book, was one to which his critics, notably Jacob Viner, took exception.[126] Unification, Heckscher insisted, was not achieved in England by deliberate governmental policy; the Statute of Artificers of 1563 was an example of bold planning in this direction, but it was unique—the destruction of medieval particularism and universalism was largely the result of a series of decisions reached in the common law courts. Although Heckscher maintained that the mercantilist attitude toward *means* was more significant than the *aims* of mercantilist policy, he insisted that the conception of society posited by mercantilism was one which had substituted amoral ends and *raison d'état* for medieval religious and ethical attitudes.[127] The underlying idea of mercantilism was that people should be taken as they are, and that what ought to be considered was social causation, not moral imperatives. After quoting several sixteenth- and seventeenth-century writers to illustrate this point he concluded that there was a very strong emphasis on causality in mercantilist thought and that (as in *laissez-faire* theories) writers held that legislative interference with economic law could only result in misfortune.

Belief in the economic and social causes of crime lay behind the savage Tudor criminal statutes. Heckscher quoted Sir Thomas More, Clement Armstrong, and *The Discourse of the Common Weal* to illustrate the spreading preoccupation with the causes behind social phenomena.[128] This new attitude, so important for the development of historiography, was later to be examined in detail by Arthur Ferguson in *The Articulate Citizen of the English Renaissance* (1965). Perhaps the most significant piece of contemporary evidence was Gresham's "Memorandum for the Understanding of the Exchange," which attempted for the first time to explain market fluctuations in terms of cause and effect. As Raymond de Roover noted, it was this new approach to economic problems that constituted the originality of the early mercantilism.[129]

The fullest criticism of Heckscher's thesis to date has been B. E. Supple's *Commercial Crisis and Change in England 1600–1642* (1959). In his brief review of the earlier criticisms of Heckscher, Supple stressed the idea that mercantilism had been erroneously defined by the traditionalists—specifically by Heckscher—who attributed a great deal too much to conscious thought and policy on the part of the government, and much too little to the influence of the economic environment. Supple insisted on short-term responses to immediate economic problems: mercantilist doctrines were not the spontaneous products of an ideal of society, nor were they evidence for the continuity of medieval concepts; Tudor and Stuart governments simply responded to the immediate problems of dearth, order, employment, security, etc. The strategic roots of certain policies and the economic roots of others were a sufficient explanation of policies designed to protect, for example, shipping and the wool trade.[130] From the point of view of policy, Supple's "environmentalism" posed a very real historiographical challenge; from the point of view of ideas, Heckscher's study remains indispensable.

Whatever the relative importance of ends and means, or of policies and ideas, there can be no doubt that the production and sale of wool and woolen textiles occupied a position of unique importance in the English economy during the medieval and the mercantilist period. The sale abroad of woolen goods was the biggest single item of trade. The merchants of the staple as well as the various companies trading to different parts of the world dealt largely in wool. About four-fifths of the value of English exports in Henry VIII's reign were accounted for by the products of this single industry, and the home market absorbed another large part of the national production. The woolen industry remained, throughout the Tudor period, the largest and most diversified of English industries, and it probably absorbed the highest proportion of merchant capital.

The importance of the wool trade in the Middle Ages was emphasized by Stubbs, gracefully clarified by Eileen Power in the Ford Lectures for 1939, and has since been reassessed in the pages of the *Cambridge Economic History of Europe* (Vols. I and II; 1941, 1952) and elsewhere.[131] For the Tudor period the works of P. J. Bowden, *The Wool Trade in Tudor and Stuart England* (1962), and G. D. Ramsay, *The Wiltshire Woolen Industry in the Sixteenth and Seventeenth Centuries* (1943), supplemented and in part supplanted the earlier studies of Heaton and Lipson, although the latest edition of Lipson's *The Economic History of England* (1949) provides a valuable general introduction.[132] A *Treatise of Commerce*, published in 1601 by John Wheeler, secretary of the Merchants Adventurers of England, naturally noted the importance of wool in foreign trade, this book was the earliest example of corporation publicity in English, and it was also one of the earliest attempts to deal with problems of economic history and social policy.[133] In general the history of foreign trade in early Tudor England has attracted less attention than Elizabethan trade— mostly because the records are fewer for the earlier period. Spanish trade was dealt with by G. Connell-Smith in *The Forerunners of Drake* (1954); and T. S. Willan discussed the Elizabethan trade with Russia in *The Muscovy Merchants of 1555* (1953) and in *The Early History of the Russia Company 1553–1603* (1959). The Tudor interest in Russia was not confined merely to trade, although Russia remained terra incognita to most Englishmen in the sixteenth century. The historical sketch by Giles Fletcher, *Of the Russe Commonwealth* (1591), was in part a contemporary travel account, which added to the information in Hakluyt, and in part an early attempt to write sociological history. In *Studies in Elizabethan Foreign Trade* (1959), T. S. Willan illuminated the problem of the interlopers, whose activities were a serious problem for the regulated companies—the joint stock companies were designed to limit competition, and their form of organization was a true innovation.[134] Finally, the work of G. D. Ramsay, especially *English Overseas Trade during the Centuries of Emergence* (1957), directed attention to some of the broader aspects of trade and policy.

In this somewhat titular survey of Tudor economic history since the 1930s, general trends have been neglected. The importance of such trends for political and administrative history is evident—price inflation, industrialization, and mercantilist ideas all affected Tudor government; and political historians cannot explain policy unless they can at least come to terms with the specialized research in economic historiography. It is obviously dangerous to generalize about recent trends of interpretation, since no two historians would agree on all points, but the effort must be made, if only because it is by a kind of generalizing that historians assimilate special and technical studies. There is an obvious sense in which statistical research has tended to receive more and more attention, and wider acceptance—statistics may not tell the whole truth, but they tell the kind of truth that cannot be told by other means. Large-scale correlations between historical movements have become more common, as prices, depressions, births, and deaths have been related to each other in ever more complex ways. Instead of depending on nineteenth-century formulas—whether Whig, Marxist, or Positivist —economic historians have tended to reach out for new formulations and to draw upon economic and sociological theory for some of their explanatory concepts. While no single book or article is "typical" of current trends, it is nevertheless possible to select one or two which illustrate primary concerns and the methods of approach (if not the conclusions) which would be acceptable to most members of the profession.

As illustrations of the statistical concerns and speculations of economic historians the articles by E. H. Phelps Brown and Sheila V. Hopkins in *Economica* (1955–1956–1957) are representative of some of the most important trends in recent research. Drawing upon Thorold Rogers for their statistics on wages paid to building trade workers in the period before 1700, Brown and Hopkins tried to avoid any mechanical treatment of the series; but they concluded that, despite regional variations, wages did not change greatly from around the time of Agincourt until the Reformation, and that wages did not, on the whole, reflect variations in the cost of provisions.[135] In "The Price of Consumables, Compared with

Builders' Wage Rates" (1956), they attempted to construct a kind of cost-of-living index. They accomplished this notoriously difficult statistical-historical task by ignoring the modern concept of real wages (i.e., the actual purchasing power of money received as wages) and concentrating instead on an aggregate price per year for a composite commodity, made up of the same amounts of some of the main heads of consumption. There was a remarkably steep increase in the "cost of living" thus defined in the century from 1500 to 1600.[136] The rather complex set of assumptions upon which their arguments were based could be challenged, but their attempt to make up a cost-of-living index was significant; historians who remain unconvinced by the Brown-Hopkins argument must now specify their reasons for dissent. In "Wage Rates and Prices: Evidence for Population Pressure in the Sixteenth Century" (1957), Brown and Hopkins argued that the cause of the progressive contraction of the purchasing power of building craftsmen in the sixteenth century—a contraction which they described as catastrophic and unlike anything else in wage history—was caused by population pressure. This "Vital Revolution," as it has been called, accounted for other changes as well: those who could share in the higher real earnings of farming found their incomes, and hence their status, transformed.[137]

The problem of inflation was attacked from a different viewpoint by Y. S. Brenner in "The Inflation of Prices in Early Sixteenth Century England" (*Economic History Review*, 1961), in which he reached similar conclusions about the importance of population pressure; but Brenner challenged the idea that all prices could be lumped together in the price rise.[138] Despite their differences, Brenner, Brown and Hopkins, and many other writers in economic history have come to believe that there was a close causal connection between the behavior of the economy and the two-fold rise in population in sixteenth-century England. Other historians have accepted the population pressure argument and applied it to political and social history, but the danger of allowing demographic growth to become a formula answer to historical problems is no less than the danger of accepting any other formula as a dogma. In an important as well as entertaining essay of reappraisal —"The Sixteenth and Seventeenth Centuries: The Dark Ages in English Economic History?" (*Economica*, 1957)—F. J. Fisher surveyed the controversies and trends of a decade ago and concluded that after all allowances were made for the importance of new demographic evidence, for industrialization, and for other innovations in the Tudor period, the really significant economic changes did not occur then but only much later, in the last decades of the seventeenth century.[139] Partly for this very reason he concluded that an understanding of the economy of Tudor and Stuart England was likely to be a good preparation for understanding the problems of economic backwardness in the modern world. The importance of the Tudor period has been reasserted, however, by Eric Kerridge in his recently published *The Agricultural Revolution* (1968).

Elizabethan England should be regarded as a revolutionary age: that was the point that Sir John Neale was anxious to make in his Creighton Lecture of 1950; and "Government," he was convinced, "was a principal, if not the principal ingredient of national greatness." [140] The queen's personal decisions controlled a wide range of governmental and administrative activities; she was strong of will and politically astute—"typically Tudor," one might say. Elizabethan England without the Elizabethan political scene would be incomprehensible.[141] Only a very foolish historian indeed would neglect political and administrative history, but this fact is obviously a truism; it can serve only to explain why, in a book on historiography, it should be unnecessary to emphasize political history. Whole libraries of books attest to the industry of historians in describing past politics; and the bone structure of Leviathan is well known. The danger is that other kinds of historiography may continue to be thought of as mere maidservants to the state and the politicians. The need is for more books, like those by Sir John Neale on the Elizabethan Parliaments, which make use of political history to illuminate national life. In the following sections some basic interpretations of the history of the Tudor state will be outlined, and some illustrations of the modern biographical approach to history will be given, but nothing like a survey—even of methods and controversies—will be found. A topical rather than a chronological approach will permit at least more attention to be paid to methodological criteria. The Reformation Parliament was not less significant than the Elizabethan Parliaments, but it is less well documented, and there is little likelihood that identical techniques can be used to study Henrician and Elizabethan problems. The output of print and the preservation of manuscripts went on apace in the sixteenth century—with consequences for the modern historian, who must suit his methods to the quantity and quality of his evidence.

The predecessors of Neale were apt to describe the personal monarchy of the sixteenth century "in terms of what the monarch could and could not do according to the law and custom of the constitution, plus a factual account of what was done." [142] This approach did not exclude specialized studies of the constitution, of political thought, and of all sorts of factual questions having to do with, for example, the making of statutes, free speech in Parliament, privileges of members, crown influence through royal boroughs, the role and influence of members of the council who were also M.P.'s, etc. Neale's approach was, nevertheless, a significant innovation, for he directed attention to the problem of clientage as a response to the system of personal monarchy: "I see the monarch as the principal dispenser of patronage in society, and I want to discover the effect of the competition for this patronage on the structure of Court life, of politics, and of national life in general." [143] The results of Neale's biographical approach to political history were presented in *The Elizabethan House of Commons* (1950) and in *Elizabeth I and Her Parliaments* (2 vols., 1953, 1957) Neale's articles rounded out this extraordinary achievement, based on meticulous archival and library research. More than most English historians, Neale drew parallels between past and present, deliberately employing analogy to drive home his point that the past is not remote from the present but helps to explain it and is in turn explained by it. Hitler taught a lesson that Tudor historians were obliged to learn: "Revolutions are not explained by statistics, but by leadership, organization, intensity of conviction, passion and purpose." [144]

In *The Elizabethan House of Commons,* Neale saw the lower house as a reflection of society at large—parliamentary history became a part of social history. The structure and manner of working of the House, the quality of the members, their social backgrounds and electoral activities, the borough patrons and their influence in specific elections, procedures within the house, and the role of governmental influence—these were the themes developed by Neale. An intimate description of the officials, ceremonies, procedures, manners, conventions, and style of speaking in the House could not be written before the reign of Elizabeth, because the evidence simply did not exist. The House of Commons reached maturity in Elizabeth's reign, and "it was not from the Stygian darkness of Tudor despotism that early Stuart parliaments emerged. They succeeded to a rich heritage, to great traditions." [145] As he pointed out, the growth in size of the House during the sixteenth century was one of the most arresting, puzzling, and important facts in parliamentary history. From 296 members at the beginning of the century, the House grew to 462 at the end; the additions under Henry VIII of seats for Wales, Monmouthshire, and Cheshire presented no problems but the rest did:

> It used to be thought that the motive for creating these additional seats was to pack parliament. Had it been so, we might expect to find the new constituencies more or less consistently returning royal nominees or out-and-out government supporters. In fact, they did not. By this obvious test the theory breaks down, sometimes quite ludicrously; and as our narrative proceeds its essential fallacy will become increasingly clear.[146]

The theory of a "Tudor despotism" got short shrift from Neale, who showed that the real influence of the Crown on elections was limited, and that the preparation and presentation of a program by the queen's councilors and servants was necessary for the proper working of Parliament. Vulgar corruption did not occur until after Elizabeth's death; and crude electoral methods, which had been practical earlier, were not necessary and were not employed by Elizabeth.[147] The election of royal officials and courtiers was, at best, a haphazard business. The quality of the House, especially the educational attainments of the members, has already been alluded to; legal training in particular was valued, along with birth, education, expert knowledge, experience, and character.[148] In truth, the Elizabethan House of Commons was a reflection of Elizabethan society: this became evident in each of the sessions of Parliament.

In *Elizabeth I and Her Parliaments*, Neale moved from analysis to chronological narrative—to constitutional and parliamentary history in the strict sense. These volumes caught the drama of parliamentary history; the issues as they emerged in day-to-day debate were revealed in clear detail through newly discovered sources. Neale began with a drastic reinterpretation of the Anglican Church settlement of 1559 and then proceeded to discuss in turn each of the Parliaments of the reign. He focused his narrative on the relations between Crown and Parliament, not only to provide thematic unity, but also in order to reveal the significance of the Elizabethan period in constitutional history, and to disprove the old myth that Stuart Parliaments had few roots in the sixteenth century. Working very often from manuscript sources, especially newly discovered diaries kept by members of Parliament, Neale was able to get at the original documents which lay behind the parliamentary materials printed in Simonds D'Ewes great seventeenth-century work, *The Journals of all the Parliaments during the Reign of Queen Elizabeth* (1682). Before Neale wrote, the principal sources for Elizabethan parliamentary history had been the printed —and therefore derived—collections such as (in addition to D'Ewes) Browne Willis's inaccurate *Notitia Parliamentaria* (3 vols., 1715–1750); Hayward Townshend's *Historical Collections* (1680); *The Lords Journals*, which, as Pollard demonstrated, were inaccurate and scandalously misleading; *The Commons Journals*, analyzed by Neale; and *The Statutes of the Realm*, which told little about the actual procedures in Parliament.[149] Historians before Neale had, of course, gone to the archives, but Neale was the first to dig out the forgotten diaries and track down little known biographical facts about the members; his narrative was constructed very largely from manuscript sources which had been neither printed nor used by earlier historians.

The first volume of *Elizabeth I and Her Parliaments* covered the years from 1559 to 1581, a period with its own unity, deriving from the fact that Parliaments were concerned with issues of religion, or with the "settlement" of Church and state. The pattern of the reign was set in the first Parliament, which, as Neale conclusively demonstrated, was revolutionary.[150] In his Introduction to the chapters dealing with the Parliament of 1559, Neale traversed the earlier history of parliamentary procedure in an essay remarkable for its compression and clarity. The idea that Parliament was a high court held revolutionary possibilities, and it was precisely this idea that was developed in connection with parliamentary claims to free speech and the right to imprison offenders against its power and dignity. Between 1515 and 1558 these ideas had gained ground until, under Elizabeth, Arthur Hall scornfully alluded to the lower house as a new person in the trinity. He was a better historian than he, or his contemporaries, realized: "In place of the simple medieval conception of a High Court of Parliament, these [Elizabethan] men were formulating a mystical creed, which might be expressed as follows: The House of Lords is a court; the House of Commons is a court; and yet there are not two courts but one court, the High Court of Parliament." [151] Henry VIII had built up the power of Parliament, but it was not until 1559 that Parliament asserted itself in a revolutionary way. The theme of revolution—percurrent in Neale's volumes—was best illustrated in the opening session of the new reign. The House was militantly Protestant, but the queen was not just a *politique* but a ruler with principles and purpose.[152] She retained the affection and admiration of even the later Puritan extremists, including that most vociferous Puritan, Peter Wentworth, but she did not suffer reformers gladly. The strong Protestants of 1559 were not hesitant about launching a positive program to realize the Protestant destiny. "Having little historical sense and a convenient memory for precedents," Neale wrote, "they read into the vague phrase 'freedom of speech' a meaning that was bound, if it prevailed, to lead to the destruction of personal monarchy as the Tudors knew it, and to the evolution of parliamentary government as the modern world has known it." [153]

A revolutionary spirit manifested itself from the very beginning of the session in 1559. It was not surprising under the circumstances that the majority were swept along by the religious radicals. Neale dismissed as a legend the older view that Elizabeth had packed this Parliament. But why the revolutionizing succeeded remained a question. The queen had not expected anything like a Bill of Uniformity which would run parallel to the Bill of Supremacy: "Royal supremacy, yes; but no Protestant Prayer Book." [154] The queen would have preferred constitutional procedures, by which the actual settlement of religion would have been accomplished at a later session and under the auspices of Convocation. The settlement of 1559 was in fact carried by revolutionary tactics, developed in and by the House; the queen, faced by the challenge, changed her mind and in so doing altered the pattern of the religious settlement. She was helped to her decision by the news that France had signed the peace of Câteau-Cambrésis—her throne thus secured, she was free to follow her political instincts. The Acts of Supremacy and Uniformity contained safeguards against radicalism, but they were essentially radical achievements. Compromise came in the form of the Elizabethan Prayer Book.[155] Yet Elizabeth's instinct for a political settlement was sound—the Acts of Supremacy and Uniformity made possible a conservative and comprehensive Church. No subsequent Elizabethan House of Commons would have agreed to the Prayer Book of 1559 without bitter struggles. Elizabeth's timing was superb, but the paradox remained: the queen was the conservative, whose art was to keep the love of even her radical subjects.

The *via media*, which some historians had more or less accepted as inevitable, was shown by Neale to have depended very much on politics and on political compromise. The next turning point in the reign occurred in 1568, when Mary fled Scotland and came to England; the central period of storms and "cold war" had begun.[156] The final period began in 1584, with the coming of the decisive showdown with Puritanism and open warfare with Spain. In concluding his first volume Neale stressed the revolutionary nature of the religious struggles and the great importance of the queen's personal rule. The true conservative must stand against all forms of zealotry; and since Elizabethan society, as mirrored in the House of Commons, was overwhelmingly Puritan in its sympathies, it was up to the queen to restrain and direct this revolutionary energy. The queen was directly and personally responsible for decision making, and she showed herself to be a conservative in the best sense:

> In our parliamentary history the person of the Queen is seen isolated in a unique and most significant way. On the Succession Question in 1566 she stood alone, against her Council (including Cecil) and her Parliament (including the Lords). In 1572 she withstood even more impassioned and concerted pressure and saved the life of Mary Queen of Scots: as Cecil bitterly remarked, the fault was not in "us that are accounted inward councillors," but in "the highest" . . . Had it not been for her, the broad way of English life would have been narrowed and an experiment made with what we today term the ideological State. The instances are too numerous, the whole story too consistent, to leave any doubt about the personal nature of Elizabeth I's rule.[157]

This was a long way from Froude's conception of the queen as essentially dependent upon the advice of Cecil, or from Creighton's cold and hesitant queen.

Neale's second volume opened in crisis, with an invisible threat —treasonable words, spoken by trained priests of the Counter Reformation. There was also the threat of war with Spain, and the constant danger of plots against the life of Protestant Elizabeth on behalf of Mary Queen of Scots, now the prospective Catholic queen of England. If the historic themes were the same as those of the earlier years, it was nevertheless during the last two decades of the reign that a climax was reached. England united to confront Catholic Spain, but from a constitutional point of view the most important resolution was that which broke the "classical" organization of Puritanism. Neale described the Puritan "classis" movement as "a case study in revolution"; but he also contended that "the art of opposition, which might be considered the outstanding contribution of the Elizabethan period to parliamentary history," was largely learned from Puritans or inspired by them.[158] In reflecting on the whole of the Elizabethan period, on the great names and on parliamentary names that were his own discoveries, Neale concluded that the dynamic of the age lay in the fact that it had emancipated itself from the past, which could no longer cause nostalgic yearnings.[159] Parliament's claim to freedom of speech, made by Sir Thomas More in 1523, was only fully exploited by the radicals during Elizabeth's reign. The model parliamentarians were all men of character, however, deeply committed to argument from precedent, and well versed in the history and procedures of Parliament. They may have been hopelessly lacking in historical perspective, but they were, on the whole, responsible and fearless in the defense of liberty.

Neale's interpretation of the character and role of Elizabeth was straightforward: Elizabeth was a great queen. The evidence in *Elizabeth I and Her Parliaments* supported the argument first advanced in *Queen Elizabeth* (1934). Aside from relatively minor criticisms, this view has been accepted; no large-scale challenges to the Neale thesis have been forthcoming. Some historians have continued to express doubts about the queen's share of responsibility, but Neale's views about the role of Parliament in the later sixteenth century have not been challenged. Perhaps one reason is that Neale did not deal with Elizabethan constitutional ideas but with parliamentary realities. English constitutional history had long suffered from myth making, especially from the myths of Elizabethan and Stuart antiquaries—men like Cotton and Coke, D'Ewes and

Prynne, who read into the Middle Ages a golden age of parliamentary liberty. In their fashion, they set history in bondage to a set of parliamentary myths, the influence of which, as Neale observed, has not easily spent itself.[160]

Stubbs and E. A. Freeman looked for instances of the power of the commons in the thirteenth century—an example, perhaps, of the persistence into the Victorian period of habits of thought and the lawyer-like love of precedents that flourished in the sixteenth century. In *The Growth of English Representative Government* (1948), George L. Haskins drew attention to the importance of historical myths in perpetuating men's sentiments about representative institutions, and to how fictions were elaborated to explain changes in old and familiar concepts.[161] Too often, when an institution was studied, it was studied in isolation rather than in relation to society, for whose sake it existed and functioned. Earlier historians had, for the most part, ignored the social setting of Parliament—Neale did not; and it is evident that the constitutional history of Elizabeth's reign can no longer be understood in the old ways.

The fifteenth century bridged the gap between two views of Parliament—the older one of Parliament as the king's high court of justice, the newer one of Parliament as an assembly representing the communities of the realm, a joint enterprise of king, lords, and commons. C. H. McIlwain's ideas about fundamental law and his argument that the Tudor Parliament was an essentially medieval high court, revealed at its best the older constitutional historiography, which was principally concerned with legal ideas, historical definitions and distinctions, and precedents.

In *The High Court of Parliament and Its Supremacy* (1910), McIlwain put forth his basic argument that Parliament was above all a "court of justice" in the Middle Ages and that it was the *fusion* of indefinite powers that was the fundamental fact about the institutions of central government in medieval England.[162] Not merely in Parliament but in the king's other courts this was true; even Coke, according to McIlwain, failed to grasp a distinction between legislation and judicature. "It is the central thesis of this essay," he wrote, "that the utterances of contemporaries show that in the Tudor and even in a large part of the Stuart period, men had not yet reached this clear distinction." [163] Parliament, in short, was not yet thought of as a legislature in the modern sense, and the courts themselves were still regarded as having "legislative" functions. McIlwain was reacting against an earlier view which had seen modern sovereignty in the actions of Henry VIII in Parliament.[164] The view presented by McIlwain was that Parliament did not "make" law, it "declared" it; Parliament was a "supreme" court in the sense of a court of last resort.[165] The idea of "making" law was alien to medieval Englishmen, who conceived of the law as customary and unchanging, having therefore an inviolable quality. Hence there emerged the idea of fundamental law, from which Englishmen derived indefeasible and inalienable rights. The idea of fundamental law was embodied in "the tough old common law," in certain statutes, and especially in Magna Carta.[166] McIlwain was undoubtedly correct in insisting that custom was enormously important, and that Tudor lawyers gave a sharper outline to fundamental law than medieval lawyers had done. He was perhaps correct in arguing that what was needful in order to understand the Tudor constitution was a more thorough understanding not of its modern innovations but of its medieval heritage.[167] But at this point his critics began to object that there was after all much in the Rolls of Parliament that would become incomprehensible unless medieval Parliaments did somehow legislate. Sir William Holdsworth in particular denied that there was any fundamental law in the sense of a law that limited the competence of Parliament. The real point, as G. R. Elton noted, was that there was a difference between theory and practice.[168] McIlwain had denied that any true theory of sovereignty existed before the seventeenth century because theories of fundamental law persisted. He was primarily concerned with theory. Constitutional historians such as Neale and Elton were to see Parliament in its whole social setting; for them actual Parliamentary practice provided the clue to the meaning of theory.

The importance of practice and of a "hardheaded" approach to historical problems stands in no need of recommendation—the works of Neale, and of Elton and others have corrected much that was wrong, and clarified much that was muddled. But there are still reasons to return to the influential interpretations of McIlwain, who not only saw the great issues of constitutionalism as they had been realized in European and American history, but who provided historians and lawyers with prime arguments about the rule of law. In *Constitutionalism Ancient and Modern*

(1947), he described in classic fashion a distinction which was fundamental for an understanding of the Tudor constitution, especially in relation to the breakdown which occurred in 1641:

> It seems reasonably certain that the line so clearly drawn by Bracton between *jurisdictio* and *gubernaculum* in the thirteenth century still remains at the end of the sixteenth the main clue to the riddle of the English constitution. At the close of Elizabeth's reign, with only a few exceptions men seemed to accept, almost as fully as Bracton, the twofold theory that the king is under law and yet under no man, that private right is determinable and enforceable by law, and is under the control of courts and parliaments; while "matters of state," or the "transforming of the Commonwealth," are things "neither pertaining to them nor within the capacity of their understanding." The latter are a part of "the Prerogative Imperial," which is and ought to be "absolute" and "not disputable." But this delicate balance between jurisdiction and government could only be kept if the head and the members of the commonwealth remained "conjoined and knit together into one body politic," as Henry VIII said.[169]

The controversy about McIlwain's conception of fundamental law has been summarized by J. W. Gough in *Fundamental Law in English Constitutional History* (1955). McIlwain's influence was felt by those who disagreed with him no less than by those who shared his views. W. S. Holdsworth in his *History of English Law* and Theodore Plucknett in *A Concise History of the Common Law* both argued against McIlwain; Sir Charles Ogilvie on the whole supported his position in *The King's Government and the Common Law 1471–1641* (1958), but he was more concerned than McIlwain had been with the part played by procedure and practice in the courts of justice, and with the organic connection between various social, economic, and political crises and the deformities and injustices of the legal system itself. The most thorough and enlightening example of such a "connective" approach to legal history, applied to the history of the Court of Wards, was Joel Hurstfield's *The Queen's Wards* (1958). Tracing the history of the court from its founding under Henry VIII, to its maturity under Elizabeth, Hurstfield was able to illuminate some of the most important problems of Elizabethan public life.

Frederick C. Dietz's *English Public Finance 1485–1641* (1921 and 1932; 2nd edition, 1964), although now outmoded in some of its interpretations ("the revolution of 1485," for example, is no longer acceptable), and although limited in its discussion of Tudor revenues (the sections on the wardrobe and chamber administration have been superseded), is still an important and valuable study, illuminating constitutional history. To explore in detail the complexities of legal and constitutional history is, however, beyond the scope of this chapter. In many areas of legal and administrative history, books of special merit have appeared during the past half century which have revealed not just the changing operations of the Tudor state but also the pools of ignorance that cover many parts of administrative history.

Tudor diplomatic history, unlike the history of law, remained a relatively neglected field between the wars. Neale's essay, "The Diplomatic Envoy," provided a short general introduction to the problems of Tudor diplomacy.[170] Garrett Mattingly's *Renaissance Diplomacy* (1955) discussed the general European setting of diplomacy. R. B. Wernham's *Before The Armada: The Emergence of the English Nation 1485–1558* (1966) provided the best general account of English foreign policy, especially for the Elizabethan period. Wernham did what a good diplomatic historian must— made sense of the connections between foreign and domestic policy. Especially valuable was his handling of the diplomatic revolution by which Spain replaced France as England's great enemy. The cycles of commercial expansion and contraction between about 1540 and 1580 were at least as important in their influence on policy as the old-fashioned factors of war and dynastic ambition. The dependence of English trade on the Antwerp market, for example, was unpleasantly apparent in the commercial crisis of 1550–1552, which marked the beginning of a new direction in English foreign policy.[171]

The best modern account of the Armada is Garrett Mattingly's *The Armada,* published in 1959. J. A. Williamson's *Hawkins of Plymouth* (1949) was a revealing biographical study; and A. L. Rowse's *The Expansion of Elizabethan England* (1955) and Thomas Woodroofe's *The Enterprise of England* (1958) were important in helping to revise, along with Mattingly, the views of Sir Julian Corbett in *Drake and the Tudor Navy* (1899). M. Oppenheim's monumental study, *The History of the Administration of the Royal Navy 1509–1660* (1896), has not been supplanted but must now be supplemented; the best modern survey is by G. J. Marcus, *A Naval History of England, The Formative Centuries* (1961). Students of military history have been scarcely less active in describing the policies and activities of the army. C. G. Cruickshank's *Elizabeth's Army* (1946; revised, 1966) has become a standard work; and Cyril Falls, noted for his analyses of strategy and tactics, produced *Elizabeth's Irish Wars* in 1950 and *Mountjoy: Elizabethan General* in 1955. Michael Roberts in *The Military Revolution 1560–1660* (1956) described the theoretical and practical innovations of the age.

The civil service of Elizabeth has received no treatment comparable to that by G. E. Aylmer in *The King's Servants, The Civil Service of Charles I, 1625–42* (1961), which contained, however, useful observations on Tudor government in a chapter on "Chronological Perspective." Among the many discussions of Tudor administrative history (aside from Elton's works, which will be discussed later) were articles by William Huse Dunham, Jr., especially his "Henry VIII's Whole Council and Its Parts" (*Huntington Library Quarterly*, 1943), and Lawrence Stone's "State Control in Sixteenth Century England" (*Economic History Review*, 1947).[172] E. P. Cheyney's *A History of England, From the Defeat of the Armada to the Death of Elizabeth* (2 vols., 1914–1926) completed Froude, and was especially valuable for its discussion of Elizabethan institutions. Some of the most constructive articles covering different aspects of the Elizabethan state were those collected by S. T. Bindoff, Joel Hurstfield, and C. H. Williams in *Elizabethan Government and Society, Essays Presented to Sir John Neale* (1961). The deserts in Tudor administrative history are perhaps now less evident than the cultivated fields, but until more administrative records are studied there can be no thorough history of the public records and record keeping in the sixteenth century.[173] A number of excellent studies have been made, such as Hubert Hall's *Studies in English Official Historical Documents* (2 vols., 1908–1909) and his *Repertory of British Archives* (1920), but record keeping in relation to law and especially historiography remains relatively uninvestigated.[174]

The administrative history of early Tudor England has been virtually rewritten, by G. R. Elton, W. C. Richardson, Joel Hurstfield, and other scholars during the past twenty years. Although Elton and Richardson have disagreed in some of their conclusions—arrived at independently, and in part on the basis of different evidence—they agreed at least in this, that during the Tudor period revolutionary changes took place in administrative practices. Richardson's *Tudor Chamber Administration 1485–1547* (1952) was roughly contemporary with Elton's *The Tudor Revolution in Government* (1953). Richardson showed that the financial arrangements of Henry VII constituted what might be called a revolution in administrative method. By developing the chamber as the primary supervising body for dealing with revenues from crown lands and other sources, Henry VII laid the foundation for the chamber system. Richardson revived in a sense the "New Monarchy" thesis. Elton, on the other hand, argued that the crucial period of change took place during the 1530s and that the prime mover was Thomas Cromwell. Richardson saw in the period from 1485 to 1555 administrative continuity, and unity of development. Elton maintained that Cromwell's reforms constituted the first and the only true revolution in Tudor government. The Court of Augmentations, established in 1536 to handle the properties that accrued to the Crown as a result of the dissolution of the monasteries, was the subject of Richardson's *History of the Court of Augmentations 1536–1554* (1961), a monumental study devoted to the complicated workings of a single government agency. Like Elton, Richardson based his account on record research; original sources were decisive. The most significant differences between Elton and Richardson still centered on the question of *when* the Tudor transition took place, but that question must be referred to interested specialists. For the general reader, and for the student of historiography, the more theoretical questions raised in the course of a debate on "Tudor revolution" in *Past and Present* (1963–1965) point to some of the crucial methodological problems of current historiography.

The "essence" of any historian's interpretation can seldom be satisfactorily conveyed in a few unequivocal propositions; and the particular field of history in which a historian writes may be so little understood in its ramifications, or so subject to change in its methods, that the general reader must look for special enlightenment before he can begin to assess controversies, especially those as wide-ranging as the *Past and Present* debate on "Tudor revolution." In administrative history, the generalizations of 1940 are almost as outdated as those of 1840, and the tasks ahead appear even greater than the tasks that have been accomplished.[175] Elton's arguments, like those of any good historian, have changed and developed over the years. Fortunately he has not only been explicit about the reasons for his own changes of opinion but has also provided a most useful account of "The Problems and Significance of Administrative History in the Tudor Period." Administrative historians, Elton noted, quoting Hurstfield, have passed beyond the stage when "The machinery alone, however intimately understood, can answer the questions." The essence of administrative history has become "the analysis and description of past administrative processes, the discovery of principles implicit or explicit in the conduct of government, and an understanding of the manner in which the theoretical mechanism operated in practice." [176] Beyond this, recent administrative historians have been moved to study the history of ideas—that is, "ideas of law and legislation, ideas concerning the purpose of the state, ideas of opposition and resistance." [177] Knowledge of economic history was obviously essential, but the administrative historian also has had to take account of personal, family, and social relationships. Indeed "the historian of administration who overlooks the fact that it is people who administer is himself best overlooked." [178] Elton went on to outline the areas in which much more work remains to be done—the history of the Council, the history of the Exchequer and the Treasury, and the history of the courts of law, other than those studied with such care by Hurstfield, Richardson, and a few other historians.

The Tudor Revolution in Government (1953), and *England under the Tudors* (1963), plus *The Tudor Constitution* (1960) and various articles formed the basis of Elton's interpretation of the Tudor age. Attacking Elton in the pages of *Past and Present*, G. L. Harriss and Penry Williams argued the medievalists' case against a "revolution" in Tudor history. Elton had attacked the "New Monarchy" thesis, and written that "In the last analysis, Henry VII, because he used the old household methods, failed to lay the foundations of a really reformed household." [179] This was acceptable enough to Harriss and Williams, though it might not square with Richardson; Henry VII "restored but did not innovate," according to Elton.[180] The true turning point was the Reformation, which was not caused by the intellectual Renaissance.[181] In the last analysis it was Cromwell who "founded the modern constitutional monarchy in England and organized the sovereign national state." [182] The essential ingredient of the Tudor revolution "was the concept of national sovereignty." [183] Earlier ideas of what the precise character of early Tudor sovereignty was and who exercised it were demonstrably wrong, according to Elton, at least insofar as they posited a Tudor despotism.[184] Henry VIII and Cromwell based themselves on the historic past, on constitutional propriety, and on the law. Parliamentary supremacy and the rule of statute were the great results of the Tudor revolution, but "while the Tudor state in practice worked on the principle that statute was supreme—that parliament was sovereign—conservatism prevented a full realization of what may be called a native theory of sovereignty." [185] It may be seen that Elton extended very considerably the thesis he first put forward in connection with administrative history in *The Tudor Revolution in Government*. Elton summed up his argument when he affirmed that Elizabeth's government was not medieval government at all, but the "first phase of modern government," resting on principles and offices given a new twist in the 1530s.[186] The Cromwellian revolution was thus conservative and "historical," but a true revolution for all that.

The initial attack of Harriss and Williams, directed against this general interpretation, began by acknowledging that the emergence of modern national government could be described neither in exclusively "revolutionary" nor "evolutionary" terms. Harriss and Williams maintained, however, that later medieval government was "essentially national and bureaucratic, resting upon the developed machinery of the exchequer, the central role of the privy seal, and a council with regular meetings, fixed membership, and wide functions." [187] Other arguments supported this same idea of continuity. Elton's first reply was essentially a reassertion of his earlier position, despite some concessions to continuity: "Revolutions do happen, even in the most continuous of societies, but when they happen without disturbing the outward structure they become harder to tell, and disagreement as to their reality will continue." [188] This was to raise the question of definition, and it quickly became clear that historical definitions were one of the prime sources of disagreement between Elton and his critics. The rebuttals by Harriss and Williams will repay closer study because they reveal why, even among scholars who are equally dedicated to the pursuit of true explanations, significant differences can persist. It may be seen that the controversy turned largely upon the following points: (1) the argument about the meaning of precedents, (2) definitions, (3) theory versus practice, involving questions of relevance, (4) the significance of historical "types" and orienting statements, and (5) chronological continuity versus change, as inferred from a study of particular sources.

One of the keys to Elton's argument about sovereignty was the meaning of the word "empire." Elton contended that it was endowed in the 1530s with new "territorial" significance; Harriss wrote that "the semantic history of the term as traced by R. Koebner shows that the transition from 'authority' to 'territory' was not *'unprecedented'* [italics added]." [189] A related argument was that the restoration of exchequer supremacy in 1554 should not be regarded as "the culmination of quite different sorts of changes in the 1530s; nor does the Elizabethan system of finance seem *essentially different* from the medieval" [italics added].[190] Here everything depends on how much weight to give to precedents—and there are no scientific rules by which to settle this question. In the matter of definitions, Harriss was equally firm: "The question to which I addressed myself was whether these considerable changes in the Church [Reformation statutes] amounted to a revolution in the nature of the state, and more specifically in what sense they marked the birth of national sovereignty." [191] The obvious question is what was meant by, and what were the connotations of, such terms as "revolution," "sovereignty," etc. As long as historians must reckon with "in what sense" a word is used, there is the possibility of disagreement; a purely denotive language for history is not available. And even if such a language were available to historians it would not eliminate the historian's task of assessing significance; the flexibility of everyday language is what enables historians to deal with long-range problems of change, crisis, revolution, and evolution. Even the most sociologically oriented historians have had to interpret the evidence for revolution in historical perspective, in the light of "significant" change. In practice, Elton, Harriss, and Williams have all sought the meaning of changes in relation to their understanding of continuities. Elton recognized the beginning of "modern" trends or continuities in the Tudor period, while Harriss and Williams recognized the continuation of medieval trends. They have not quarreled merely about the semantic definition of revolution, but about the meaning of historical facts which establish precedents or consequences. This most important area of disagreement was not confined to the Tudor period and Tudor evidence but encompassed what came before and after: the scope for disagreement was widened in principle to include many centuries of English history. Thus a disagreement about the revolutionary nature of Tudor chamber administration might hinge on disagreements about the essential nature of the medieval constitution or the modern state. And revolution itself might take place over a more or less extended period of time—the time scale of revolution was at least a problem, albeit not an explicitly stated one. Elton and his critics understood each other, but they did not agree about the significance of the Reformation changes. However, in a book on historiography it is enough to identify areas of disagreement; it is not necessary to rewrite English history. Every historian does that in his own mind when he reads a new interpretation, a new monograph, or an old document. In this sense at least all history is, indeed, the history of thought.

The argument about contemporary theory versus practice is a special case of general arguments about relevance. Harriss complained that he thought Elton had interpreted statutes only through the minds of the legislators and that he forgot those for whom the laws were made. Moreover:

> Dr. Elton would claim that there was a world of difference between such a [medieval] *"de facto* sovereignty"* which limited papal interference, and the true sovereignty achieved by abolishing papal authority. In theory, yes; but in practice, to limit papal authority was by that much to abolish it, and in the political context the difference amounted to little more than a decision whether the spiritual jurisdiction touched the regality or not.[192]

Here the relevance of practice to theory is explicitly the issue, not just the facts as such. Elton was perhaps right to reply that "This controversy, like most, consists largely of people talking past each other." [193]

Although neither Elton nor his critics were concerned with ideal types or orienting statements in the manner of Weber or Marx, it is worth noting that Harriss invoked historiographical principles which took the form of general orienting statements: "The actual must always be historically more significant than the potential . . ." and "The *true pattern* [italics added] of medieval government must be sought elsewhere [than in the Household]."

The emergence of the nation state could be studied only in terms of centuries, not decades; and the time scale of significant change was as a rule long, not short: "Rarely are the really profound changes achieved by a Revolution." [194] Penry Williams concluded his essay by saying that he believed Elton had treated the Middle Ages "as if they were static." [195] Presumably he meant that Elton had not given enough weight to the medieval precedents for "Tudor revolution." Whatever else such passages indicate, they show that debates in history do involve issues of philosophical moment, and that modern historians are constantly coming up against the basic problems dealt with by the general theorists of the profession. In the broadest sense the debate was about the problem of continuity. Despite the importance of historical theory, despite the need for philosophical clarification—in this as in other historical debates— the fundamental, ultimate resolution of the issue could come only from a detailed study of the original sources of English history. Special studies may reveal special chronologies, and the sources of innovation and precedent may be marshaled differently by different specialists. General interpretations are nevertheless a necessity; and coherence then becomes the essential test. This was the point that Elton made in his concluding remarks: "while some things have been stated which underline the element of continuity in the story, I venture to suggest that other work, for instance in the history of the church, of society, of the parts of the realm, of finance, or of thought (work already published or at present proceeding) is enlarging and deepening the interpretation which I put forward a decade ago." [196]

Further comments on the historiography of the Tudor state must of necessity be brief. Law, diplomacy, and war constituted three of the main activities of the Tudor state, and in each scholars have observed that contemporaries were much concerned with classical ideas and models, or with precedents having the authority of antiquity. Ideas of "reason of state," and of power politics, emerged along with revolutionary advances in military and naval power and tactics. In *The Holy Pretense* (1957), George Mosse analyzed the emerging idea of "reason of state," adding to the pioneering interpretations of Meinecke in *Die Idee der Staatsräson in der Neuern Geschichte* (1924)—the title changed in translation to *Machiavellism*. The chapter on "Politics and War" in Michael Walzer's *The Revolution of the Saints* drew attention to the fact that the new warfare "had been launched under the aegis of ancient Rome: Roman drill, Roman discipline, Roman tactics—all were enthusiastically praised by Renaissance writers." [197] The military rhetoric of Calvin and the Marian exiles gave way in the early seventeenth century to a more optimistic and historical theory of Christian warfare; but the importance of tradition and precedent, for both soldiers and saints in the Tudor period, was very great. The broad intellectual appeal of historical precedents was one of the themes running through James Kelsey McConica's *English Humanists and Reformation Politics* (1965), a book which revealed the extent of the influence of intellectuals (especially Erasmians) on the early Tudor state. Some of the most revealing remarks, however, were made by sixteenth-century European writers on diplomacy:

> Ambassadors became a necessity among men when Pandora's box was opened and the evils escaped into the world. So say sixteenth-century authors of manuals for ambassadors, claiming an antiquity for the art of diplomacy as remote as society itself and the distinction between *meum* and *tuum*. They might have added that it was the reopening of Pandora's box, when princes were consolidating the nation-state, that made resident ambassadors a necessity in Europe and gave the art its modern significance.[198]

The theme of antiquity in the literature of change is one of the most notable features of Tudor history.

Tudor biography has dealt primarily with monarchs, ministers, and the upper ranks of society. The bibliographical history of the lives of individual monarchs need not be repeated here—some of the more important lives have already been mentioned. The ministerial biographies by Conyers Read, *Mr. Secretary Walsingham and the Policy of Queen Elizabeth* (3 vols., 1925), *Mr. Secretary Cecil and Queen Elizabeth* (1955), and *Lord Burghley and Queen Elizabeth* (1960) are well known. Although nothing like as complete a set of studies of royal officials exists for the earlier period, there are a score or more of notable studies of the great and near great. Pollard's *Wolsey* must now make way for Charles W. Ferguson's *Naked to Mine Enemies* (1958). Cromwell has been reinterpreted by Elton in *The Tudor Revolution in Government* and, more recently and succinctly, by A. G. Dickens in *Thomas Cromwell and the English Reformation* (1959). R. B. Merriman in *The Life and*

Letters of Thomas Cromwell (2 vols., 1902) proved to be an un-sympathetic biographer, but a diligent though by no means defini-tive editor. However, his remarks on foreign policy are still valu-able. Elton's articles on Cromwell are essential because they define the revisionist interpretation of Cromwell's importance.[199]

Sir Thomas More has perhaps become the most attractive figure of the Tudor age to twentieth-century biographers. The "Sir Thomas More Project" at Yale University now aims at publishing an edition of his complete works in fourteen volumes. A *Prelimi-nary Bibliography* by R. W. Gibson and J. Max Patrick appeared in 1961, followed by the *Selected Letters*, edited by Elizabeth Francis Rogers, and *The History of King Richard III* in a splendid text (with an indispensable introductory essay) by Richard S. Sylvester in 1963. Among the many recent studies, *Sir Thomas More and Erasmus* (1965) by E. E. Reynolds linked the careers of the two best known humanists of the age. And, of course, no student of More can afford to neglect the contemporary accounts by Roper and Harpsfield.[200] The latter's *Life* was first published in 1932; Roper, who had written to provide information for Harpsfield, was first published in 1626. Biographers of other Tudor intellectuals have seldom been able to rely on contemporary historical accounts. Clerical writers have been often studied because their views helped to define the Reformation, but full-scale biographies are in many cases still lacking. Secular intellectuals have begun to be reappraised in books such as E. E. Lehmberg's *Sir Thomas Elyot, Tudor Human-ist* (1960) and John Burton's *Sir Philip Sidney and the English Re-naissance* (1954). Mary Dewar began a task of major rehabilitation in *Sir Thomas Smith, A Tudor Intellectual in Office* (1964), which will be followed by a volume on Smith's main works. The men surrounding Cromwell and who gave him intellectual support were first studied by W. Gordon Zeeveld in *The Founda-tions of Tudor Policy* (1948). Sir Robert Cotton, the most influen-tial antiquary of the age, belongs properly to the seventeenth cen-tury, but his ancestry and early collecting habits were discussed by Hope Mirrlees in *A Fly in Amber* (1962), accurately described as an "extravagant biography."

Thomas Howard, Fourth Duke of Norfolk, was perhaps the earliest Englishman outside the royal house of whom a full-scale biography could be written; yet only recently was this done, by Neville Williams in *Thomas Howard, Fourth Duke of Norfolk*

(1964). The book illuminated not only politics but the significance of the College of Arms, refounded by the duke in 1555. Leicester, Essex, and several of the lesser noblemen, politicians, and courtiers attracted biographers in the late nineteenth or in the twentieth century. Two works of reference can be called essential despite errors: G. E. Cockayne, *Complete Peerage of England, Scotland, and Ireland, Extant, Extinct, and Dormant* (13 vols., 1910–1949), and J. E. Doyle, *The Official Baronage of England 1066–1885* (3 vols., 1886).

The tradition of short lives, inherited from the Middle Ages, became in the Renaissance a prominent literary genre. Any survey of Tudor biography must take into account the splendid series of Tudor portraits in Thomas Fuller's *The Worthies of England* (1662), as well as the apt if often apocryphal sketches in John Aubrey's *Brief Lives*. The biographies in Foxe's *Book of Martyrs*, and the shorter "characters" in Camden's *Annals* and in the works of earlier and later historians, still provide useful information and anecdotes. The twentieth century has witnessed a revolution in biography, but the classic methods have not been rendered obsolete. Lord Herbert of Cherbury began his *Life and Reign of King Henry the Eighth* with a comment which all good biographers still must ponder:

> It is not easie to write that prince's history, of whom no one thing may constantly be affirmed. Changing of manners and condition alters the coherence of parts, which should give an uniform description. Nor is it probable that contradictories should agree to the same person: so that nothing can shake the credit of a narration more than if it grow unlike itself; when yet it may not be the author, but the argument caused the variation. It is impossible to draw his picture well who hath several countenances.[201]

Perhaps the most promising trend in biography during the past half century has been the growth in awareness of the complexities and differences of attitude within Tudor society, and recognition of the sovereignty of original sources. The latter point appears so obvious to twentieth-century professional historians that they sometimes forget how long and hard the road was from medieval legendary saints' lives to modern source-based lives of saints, kings, and ordinary men who wore "several countenances."

Many of the great document publications begun in the nineteenth century have been continued, with notable additions, in the twentieth century. New kinds of collections have also appeared. Reflecting the growth of history courses in colleges and universities during the past seventy-five years are the now familiar historical collections chosen for the benefit of teachers and students. These constitute, although perhaps less obviously than the series publications or calendars of state papers, a significant contribution to Tudor historiography. Not only have such collections usually been accompanied by commentaries or introductions, but the choice and editing of the documents reflect current historiographical interests, standards, and interpretations. For all but a very few students these books are the first and often the last contact with the sources. G. W. Prothero in 1884 published his *Select Statutes and Other Constitutional Documents 1559–1625* in order to fill the gap between Stubbs' *Select Charters* and S. R. Gardiner's *Constitutional Documents of the Puritan Revolution*. He made roughly the same assumptions that Gardiner and Stubbs made; and he abbreviated the documents themselves in accordance with what he thought most important in them, leaving out, for example, the revealing preambles to statutes. A comparison of his work with that of J. R. Tanner uncovers many historiographical changes between 1884 and 1922, when Tanner first published his *Tudor Constitutional Documents A.D. 1485–1603*. Tanner not only provided important historical commentaries, but much broader coverage of the courts and administration, as well as selections illustrating finance and local government. He omitted, however, documents dealing with the military system, and did not duplicate the extracts from political writers (with minor exceptions) found in Prothero. By 1934, when Kenneth Pickthorne published his *Early Tudor Government, Henry VIII*, the trend toward a broader interpretation of constitutional history was well established. Pickthorne's textbook contained no documents, but it was geared to the concept of constitutional history found in Tanner; Pickthorne's *Henry VII*, published in 1949, followed the same principles and was meant as an introduction to the more detailed history of the reign of Henry VIII.

Having originally intended to bring Tanner up to date, G. R. Elton discovered that it was no longer possible merely to revise the work of a scholar who had begun his own lecturing career over seventy-five years earlier. Elton's *The Tudor Constitution: Docu-*

ments and Commentary (1960) provided a fresh perspective, based on the broad concept of constitutional history that Tanner, Pollard, and others had established. Elton, however, deployed many of the newer interpretations of Tudor constitutional, and especially administrative, history. The record of historiographical progress stood revealed in the choice of documents no less than in the commentary. By paying close attention to original and derived sources Elton was able to correct errors in Tanner's transcripts and, in the case of the Treasons Act, to substitute for black arts the common imaginings of men—the Treasons Act of 1534 did not fulminate against those who "by crafty images invent, practice or attempt any bodily harm [etc.]," but against those who "by craft imagine, invent [etc.]." [202]

As a bibliographical and documentary guide to most of the topics discussed under "Society, the State, and the Individual" the recently published collection of *English Historical Documents*, Vol. V, *1485–1553* (1967), by C. H. Williams, stands alone. The objective of the editor was not merely to exemplify different aspects of Tudor society but to illustrate the various types of sources. The opening section of historiographical excerpts points up the importance of reading contemporary historians and chroniclers; the bibliographical essays for all sections are full and revealing; the documents are edited with care. Yet, like all such collections, this was a compromise—efforts to avoid specialization have their own inevitable limitations. Whenever scholars have attempted to illustrate the complexities of historical transactions they have had to sacrifice contextual fullness; whenever they have sought to provide broader perspectives they have had to sacrifice complexity. If *Tudor Economic Documents*, edited by R. H. Tawney and Eileen Power in three volumes in 1924, represented the one alternative, then the *English Historical Documents* series represents the other. [203]

What is true of selections of Tudor documents is true of selections from Tudor literature, and is no less true of written histories—there can be no single approach, no one true way to study or write history. If the history of historiography proves anything it is that orthodoxy has not been the mother of progress. It also proves something else—the responses and questions of each generation are determined not merely by the limited experience of each generation but by the historiographical traditions established by the living and the dead. A collection of historical documents may appear to be a summary of what one generation finds worthy of note in another, but to assert that new collections must be made, and histories rewritten, because new readers believe that the old books are full of things unworthy of note, is simply to miss the point. The reason for revision lies in the very nature of the historian's craft. Historians have been concerned with the world that is present to their senses, and have seen in the past the problems, fears, and promises of their own times; but they have also responded to the problems of other ages, and to the promise that scholarship holds of discovering some part of the past as it really was.

The move to broaden the study of administrative history has been no less significant than the increasing interest in governmental administration itself during the last fifty years. It has always been easy to see the present in the past; and present-day complexities might be thought of—plausibly, though inaccurately—as the reason why historians have come to recognize more and more complexity in the past. But the answer to historical solipsism is found by reflection on good history, and on the continuities of method and argument in historiography. The present, except to the arrogantly inexperienced or to the very young, exists under the domination of history and binds thought and action accordingly. No present age is entirely its own master, being subject to accidents that the past has defined as possible, and that the future may or may not define as real. All that can with certainty be said is that different forms of historical consciousness have produced different reactions to the real crises and to the everyday work of societies. It will be the purpose of the last chapter of this book to examine instances of the growth of historical consciousness, and to suggest reasons why modern ideas of history and historical consciousness grew apace in Tudor England.

NOTES

1. See, for example, Abraham Kardiner and Belward Preble, *They Studied Man* (New York, 1963), an analysis of anthropological writings. Sociological tradi-

tions are examined by Robert A. Nisbet, *The Sociological Tradition* (New York, 1966).

2. See Erich Fromm, *Marx's Concept of Man: With a Translation from Marx's Economic and Philosophical Manuscripts*, trans. by T. B. Bottomore (New York, 1961), pp. 105, 134–136. See also *Writings of the Young Marx on Philosophy and Society*, edited and translated by Lloyd D. Easton and Kurt H. Guddat (New York, 1967).

3. *Ibid.*, p. 105.

4. See *Karl Marx: Selected Writings in Sociology and Social Philosophy*, ed. T. B. Bottomore and Maximillien Rubel (London, 1963), p. 167.

5. Karl Marx and Friedrich Engels, *The German Ideology*, Parts I and III, ed. and with an Introduction by R. Pascal (New York, 1947), p. 15.

6. Fromm, *op. cit.*, p. 216; see also p. 203; Marx and Engels, *op. cit.*, *passim*.

7. For discussion of "orienting statements" see George C. Homans, *The Nature of Social Science* (New York, 1967), pp. 14 ff.

8. Leonard Krieger, "The Uses of Marx for History," *Political Science Quarterly*, LXXV, No. 3 (1960), 355–378.

9. Kurt Samuelsson, *Religion and Economic Action* (New York, 1961), p. 150.

10. Ephraim Fischoff, "The Protestant Ethic and the Spirit of Capitalism: The History of a Controversy," *Social Research*, XI (1944), 61–77; reprinted in Robert W. Green (ed.), *Protestantism and Capitalism, The Weber Thesis and Its Critics* (New York, 1959). The most recent collection of articles with commentary is S. N. Eisenstadt, *The Protestant Ethic and Modernization: A Comparative View* (New York, 1968); see esp. S. N. Eisenstadt, "The Protestant Ethic Thesis in an Analytical and Comparative Framework," pp. 3–45. Also Reinhard Bendix, *Max Weber: An Intellectual Portrait* (New York, 1962), pp. 46 ff.

11. Marx and Engels, *op. cit.*, p. 30; cf. Harry B. Acton, *The Illusion of the Epoch* (London, 1955).

12. Fromm, *op. cit.*, p. 137.

13. See Henry Thomas Buckle, *History of Civilization in England* (New York, 1910), II, 250; also 257.

14. *Ibid.*, I, 162; see also 113, 183–186, and *passim*.

15. Buckle's thought is discussed in some detail by Giles St. Aubyn, *A Victorian Eminence* (London, 1958).

16. See Buckle, *op. cit.*, I, 279.

17. *Ibid.*, pp. 210–211.

18. *Ibid.*, p. 210; cf. 184.

19. *Ibid.*, pp. 184–185.

20. Max Weber, *The Protestant Ethic and the Spirit of Capitalism*, trans. Talcott Parsons, with a Foreword by R. H. Tawney (New York, 1948), p. 44.

21. Buckle, *op. cit.*, II, 457; also 248–256.

22. See *ibid.*, pp. 322–323.

23. *Ibid.*, pp. 317, 318 ff.

24. *Ibid.*, I, 106; cf. St. Aubyn, *op. cit.*, p. 186.

25. In addition to the books cited in note 10 above, the reader should consult Talcott Parsons, *The Structure of Social Action* (Glencoe, 1949); and see Bendix, *op. cit.*, pp. 50–78, 358–359, 373.

26. See Arnold Bergstraesser, "Wilhelm Dilthey and Max Weber: An Empirical Approach to Historical Synthesis," *Ethics*, LVII (January 1947), 92–110.

27. Weber, *op. cit.*, p. 183.

28. Bendix, *op. cit.*, p. 46.

29. Max Weber, *On the Methodology of the Social Sciences*, trans. and ed. Edward A. Shils and Henry A. Finch (Glencoe, 1949), pp. 92–93.
30. Weber, *Protestant Ethic*, pp. 90–92; see also Max Weber, *The Sociology of Religion*, trans. Ephraim Fischoff (Boston, 1964), p. xxi, Introduction, by Talcott Parsons; and Max Weber, *The Theory of Social and Economic Organization*, trans. A. M. Henderson and Talcott Parsons (Glencoe, 1947), pp. 109 ff.
31. Max Weber, *General Economic History*, trans. Frank H. Knight (Glencoe, 1950), p. 354.
32. G. R. Elton, *The Tudor Revolution in Government* (Cambridge, 1953), p. 415. t is worth noting that Elton avoided the use of the term "rationalization."
33. Weber, *Protestant Ethic*, p. 55.
34. *Ibid.*, pp. 58–59.
35. *Ibid.*, pp. 63 ff.
36. *Ibid.*, pp. 76–77.
37. Useful bibliography is contained in the books about Weber already cited. Two articles are helpful in giving perspective: Sidney A. Burrell, "Calvinism, Capitalism and the Middle Classes: Some Afterthoughts on an Old Problem," *Journal of Modern History*, XXXII (1960), 129–141; and Leonard J. Trinterud, "The Origins of Puritanism," *Church History*, XX (1951), 37–57.
38. See Ernst Troeltsch, *The Social Teachings of the Christian Churches*, trans. Olive Wyon (London, 1931), I, 30, and II, 1002–1004, for Troeltsch's comments on definitional questions and Marxism.
39. *Ibid.*, II, 1002.
40. *Ibid.*, p. 1003.
41. *Ibid.*, I, 333.
42. *Ibid.*, pp. 354 ff.
43. *Ibid.*, p. 336.
44. Cf. *ibid.*, p. 337. The definition of "pattern variables" may be found in Talcott Parsons, *Toward a General Theory of Action* (New York, 1962), pp. 77, 81–82, 90, 94, 99, 117, 177, 216, and *passim*. Troeltsch used the term "universalism" in a much more restricted sense.
45. Troeltsch, *op. cit.*, I, 338–339.
46. *Ibid.*, II, 993–994.
47. *Ibid.*, p. 678.
48. *Ibid.*, p. 681.
49. Cf. *ibid.*, pp. 656–672, 696–710.
50. *Ibid.*, p. 657.
51. See Horton Davies, *The English Free Churches* (Oxford, 1952), esp. p. 50.
52. Troeltsch, *op. cit.*, II, 915; see also 467–515, 644–655, 915–917.
53. *Ibid.*, p. 916.
54. Ernst Troeltsch, *Protestantism and Progress* (Boston, 1958), pp. 138, 175.
55. Weber, *Protestant Ethic*, p. 1.
56. R. H. Tawney, *Religion and the Rise of Capitalism* (New York, 1947), Introduction, p. 1.
57. *Ibid.*, p. 8.
58. See F. J. Fisher, "Tawney's Century," in *Essays in the Economic and Social History of Tudor and Stuart England*, ed. F. J. Fisher (Cambridge, 1961), p. 1.
59. Tawney, *Religion and the Rise of Capitalism*, pp. 62, 27 ff.
60. See Christopher Hill, "Protestantism and Capitalism," in Fisher (ed.), *Economic and Social History*, pp. 15–39.

61. Tawney, *Religion and the Rise of Capitalism*, pp. 76–77; see also p. 81 for his note on Troeltsch.
62. *Ibid.*, pp. 124–128.
63. *Ibid.*, pp. 149, 158–159, 165.
64. *Ibid.*, p. 176.
65. *Ibid.*, p. 176.
66. W. K. Jordan, *Philanthropy in England 1480–1660: A Study of the Changing Pattern of English Social Aspirations* (London, 1959), p. 15.
67. *Ibid.*, p. 154.
68. See the statistical appendices, *ibid.*, pp. 330–337, esp. Table VII, p. 377.
69. *Ibid.*, pp. 322–365.
70. *Ibid.*, p. 145.
71. *Ibid.*, pp. 77 ff. and 109 ff.
72. *Ibid.*, p. 31.
73. *Ibid.*, p. 152, and see pp. 151–154, 182.
74. *Ibid.*, pp. 186–188.
75. *Ibid.*, p. 215.
76. *Ibid.*, pp. 215–239.
77. See, for example, the critical review by D. C. Coleman in *The Economic History Review* (hereafter *EcHR*), 2nd ser., XIII (1960–1961), 113–115; cf. XIV (1961–1962), 138–140; XV (1962–1963), 155–156, 376–377, 541.
78. Jordan, *op. cit.*, p. 32.
79. *Ibid.*, pp. 31–40; see also W. K. Jordan, *The Charities of Rural England, 1480–1660* (London, 1961), pp. 9–12.
80. Jordan, *Philanthropy*, p. 37; see also pp. 93–142.
81. Lawrence Stone, *The Crisis of the Aristocracy, 1558–1641* (Oxford, 1965), pp. 1–3. For a critical review of this book see the *Times Literary Supplement*, April 7, 1966.
82. Stone, *op. cit.*, p. 2.
83. *Ibid.*, p. 3.
84. *Ibid.*, pp. 3–4.
85. *Ibid.*, pp. 44–49.
86. *Ibid.*, p. 5.
87. *Ibid.*, p. 6.
88. *Ibid.*, p. 15.
89. *Ibid.*, p. 55.
90. *Ibid.*, p. 128.
91. *Ibid.*, p. 149.
92. *Ibid.*, p. 156; also Chap. 4 *passim*.
93. *Ibid.*, p. 13.
94. *Ibid.*, p. 242.
95. *Ibid.*, p. 672; Chap. 12 *passim*.
96. See Lawrence Stone, "The Educational Revolution in England 1560–1640," *Past and Present*, No. 28 (July 1964), pp. 41–80.
97. See Stone, *Crisis of the Aristocracy*, p. 709.
98. *Ibid.*, p. 722.
99. See esp. Theodore K. Rabb, *Enterprise and Empire: Merchant and Gentry Investment in the Expansion of England 1575–1630* (Cambridge, Mass., 1967), esp. pp. 133–190. Rabb's book appeared after this chapter was written; see also the *ACLS Newsletter*, Special Supplement (June, 1966), "Computerized Research in the Humanities."

100. See also by Hoskins, *Essays in Leicestershire History* (Liverpool, 1951), and *Devonshire Studies* (1952); *Studies in Social History*, ed. J. H. Plumb, is also valuable.

101. Mildred Campbell, *The English Yeoman* (London, 1960), p. 27.

102. Sylvia L. Thrupp, *The Merchant Class of Medieval London 1300–1500* (Ann Arbor, 1962), p. 314 and *passim*.

103. Augustus Jessopp, *One Generation of a Norfolk House* (New York, 1914), p. 333.

104. Based on this book was Emmison's *Tudor Food and Pastimes* (London, 1964).

105. There are a number of guides to local archives; one of the most recent is F. G. Emmison, *Archives and Local History* (London, 1967). On the history of the heralds see Anthony Wagner, *Heralds of England: A History of the Office and College of Arms* (London, 1967).

106. Cf. A. L. Rowse, *The English Spirit* (New York, 1946), pp. 97–110.

107. See esp. the discussion in Penry Williams, *The Council in the Marches of Wales* (Cardiff, 1958), p. 47.

108. Ralph Griffiths, "The Rise of the Stradlings of St. Donats," *Morgannwg: Transactions of the Glamorgan Local History Society*, VII (1963), 15–47, describes, among other things, the concern with history.

109. Glanmor Williams, *Owen Glendower* (Oxford, 1966), p. 60.

110. See also R. Dudley Edwards, "Ireland, Elizabeth I, and the Counter-Reformation," in *Elizabethan Government and Society: Essays Presented to Sir John Neale*, ed. S. T. Bindoff *et al.* (London, 1961), pp. 315–339.

111. Earl J. Hamilton, *American Treasure and the Price Revolution in Spain, 1500–1650* (Cambridge, Mass., 1934), p. vii; see also pp. 300–302.

112. See Earl J. Hamilton, "American Treasure and the Rise of Capitalism, 1500–1700," *Economica*, IX (1929), 338, 344–346.

113. John Maynard Keynes, *A Treatise on Money*, Vol. II, *The Applied Theory of Money* (New York, 1930), p. 154.

114. Hamilton, "American Treasure and the Rise of Capitalism," *passim*.

115. Keynes, *op. cit.*, II, 156–157.

116. John U. Nef, *The Rise of the British Coal Industry* (London, 1932), I, 162–189 and *passim*.

117. *Ibid.*, pp. 350–448.

118. *Ibid.*, II, 44.

119. See John U. Nef, *Industry and Government in France and England, 1540–1640* (Ithaca, 1957). This book contains references to other important essays by Nef (see p. 2 note).

120. *Ibid.*, pp. 55–56, 104–105, 144–145.

121. See Eric Kerridge's review of Ramsey's *Tudor Economic Problems* in *History*, XLVIII (1963), 372.

122. Stone, *Crisis of the Aristocracy*, p. 10.

123. See Eli Heckscher, *Mercantilism*, trans. Mandel Shapiro, (London, 1934), I, 415–436, 451, 468–470.

124. See the Historical Association pamphlet by Charles Wilson, *Mercantilism* (London, 1958), p. 8 and *passim*; and Eli Heckscher, "Mercantilism," *EcHR*, VII (1936), 44–54; cf. C. Wilson, "Mercantilism: Some Vicissitudes of an Idea," *EcHR*, 2nd ser., X (1957–1958), 181–188.

125. Heckscher, "Mercantilism," p. 54; cf. D. C. Coleman, "Eli Heckscher and the Idea of Mercantilism," *Scandinavian Economic History Review*, V, No. 1 (1957), 3–25.

126. See the review by Viner, reprinted in Jacob Viner, *The Long View and the Short* (Glencoe, 1958), p. 409.

127. Heckscher, "Mercantilism," pp. 45–49.

128. Heckscher, *Mercantilism*, II, 312–313.

129. See Raymond De Roover, *Gresham on Foreign Exchange* (Cambridge, Mass., 1949), p. 281 and *passim*. The authorship of this tract has been disputed by Mary Dewar, who attributed it to Sir Thomas Smith, and by Daniel R. Fusfeld, who attributed it to Sir Richard Martin. See the discussion in *EcHR*, XX, No. 1 (April 1967), 145–152.

130. See B. E. Supple, *Commercial Crisis and Change in England 1600–1642* (Cambridge, Mass., 1959), pp. 225–227, and Chap. 10 *passim*. But cf. Heckscher, *Mercantilism*, I, 470 and *passim*. Heckscher was not unaware of the influence of the environment.

131. See Eileen Power, *The Wool Trade in English Medieval History* (Oxford, 1941).

132. See also E. Carus-Wilson, *Medieval Merchant Venturers* (London, 1954); Herbert Heaton, *The Yorkshire Woolen and Worsted Industries* (Oxford, 1920); and E. Lipson, *English Woolen and Worsted Industries* (rev. ed.; London, 1953).

133. See John Wheeler, *A Treatise of Commerce*, ed. George Burton Hotchkiss (New York, 1931); the editor makes the point about corporation publicity.

134. Cf. Heckscher, *Mercantilism*, I, 399 ff.

135. E. H. Phelps Brown and Sheila V. Hopkins, "Seven Centuries of Building Wages," *Economica*, n.s., XXII (1955), 195–206, esp. 196–202.

136. E. H. Phelps Brown and Sheila V. Hopkins, "The Price of Consumables, Compared with Builders' Wage Rates," *Economica*, n.s., XXIII (1956), 291–314.

137. E. H. Phelps Brown and Sheila V. Hopkins, "Wage Rates and Prices: Evidence for Population Pressure in the Sixteenth Century," *Economica*, n.s., XXIV (1957), 289–299.

138. Y. S. Brenner, "The Inflation of Prices in Early 16th Century England," *EcHR*, 2nd ser. XIV (1961), 225–239. See also Y. S. Brenner, "The Inflation of Prices in England, 1551–1650," *EcHR*, 2nd ser. XV (1962), 266–284; and J. D. Gould, "Y. S. Brenner on Prices: A Comment," *EcHR*, XVI (1963), 351–360; J. D. Gould, "The Price Revolution Reconsidered," *EcHR*, XVII (1964), 249–266; and Y. S. Brenner, "The Price Revolution Considered: A Reply," *EcHR*, XVIII (1965), 392–396. The journal literature on this subject is very large, as a glance at the items listed in the bibliographical essays in the *Economic History Review* will show. Only two other articles can be noted here: Eric Kerridge, "The Movement of Rent 1540–1640," *EcHR*, V (1953), 16–34; and Habbakuk, "The Market for Monastic Property, 1509–1603," *EcHR*, X (1958), 362–380. An important book which provides a basis for comparison is Herman Van Der Wee, *The Growth of the Antwerp Market and the European Economy* (The Hague, 1963). This massive three-volume study of Antwerp from the fourteenth through the sixteenth centuries contains masses of statistics (in Vol. I), plus an analysis of the processes of economic growth (Vol. II), and a set of graphs based on comparative statistical research (Vol. III).

139. F. J. Fisher, "The Sixteenth and Seventeenth Centuries: The Dark Ages in English Economic History," *Economica*, n.s., XXIV (1957), 2–18.

140. J. E. Neale, *Essays in Elizabethan History* (London, 1958), pp. 28, 42, and 21–44 *passim*.

141. Neale, "The Elizabethan Political Scene," *ibid.*, pp. 59–84.
142. Neale, "The Biographical Approach to History," *ibid.*, p. 235.
143. *Ibid.*
144. Neale, "The Elizabethan Age," *ibid.*, p. 23; see also J. E. Neale, *The Elizabethan House of Commons* (New Haven, 1950), p. 15. There is a later revised edition of *The Elizabethan House of Commons* published in Peregrine Books by Penguin (London, 1963) which differs in pagination and contains some revisions based on later research. Further references will be to the New Haven 1950 edition, but quotations have been checked against the 1963 edition.
145. Neale, *Elizabethan House of Commons*, p. 320; cf. Introduction, pp. 15–17, and Chap. 1 *passim*.
146. *Ibid.*, p. 141.
147. *Ibid.*, pp. 245, 282–300.
148. *Ibid.*, p. 319.
149. See A. F. Pollard, "The Authority of the Lords Journals in the Sixteenth Century," *Transactions of the Royal Historical Society*, 3rd ser., VIII (1914), 17–39.
150. J. E. Neale, *Elizabeth I and Her Parliaments 1559–1581* (London, 1953), pp. 420, 417–424 *passim*.
151. *Ibid.*, p. 19.
152. See Neale's estimate of Elizabeth's character in J. E. Neale, *Elizabeth I and Her Parliaments 1584–1601* (London, 1957), p. 439.
153. Neale, *Elizabeth I and Her Parliaments 1559–1581*, p. 28.
154. *Ibid.*, p. 53.
155. *Ibid.*, p. 78.
156. *Ibid.*, p. 178.
157. *Ibid.*, p. 419.
158. Neale, *Elizabeth I and Her Parliaments 1584–1601*, p. 436.
159. *Ibid.*, p. 434.
160. See "The Commons Privilege of Free Speech in Parliament," in *Tudor Studies Presented to A. F. Pollard*, ed. R. W. Seton-Watson (London, 1924), pp. 257–286, 257.
161. George L. Haskins, *The Growth of English Representative Government* (Philadelphia, 1948), pp. 127–130.
162. C. H. McIlwain, *The High Court of Parliament and Its Supremacy* (New Haven, 1910), pp. 119, 133–134, 148.
163. *Ibid.*, p. 134. McIlwain's essays, esp. "Whig Sovereignty and Real Sovereignty," should also be consulted; these are conveniently gathered in C. H. McIlwain, *Constitutionalism and the Changing World* (Cambridge, Mass., 1939).
164. See McIlwain, *High Court of Parliament*, Chap. 5 *passim*, and pp. 119–127, 140–147.
165. *Ibid.*, p. 110.
166. See *ibid.*, pp. 50–54.
167. McIlwain, "The Historian's Part in a Changing World" in *Constitutionalism and the Changing World*, p. 19.
168. See W. S. Holdsworth, *A History of English Law* (London, 1922–1952), II, 441 ff.; G. R. Elton, *The Tudor Constitution: Documents and Commentary* (Cambridge, 1960), 228–234.
169. C. H. McIlwain, *Constitutionalism Ancient and Modern* (Ithaca, 1947), p. 111.
170. See Neale, *Essays*, pp. 125–145.
171. R. B. Wernham, *Before the Armada: The Emergence of the English Nation 1485–1588* (New York, 1966), p. 205.

172. But cf. the rejoinder in G. R. Elton, "State Planning in Early Tudor England," *EcHR*, 2nd ser. XIII, No. 3 (1961), 433–439.
173. The works of G. R. Elton, Joel Hurstfield, G. E. Aylmer, W. C. Richardson, and others have done much to close this gap, but many departmental and legal records have been only haphazardly explored from the point of view of record-keeping.
174. There is a brief survey in F. Smith Fussner, *The Historical Revolution* (London, 1962), pp. 69–91.
175. This is not to minimize the importance of Kenneth Pickthorne's *Early Tudor Government Henry VII* (1949) and *Henry VIII* (1934), both general text-books based on printed sources. The exploration of administrative archives has, however, radically changed older interpretations.
176. G. R. Elton, "The Problems and Significance of Administrative History in Tudor England,'" *Journal of British Studies*, IV, No. 2 (1965), 18.
177. *Ibid.*, p. 18.
178. *Ibid.*, p. 19.
179. G. R. Elton, *England under the Tudors* (London, 1963), p. 57.
180. *Ibid.*, p. 66.
181. *Ibid.*, p. 111.
182. *Ibid.*, pp. 129, 133.
183. *Ibid.*, p. 160.
184. *Ibid.*, p. 165.
185. *Ibid.*, pp. 165 ff., 402.
186. *Ibid.*, p. 417.
187. Penry Williams, "The Tudor State," *Past and Present*, No. 25 (July 1963), p. 54.
188. G. R. Elton, "The Tudor Revolution: A Reply," *Past and Present*, No. 29 (December 1964), p. 49.
189. G. L. Harriss, "A Revolution in Tudor History?" *Past and Present*, No. 31 (July 1965), p. 87.
190. Penry Williams, "A Revolution in Tudor History?" *ibid.*, pp. 94–96, from p. 95.
191. *Ibid.*, p. 88.
192. *Ibid.*, p. 89.
193. G. R. Elton, "A Revolution in Tudor History?" *Past and Present*, No. 32 (December 1965), p. 103.
194. Harriss, "Revolution in Tudor History?" pp. 89, 92, 94.
195. Williams, "A Revolution in Tudor History?" p. 96.
196. Elton, "A Revolution in Tudor History?" p. 109.
197. Michael Walzer, *The Revolution of the Saints* (Cambridge, Mass., 1965), p. 289.
198. Neale, *Essays*, p. 125.
199. See the following by G. R. Elton: "King or Minister, The Man behind the Henrician Reformation," *History*, XXXIX (1954); "The Political Creed of Thomas Cromwell," *Transactions of the Royal Historical Society*, 5th ser., VI (1956); "The Evolution of a Reformation Statute," *English Historical Review*, LXIX (1949); "Parliamentary Drafts, 1529–1540," *Bulletin of the Institute of Historical Research*, XXV (1952); "Thomas Cromwell's Decline and Fall," *Cambridge Historical Journal*, X (1951); "The Commons Supplication of 1532," *English Historical Review*, LXVI (1951); and *Star Chamber Stories* (London, 1958). Cf. J. P. Cooper, "The Supplication against the Ordinaries Reconsidered," *English Historical Review*, LXXII (Oct., 1957), 616–641; and

T. M. Parker, "Was Thomas Cromwell a Machiavellian?" *Journal of Ecclesiastical History*, I (1950). See also "Why the history of the Early-Tudor Council remains unwritten," *Annali della Fondazione italiana per la storia administravita*, I (1964), 268–296.

200. The first accurate editions were published in 1932 and 1935 by the Early English Text Society.

201. See Edward Lord Herbert [of Cherbury], *The History of England under Henry VIII* (reprint, London, 1870), p. 109.

202. Elton, *Tudor Constitution*, p. vi.

203. Cf. Elizabeth M. Nugent, *The Thought and Culture of the English Renaissance* (Cambridge, 1960), selections of Tudor prose.

5

Reconnaissance:
Tudor Writers and the
Expansion of History

THE EXPANSION OF ELIZABETHAN ENGLAND took place swiftly, midway in the Age of Reconnaissance. That period of discovery, exploration, and settlement lasted from about 1450 to 1650. It saw Europe rise to a commanding position in the world, establish the footholds of colonial empires, and bring together science and tech nology in a new, characteristically modern alliance: the expectation of progress supplanted the older, authoritative doctrine of the world's decay. As Elizabethan England "wheeled to the west," its fortunes changed; and reorientation toward the New World was symbolic as well as politic: cultural expansion accompanied the westward economic expansion, bringing a new sense of possibilities, a new awareness of history, and surprising views of a wider world.[1] The expansion of English society, first into the margins of backward areas at home—Cornwall, Wales, the Borders; Ireland by conquest and colonization—then, via the North Sea into Russia; across the Atlantic to the Americas, and into the Pacific—eventually to the Antipodes, and the Far East: this was the theme of A. L. Rowse's *The Expansion of Elizabethan England* (1955). The European cultural and economic setting of that expansion was the subject of J. H. Parry's *The Age of Reconnaissance* (1963), a book which defined "Reconnaissance" in intellectual as well as physical terms:

It was a principal task of the Reconnaissance to challenge belief in the necessary superiority of ancient wisdom. Not only in the specific field of geography, but in almost every branch of science, at some time during our period there came a moment when Western Europe, so to speak, at last caught up with the ancient world, and a few bold men, understanding and revering what the ancients had taught, were, nevertheless, ready to dispute their conclusions. So in the process of Reconnaissance, explorers by sea, pushing rashly out into a world unknown, but for Ptolemy, and finding it bigger and more varied than they expected, began first to doubt Ptolemy, then to prove him wrong in many particulars, and finally to draw on maps and globes a new and more convincing picture. Similarly, but independently, Copernicus and his successors . . . began timidly and tentatively, first, to question, then to dismantle the Aristotelian-Ptolemaic geocentric scheme of the universe, and to postulate a heliocentric system in its place.

In both areas, Parry concluded, the movement from doubt to discard and replacement was similar: "Eventually, in all branches of science, Reconnaissance became Revolution." [2]

Only very slowly did a technological and scientific attitude develop in Europe during the Reconnaissance. The principle of verification by empirical test, by going directly to the relevant sources, was recognized only in a limited number of fields. Scholars of the fifteenth century had no reliable means of criticizing Ptolemy or Marco Polo; and even in the sixteenth century paintings of African animals were sometimes based on nothing more than descriptions and confident ignorance. Hence the importance of territorial reconnaissance:

Geographical exploration, with its associated skills of navigation and cartography, was not merely the principal field of human endeavor in which scientific discovery and everyday technique became closely associated before the middle of the seventeenth century; except for the arts of war and of military engineering and (to a very limited extent) medical practice, it was almost the only field; hence its immense significance in the history of science and thought.[3]

The vital technical superiority of Europeans in guns and ships "ensured the continuous development of the Reconnaissance and the permanence of its results." [4] Different aspects of the Reconnaissance have attracted different kinds of scholars: geographers, cartographers, military and naval historians, as well as economic historians, and historians of science and culture have put forth revisionist views in recent years. In line with contemporary trends toward the study of world history, a number of books and essays have appeared which assess the impact of Europe on Asiatic societies. The Global History Series of paperbacks, edited by Leften Stavrianoes, is indicative of the trend; and the volume edited by Joseph R. Levenson, *European Expansion and the Counter-Example of Asia, 1300–1600* (1967), provides useful selections from articles and books, most of which were published after 1945. The technological superiority of Europe was not by any means absolute, and some historians were inclined to attribute European successes to superior determination; but the inadequacy of this view was demonstrated by Carlo Cipolla in *Guns, Sails, and Empires* (1965), a study of technological innovation in the early phases of European expansion from 1400 to 1700.[5] Two general surveys of cartographical art and science were R. V. Tooley's *Maps and Map-Makers* (revised edition, 1952) and G. R. Crone's *Maps and Their Makers* (1962), both containing helpful bibliography. E. G. R. Taylor's *Tudor Geography 1485–1583* (1930) and *Late Tudor and Early Stuart Geography 1583–1650* (1934) provided a scholarly perspective on Hakluyt as a geographer. The navigational problems of Elizabethan seamen were discussed at length, and with great technical expertise, by David W. Waters in *The Art of Navigation in England in Elizabethan and Early Stuart Times* (1958).

A. L. Rowse in *The Elizabethans and America* (1965) disputed the orthodox nineteenth-century version of American history which dated the beginnings of America from the landing of the *Mayflower*. Urging instead that the Elizabethan expansion of the 1580s was the true and vital beginning of much that was characteristically American, Rowse wove his argument around the fact that New England had Elizabethan England behind it, especially the Elizabethan enthusiasm for education, and the opposition faith—Puritanism—with the Puritan's commitment to a learned ministry and to Godly Thorough Reformation.[6] Perhaps the most interesting lectures were those on "Ralegh, Hakluyt and Colonization" and "America in Elizabethan Literature, Science, and the Arts." In the former Rowse called attention to the remarkable conjuncture of the 1580s, when many currents were beginning to meet and swirl together: poetry and the drama, the English colonization of

America, the Spanish conflict, and the first great historical and geographical works, epitomized in Hakluyt's *Principal Navigations*. The idea of America in English writings of the period was discussed more fully by Gustav H. Blanke in *Amerika im Englischen Schriftum des 16. und 17. Jahrhunderts*. The image of the New World was at least as significant as the actual facts about it—"in what part of the newe world Utopia is situate" More did not tell his readers, but the image of Utopia clung to America despite the facts.[7] "That great antiquity America lay buried for thousands of years; and a large part of the earth is still in the Urne unto us," Sir Thomas Browne would write in 1658. The quest for new land, for discovery itself, was greatly stimulated by Hakluyt and other writers of his generation. Yet we are left with a question about the meaning of "discovery"—did the early explorers "discover" what they did not seek? [8] And were discoveries in science, literature, and the arts parts of a larger pattern of discovery—an intellectual universal—or were they still unrelated, nominalistic accidents? The answers are by no means clear, but the questions themselves raise further issues for historiography.

Since it is clear that expansion did not take place at the same rate, or at the same time in different fields, and since the "even-flow" of time was roiled in the 1530s and again in the 1580s, it might seem that no generalizations about the Reconnaissance can do justice to the complexity of change in the period. The warrant for such pessimism does not lie, however, in the facts of change. Discoveries of new lands, or of new methods of sailing, fighting, manufacturing, or governing, discoveries of new powers in the imagination, and in the English language—these did expand the sense of intellectual possibility, the belief in future growth, and indirectly the remembrance of things past. The very fact that men were being challenged in ways that were not again to be so disturbing to imaginative minds until the twentieth century was reason enough for there to be reassessment; and attempts were made both to reassert traditional values and to move further into unknown waters, and strange seas of thought, using methods that had worked in earlier explorations. The reassertion of tradition in times of crisis was nothing new; but traditions alone, the authority of antiquity or of religion alone, seldom have deflected movements of revolutionary change. J. R. Hale's tough-minded analysis of the use of gunpowder during the Renaissance disposes of the nostalgic arguments of some historians that Christian ethics were an effective restraint on the use of firearms.[9] The greatest challenge to Europe's conscience before the atomic bomb, according to Hale, was the Renaissance use of gunpowder in weapons of war, but the new technology soon created its own traditions; and firearms were neatly accommodated by the European conscience and by the European imagination. It will thus not do to argue that traditions alone, whether of ancient or of recent times, can withstand the forces of change. It would be equally wrong, however, to deny or to underestimate and misunderstand the significance of traditions in European society in the sixteenth century. It will be the purpose of the first section of this chapter to illustrate some English explorations and traditions, then to define some of the mechanisms by which intelligence gathered by one kind of reconnaissance was made available for the exploration of other fields. Following this will be sections dealing with particular aspects of Tudor historical writing and thought: the Early Humanists and the Study of History; Chronicles and Chroniclers; Biographers and Antiquaries; the Reformation Uses of History; and finally, Tudor Descriptions—Topography, Customs, and Territorial Histories.

Except in religion and the arts of government England under the earlier Tudors moved slowly in its reconnoitering of new ground. Comparatively little was accomplished in maritime exploration before the mid-sixteenth century. Print, while revolutionary in its cumulative effects, did not immediately overthrow old ideas; the fine fluency of the later Elizabethans in literature, seamanship, and adventure was scarcely evident under the first of the Tudors. Stability was the great achievement of Henry VII, and legitimacy depended on it. Not the least of the achievements of Henry VIII and his successors was the maintenance of legitimacy—the national monarchy, national law, and national religion. Each might change in particulars, but all three were accepted and supported by the people at large. In its simplest definition legitimacy meant a right of royal hereditary succession. The recognition of that right was as much the result of political skill as of propaganda. It has been said that Tudor Englishmen valued order and supported the dynasty because they had so recently experienced disorder. This is a half truth: the Wars of the Roses were "ancient" by the time Henry VIII died; what mattered was respect for dynastic principles, and for the rule of law. History has always taught the lessons of disorder, but history has been quiet about how to maintain order in the midst of change. It is virtually impossible for the modern Tudor historian to measure the intensity of a psychological attitude, or to calculate precisely the effects of a sense of stability and legitimacy on behavior, but as a historian he must reckon with such considerations. Conjectural reasons suggest that the Elizabethans felt freer to assert themselves, to experiment in dress, in speech, and in behavior, because they felt relatively secure in basic political and social roles and rights.[10] The legitimacy of Tudor rule was recognized by the majority of Catholics and Puritans as well as by those who wore their Anglicanism with indifference; that fact in itself was a tribute to Tudor success in ruling with restraint. The concept of a divine right of kings, refurbished in England in the sixteenth century, masked to some extent the underlying weakness of the monarchy. The increasing complexity of Tudor society made it more and more difficult to achieve success by resolute expedients; and, in the long run, the monarchy was faced by the same crisis that Lawrence Stone described in *The Crisis of the Aristocracy*. The machinery of government creaked on, then finally broke down in the 1640s. The long-term crisis of the monarchy was compounded by Reformation international politics, by the emergence of pressure groups both in and out of Parliament, and by the unrelenting pressures of population and inflation. In the post-Reformation century a crisis of confidence was likely to occur, but the question remains, why should Edward, Mary, and Elizabeth have been spared the consequences of the crisis? No simple answer can be given, but the existence of a sense of legitimate order was probably not irrelevant to Elizabethan achievements in government and the arts. Although the word "anomie" had appeared in the language by 1591, it did not yet have its modern connotations; men and women to a large extent accepted their roles in society.

Puritans like Philip Stubbs might rail at the wickedness of the world, but the author of *The Anatomy of Abuses* (1583) remained a loyal Englishman. Many of the abuses he described were real enough, although admonitions to the rich to care for the poor were scarcely original; the vocabulary was Elizabethan but the sins were pre-Christian. "Take heed, therefore, you rich men, that poll and pill the poor, for the blood of as many as miscarry any manner of way through your injurious exactions, sinister oppressions, and indirect dealings, shall be poured upon your heads at the great day of the Lord," Stubbs wrote, and took satisfaction in the thought that the Lord would remove those who massacred the poor, either by enclosures or other means.[11] There were critics enough and enough things to criticize in Elizabethan England, but the abuses were marginal compared with the accomplishments.

Sharp contrasts between old and new, between antiquity and modern practices, and between traditional authority and attacks on that authority, powerfully stimulated further exploration and experimentation. A sense of legitimacy, respect for tradition and convention, and a readiness to explore, or to borrow new techniques, were not necessarily in conflict. Scholars borrowed from one another, amassed information on all sorts of subjects, and communicated with each other much more extensively in 1600 than in 1500. New techniques invented in one field could be tried in others, thanks in large part to the greater ease of exchanging ideas that print permitted. Anomalies of one sort or another became more and more apparent to men who were accustomed to searching the past for authoritative answers. In history, science, medicine, exploration, and other fields, traditions played a double role: as "standards" they defined accepted methods, norms, and ideas, allowing comparisons, and therefore modifications, to be made; as "legitimizing concepts" they provided psychological security, allowing not only a blind adherence to old ways but also the trial of new methods. Obviously no traditions can persist without change, but the more rapid the rate of change the more readily did Tudor Englishmen embrace religious and secular traditions and look for continuities—if not with medieval times, then with antiquity. These complex relationships cannot be explored in detail, but some of them can be illustrated in Tudor history and historiography.

The recent article by Elizabeth Eisenstein, "Some Conjectures about the Impact of Printing on Western Society and Thought: A Preliminary Report" (1968), analyzes some of the ways in which printing affected intellectual and political traditions, both by creating new conventions and by fixing the old: "The preservation of the old, in brief, launched a tradition of the new." [12] The article is essential reading for anyone interested in historiography and the growth of historical consciousness; the ways in which print changed men's lives have seldom before been carefully analyzed, and the "further work" that remains to be done will assuredly start from these conjectures. One of the effects of the increased output of print was that many more books could be seen or acquired by scholars than was possible in the era of manuscript learning, when "wandering" was a necessity for scholars who wanted to consult a variety of books. The development of cross-referencing not only ended the day of the glossator but made possible a far wider comparison of texts, which facilitated new intellectual combinations.[13] The significance of this for the development of historiography was incalculable—combinatory intellectual activity was the reagent of change. Cross-cultural interchanges "stimulated mental activities in contradictory ways" according to Eisenstein, who pointed out that "certain confusing cross-currents may be explained by noting that new links between disciplines were being forged before old ones had been severed."[14]

Print not only created its own new conventions and traditions but fixed and extended in time older traditions and world views. Traditions were "age-old" after only forty years in the Middle Ages.[15] The printing press made available to poets, historians, and other intellectuals the views of ancient and medieval writers in a way that was inconceivable prior to the age of incunabula. The possibility of successive generations building on the work of their predecessors was enhanced, just as chronological awareness was extended by the availability of the printed book.[16] Typographical fixity was essential to the development of humanistic scholarship and its auxiliary sciences: paleography, philology, archaeology, numismatics, etc.[17] The concept of "immemorial custom" was in some ways rendered more, not less, potent by the fact that printed statutes existed and could be cited by page numbers. Precedents took on new meaning, and a new aura of respectability, when they appeared in print, if only because print concealed the true antiquity of the original and gave currency to myths. In his essay on "Magna Carta and British Constitutionalism" (1965), William H. Dunham, Jr., called attention to the importance of constitutional myths that were the product of Tudor lawyers, historians, and chroniclers. Caxton, the printer, in 1480 had stressed the contractual nature of the Great Charter; and a century later, in 1577, Holinshed located Henry III's granting of the 1125 charter at a Parliament. Lambarde and other Elizabethans created the myth of the antiquity of Parliament and shaped the convention that the Charter was made by the common consent of the realm; they thus demonstrated again how bad history might make good law.[18]

"Veneration for the wisdom of the ancients was not incompatible with the advancement of learning," Eisenstein concluded, "nor was imitation incompatible with inspiration." [19] In the sixteenth century the ancients could provide more familiar quotations, symbols, stereotypes, and traditions than ever before; intellectuals profited accordingly. The expression of opinions about the Church was no longer confined to a few intellectual leaders and their followers—Lollardry became a public tradition in the sixteenth century by virtue of the job printers.[20] Even more important was the fact that Elizabethan education, family life, and class consciousness were influenced by the new medium. Traditions could be more readily transmitted, established, or reinforced in a reading culture. Even the rise of science may have owed more to the geography of the printing press than to the accident of individual genius.[21]

If older ideas were given greater permanence as the result of printing, it is also true that print greatly facilitated comparisons, and that new ideas and attitudes spread quickly—not only among intellectuals but through the ranks of the occasional readers. The printing press made it easier for the barely literate to acquire ideas about the wider world and about history. A medieval cathedral was in some sense a teaching instrument, with stories told in stone and glass, but it was at best a poor substitute for teaching with woodcuts and printed propaganda. Every increase in the size of the "mass audience" has resulted in new opportunities as well as new problems: the growth of literacy provided the context which made possible broad-based scholarship. With the emergence of a larger reading public in Tudor times went the now familiar increases in University attendance and the emphasis on a learned ministry. Puritanism in particular contributed to the demand for higher clerical education. Gentlemen who attended universities had, at the very least, to pretend to think that books were important. That the long-term results were always favorable to learning may not be beyond dispute, but that is not the question at issue. Unless the whole root system of education was nourished, the trunk and the highest branches of scholarship would have been stunted; print nourished the entire tree.

The emergence of a broader based historiography and of new intellectual interests in Tudor England can be illustrated by the Elizabethan history play, by the literature of travel and discovery, and by recent historical and bibliographical studies of the origins of modern disciplines. The Tudor history play has attracted relatively little attention: except for articles and books on subjects such as the influence of John Foxe or of Holinshed and Hall on Shakespeare, or the influence of English legal history on Tudor plays, or attempts to define the history play in Tudor times, modern literary scholars have until recently virtually ignored the relationships between historiography and the drama.[22] Lily B. Campbell's *Shakespeare's Histories, Mirrors of Elizabethan Policy* (1947) and E. M. W. Tillyard's *Shakespeare's History Plays* (1944) are the books that have shaped most students' attitudes; recent studies have expanded on their themes, and developed new ones, as M. M. Reese did in *The Cease of Majesty* (1961) and Irving Ribner in *The English History Play in the Age of Shakespeare* (1957). But no books have thus far appeared dealing in detail with the causes of the popularity of history plays and with the unique problems of "historical drama." Editors, especially of the Variorum edition of Shakespeare, have dealt with textual problems, borrowings, and transformations of plot and character.[23] Literary critics have tended to stress literary themes and conventions, symbolism and imagery, without inquiring very thoroughly into the origins and causes of the literary concern with historical tradition. A great amount of criticism has gone to show that Shakespeare was not really interested in history so much as in irony, myth, ritual, philosophy, tragedy, comedy, sex, sin, and salvation. Yet even the most "thematic" critics have had to come back finally to history (even if they choose to call it myth) in interpreting Shakespeare's history plays.[24]

The Tudor interest in history was not simply the outcome of Tudor patriotism, but there is a sense in which Tudor historical consciousness shaped both patriotism and Elizabethan dramatic attitudes. The work of E. M. W. Tillyard and Lily B. Campbell had the salutary effect of making clear how much Shakespeare's history plays, especially the Henry VI–Richard III tetralogy, owed to the common Tudor concepts of historical order. Only against the concept of providential historical order could Shakespeare's images of discord and his treatment of murder, revolt, and war be understood. Earlier chronicle plays were usually spoiled by simple-minded borrowings from the chronicles; Shakespeare transformed his sources.[25] In the process of writing *Henry V* he moved from history toward tragedy. The argument that Shakespeare only discovered the way to tragedy after he had exhausted the possibilities of the history play was outlined by Harley Granville-Barker, who proposed that the turn away from history was crucial to Shakespeare's realization of his full potential as a dramatist.[26] In "From *Henry V to Hamlet*" (1933), Granville-Barker was, in effect, elaborating on an earlier view, expressed less subtly by George Pierce Baker in *The Development of Shakespeare as a Dramatist* (1916).[27] The idea was that history was inimical to tragedy, that the plot defined the characters, and that historical characters could not be truly tragic. Recent critics, especially A. P. Rossiter and M. M. Reese, have moved beyond Tillyard and Campbell, arguing that Shakespeare's histories did not offer the moral certainties, historical legitimacies, and providential absolutes enshrined in the prefaces to Tudor chronicles; instead Shakespeare left his readers with a sense of irony, of ambiguity, and of dialectical development. Rossiter, for example, in *Angel with Horns* (1961) proposed that Shakespeare was led to write *comic history*, not moral history, in *Richard III*, and that in this play the sense of irony was crucial. His argument points, however, to the importance of the history play in Shakespeare's development, as well as to Shakespeare's contributions to historical understanding. Shakespeare learned something about tragic irony by contemplating historical irony; he transformed Holinshed and Hall, as he did other sources, by reading them with imagination. In history were the same themes and subtleties that he orchestrated in the great tragedies and comedies. Continuity of development has been masked by the sharp division into "Comedies, Histories, and Tragedies."

Shakespeare's conception of Richard II as a poetic, frivolous, and unstable king has not yet been driven from the mind by record research. The weakness of Richard was necessary to Shakespeare's imperial theme; but historians, by and large, have accepted the Shakespearian Richard. In his study of *The Royal Policy of Richard II* (1968), R. H. Jones righted the picture of Richard as a feckless monarch and paid tribute to Shakespeare's compelling success in impressing an image of weakness on the king.[28] Shakespeare's contribution to Elizabethan ideas of history is, however, even more interesting than his distortions of character for dramatic effect. What he achieved was historic verisimilitude: probable, live kings; not player kings dressed up from the chronicles. The history plays of Shakespeare taught Elizabethans much, including the idea that "there is a history in all men's lives, figuring the nature of the times deceas'd." More importantly, Shakespeare's histories dealt with the historically unique problems of kingship. The succession, legitimacy, royal power, and politics were the true imperial themes. Kings might be like other men in their tragedies; in their public roles kings held power and office that could make or break the state. History plays explained to Elizabethan Englishmen the unsuspected problems of majesty; comparisons between past and present —between Macedon and Monmouth—were necessary for an understanding of both. The lines on ceremony spoken by Henry V before Agincourt revealed a human king, who in the end soliloquized on the responsibilities of kingship: "what watch the king keeps to maintain the peace, whose hours the peasant best advantages." [29]

The ironies, surprises, and problems produced by the "hatch and brood of time" were history, even if not always history warranted by the sources. The modern record-minded historian must interpret character and circumstances in the light of all the evidence; Shakespeare invented character and circumstance when necessary to make plays that could move men and help them understand the past as present. Shakespeare's subtlety about history was worth more at the time than Hall's facts, or even the best historian's interpretations.

A mere chronicle play might contain such lines as these on Henry VIII and his children:

> When he had reign'd full thirty-eight years,
> Nine months and some odd days, and was buried in Windsor,
> He died and left three famous sprigs behind him.
> Edward the Sixt:
> He did restore the gospel to his light
> And finish'd that his father left undone;
> A wise young prince given greatly to his book.
> He brought the English service first in use
> And died when he had reign'd six years five months
> And some odd days and lieth buried in Westminster
> Next after him a Mary did succeed,
> Which married Philip King of Spain.
> She reig'ned five years four months and some
> Odd days and is buried in Westminster.
> When she was dead her sister did succeed.[30]

As Tillyard observed, only a very serious desire for facts could have tolerated such writing. Shakespeare's history plays, and a few by Marlowe, Jonson, and their contemporaries, are far different from the mere chronicle plays of the period, yet from Bale's *King Johan* to the decline of the history play in the seventeenth century the theater taught history: no one can pretend to understand Tudor ideas of history without reading plays.[31] Rosalind in *As You Like It* noticed how "Time travels in divers paces with divers persons"; [32] and the problems of the state run through all the great tragedies.[33] Elizabethan images of the Puritan, the Jew, and of all manner of "types" are reflected in dramatic literature. Plays are thus true sources, though of a peculiar kind—worrying them for direct evidence of what people were really like often results in a noseful of false inferences as sharp as porcupine quills. But perhaps nowhere else can one discover as much about how Elizabethans thought and what their ideas and attitudes were toward the past and its lessons:

What stratagems, how fell, how butcherly,
Erroneous, mutinous and unnatural,
This daily quarrel doth beget! (*3 Henry VI*, 2.5.89)

The Elizabethans were interested in the large and important lessons of history—they were certainly not morally neutral observers of the evil that men do. The causes of events were still thought to be personal and dramatic, even if the consequences were not humanly controllable. History and tragedy were closer together than was ever imagined by most literary critics. The subtle ironies of history led to the deepening awareness of freedom and necessity, of human passion, reason, and pity, that informed the great tragedies. *Macbeth, Hamlet, Othello, Lear, Antony and Cleopatra*: all were plays about leaders of the state, and about the forms of corruption in the state. All were "myth-historical" tragedies—tragedies that illuminated the motives, cues, and passions of history. In this sense Shakespeare can be called a very great historian.

To understand Elizabethan drama in its historical setting some knowledge of the stage and its conventions is a necessity. E. K. Chambers' four-volume work on *The Elizabethan Stage* (1923-) remains an essential work of reference. The most recent and challenging reinterpretation of the design of Shakespeare's theatre occurs in a study of *The Art of Memory* (1966) by Frances Yates. Occult memory and Ramist memory were in conflict—both were "modern," yet both had strong links with the past, as did Fludd's Memory Theatre, which, according to Yates, provides the clue to the construction of the Globe Theatre.[34] In *The Idea of a Theatre* (1949), Francis Ferguson had stressed the fact that in *Hamlet* all the religious, cultural, and moral values of tradition were at stake in the action, and that ritual elements in the play were crucial—a point which was considerably strengthened by the research of George Riley Kernodle, set forth in *From Art to Theatre* (1944). Traditional elements, such as theatre forms based on Vitruvian reconstructions of ancient theatres, or—within the plays—dumb shows, and the deliberate exploitation of a multilevel stage for symbolic effect: these elements of the Elizabethan theatre were being combined in new ways which suggest that, in the broadest sense, Tudor Englishmen were becoming conscious of historical continuities in a fashion in which their ancestors had not been. "Traditions" were being consciously exploited to produce new ideas of the theatre. Medieval mystery plays were "universal" and ritualistic in the Christian sense, like *Everyman*; the Elizabethan dramatists were boldly using a variety of elements from the past, including specific ideas of history.[35]

The popularity of history outside the theatre can be inferred not only from the manuals of history described by Louis B. Wright in *Middle Class Culture in Elizabethan England* but by the growing interest in pamphlet literature, and in books on travel, discovery, and current events. In *Images of a Queen* (1964), James Emerson Phillips traced in detail the interpretations of the character and importance of Mary Stuart in sixteenth-century literature.[36] The Queen of Scots became a symbol—either Circe or Saint—in Reformation controversies. Mary's contemporaries shaped their portraits of the queen in terms of their political and religious fears and hopes. No one would deny that symbolism and allegory were important, but it is sometimes not sufficiently appreciated that Mary Stuart's life was thought to represent a lesson of history.[37] Spenser's Duessa in *The Fairie Queene* offended James VI because James recognized the real queen, his mother—the allegory was offensive as history. Literature and historiography alike might be subversive of state policy. Correspondence between past and present was but one aspect of the general Elizabethan doctrine of correspondences.

In *The Enchanted Glass* (1936), Hardin Craig analyzed different aspects of Tudor consciousness, especially the powerful attractions of antiquity, the effects of a mechanistic psychology, the rhetorical uses of history, and the ways in which symbolism and history, similitude and tradition, could be combined.[38] On a more prosaic level, the activities of publishers and professional writers helped to set the taste for history by purveying what the audience or the patrons wanted. The importance of novelty, of fashion, was perhaps part of the Elizabethan attitude toward change—an ambivalent attitude, certainly, which embraced mutability while deploring it. In *The Professional Writer in Elizabethan England* (1959), Edwin Haviland Miller took note of this aspect of Elizabethan opinion, which may have had something to do with the popularity of travel literature.[39] The fullest account of the general processes by which Europe came to be acquainted with Asia was given by Donald F. Lach, in Volume I of *Asia in the Making of Europe* (1965).[40] The maritime exploits of captains such as Grenville, Drake, and Ralegh, of course, made news; and more will be said later of Hakluyt as journalist and historian. The amount of historical, anthropological, and ethnographical information in Elizabethan travel literature was considerable, but it has not been extensively analyzed. The multiplication of collections of customs during the sixteenth century was a noteworthy European phenomenon; and although most collectors sought merely new "curios," some, such as Sebastian Münster, attempted classification and description. In *Early Anthropology in the Sixteenth and Seventeenth Centuries* (1964), Margaret T. Hodgen discussed some of the works that laid the foundations of early anthropology, comparative religions, anthropogeography, and related studies. The movement toward organized inquiry, formulation of problems, and choice of organizing ideas began in the sixteenth century. The connection between historical and anthropological thought was, as the author pointed out, very close; and the place of the savage in the chain of being and in history remained a crucial intellectual problem.[41] Various attempts were made to explain cultural diffusion, usually on a Biblical and Trojan basis; one aspect of this was analyzed by T. D. Kendrick in *British Antiquity*. Contemporary history, as might be expected, was watched with considerable interest. French history in particular formed the basis of new and significant political thought, especially in the seventeenth century, as was demonstrated by J. H. M. Salmon in *The French Religious Wars in English Political Thought* (1959). French conflicts had become well established in English historical consciousness during Elizabeth's reign—a fact which was accounted for in part by Elizabethan reverence for French culture, and in part by the already established habit of drawing historical parallels and lessons from history.[42]

What was and was not characteristic of English historiography during the sixteenth century is a question that takes precedence over the discussion of what changed, how and why innovations were made, and what were the patterns of change. Different types of historical writing had different histories—each will be illustrated, but none can be described in detail. A general outline of patterns and trends will serve to introduce representative selections of Tudor historical writing. Ralegh once observed that the "industry of an historian having so many things to weary it, may well be excused, when finding apparent cause enough of things done, it forbeareth to make further search." [43] This disarming remark was intended to legitimize conjecture, not laziness. Lacking a range of studies of the different branches of thought in relation to each other, especially in the Tudor period, historians have not been able to solve the definitional, much less the causal problems of the climate of opinions. Such problems are not, however, in principle insoluble. Important similarities between the scientific and the historical revolutions at the end of the Renaissance have been pointed out by G. Wylie Sypher; and Toulmin and Goodfield have convincingly argued that "throughout the centuries of intellectual endeavour, the growth of men's historical consciousness across subjects ranging from physical cosmology at one extreme to theology and social history at the other took closely parallel forms." [44] What is lacking is an intensive study of the growth of historical consciousness in English society during the early modern transition period.

What was *not* characteristic of English historiography under the Tudors can be stated succinctly: there was, as Bacon observed, no history of learning and the arts. This meant no history of science, of technology, of philosophy, or of art and literature, and, of course, no distinctive economic history; the history of trades was to be a Baconian contribution. There was virtually no original speculation by Englishmen about the theory or philosophy of history, although works by continental scholars, notably Bodin, were known and read in England.[45] Modern fields of specialization had not yet developed—historiography, as a mirror of the times, reflected the humanist ideal of the "complete" man.

Continuity was more important than change, and the "search for uniformities" predominated over appreciation of the unique among sixteenth-century English historians.[46] Most characteristic, perhaps, was the persistence of medieval ideas and attitudes. History embodied, no less than rhetoric, the continuity of the old European tradition.[47] The moral and prudential values of history were especially stressed by Elyot and the humanists.[48] Yet, in the world view of Elizabethan intellectuals, "original sin and the decline of the world from a golden age were general assumptions." And, as Franklin Baumer went on to point out, "the method of knowledge was authoritarian, theology was the queen of the sciences, and it was unthinkable to all but a daring few that historiography and political and economic thought should be unrelated to it."[49] Notable exceptions do not disprove this simple rule—it is significant that no one explicitly denied a providential framework for history.

English common law profoundly influenced historiography and historical attitudes. The law itself rested on precedents of record (so that archival research was encouraged); and the legal doctrine of *jus non scripta* was one that demanded explanation and elucidation in historical form. This is not to say that the common lawyers were practicing historians, trying to ascertain the truth about the past. They were not. They were lawyers first, and they became antiquaries or historians because they assumed that facts and precedents from the past must be relevant to the present: arguments from precedent had long been characteristic of the common law. Common lawyers were not, however, wholly isolated from the influence of humanism and continental learning, and the Elizabethan legal antiquaries knew very well how to plant the sharpened stakes of historical argument.[50]

Even Coke, who was thoroughly insular in outlook, felt obliged to account for historical anomalies. English law, although based on custom, was known to resemble Norman law. Coke was to argue that the unwritten English laws must have been "imposed" on Normandy. William the Conqueror discovered English law and said to himself: Behold, it is good—it must be exported to Normandy! In order to account for similarities between the two sys-

tems of law (English and Norman, after the conquest), Coke was
prepared to argue historical nonsense.[51] Brady's retort in 1685 was
crushing: "it would have been a greater difficulty than the Conquest of *England*, to have imposed the *English* Laws upon so stub-
born a people as the *Normans* were, especially at that time
when the Conqueror had much to do to keep them in subjection
. . ."[52]

Coke was notoriously fond of criticizing historians for their ignorance of the law, but he himself was a "historical lawyer" who
did not disdain arguments drawn from the Stoic traditions of
Roman law.[53] Reason upheld authority, and the laws of England,
leges non scripta, were "divinely cast into the hearts of men, and
built upon the immoveable Rock of Reason." [54] The men of the long
robe, however, had their own political and professional reasons
for clinging to the doctrine of custom. It was an antidote against
arbitrary "regal Government," and a justification for new rights
and liberties claimed in the name of "the most ancient and original
constitution of this kingdom." [55] Insofar as custom became a shib-
boleth, it doubtless did inhibit the acceptance of continental learning, but Coke was not being entirely cantankerous when he
squeezed awkward historical facts into a familiar but wrong interpretation. As Christopher Hill observed, it was largely owing to
Coke that "the struggle of common lawyers and Parliamentarians
was given historical significance and dignity, the prestige of a thou-
sand-year-old tradition." [56]

Ecclesiastical history was dominated by Reformation controversy. By the very act of making the Reformation, Henry VIII made
a history of the pre-Reformation, "establishing causes, motives
and significances." [57] His claim to be redressing the usurpation
of a foreign power was orthodox Protestant doctrine, propagated
by most authorities, including Foxe.[58] In the Catholic version
of Reformation history, given currency by Nicholas Sander in
1585, Henry VIII was a wicked, usurping tyrant, who "all this
while used all possible dissoluteness amongst the Queen's maids." [59]
The Catholic attempt to make Henry odious by comparison was,
however, doomed to failure in England. William Haller rightly
observed that "the bible, the prayer-book, the pulpit and the
book trade, working together, were to produce a change in the
mental lives of the people basic to the whole process of change to
come." [60] Foxe's *Book of Martyrs* made a fundamental contribu-

tion by persuading Englishmen that "to hold faithfully to the idea of history thus conceived was to be of the true Church which had come down in the process of time from the prime witnesses of the unique event which gives history its meaning and reveals its purpose." [61]

Even before Foxe wrote, Protestant tractarians had been mustering precedent and example to show that the new Protestants had had forerunners in the old Lollards, and that "it ys no new thinge, but an olde practyse of oure prelates . . . to defame the doctrine of christe with the name of new learninge and teachers thereof with the name of new masters." [62] William Tyndale, translator of the Bible; William Thynne, editor of Chaucer; John Gough, bookseller with reformist sympathies; John Leland; and, above all, John Bale had prepared the way for Foxe. Bale was perhaps the first to see that "the exile of the papacy from England meant the ending of a whole historical tradition, and that the advent of a Protestant settlement meant the need to reshape and rewrite English chronicles with a new, reformist outlook." [63]

The characteristic purpose of history, in whatever form it was written in the mid-sixteenth century, was to uphold and justify religion, law or country. All prefaces praised TRUTH; but nearly all texts ignored the awkward consequences. Still, by the end of the century, the learned world was becoming habituated to critical arguments founded on records and historical precedents. A search for recorded precedents dominated the political and religious controversies of the time. [64] Legends of British antiquity were gradually ignored, but common law myths of "Custom and the Immemorial" persisted, while Coke built his reputation on arguments from records. Advances in philology made possible the seventeenth-century breakthrough in knowledge of medieval and Anglo-Saxon history. Remote antiquity, however, still lay buried: the archaeologist's spade was not yet a weapon against myths sanctioned by manuscripts.

The Society of Antiquaries, founded in the mid-eighties, was characteristic of both the old and the new in historical scholarship. Most of the antiquaries were common lawyers, who brought with them their prejudices in favor of antiquity; they persistently antedated historical origins, but at least these men set great store by original research. In dealing with the early history of Parliament and the law, they failed to keep strictly to the sources and sometimes violated a sensible rule against conjecture. Dodderidge voiced the common opinion (which was the common law opinion) when, in discussing Parliament, he said, "So by looking back, it is easy to see the great antiquity of this high court, delivered as you see, from before the Romans; but never so dignified as since Queen Elizabeth's time." [65] Camden, who was not a common lawyer, knew better: he was careful to speak of "Parliament-like" assemblies before the Conquest. But what mattered was the fact that the antiquaries gathered in order to discuss scholarly questions on the basis of scholarly evidence as they understood it. This in itself was an important service to the wider community of learning; the antiquaries helped to establish a sound tradition of cooperative research; and they passed on to others their concern with discussion, evidence, and criticism.

Medieval historiography, as V. H. Galbraith observed, followed the fortunes of monasticism. [66] The suppression of the monasteries affected historiography in at least three ways: vast quantities of original records were thrown on the market as an unwanted surplus; the link binding historical research to the Church was broken; and owners of monastic lands acquired a vested interest in legal and historical scholarship justifying the Reformation. It took time for these changes to take effect: not until about 1560 did the English make serious efforts to halt the dispersal of records. Archbishop Parker was responsible for a new official attitude toward monastic and public records—they were to be preserved for the sake of their importance in controversy. Cecil and other officials shared his concern with stockpiling records for use as ammunition in the wars of truth. Private scholarly libraries also began to grow at this time: the impetus to collect was part of the impetus to convert. Along with the growth and consolidation of private libraries went improvements in public record keeping. All these changes made it easier for historians to engage in original research and to develop new skills. Access to the archives was indeed a strategic necessity: historiography could advance only through the Elizabethan record offices. Fortunately the record keepers themselves were history-minded men.

Historical scholarship, of course, did not survive on documents alone. A community of historians was necessary, as well as the habit of scholarly communication. The universities did not as yet provide for the needs of historians, who had to depend on patronage and self-help. Correspondence flourished: Camden's letters alone indicate the growing importance of foreign (especially French) influence on English scholarship. By 1600 the secular historical community in England was self-sustaining, its leaders receptive to new ideas from abroad. Finally, there were significant changes in the long-range "weather patterns" of the climate of opinion itself. In science, in religion, in politics, as well as in history and philosophy, all kinds of authorities were coming under attack in the sixteenth century. When Digges referred to the *"monstrous system* of Celestial globes . . . fashioned by the ancients" he was voicing a creative minority's discontent with ancient authority.[67] His attitude was increasingly heard, and it would eventually prevail.

Three basic patterns of change may now be suggested: (1) adaptation, (2) accretion, and (3) anomaly. Adaptation was characteristic of sixteenth-century scholarship—scholars borrowed and adapted each other's ideas almost as freely as they "imitated" the ancients. Accretion, or the collecting of information and manuscripts, was not confined to the early humanists; many Tudor scholars and gentlemen made collections on particular topics, some of which paved the way for revisions of accepted opinion. The pattern of accretion entailed the idea of verification from sources, even if the sources were derived or if, as in the case of Vesalian anatomy, they were "original" human cadavers. Anomaly was one of the patterns of change, since in nearly every field recognition of anomaly suggested new research problems. Vesalius perceived anomaly when he compared bodies and books—Galen's authority was undermined by dissection. Copernicus saw anomalies in the Ptolemaic system, which required ever more complicated calculations, but the Copernican "revolution" was not sudden, partly because his critics could point to anomalies in his own argument.[68] The sense of anachronism depended on the recognition of anomalies in the traditional interpretations of the history of earlier periods. Ultimately the authority of any interpretation or theory was no greater than the authority of the facts supporting it; yet the facts could not be understood, or even collected, without some theory. In *The Structure of Scientific Revolutions*, Thomas Kuhn observed that "no natural history can be interpreted in the absence of at least some implicit body of intertwined theoretical and methodological belief that permits selection, evaluation and criticism." [69] The same thing could be said of civil history, although there are obvious differences. Scientists become aware of anomaly against the background provided by a scientific paradigm—that is, against the shared rules, explanations, and standards of scientific practice which constitute a particular research tradition. In history, anomaly is recognized against the background of accepted interpretations (or "paradigms"), and against currently accepted standards and methods of historical verification.

The best example of a sixteenth-century historical "paradigm" is probably the English common law doctrine of custom, which asserted that the laws of the constitution were more ancient than any records.[70] At the end of the sixteenth century Lambarde, in *Archeion*, made this point in connection with the pre-Conquest history of Parliament: "Now as these written *authorities*, do undoubtedly confirme our assertion of this continuance of this manner of *Parliament:* So is there also unwritten *Law*, or *Prescription*, that doth no less infallibly uphold the same." [71] Lambarde himself was aware of anomaly (as some of his revisions indicate), yet neither he nor his successors gave up the theory, or paradigm, until forced to do so much later by an overwhelming awareness that the facts would not fit, and that other explanations were simpler.[72] In the meantime, it was awareness of anomaly that focused attention on the need for new, specialized studies; these culminated in Spelman's "theoreme" of feudalism in the seventeenth century—a new interpretation which challenged the old paradigm of "Custom and the Immemorial." [73]

Not every historian had to face problems of anomaly, which occurred mostly in legal and ecclesiastical history or controversy. In the case of territorial history—in the works of Stow, Camden, and the chroniclers, for example—the pattern of accretion was most evident. The *chronicle* or *survey* form was like shelving, on which a variety of facts could be stored: major changes of interpretation were seldom necessary. The incentive to add new facts—or simply to collect information and manuscripts—lay near the heart of the antiquarian movement of the age; and most good historians were also good antiquaries. In medicine, astronomy, and botany, as well as in Reformation theology, collections of sources and new facts lent support to new interpretations.[74]

The pattern of adaptation (including imitation and borrowing, which formed the basis of originality), showed up most clearly in the areas of style and method. Camden's *Britannia* was, in form, a large-scale "survey"; Lambarde's *Perambulation of Kent* was the model for later county surveys and histories; Stow's *Survey of London,* to some extent an imitation of medieval town history, in fact revealed how a town history should be written. The classical historians were deliberately taken as models; and classical history and theory provided Elizabethans with standards of judgment, as well as examples of philosophical precept.[75] Adaptation could and often did involve comparison—Bacon's concern with comparative natural and civil history owed something to the humanistic and Reformation interest in comparison and argument from analogy.

Method was obviously a crucial problem; and here the pattern of adaptation was most evident. The methods of comparison employed by French jurists were borrowed or imitated by Camden, Spelman, and other scholars. The use of philological evidence in the *Britannia* illustrates the close connection between philology and history. "It is a greater glory now to be a linguist than a Realist," Camden once remarked; but none knew better than he how to make use of philology.[76]

The pattern of adaptation was in one sense routine and obvious; in another sense it was an act of imagination, of connection, a part of creative scholarship and original thought. Historians and antiquaries could easily see the relevance of philology to history, but they were beginning to take an interest in many other ideas drawn from the stores of "general knowledge." Even a very brief survey of writers and patrons with historical interests will reveal that there was a great deal of "intellectual mobility" in sixteenth-century England. It was not an age of specialization and concentration but rather of "decompartmentalization," of expansion and broadening interests.[77] Among the Tudor schoolmasters, teachers, and university members were many able and intellectually versatile men, with strong humanistic interests. Even in the backward North and in Wales it was possible to get a good Tudor education; and in Yorkshire and elsewhere the gentry were "becoming increasingly aware both of the value of education and of their own social and administrative obligations." [78]

Camden and Sir Henry Savile illustrate different aspects of the trend toward combined intellectual operations. And William Salesbury, who radically influenced Welsh history by reshaping the Welsh literary tradition, was the embodiment of Protestant humanism in a Welsh setting: he was "a typical Renaissance polymath with a protean range of scholarly enquiry and equipment: linguist, lawyer, theologian, historian, scientist, litterateur, author and translator." [79]

Richard White (1539–1611) was a jurist and historian who became professor of civil and common law at Douai, and a priest after the death of his second wife. In his study of British history he had the encouragement of Thomas Goldwell (Bishop of St. Asaph), Sir Henry Peachan, and Sir Francis Englefield, former Privy Councillors to Queen Mary, as well as the benefit of correspondence with Cardinal Baronius. Clearly the Catholic interest in English history was no less significant, though less well publicized, than the Protestant.

Clement Adams (1519–1587) was a schoolmaster and author who "cut" the famous Cabot "mappe monde," which showed the Cabots' Atlantic explorations. Adams left an account in Latin of the first English trading voyage to Russia (written from dictation by Richard Chancellor, according to Richard Eden, the founder of British geography). This account was first translated and printed by Hakluyt. Such men were aware of the importance of discovery in a variety of historical fields. Whether or not they *taught* history, they at least did communicate their findings—and probably their enthusiasms—to a wider audience. They formed nuclei of personal intellectual influence in Tudor society.[80]

Royal officials were important members of the informal communications network that was slowly being built up among Tudor intellectuals. It is well known that Cromwell and Burghley were collectors with strong historical interests, and that both were important patrons of learning.[81] Burghley's private secretary, Richard Eden (d. 1576), is particularly interesting as an example of a minor Tudor official with eclectic scholarly interests: he translated Münster's *Cosmography* in 1553, wrote "The Decades of the Newe Worlde, or West India" in 1555 (when he escaped from a charge of heresy), revised Geminus's *Anatomy* in 1559; translated Martin Cortes's *Arte de Navigar* in 1561, and in 1574 translated John Taisner's *De Natura Magnetis*.

Sir Thomas Smith, ambassador and author of *De Republica Anglorum* and other works, may be the best known example of a Tudor intellectual in office. The rival of John Cheke as a classical scholar, he had the reputation of being an accomplished "physician, mathematician, astronomer, architect, historian and orator." [82] Appealing often to history to support his arguments in *De Republica Anglorum*, Smith was one of the first to compare English and continental law, and to stress the idea that historical change might be natural, not the result of political ambition or malice.

Turning to the medical profession, one is struck immediately by the number of doctors (or men with medical training) who were also interested in antiquities. Many of these men had received some training on the continent, often in Italy, and many were avid collectors of information, believing implicitly that the accumulation of facts would produce useful knowledge.[83] John Caius (1510–1575) was an outstanding English scholar-physician. After studying anatomy under Vesalius he toured Europe to meet important scholars. His conservatism in preferring Galen to Vesalius only illustrates a sixteenth-century paradox: intelligent men often united credulity with skepticism, and contributed to progress while holding firmly reactionary beliefs. In his early work on *The Sweate* (1552), he drew upon the connections between history and medicine; in his later years he wrote a partial history of Cambridge University.[84] A somewhat younger contemporary and friend of Caius, Thomas Hatcher, was trained in both law and medicine but practiced neither profession. He became chancellor of Cambridge University and a well-known antiquary, who was a friend and correspondent of John Stow. It was still relatively easy for scholars and physicians to exchange places—medical knowledge was textual, and scholarly competence was at least as important as experience. "Empiric" remained a synonym for quack. Yet the changes in London science and medicine in the later sixteenth century were contributing to an "intellectual revolution." [85]

Churchmen, like lawyers, were directly concerned with traditions and historical controversy. Merchants and businessmen were frequently mindful of the past as patrons of learning; but most often, perhaps, they responded to religious views—in particular to the Puritan criticism, or Anglican defense, of the Church. In this context it is essential to bear in mind that the Church was still an eminent intellectual institution. Prebends and church livings fell to many with a talent for controversy. And sometimes a cleric's knowledge was of interest to practical-minded laymen: Hakluyt was asked by a committee of the East India Company in 1601 to name the "principal places in the East Indies where trade is to be had." [86] The economic problems of the Church limited rewards, but no other institution provided for the needs of so many Tudor intellectuals: Bale, Leland, Parker, Nowell, Foxe, Hooker, Norden, Hakluyt, and Harrison were only a few of the better known writers connected with the Church. And clergymen seem to have been on the whole less specialized than lawyers—they became botanists, topographers, physicians, and astronomers as well as theologians, poets, antiquaries, and historians. Unfortunately it is not yet possible to say exactly how the role of clerical intellectuals was changing. [87]

Within the merchant class of Tudor England the booksellers and publishers were directly concerned with intellectual production. As book- and businessmen they were largely responsible for what was published; they regulated, subject to government censorship, the flow of communications to the public. Two publishers deserve special mention: Reyner (or Reginald) Wolfe and Richard Grafton. Wolfe, a native of Strasbourg, was related to John Wolfe of Zurich, who became host to many English Protestant refugees, including John Jewel. Reginald Wolfe became royal printer to Edward VI; and, despite his Protestantism, he figured in the original charter of the Stationers' Company in 1554. [88] The patron and benefactor of many authors, he proposed a universal history and cosmography which served as the starting point for Holinshed's *Chronicles*. Richard Grafton, best known as a chronicler, was in fact a prosperous London merchant who arranged for the printing of the Bible in English; he must have known his way through the private passageways of power in the 1530s and 1540s. Although inferior to Stow as a scholar, his own *Chronicle* was useful; and he was in a far better position to promote historical studies. [89]

At this point a brief summary may help to clarify the argument that these specimen biographies are meant to illustrate. A disclaimer must be entered at the start: problems of adaptation and change cannot be solved by merely correlating the various interests and activities of intellectuals. That intellectual mobility was evident in many careers can easily be shown; direct evidence of the extent, nature, and motives for borrowing is harder to come by. The correspondence of Erasmus, More, and Camden is revealing, but these men were scarcely typical. A biographical history of Tudor historiography might reveal much that is now hidden; but lacking this—and lacking reason to believe that there are masses of

original letters and papers by Tudor intellectuals waiting to be discovered—historians today must be content with generalizations
and conjectures.

Two professional fields influenced history steadily: law and theology. And historical arguments suffused theology and the law. Science was not yet defined as a separate profession; its influence on
history was less certain. It may be that the Copernican revolution
affected historians only indirectly, as a kind of fallout from the climate of opinion. Or it may be (as some recent historians of science
have held) that there was a closer connection between the methods of history and of science. This is still a dark plain, on which
anyone may stumble. What seems reasonably certain is that by the
late sixteenth century English historians were beginning to change
their ways and amend their methods. The process they followed
was not unique; others had already learned "first to doubt, then to
inquire, and then to discover." [90] Boundaries between different
scholarly fields could still be crossed with ease by men who were
not yet fenced and confined by their specialties; the various professions were only beginning to develop signs of "professionalism."
Historians borrowed freely, but their imitation of classical models
is still less than perfectly understood; and the borrowing of French
juristic techniques and styles of argument by Elizabethan and
Stuart historians has only recently attracted attention. The patterns
of adaptation, accretion, and anomaly can at best suggest the nature
of the changes that took place in Tudor historical thought; the
complexities of change, and the motives of innovation, remain to be
uncovered.

Since historiography exerted its influence on other intellectual
fields—and on politics as well—another question that must be
asked is: "What were the functions of historical evidence and argument in areas outside of history?" Quite obviously there are as
many answers to this question as there are fields of inquiry touch-
ing the past. The crucial *generalization* has been made by J. G. A.
Pocock in his essay on "The Origins of the Study of the Past":

> A society normally consists of a number of continuous activities and
> a number of continuous structures, and if the function of the past is
> to ensure continuity, it may be predicted that any society may have
> as many pasts as it has elements of continuity, and that different in-
> dividuals may be aware of different pasts, varying as they are asso-

ciated with different activities, structures or other elements of continuity.[91]

The complex awareness of a "past-relationship" is characteristic of all modern societies; and it is precisely in the midst of change that this awareness has been most highly cultivated and prized.

In traditional societies, relationships between past and present were apt to be taken for granted, not investigated as problems. Medieval art forms reflected the rudimentary sense of anachronism in medieval society. Although this was also true to a degree of Tudor art forms, and although Tudor society was in many ways still traditional, indeed medieval, there were crucial differences. Many of these differences have been investigated by Tudor historians, whose findings have already been summarized. The argument here is that Tudor society was characterized by a greater degree of historical consciousness than, for example, Lancasterian society had been. The evidence for this view is not statistical (nor could it be in any very meaningful sense) but rather presumptive: that is, the evidence depends on the coherence of sources and secondary works which support the generalization. The expansion of historical investigation in the sixteenth century, the extension of the idea of verification by appeals to original sources, the emergence of the history play, and the development of historical controversy about the Church—these go together, and are not characteristic of an earlier, more traditional society. The medieval Church thought of tradition in terms of the writings of the fathers and the succession of the popes; the Reformation necessitated a much wider appeal to historical evidence. Historical consciousness, like other "instrumental concepts," will prove useful to the extent that it helps to make sense of a multitude of details and problems in a particular period. It is a heuristic device, not a fact about Tudor society in the sense that Henry VIII's right arm was a fact.

At the time of the Reformation, when the traditional relationship between past and present was ruptured, the first instinct of the political intellectuals was to restore it.[92] This required a vastly more complicated kind of argument than at first sight appeared. It was not enough, though it was important, for Cromwell to arrange for the republication of Marsiglio's *Defensor Pacis*. The doctrine of papal usurpation was useful but not decisive. With the advent of Protestantism in England a new element was introduced, which laid bare the truth of Hobbes's observation: "No man can have in mind a conception of the future for the future is not yet. But of our conceptions of the past we make a future." [93]

One of the many pieces of evidence that suggest how deeply historical argument had penetrated Protestant theology by the early seventeenth century was the catechetical work, A *Body of Divinitie* (1614). Attributed to James Ussher (who repudiated it), the book held that the Bible was validated by the uniform testimony of men in all ages. In the beginning of the world God "delivered his Word by *Revelation,* and continued the knowledge thereof by *Tradition.*" [94] The crucial question was this: "If that the Scripture can be written by men which are subject unto infirmities, how can it be accounted the word of God?" The answer was a circular one: generations of men have testified to the truth and authority of Scriptures; and "we may learn out of the testimonies themselves . . . that God hath established them for ever." Among the many reasons for believing them was that "the writers of the Holy Scriptures are the most ancient of all others." [95] Although not historically or methodologically convincing, this argument at least did embrace history and touch on problems of method. It was characteristic that an appeal should be made to that which was "most ancient." In the statutes of the realm, and in the writings of humanists, heralds, lawyers, and churchmen, ancientness implied virtue; truth was warranted by length of pedigree as well as by reason or evidence.[96] The assumptions of the common lawyers in particular were Burkean: long continuance was presumptive evidence of excellence and rationality. Sir John Davies spoke of *ius non scriptum* as a *"peculiar invention* of this Nation, and delivered over from age to age by *Tradition,* for the common lawe of England is a *Tradition*—learned by *Tradition* as well as by Books." [97] Both Protestants and Catholics were inclined to share such admiration for tradition, although only up to a point. The appeal to the past was useful, but faith was crucial; Protestants in particular raised faith above reason. Against the papists "who teach that the Scriptures receive their Authority from the Church," it was urged that the final testimony of God's spirit was in the "hearts of his faithful, as it is proper to the Word of God," this conviction being greater than "any humane Perswasions grounded upon reason or witnesses of men." Thus ultimately "All traditions, revelations, decrees of Councels, opinions of Doctors, etc., are to be embraced so farre forth as they may be proved out of the Divine Scriptures, and not otherwise . . ." [98]

The corruption of primitive nature was a doctrine that took many forms, and it helps to explain the sixteenth-century worship of antiquity. The fall of man implied a theory of progressive degeneration, as did the pagan idea of a golden age. But it was the worship of antiquity that made the conservative seventeenth-century bishop, Godfrey Goodman, hold so stubbornly to the theory of decay.[99] The immediate problem for sixteenth-century religious controversialists was to assess responsibility. Archbishop Parker concurred with Lambarde that the "Popish party" in the eleventh century had labored "under pretence of correcting, to corrupt all the ancient writings, to make them look more favorably upon their backsliding church and sophisticated doctrines." [100]

Concern with the sanctions of antiquity was thus part of the intellectual ferment of the age. Christians even before St. Augustine had stressed the continuity of divine tradition. But after the Reformation, when there was no longer a single head governing the visible Christian Church, Protestants as well as Catholics had to distinguish between the practice of antiquity and "the practice of approved antiquity." [101]

The "historical" attack on the authority of the pope in the Act in Restraint of Appeals had consequences that are difficult to assess but that cannot excusably be ignored. The "imperial crown" became an accepted title, referred to in statutes, speeches, and books.[102] From 1533 onward English historians tended to build their interpretation of the Act of Appeals on a new and in some ways mistaken reading of the medieval statutes of praemunire.[103] Most sixteenth-century statutes were concerned with the reformation of abuses, with finances, or with remedial legislation. But the great acts redefining the constitution under Henry, Edward, Mary, and Elizabeth were broader in scope. Like many of the Tudor proclamations, which in effect were also legislative, their preambles appealed to historical precedents as an important justification for policy changes. The Edwardian act of uniformity, for example, spoke of having "aswel eye and respecte to the moste syncere and pure Christian Religion taught by Scripture, as to the usages in the Primatyve Churche . . ." [104] The preamble to the act declaring Mary legitimate outlined a whole Catholic theory of the Reformation; and the first act of Elizabeth's first Parliament began with a historical explanation of how England had prospered under Henry VIII and suffered misfortune when "usurped" and foreign powers were brought back under Philip and Mary.[105] These appeals to the past were symptomatic of the growing concern with historical precedents and arguments in both Church and state. The harrowing of tradition was preparing the ground for historical politics, and a new historiography.

Diplomats, like lawyers, had long been accustomed to cite precedents and reasons for doing what they wanted to do. But when Henry VIII undertook to justify his war with the Scots in 1542 he spoke directly of history as the proof of his case. The royal declaration asserted that the kings of Scotland had always acknowledged the kings of England as their superior lords, and that this was proved both by documents (i.e., precedents) and by history. Appropriately the humanist classical phrases about history were invoked:

> First as concerning histories, which be called wytnesses of times, the light of truth, and the life of memorie, and finally the convenient ways and means whereby the Things of antiquitie maye be brought to men's knowledge, They show as playnely This matter as could be wyshed or required, with such a consent of wryters, as could not so agree upon an untruth, conteyning a declaration of such matter as hath most evident probabilitie and apparauence.[106]

The discussion of evident probability began with Brute and his children's inheritance—but then this was not yet considered a frivolous argument.

Finally, and not least importantly, there was the constant if imponderable influence of the English Bible and the habit of Bible reading in England after the Reformation. The radical distinction between the Bible as history and the Bible as doctrine, or between the literal sense of a passage and the historical sense, is modern; Luther and the Reformers would have none of it.[107] It has been argued that modern historical method grew up in response to the hermeneutical tasks of interpretation.[108] Although that is by no means the whole story, it is true that historiography was profoundly influenced by Biblical scholarship and by the printing of large numbers of vernacular Bibles. Not only did Biblical scholars, especially Protestants, have to contend with the problems of translation and historical identification, but both they and the common readers were committed to understanding the Bible as the literal historical truth; the "factualness" of the Bible confirmed the reader's faith in its divine inspiration. Christ's admonition to search the Scriptures (John 5: 39) was taken to heart by a Protestant nation. The story of the Lollard Bible, told by Margaret Deanesley in *The Lollard Bible and Other Medieval Biblical Versions* (1920), has since been taken up and expanded; and the *Cambridge History of the Bible* (1963–) is only the latest in a long line of books on the making of the Bible. Surprisingly little attention has been paid, however, to the fact that the English Bible in the sixteenth century was read and understood—and indeed searched—as history and for the sake of historical examples. Moreover, in the Preface to the Geneva Bible (1560) it was explained that "certeyne mappes of Cosmographie" had been added, "which necessarely serve for the perfect vnderstanding and memorie of diuers places and countreys, partely described, and partely by occasion touched, boothe in the old and newe Testament." [109] Englishmen became "the People of a book, and that book was the Bible." Gradually Biblical stories and Biblical cadences permeated English literature and thought. The official beginning of the process was an act of state which, according to Froude, "laid the foundation-stone on which the whole later history of England, civil as well as ecclesiastical, has been reared." [110]

The full history of the uses of scriptural history remains to be written, but clearly the historical consciousness of Englishmen was rapidly expanded by the "open Bible." [111] The sharing of the Bible was perhaps even more significant than the controversies provoked by competing translations and interpretations. The Bible rather than the classics was the source of much that was most characteristic in English political theory, and in English attitudes toward the past.[112]

It has been suggested that a society is "modern" when it becomes conscious of its past, "when this past is shared by the vast majority of the society, and when it can be used as a national basis to determine and validate behaviour." [113] The contribution of Tudor intellectuals to this idea of the past is unquestionable.[114]

Several reasons for the changes in Tudor historiography and for the expansion of historical consciousness have been given in the preceding pages. In the rest of this chapter the focus will be on examples of different types of Tudor historiography; the choice of examples is, of course, arbitrary. No attempt can be made to survey the history of English historiography from 1485 to 1603, since obviously that would require another book. Although different types of historical writing emerged and developed at different times, a purely chronological approach (suggesting a sequence of types) has not been attempted. Only five types of Tudor historical writing will be discussed: (1) humanist history, (2) chronicle history, (3) biography, (4) polemics, and (5) descriptive history, or survey. Few writers since Sir Francis Bacon have written on the genera and species of historical writing; and there are few modern studies of the intellectual traditions which influenced Tudor historians. C. L. Kingsford's *English Historical Literature in the Fifteenth Century* (1913) provides an indispensable introduction; F. S. Fussner's *The Historical Revolution* (1962) contains a chapter on the varieties of history in the early seventeenth century, as well as chapters on Stow and Cotton, but does not emphasize the period before 1580. The mid-century decades have been only very haphazardly explored. The main chronological outlines of Tudor historiography are known, thanks in part to biographical articles, a few books on major historians, and editorial introductions to a few important works. G. G. Coulton's chapters in *Medieval Panorama* (1938) on the importance of the open Bible and the searching of Scriptures in the vernacular contain important insights into the significance of Bible-reading habits for historiography. C. A. Patrides in *The Phoenix and the Ladder* (1964) discusses the rise and decline of the Christian view of history. Only F. J. Levy's *Tudor Historical Thought* (1967) covers the entire Tudor period; but while this book provides a kind of aerial survey of Tudor historical writing, it does not attempt to measure the contour elevations of the social ground—the context of historiography. In short, there are discoveries still to be made and revisions still to be published.

All of the early Tudor humanists wrote under the influence of ancient or foreign models. Polydore Vergil and Sir Thomas More represented early humanist history at its best; Sir Thomas Elyot, diplomatist, translator, and political theorist, expressed the humanist attitude toward history as an educational force. Polydore Vergil's life and writings can now be studied in Denys Hay's *Polydore Vergil, Renaissance Historian and Man of Letters* (1952) and in Hay's edition of the *Anglica Historia* (1950), covering the years from 1485 to 1537. A valuable Tudor translation of parts of the *Anglica*

Historia was edited by Sir Henry Ellis for the Camden Society in the nineteenth century.[115] The importance of Vergil's criticism of the British history myths has been put in historical perspective by Sir Thomas Kendrick in *British Antiquity*. The *Anglica Historia* was not only representative of Italian humanist attitudes, and important because it exerted a powerful influence on subsequent historiography, it was also a most valuable source for the reigns of Henry VII and Henry VIII. Vergil's manuscript, covering events up until 1513, was written in 1512–1513; the first edition was printed at Basel in 1534, covering events up to 1509; only in the third edition (Basel, 1555) were events brought down to 1538. In his use of evidence, Vergil demonstrated that he was a true humanist, who sought information from all kinds of sources, but who nevertheless eschewed the barbarity of long textual quotations. Depending primarily on standard ancient writers for the early history of Britain (as all historians had to do before archaeological techniques were invented), Vergil was sensible and shrewd, although he did not add much to what medieval historians had known. The case was different when he came to deal with the medieval chronicles and with contemporary events.

Vergil made good use of manuscripts and printed sources, but he was especially perceptive in his treatment of linguistic and oral traditions, in his use of the memories of his older contemporaries, and in his direct observation of English customs.[116] Structurally the superiority of Vergil's narrative to earlier monastic chronicles is apparent, although it took at least a generation for this superiority to be recognized. Vergil's critical attitude toward British myths was to some extent the result of his detachment as an Italian, but the viewpoint of Urbino would have meant little had he not absorbed the humanist traditions of source criticism. In his treatment of the Brute legend and in his discussions of contemporary Tudor history one may observe the ways in which his mind worked. He could be swayed by passion, as is evident in his treatment of Wolsey (whom he detested, not without reason, for having arranged his arrest); but Olympian detachment about one's own enemies is seldom possible. Vergil's skepticism about the Trojan ancestry of the British was based on a number of common-sense arguments, rather than on the marshaling of original historical sources. Like most sixteenth-century historians he spoke often of truth, yet admitted that in many areas truth could scarcely be known. Conjectures were inevitable.

Many writers, including some of the best antiquaries, believed in the Trojan myth. The "British History" of Geoffrey of Monmouth was accepted and reiterated, with varying degrees of subtlety, by Caxton, Grafton, Leland, Bale, and others, and treated with varying degrees of skepticism, but not rejected, by Fabyan, Twynne, Rastell, Elyot, and probably More and Colet. "Historie is a full rehersall and declaration of things don, not a gesse, or divination," Vergil wrote, but this seemed to mean that he would present all arguments, including those he in fact rejected: "I will nether affirme as trew, nether reproove as false, the judgement of one or other as concerning the originall of soe auncient a people, referring all things, as wee have don hertofore, to the consideracion of the reader." [117] Vergil did, however, give reasons for preferring his own view that the original inhabitants of Britain were not the descendants of the Trojan Brute. Ancient writers had failed to mention Brute; and, since Albion was visible from the shores of France, "it is not to bee thought that at enie time it lacked inhabitants, which might then receave them when all other londes didd, not awayghting or intertaining the exiled or hurtful roge runninge awaye owt of Spaine, Germanie, Fraunce, or Italie, as late Historiens make reporte." [118] Nothing was more obscure, uncertain, and unknown than the affairs of the British from the beginning; the "newe historie" of Geoffrey and his followers, including Fabyan, was to be included, not because it was true, but because this was required by wisdom and the times.[119] Vergil was not an utter iconoclast, as he has sometimes been pictured, nor was he entirely emancipated from medieval credulity (as Denys Hay has shown), but he introduced more into the writing of English history than the mere exercise of logic.[120] The complexity of Vergil's thought, unlike that of the best modern scientific or sociological historians, was a humanistic mixture of verifiable and unverifiable beliefs. Making use of a number of different traditions dating from different times, he showed himself to be both a skeptic and a true believer, a reformer and a conservative, a shrewd historical critic and a naïve antiquary.

In *De Inventoribus Rerum,* a book on the origins of customs, inventions, laws, arts, sciences, religious beliefs, towns, and time, Vergil was original—in making such a collection and in his promise of comparative history—and quite old-fashioned (a kind of Renaissance Isidore of Seville) in his search for "originators" or individual inventors.[121] The concept of historical process (or even the idea of necessity as the mother of invention) was still foreign to Vergil, who nevertheless, with all his inconsistencies, was a salutary influence on English historiography. One comment he made was ironically appropriate: "I thincke it mei parte severallie to open bothe the newe and oulde, that the more mei travaille is, the more plesure the reader maye conceave, when in reading he shall note somme things worthie credite, somm worthie favor, and somme meete to be laughed at." [122] Vergil's own work contained, however, more things worthy of credit than meet to be laughed at.

The explanations that Vergil offered ranged from straightforward diplomatic or political analyses to the presumed workings of evil spirits.[123] He combined a traditional belief in portents with an equally traditional belief in the operations of divine providence; he was given to pointing the political and religious morals of history; and he drew the characteristic parallels of the humanist, although, in order to avoid trouble, he preferred to find his analogues in antiquity rather than in the present. Contemporary history was and remained a dangerous game. Ralegh best characterized it: "Whosoever, in writing a modern history, shall follow truth too near the heels, it may happily strike out his teeth." [124] Vergil was not afraid to express his opinion of Wolsey, for this was safe in 1534. In describing Wolsey and interpreting his actions Vergil was often unjust, usually uncharitable, and almost never subtle or perceptive. The limitations of his psychological explanations were nowhere more apparent; he was willing to make psychology conform to personal animosity, and to subordinate explanation to rhetoric in his treatment of the cardinal:

> The enjoyment of such an abundance of good fortune is to be reckoned most praiseworthy if it is showered upon sober, moderate, and self-controlled men, who are not proud in their power, nor are made arrogant with their money, nor vaunt themselves in other fortunate circumstances. None of these characteristics could be described in Wolsey, who, acquiring so many offices at almost the same time, became so proud that he considered himself the peer of kings . . . His own odiousness was truly complete, because he claimed he could undertake himself almost all public duties.[125]

This was the view of Wolsey which passed into the main stream of English historiography.

The organization of the *Anglica Historia*, proceeding by kings' reigns after the introductory description of the land and the people, owed something to medieval works, and more perhaps to the precedent of Suetonius. From the point of view of Tudor historiography, the organization of the work was less important than Vergil's critical asides, factual details, and new interpretations. Even Vergil's detractors found his book indispensable; and the best chroniclers, such as Hall, took from Vergil concepts which leavened their own work.[126] Before Vergil wrote, English printed historiography was best represented by "Caxton's Chronicles," by Fabyan's *Chronicle* (1516), and perhaps by Arnold's dull London *Chronicle* (1502). More's *History of King Richard III* was not printed until 1557 (in English), although More had begun the composition in 1513. The influence of Vergil's humanism can be traced in Hall's *Chronicle*, first published in 1548—a work which remained a standard throughout the Tudor period and beyond. Hall derived from Vergil three fundamental notions, which Denys Hay has identified: history was the record of the past set forth in a form designed to preserve the memory of fame and glory, it was "memory by literature"; history was nevertheless based on a critical use of sources; and history must have an argument.[127] In the long run these ideas would revolutionize English historiography; in the process each idea would be transformed: literature, science, and a philosophy of history would result.

The Tudor version of fifteenth-century history, fixed by Hall, was thus indirectly the product of Polydore Vergil's pen. The Tudor picture of Richard III was, to an even greater extent, set by Vergil and by Sir Thomas More, whose influence on Tudor writers, including Shakespeare, confirmed the image of the usurping, crook-backed villain.[128] The publication history of More's *History of King Richard III* indicates something of its importance: English versions of the manuscript were incorporated into "Hardyng's Chronicle" in 1543, into "Halle's Chronicle," printed by Grafton in 1548 and 1550, and into Rastell's edition of *The Workes of Sir Thomas More, Knyght* in 1557. The peculiarities of More's Latin and English texts, and the problems of method, dating, sources, and influence have been dealt with in matchless detail and clarity by Richard Sylvester in his edition of the *History* (1963). The Tudor chroniclers wanted More's *History* for three reasons: More's information was grist for the chronicler's mills; the portrait of Richard was unsurpassed as propaganda for the Tudors; and the moral lessons satisfied the moralizing taste of the age. The pattern of accretion in historiography can readily be illustrated by the use made of More's manuscript by chroniclers to build up the history of Richard III; Grafton, for example, edited More's manuscript and interpolated passages in order to adapt it to the chronicle form, in which conveying information was the primary goal. The literary virtues of More's *History* may have impressed the chroniclers, but certainly the book's moral judgments were most highly prized.

It would be almost impossible to overestimate the Tudor taste for moral and political sermonizing. Hall's chronicle, published as *The Union of the Two Noble and Illustre Famelies of Lancaster and Yorke*, began with a series of historical arguments designed to acquaint readers with ancient and modern precedents against rebellion, in countries throughout Europe; the worst consequences were, of course, to be illustrated in the quarrels between Lancaster and York. Nearly all writers, including Vergil, More, and the humanists, believed that history had lessons to teach, and that one of the prime duties of a historian was to extract these lessons. Readers of Grafton's *Chronicle* were told in 1569 a few of the things that could be learned from history:

> Kings maye learne to depende upon God, and acknowledge his governance in their protection: the nobilitie may reade the true honor of their auncestours: The Ecclesiasticall state maye learne to abhorre trayterous practices and indignities done against kings by the Popishe vsurping clergie: high and lowe may shonne rebellions by their dreadfull effectes, and beware how they attempt against right, how vnhable soeuer the person be that beareth it . . .[129]

More's *History of King Richard III* was as Hyperion to a satyr when compared with any Tudor chronicle, but More's superiority was literary; he shared with the chroniclers a taste for historical villains and moral certainties.

More was considerably less critical of his sources than Polydore Vergil, although both men made important contributions to historiography. An accurate reporter of contemporary opinion about Richard III, More knew how to write sustained narrative, and he was probably right to call his book *The History of King Richard III*. It was more than just biography; and although it was also, to a degree, a tract of the times, it remains a great literary portrait. Having profited from reading the classical historians—especially

Thucydides, Sallust, Suetonius, and Tacitus—More was able to adapt their devices and express the irony of history as no Englishman had done before him. More's sense of irony was apparent throughout the narrative; he used irony to make the Erasmian, humanist point that *realpolitik* was essentially wicked and self-defeating. Sylvester has pointed out how the irony grew out of the structure of historical facts. The ironic historian contrasted the smooth-flowing calm suface of events with the vicious, deadly currents beneath; and he counted on his readers' being able to recognize literary and historiographical reflections.[130] A single great sentence did not make the narrative great, but More knew how to create the most effective setting for such a telling sentence: "And so they said that these matters bee kynges games, as it were stage playes, and for the more part played vpon scafoldes." [131]

Kings' games were the subject of the book; Richard played them with villainous pleasure, but his own days were numbered. The murder of the princes in the Tower was tragically inevitable. More prefaced the story with a remark calculated to insure the reader's belief in Richard's guilt: "I shall rehearse you the dolorous end of those babes, not after euery way that I haue heard, but after that way yt I haue so hard by suche men & by such meanes, as me thinketh it wer hard but it should be so." [132] Taken by a traitorous tyrant, and murdered for ambition's sake, the princes were victims, whose fate in a providential universe all men should ponder: "God neuer gaue this world a more notable example, neither in what vnsuretie standeth this worldly wel or what mischief worketh the prowde enterprise of an hyghe heart, or finally what wretched end ensueth such despiteous crueltie." [133] This was a lesson that More thought England should learn—tyranny had existed before Henry VII, and it might return; the problem of tyranny was the unifying theme of the narrative.[134] What More did for English historiography was to make history truly a part of literature: Richard III recalled Tiberius, and More's narrative skill recalled that of Tacitus. If Polydore Vergil represented the humanist as historical critic, More represented the humanist as literary artist —and Elyot, the humanist as educator.

The Book Named the Governor was published by Elyot in 1531; it was one of the most influential works of the early Tudor period. Elyot's career has been described in detail by S. E. Lehmberg in *Sir Thomas Elyot, Tudor Humanist* (1960), which provides the best bibliographical survey of Elyot's works, and of works about Elyot. Lehmberg also edited the Everyman edition of the *Governor*, which was the first edition to adopt modern spelling. In his introduction, Lehmberg pointed out how Elyot first defined the virtues of a governor and then (particularly in the last two books) gave historical examples of each virtue: he noted that Elyot appeared to be more concerned with the historical illustrations than with the virtues themselves.[135] Elyot's account of Prince Hal's wrath (Book II, Chapter 6) was so well done and convincing that it was repeated by Hall, Holinshed, and Shakespeare. The historical awareness displayed by Elyot was remarkable; the *Governor* is evidence that early Tudor humanism was contributing to the growth of a new idea of history.

Elyot's purpose in writing was to employ his learning for the benefit of his country, and for the recreation and profit of all readers of noble or gentle courage. His book was filled with histories and sentences which he thought would repay careful and frequent reading.[136] Education of the governors should begin at birth "for, as some ancient writers do suppose, often times the child sucketh the vice of his nurse with the milk of her pap." [137] Beginning at about the age of fourteen young men should be introduced to cosmography, partly to prepare them for an understanding of histories.[138] The student should be taught to note and mark "not only the order and elegancy in declaration of the history but also the occasion of the wars, the counsels and preparations on either part, the estimation of the captains, the manner and form of their governance, the continuance of the battle, the fortune and success of the whole affairs." Similarly the causes of prosperity and decay in civil affairs should be noted; then "surely if a nobleman do thus seriously and diligently read histories I dare affirm there is no study or science for him of equal commodity and pleasure, having regard to every time and age." [139] Here were the conventional humanist reasons for studying history, and the characteristic sixteenth-century assumptions about the relation of past to present.

Elyot believed that the lessons of history could easily be lifted out of the works of ancient historians or medieval chroniclers. He had nothing to say about the differences between past and present experience, or about the unique problems of each age. Continuities were taken for granted; discontinuities were ignored. Only a very few writers of the sixteenth century perceived that there could be serious problems of discontinuity. The recognition of anachronism, possible to philological critics, did not destroy faith in the under- lying continuities of political and social life. Sensitivity to anachro- nism was quite compatible with historical pessimism and with the widely held doctrine of the world's decay; the idea of progress came later. Elyot was perhaps more optimistic than most Chris- tians, for he believed that men could improve themselves through education. The noblemen of his own time were less excellent in learning than the noblemen among the ancient Romans and Greeks; but the causes of this decay were pride, avarice, negligence of parents, and lack of good masters and teachers.[140] The human- ists in general shared Elyot's faith in education; but "learning" was still thought of as an island to be occupied and held, not as a pro- cess of expansion, carrying men beyond known boundaries.

In his chapter "Of experiences which have preceded our time, with a defense of histories," Elyot expressed—as well as any single writer—the characteristic Tudor beliefs about history. If his views were still somewhat unusual in 1531, they were by no means un- usual by 1601. It will therefore be appropriate to quote at some length Elyot's definition of history:

> First it is to be noted that it is a Greek name, and cometh of a word or verb in Greek, *historeo*, which doth signify to know, to see, to ensearch, to enquire, to hear, to learn, to tell, or expound unto other. And then must history which cometh thereof be wondrous profitable, which leaveth nothing hid from man's knowledge, that unto him may be either pleasant or necessary. For it not only re- porteth the gests or acts of princes or captains, their counsels and attempts, enterprises, affairs, manners in living good and bad, descriptions of regions and cities, with their inhabitants, but also it bringeth to our knowledge the forms of sundry public weals with augmentation and decays and occasion thereof; moreover precepts, exhortations, counsels, and good persuasions, comprehended in quick sentences and eloquent orations. Finally so large is the com- pass of that which is named history, that it comprehendeth all thing that is necessary to be put in memory.[141]

It is not surprising that the author of this definition inspired by the classics should also, as a Christian, have considered the Bible to be history as well as doctrine: "There is no doctrine, be it either di- vine or human, that is not either all expressed in history or at the least mixed with history." [142] Grafton's *Chronicle* referred to Moses as "the deuine Prophet and Historiographer." [143] Most of the Tudor chroniclers, polemicists, antiquaries, and educators favored the study of history, although not all would have agreed with Elyot that even lying historians might be profitable. The implications of Elyot's notion that history encompassed doctrine were just beginning to be explored in the sixteenth century. Not until Selden published his *History of Tithes* in 1618 was the threat of history to doctrine at last understood.[144]

Tudor chronicles have received much less attention than they deserve. The value of Hall and Stow to the modern historian has been noted; but even Stow's work on records is still little appreciated, despite the efforts of C. L. Kingsford, who rightly said that Stow "was the first English historian to make systematic use of the Public Records for the purpose of his work." [145] Kingsford's masterly editing of *A Survey of London* revealed the extent of Stow's record learning; and Stow's familiarity with the chronicles was traced in *English Historical Literature of the Fifteenth Century*. The earliest historical work by Stow, *A Summary of English Chronicles* (1565), was a compendium but a promising one; the enlarged editions of 1570 and 1575 showed much more evidence of independent research; and in his *Annales of England* (1592) he abandoned the cruder chronology of the city chronicle in favor of regnal years, more in keeping with the national scale of the work. It was not the history he had hoped to write, and it was uneven in value, but where he undertook his own research it was and still is of considerable interest—especially for the reign of Henry VI. For the last ten years of that King's reign Stow included in his text numerous documents, otherwise lost, which entitle this section of the work "to take rank as an original authority of importance." [146] Stow was conspicuous above all his predecessors for the care he took in providing full marginal citations of authorities. His recognition of the importance of scholarly documentation constituted a great advance in historiography. The care with which he copied and reproduced extracts from chronicles and other sources can still be admired; in fact his scholarly integrity merits imitation: not everyone has yet learned to work to Stow's standards. Apart from the question of form, Stow wrote the best history of England that had appeared up to his death in 1605.[147] The *Annales* were not, however, the most characteristic expression of

Tudor historical thought, nor was Stow's work (except perhaps for the *Survey of London*) anything like as influential as Holinshed's *Chronicles*, first published in 1578.

The original plans of Reyner Wolfe, the printer, called for the publication of a "Universal History" of the world; English chronicles were to be a part of universal history. The printers who took up Wolfe's idea after his death in 1573 were more realistic: they limited the publication to a large-scale history of England, Ireland, and Scotland. Raphael Holinshed was made responsible for the chronicles that would bear his name, but the work was accomplished by a syndicate. The principal members were Holinshed himself; William Harrison, author of "The Description of Britain"; John Hooker, alias Vowell, the Essex antiquary; Francis Thynne, attorney and later Lancaster herald; Abraham Fleming, poet and author of a history of English earthquakes; and John Stow. The details of the printing of "Holinshed's Chronicles," and of the suppression of offensive passages in the first edition may be found in the *Dictionary of National Biography*. Kingsford rightly observed that the great folios of 1578 and especially the second, enlarged edition of 1587 in three volumes constituted "the first complete history of England of an authoritative character, composed in English and in a continuous narrative, to appear in print." [148] Although on the score of originality of conception and scholarship a better claim could be made for Stow, Holinshed was first in the field and first in popularity. If Holinshed lacked Stow's impartiality, and copied Hall's prejudices about the fifteenth century without really understanding the significance of Hall's theme of union, he nevertheless provided the prime material for Shakespeare's vision of English history. It will therefore be appropriate to deal at greater length with the historical thought of Holinshed and his helpers.

Holinshed's *Chronicles* began with "An Historicall description of the Iland of Britanie; with a briefe rehersall of the nature and qualities of the people of England, and such commodities as are to be found in the same. Comprehended in three bookes, and written by W. H." [149] In the "Epistle Dedicatorie," William Harrison, the author, observed that he "neuer made any choise of stile, or words, neither regarded to handle this Treatise in such precise order and method as manie other would haue done . . ." He added that he hoped "this foule frizeled Treatise of mine will prooue a spur to others better learned, more skilfull in Chorographie, and of greater

iudgment . . ." This was not entirely the conventional self-depre-
ciation of an Elizabethan; Harrison and his fellow historians were
aware of their own deficiencies, but they also had reason to look
forward to progress in historiography. Even though the "Description" was a lively and interesting work, Harrison was right to dis-
claim literary distinction. By and large, none of the Tudor chroniclers were stylists—certainly none could write with the easy
grace and narrative brilliance of Sir Thomas More. Neither Harrison nor Holinshed attempted to explain events by their causes (the
exceptions are piddling), and in this they were typical chroniclers.
Harrison did, however, offer some observations on chronology
which he used as a pretext for making a characteristic Tudor observation:

> There is a certeine period of kingdomes, of 430 yeares, in which
> commonlie they suffer some notable alteration. And as in the afore-
> said season there is set a time to increase and decaie, so we find
> that before the execution of God's purpose doth come to passe, in
> changing the estate of things, sundrie tokens are sent, whereby
> warning is given, that without repentence he will come and visit our
> offenses.[150]

The notion of portents—tokens of wrath to come—was strong in
Tudor historical consciousness; Shakespeare in more than one play
made good use of the "precurse of fierce events, / As harbingers
preceding still the fates / And prologue to the omen coming
on . . ." [151]

Following Harrison's "Description" was Holinshed's "The Historie of England, from the time that it was first inhabited, vntill
the time that it was last conquored." Holinshed followed the "opinion of most writers" in stating that "Brute did first inhabit this
land, and called it after his owne name, Britaine, in the yeere after
the creation of the world 2855, and in the yeere before the incarna-
tion of Christ 1108." [152] This historical nonsense was still generally believed, although with misgivings by the learned. Abraham
Fleming, in his Preface, "To the Readers Studious in histories," admitted that the early chronological reckonings might not be abso-
lutely accurate but urged that the computations "were justifiable
by their originals"—a pomposity that it would be difficult to
match.[153] Following Holinshed's "Historie" (which of course
broke off in 1066) came a description of Ireland, followed by John

Hooker's translation of the Irish history of Giraldus Cambrensis, and Stanihurst's version of Campion's Irish History. The principle of description followed by chronicle was repeated for Scotland. Only in the third volume (of the second edition) was the history of England taken from 1066 up to the events of 1587. John Hooker, who was responsible for the Irish history from the death of Henry VIII to 1587, dedicated his work to Sir Walter Ralegh. The Dedication is one of the primary documents of Elizabethan historiography, for it includes nearly all the traditional beliefs about history and the uses of history: "Among all the infinit good blessings, right honorable, which the Lord God hath bestowed vpon vs, I thinke none more expedient and necessarie, than the vse and knowledge of histories and chronicles." Referring to Cicero's definition of history as "the witnesse of time, the light of truth, the life of memorie, and the mistresse of life," Hooker advised all men to have recourse to the study of histories, for St. Augustine himself had said no less: "Histories doo teach and aduertise vs as well of the things to come, as of the things past." [154]

Cicero and Thucydides, the Bible and St. Augustine, ancients and moderns—all contributed to the Tudor idea of history. Biblical precedents were perhaps especially important to a Protestant nation, but Roman and Greek examples carried great weight; presumably all nations would do well to follow the Roman practice:

> For it was a common thing among the Romans, not that onelie they would make recourse in all doubtfull matters to their owne annales: but what so euer they found in the like in anie other nation or commonwealth, which might further them in anie thing touching their owne affaires, they would draw the same into an example for themselues to follow, which was no small benefit to their commonwealth.[155]

Precedents meant much, but patriotism meant even more to the Elizabethan historians. Hooker's praise of English history and historiography was insular, and it showed that he had not really mastered French and Italian models, but his statements were none the less revealing. Every king of England, he wrote, for sundry hundreds of years had kept scribes to collect and record things done; and as time and course of years did serve, these writings were published. This extraordinary notion Hooker wisely did not attempt to document, but he went on to strike the note of patriotism:

> For this I dare boldlie saie and affirme: No realme, no nation, no
> state, nor commonwealth throughout all Europa, can yeeld more
> nor so manie profitable lawes, directions, rules, examples & dis-
> courses, either in matters of religion, or of ciuill gouernment, or of
> martiall affairs, than do the histories of this little Isle of Britaine or
> England. I would to God that I might or were able to saie the like,
> or the halfe like of Ireland, a countrie the more barren of good
> things, the more replenished with actions of bloud, murther, and
> lothsome outrages; which to anie good reader are greeuous & irk-
> some to be read & considered, much more for anie man to pen and
> set downe in writing, and to reduce into an historie.[156]

It did not occur to Hooker to ask why Ireland should have had
fewer records and fewer historians than England. That was a
question that concerned few English chroniclers in the sixteenth
century; the reason was in part that chroniclers were not true historians interested in questions of causation, and in part it was simply that moral judgments were such convenient substitutes for explanation. Ireland constituted a moral, not a historical lesson to
Hooker and to almost all his contemporaries: "I found no matter of
an historie woorthie to be recorded: but rather a tragedie of cruel-
ties to be abhorred, and no historie of good things to be followed."
The ultimate lesson of Irish history was that of the justice of God
against rebels—a lesson confirmed by the Bible and congenial to
both the Tudors and their subjects. Addressing himself to Ralegh as
one who "did not giue ouer, vntill you had recouered a land, and
had made a plantation of the people of your owne English nation
in *Virginia*," [157] Hooker asserted that the Spanish had no right to
be considered great colonizers or planters of the Christian religion
in the new world. The appeal to patriotism was strong and
proud. "This blessed plot, this earth, this realm, this England . . ."
—Gaunt's speech, without the poetry, might have come from the
chronicles.

The chronicle of England from 1066 was completed to 1578 by
Holinshed in the first edition and carried on by John Stow to 1587
in the second edition. The prefaces by Holinshed (written originally for the work as a whole) and by Stow to his own continuation of the English chronicle are no less revealing than Hooker's

dedication. Stow, as might be expected, was the more learned and the more interesting writer, especially since he attempted to define the chronicle for his readers:

> Time in Greeke is called χρόνος, whereof the word Chronicles ariseth, termed χρόνιυα, that is, obseruations of time: so that if nothing in wisedome dooth excell time, then who can but wax wise by reading and perusing the obseruations of time, which are meerelie & simple Chronicles? Chroniclers therefore deserue a reuerence of dutie, whome time hath called and culled out as it were by the hand, to vse their ministerie and seruice for the disposing and distributing of the riches of his wisdome to all ages . . .[158]

Holinshed praised the uses of the past in even more conventional language, asserting that histories and chronicles should contain praise of country, encouragement of worthy countrymen, and the daunting of the vicious by penal examples. Truth mattered, but Holinshed admitted that he had found contrariety, disagreement, negligence and rashness in the reports of his sundry authors and had therefore "in things doubtfull rather chosen to shew the diversitie of their writings, than by ouer-ruling them, and vsing a peremptorie censure, to frame them to agree to my liking: leauing it neuerthelesse to each man's iudgement, to controll them as he seeth cause." [159] While he respected the judgment of the learned he would nonetheless offer his own opinions, especially on matters which were still subject to controversy.[160]

At the end of the volume Stow appended a list of the historiographers who had contributed to the work:

> Now as Holinshed and such as with painful care and love to their countrie have thought good before me, to knit up the seuerall reigne of euerie seuerall king with a generalitie of the seuerall writers in that princes daies: So haue I beene importuned by manie of my friends, to knit up the said whole historie with a particular catalog of all such as haue purposoelie in seuerall histories of this realme, or by the waie in the histories of other countries written of England and English matter.[161]

Stow's mere catalogue was significant as an early attempt to deal with the history of English historiography.

What was perhaps most interesting about Holinshed's *Chronicles* was the projection of current interests onto the screen of the past. The taste for drum and trumpet history was not new, nor was Holinshed original, in either purpose or method. Truth, for Holinshed, was largely a matter of authority; he saw no need to seek and cite original records as evidence. Stow, accepting his role as compiler, did not attempt to identify his sources either, as he would do later in the *Survey*. The past that was being re-created by Holinshed's syndicate was nevertheless very different from that created by the medieval chroniclers, most of whom began with the creation and universal history; monkish writers on the whole were more parochial in outlook, more clerically oriented, and less interested in the problems of secular chronology. Tudor readers, if one may judge by Holinshed's emphasis, wanted to know more about recent history ("modern" history, from their point of view) than about the details of earlier events. Of the 1,592 pages in the second (1587) edition of Holinshed's *Chronicles*, over half were devoted to the Tudor century from 1485 to 1587; the preceding hundred years occupied 264 pages; and the century from 1285 to 1385 only 164 pages. The demand for a foreshortened history, with the emphasis on "recent" events, was evident. At the same time, Holinshed provided more of a sense of historical perspective: the whole medieval past of England was being made available to literate Englishmen in a way that it could not have been before the sixteenth century.

Biography as a genre was seldom clearly distinguished from history in the sixteenth century. One primary inspiration of secular biography was, in fact, secular history. Ecclesiastical biography derived from medieval saints' lives; and Foxe's martyrs were to some extent the legatees of a tradition going back at least to the ninth century, when saints' lives began to be translated into the vernacular. The medieval confusion between history and legend persisted, but was greatly diminished during the sixteenth century; Foxe in particular was a conscientious scholar. During the Renaissance European humanists, including Erasmus, became interested in biography and strove to imitate or adapt classical models, especially Suetonius, Plutarch, Tacitus, Livy, and Caesar. Vespasiano's *The Lives of Illustrious Men* was one of the earliest biographical collections, and although it remained in manuscript until the nineteenth century it was presumably known to John Tiptoft, Earl of Worcester, the fifteenth-century English patron of humanists.[162] In any case the taste for biography among the Tudors was well cultivated, by humanists, chroniclers, and antiquaries. Indeed biographical information was important to the whole antiquarian movement from the time of Leland, whose notes and plans for a topographical and biographical survey of English history were of the greatest use to later scholars. The tradition of moral tales, epitomized in *The Mirror for Magistrates*, went back as far as Lydgate and the *de casibus* tragedies of Boccaccio, although the information in *The Mirror* was taken from Hall. It is evident that the popularization of history depended in part on the popularity of biography—individuals were simply more interesting than movements; and chroniclers had not yet learned to write good narratives, much less analytical history.

The publication of North's translation of Plutarch's *The Lives of the Noble Grecians and Romans* (1579) was a landmark in Tudor biography, providing both a model for imitation and a definition of the difference between history and biography.[163] Amyot in his Preface to the original French translation of Plutarch (which formed the basis of North's text) proclaimed the manifold virtues of history and then concluded that history, "according to the diversity of the matter that it treateth of, or the order and manner of writing that it useth," had sundry names given to it:

> But yet among the rest there are two chief kinds: the one, which setteth down men's doings and adventures at length, is called by the common name of a history; the other, which declareth their natures, saying, and manner, is properly named their lives. And although the ground of them both do close very near in one, yet doth the one respect more the things and the other the persons. The one is more common, and the other more private; the one concerneth more the things that are without the man, and the other the things that proceed from within; the one the events, the other the consultations, between the which there is oftentimes great odds, according to this answer of the Persian Siramnes, to such as marveled how it came to pass that his devices being so politic had so unhappy success. "It is," quoth he, "because my devices are wholly from my own invention, but the effects of them are in the disposition of Fortune and the King." [164]

This was as clear a definition of the differences as Tudor writers ever arrived at, and it suggests not only the close connections between history and biography but also the tendency to invoke "fortune" as an explanatory concept. Fortune became, in one sense, the secular equivalent of providence. Both concepts appear in Tudor historiography, and religious polemicists naturally were even more prone than secular chroniclers to discover the hand of providence in the crises of history.

Reformation history, philology, and political theory have never been thoroughly studied in relation to each other, although the close connection between these three fields has long been recognized. Religious polemicists contributed directly to the idea of religious history and indirectly to the idea of secular history during the sixteenth century. Pontien Polman in *L'Elément Historique dans la Controverse Religieuse du XVIe Siècle* (1932) wrote the first detailed history of the Reformation uses of historical argument. H. O. Taylor's *Thought and Expression in the Sixteenth Century* (1920) and Preserved Smith's *A History of Modern Culture* (1930) were at best useful surveys. More recent studies of individuals—especially of Foxe, Jewel, Knox, Hooker, and others—provide a much clearer picture of the ways in which history entered into religious thought and was itself reshaped by religious politics. In general, Foxe described the basic Protestant idea of history; Jewel and Hooker wrote as apologists for the Anglican state Church; Sander and Cardinal Allen spoke for the Tudor Catholics; Knox represented himself, the Kirk, and some English Puritans; and William Cecil defined the position of those Elizabethan officials who were staunchly Erastian in their outlook.

The *Acts and Monuments* of John Foxe was being "vindicated" against the objections of Robert Parsons and Nicholas Harpsfield, both Tudor Catholics, by the Rev. George Townsend early in the nineteenth century. Historiographical quarrels have seldom been so long lived. The inaccuracies of the edition of S. R. Cattley and George Townsend, published in eight volumes between 1837 and 1841, were pointed out by S. R. Maitland.[165] Foxe's continuing influence on Protestant churchmen and laymen was a temptation to later editors, most of whom disregarded the text in order to "bring it up to date." A reprint of the original work is much to be desired, although the recent abridgment by G. A. Williamson provides a good sample of the Tudor materials. J. F. Mozley in *John Foxe and His Book* (1940) and William Haller in *Foxe's Book of Martyrs and the Elect Nation* (1963) reinterpreted Foxe for the benefit of twentieth-century readers, who can no longer dismiss Foxe's achievements as a historian.[166] Foxe explicitly referred to his work as "This Ecclesiasticall History," and (in the 1563 edition) he made it clear that he thought of himself as a historian who would enlighten "the unlearned sort, so miserably abused, and all for ignorance of history, not knowing the course of times and true descent of the church." [167] Foxe's purpose as a historian was, of course, to demonstrate the cruelty of the papists and the antiquity of the Protestant religion—a standard argument of Protestant propagandists in the sixteenth century. He outlined his general thesis for the benefit of the true and faithful congregation of Christ's universal Church, saying that:

> . . . if times had been well searched, or if they which wrote histories had, without partiality, gone upright between God and Baal, halting neither side, it might well have been found, the most part of all this Catholic corruption intruded into the church by the bishops of Rome, as transubstantiation, elevation and adoration of the sacrament, auricular confession, forced vows of priests not to marry, veneration of images, private and satisfactory masses, the order of Gregory's mass now used, the usurped authority and "summa potestas" of the see of Rome, with all the rout of their ceremonies and weeds of superstition overgrowing the church; all these, I say to be new-nothings lately coined in the mint of Rome, without any stamp of antiquity, as by reading of this present history shall sufficiently, I trust, appear.[168]

The Christian religion remained uncorrupted for approximately the first four hundred years, but then in Rome and elsewhere "riches begat ambition, ambition destroyed religion, so all came to ruin." [169] A true Church continued in the midst of the false "universal" Church of Rome even in the Middle Ages, until truth began to re-emerge in the three hundred years preceding the Reformation.[170] Protestantism was ancient; Roman Catholicism was the corrupt novelty. Continuities prevailed in religious, as they did in secular history.

Having begun the "Monuments" or martyrology "chiefly for the use of the English church" Foxe wrote in the tongue the people could best understand.[171] If men delighted in secular chronicles, it was the more appropriate for Christians to read about the martyrs of Christ; Christians would learn from the examples of Christian fortitude "God's mighty working in the life of man," as well as contempt of the world and the fear of God. If martyrs were to be compared with martyrs, Foxe saw no reason "why the martyrs of our time deserve any less commendation than the others in the primitive church." [172] In short, like most of the Tudor chroniclers, Foxe was primarily a "modern" historian, who provided long historical perspectives, and broad coverage, but whose first interest was in the Tudor age.

Foxe printed many original sources in his work, and by so doing he made a distinct contribution to historiography. The emphasis on evidence, whether from ancient or modern history, or from printed or unprinted sources, was not news to the humanists and other intellectuals, but Foxe made a point of printing this evidence in the vernacular for the benefit of the common reader. The importance of Foxe's influence may be gathered from the mere fact that by 1577 every office at court had either a Bible or a copy of Foxe, and often both—the reading of Foxe was next in importance only to the reading of the Bible among Protestants.[173] That Foxe himself should have recognized the significance of printing in the Reformation is not surprising:

> Printing, being opened, incontinently ministered unto the church the instruments and tools of learning and knowledge; which were good books and authors, which before lay hid and unknown. The science of printing being found, immediately followed the grace of God; which stirred up good wits aptly to conceive the light of knowledge and judgment: by which light darkness began to be espied, and ignorance to be detected; truth from error, religion from superstition . . .[174]

Foxe even suggested that printing might abolish the pope—he truly believed that the light of knowledge and Protestantism were one. The Renaissance was prelude to the Reformation in Foxe's view of history.

The note of patriotism was as characteristic of Foxe as it was of the Tudor chroniclers. Living in "these halcyon days" of Queen Elizabeth, Foxe gave thanks not only for the triumph of the Protestant religion but for the disappearance of persecution under Elizabeth—Foxe was not, by nature, a bloodthirsty man, and his ideal was a rough kind of toleration.[175] Even Anabaptists and papists were to be spared fire, for Foxe had a horror of cruelty. No one is likely to forget Bishop Hooper, who "When he was black in the mouth, and his tongue swollen, that he could not speak, yet his lips went till they were shrunk to the gums: and he knocked his breast with his hands, until one of his arms fell off, and then knocked still with the other, what time the fat, water, and blood, dropped out at his fingers' ends, until by renewing of the fire his strength was gone, and his hand did cleave fast, in knocking, to the iron upon his breast." [176] Such martyrs provided models for the faithful, as well as a reminder of the need for Christian charity: "They continued in patient suffering, when they had most wrong done unto them . . . and yet we will not forgive our poor brother, be the injury never so small, but are ready for every trifling offence to seek his destruction and cut his throat." [177] Lord Cromwell, who had profited the commonwealth more than most men, was at last the victim of persecuting envy: "where true piety seeketh most after Christ, there some persecution followeth withal." [178] The sinister councilors of kings were the true villains. The king and Parliament were essentially misguided: "they that say that princes and parliaments may be misinformed sometimes, by some sinister heads, in matters civil and politic, do not therein derogate or impair the high estate of parliaments, but rather give wholesome admonition to princes and parliament men, to be more circumspect and vigilant what counsel they shall admit, and what witnesses they do credit." [179] The medieval idea that good counsel would lead to good government was in the process of being transformed during the sixteenth century into the modern idea that what matters is the evidence, the credit of witnesses for fact as well as for moral character. In this transformation history played a key role. Haller was assuredly right to insist that "not the least important effect of the Reformation, aside from its effect on religious life as such, was to make the art and science of historiography of momentous concern." [180] Through the pages of Foxe one may trace the ways in which historical consciousness affected men and events. Foxe is thus a primary source of information about Tudor attitudes; and some of his epigrams are still disconcertingly apt: "Of immoderate liberty and too much security, followeth most commonly extreme servitude." [181]

John Jewel's *An Apology for the Church of England* was published in Lady Ann Bacon's translation in 1564. Following upon Jewel's "Challenge Sermon" of 1559–1560 the *Apology* started a controversy which eventually involved so many disputants that it is now known as "the Great Controversy." [182] The chief opponent of Jewel was Nicholas Sander, the English scholar at Louvain. In the course of time, Jewel's *Apology* became one of the main defenses of the English Church, along with Hooker's classic, *Of the Laws of Ecclesiastical Polity.* As late as 1938 copies of Jewel's *Defence of the Apology* or Jewel's *Works* (1609 or 1611) were kept chained in thirteen different cathedral or parish churches in England.[183] William Cecil wrote to Archbishop Parker to express his satisfaction with the *Apology*, and Parker himself thanked Lady Bacon for translating it.[184] It was indeed a major contribution to the Anglican quarrel with the papacy; and it influenced the whole subsequent development of Anglicanism. The extent to which Jewel made use of historical arguments is therefore of considerable interest. Although the work was properly speaking a tract, not a piece of history, it was full of historical observations and historical rhetoric. Jewel remarked on the importance of printing for Protestantism (as Foxe later did), noting that the Bishop of Rome's sayings were allowed for gospel in times past, but "Nowadays the Holy Scripture is abroad, the writings of the apostles and prophets are in print, whereby all truth and catholic doctrine may be proved and all heresy may be disproved and confuted." [185] The "high brag" of the Catholics, who said they had antiquity on their side, was dismissed by Jewel: "they have not that antiquity, they have not that universality, they have not that consent of all places nor of all times." [186] Jewel discussed most of the significant points of difference between the Anglican and the Roman Catholic Church including the all-important matter of tradition; persuasion, however, was still more important than proof.

Responding to Jewel, Nicholas Sander wrote a very different kind of book. *The Rise and Growth of the Anglican Schism,* written in Latin by Sander and completed by the missionary priest, Edward Rishton, was published at Cologne in 1585.[187] Sander sought to discredit the Anglican Church and the monarchy, asserting among other things that Queen Elizabeth's mother, Anne Boleyn, was doubly incestuous, being Henry VIII's own daughter, who was herself guilty of incest with her brother. Sander was by no means as careful a scholar as Foxe, but he did consult records and he knew the importance of presenting a reasoned case:

> The marvellous and amazing things that God wrought in that kingdom, after the beginning of the schism, for the purpose of bringing back the hearts of the children to the faith of their fathers, can never be thoroughly understood without a history of the schism; that history, strange and surprising, I shall now tell in all sincerity as I have gathered it either from public records or from the testimony, oral and written, of men of the greatest consideration, or at least from my own knowledge and observation.[188]

Sander's interpretation of events was of course colored by his prejudices. The debasement of the coinage was "a manifest judgment of God."[189] Henry VIII gave up the Catholic faith "for no other reason in the world than that which came from his lust and wickedness."[190] After a schism which lasted twenty years, the peaceful victory of Mary Tudor "was a manifest miracle wrought before all the world in favour of the Catholic faith."[191] And with the death of Queen Mary and Cardinal Pole "came the hour of Satan, and the power of darkness took possession of the whole of England."[192]

Sander's book was polemical history, written in response to Jewel's *Apology* but not addressed to the same questions that Jewel had raised. The historical rhetoric was, however, even more pronounced. *The Anglican Schism* is of interest today primarily as a specimen of the Catholic version of Tudor history. In Protestant historiography the closest approach to the work was probably John Knox's *History of the Reformation in Scotland*; but Knox's book was not published during his lifetime, and it was, as well as history, a self-justifying, highly personal account of the activities of its author. Knox spoke in the true, rude voice of the Protestant zealot—he was, at least in this, Sander's counterpart. His judgment of the Scottish Church before the coming of Mary Stuart was that, in doctrine and administration of the sacraments, it alone was pure: "For all others . . . retain in their Churches, and the ministers thereof, some footsteps of Antichrist, and some dregs of papistry; but we (all praise to God alone) have nothing within our Churches that ever flowed from that Man of Sin."[193] Purity, however, did not prevent Protestants from accepting Queen Mary and even (far worse) tolerating her religion. Thus "the Devil finding his reins loose, ran forwards in his course; and the Queen took upon her the greater boldness than she and Baal's belating priests durst have attempted before." [194] Seldom has the devil been given so much work to do as by the angry Tudor clerics. The decline of Hell in the seventeenth century was accompanied by a corresponding decline of devilish explanations in history.[195]

The controversy between William Cecil, Lord Burghley, and William Allen, the Catholic cardinal, encompassed some of the points raised by Sander—or Sanders, as Burghley referred to him in the text of *The Execution of Justice in England* (1583).[196] Cardinal Allen's *Defense of English Catholics* was a point by point refutation of Cecil's text; it appeared in 1584 on the heels of Burghley's anonymous work.[197] Both books were addressed to the question of whether or not English Catholics were being put to death because of their religion; neither argument was entirely convincing —and both authors were disingenuous.[198] In a pamphlet of only thirty-eight pages (in the original edition), it is surprising how much historical argument and reference Burghley saw fit to include. Since he could not prove actual Catholic treasons he asserted that the popes had always maintained traitors and rebels, and that monarchs had therefore seen fit to protect themselves "by laws and pragmatics both ancient and new." [199] Much of Cardinal Allen's argument was devoted to contemporary affairs, but he frequently cited Biblical history or the writings of the church fathers to support his positions; and in the latter part of the *Defense* he posed one specifically historical problem. "The Protestants cannot prove by example of all nations and times since Christ that anyone hath been deposed that was not proved to be a notorious heretic or evil man," he wrote, while "on the other side, rebels and, namely, heretics, by unlawful means deprive commonly none but innocent, just, and holy princes . . ." [200] Both Allen and Burghley were more restrained and "reasonable" than Knox or Sander, possibly because they were both astute men of affairs, anxious to impress diplomats and heads of state. In the long run the tone of rational historical argument may have helped to create an attitude of reasonableness; in any case, many Tudor Englishmen valued judiciousness and civility more than reforming zeal. They were therefore more impressed by Hooker than by his more boisterous predecessors or opponents. Cartwright in the Admonition controversy, and "Martin Marprelate" in the tracts which bear his name, alluded to historical examples, but it was Hooker who made the best and wisest use of history in his argument about the Church.[201]

It has been customary to depreciate Hooker's historical thought and to stress instead his debts to religious and philosophical traditions. The importance of St. Thomas Aquinas, Marsilius of Padua, Aristotle, and Plato in the development of Hooker's thought has been effectively demonstrated by Peter Munz in *The Place of Hooker in the History of Thought* (1952). In an appendix on "Hooker's Historical Sense," Munz stressed the fact that Hooker did indeed have a strong historical sense, but he asserted that this was unusual in the sixteenth century and could only be accounted for on the basis of Thomistic influence—Hooker's rational attitude toward history and tradition derived from medieval rationalism. Burke, the only writer with a comparable historical sense, had to appeal to irrationalism, because modern rationalism did not lend itself to a similar approach. Munz was primarily interested in the philosophical units of the history of ideas; thus the method of parallel passages could be used to demonstrate Hooker's debts to St. Thomas, even though Hooker often made a different use of the same units of argument.[202] In the context of the expanding historical consciousness of Tudor England, Hooker's historical thought perhaps deserves to be reappraised. Hooker believed that the Law of Nature and the Law of Reason were one and could be discovered, in some sense, inductively; he also maintained, however, that time changed all human arrangements, and that what was a reasonable positive law at one time might not be at another time.[203] It followed that "neither councils nor customs, be they never so ancient and so general," could prevent the Church from "taking away that thing which is hurtful to be retained." In short, "there is not any positive law of men, whether it be general or particular; received by formal express consent, as in councils, or by secret approbation, as in customs it cometh to pass; but the same may be taken away if occasion serve." [204]

The complexity of Hooker's thought rules out any simple formulas about his work; and his attempts to reconcile different and sometimes contradictory opinions led him into inconsistencies.[205] He combined learning, sympathy, and faith with a subtle awareness of historical differences and a profound conviction that reason, not will, was the ground for belief and controversy. He was an apologist for the Tudor Constitution, taking it to be ancient; and, like Burke, he could argue that "the things which so long experience of all ages hath confirmed and made profitable, let us not presume to condemn as follies and toys, because we sometimes know not the cause and reason of them." [206] Hooker's rationalism did not prevent him from appreciating the nature of historical change. God was rational, but God had not ordained absolute continuity: "God never ordained any thing that could be bettered. Yet many things he hath that have been changed and that for the better." [207] Arguments from human authority and testimony were to be considered as problems, which were subject to what might be called historical reasoning. Human testimony could be used to prove things both affirmatively and negatively—even Scripture had to be accepted on the basis of historical testimony.[208] There were degrees of belief, or of assent, even in divine matters. Human and divine history shared a common method, whatever their peculiar differences might be. "Now it is not required nor can be expected at our hands," Hooker wrote, "that we should yield unto any thing other assent, than such as doth answer the evidence which is to be had out of what we assent unto." [209]

As there were varieties of belief so were there varieties of reasons for studying Scripture. Laws, points of doctrine, prophecies (which confirmed the world's belief in things unseen) were among the reasons given for studying the books of the Bible; and not least in importance were the "many histories to serve as looking-glasses to behold the mercy, the truth, the righteousness of God towards all that faithfully serve, obey and honour him." [210] When in 1597 Hooker published Book V of his *Laws* he dedicated it to his patron, Archbishop Whitgift. The public and common good of all was the mark he aimed at "for the easier procurement whereof, our diligence must search out all helps and furtherances of direction, which scriptures, councils, fathers, histories, the laws and practices of all churches, the mutual conference of all men's collections and observations may afford." [211] In the course of this book, as elsewhere in his work, Hooker insisted on the importance of looking at all the evidence, including the historical. To judge conclusions by demi-premises and half-principles, as the Puritans did, was to "lay them in the balance stripped from those necessary material circumstances, which should give them weight, and by show of falling uneven with the scale of most universal and abstracted rules, they pronounce that too light which is not, if they had the skill to weigh it." [212] Hooker's historical sense was a tribute not so much to medieval rationalism as to the growth of historical consciousness and scholarship in the England of Elizabeth.

Under the general heading of "Descriptions" all kinds of works on topography, customs, and territorial history must be considered: descriptive writing was one of the features of Tudor historiography. The purely informational aspects of early Tudor chronicles, especially of the city chronicles, was marked; and those who talked of "mayors and sheriffs, of the dear year and the great frost" were beginning to be ridiculed by the more sophisticated Elizabethans. Still, there was much more descriptive information available to Elizabethan readers than to earlier Tudor Englishmen on subjects such as roads, towns, fairs, weights, measures, town houses and country houses, charities and businesses, local customs and antiquities, as well as the territorial features and social and economic conditions of England. The two London chronicles that Stow made the most use of in his own *Summary of English Chronicles* (1565) illustrate the descriptive aspects of the city chronicle tradition.[213] The briefer of the two manuscripts, covering events from 1547 to 1564, contained characteristic notes on the value of English money at the Antwerp exchange, and the price of a Holland cheese, as well as the uncharacteristic estimate that "In the tyme of the raigne of this qwene [Mary Tudor] there were burnyd, and som allso that died in prison for religion, lityll vnder or ouer 2040, men & women." For the following year a briefer note sufficed: "Quene Elisabeth. Leigh, Mayor, in aº lº no thing to noate." [214]

The topographical or chorographical works of Lambarde, Camden, Norden, and Stow were more or less comprehensive descriptions of counties and towns, with some historical information and notes on the local families and antiquities. Such works probably served as guidebooks and introductions to local history, but primarily they conveyed information about the history and topography of the area and about contemporary life. They are thus of considerable interest to present-day historians who want to know what the Tudors thought important in their own society and in their own past.

Norden's productions as a topographer began with *Speculum Britanniae, the First Parte. An Historicall and Chorographical Description of Middlesex* (1593) and went on to include *England: An Intended Guyde for English Travaillers* (1625). His description of Essex (1594) was actually little more than an outline, but as such revealing; and it was based on his own map of the county, which showed roads (unlike Norden's maps as published by Camden and Speed). Edited by Sir Henry Ellis for the Camden Society in 1840, the manuscript on Essex was part of a projected, but never completed, series of volumes on the counties of England. Although Norden called it "An Historical and Chorographical Description," the history in it was minimal; and the chorography was scarcely typical of the much longer works of Lambarde, Camden, and Stow. Chorography meant technically the description of an area too large to come under topography and too small to come under geography. In practice it meant any combination of descriptive notes which might define an area and its inhabitants. In *Essex* Norden merely noted terrain features and listed important houses and families. In his volume on Middlesex he described the houses, bridges, and economy of London in more detail. Lambarde, in his pioneering work *A Perambulation of Kent* (1574), had included a range of information on topics from archaeology to law, and from topography to ancient history. Lambarde's *Perambulation* has rightly been called the first county history. It was also a chorographical description—but to insist too much on the name instead of on the thing would be a mistake. History in the sixteenth century bore many titles.

The full title of the 1596 edition of the *Perambulation* drew attention to the different things it contained: *A Perambulation of Kent, Conteining the Description, Hystorie, and Customes of that Shire, Written in the yeere 1570 by William Lambarde of Lincoln's Inne Gent: first published in the yeere 1576, and now increased and altered after the Author's Owne Copie. London 1596.* The introductory remarks by Sir Henry Wotton were clear and explicit: "I know not how I may more fitly and effectually commend it than to say, that it is in substance, an historie: treating of the parts (and actions of greatest weight a good time together, done by the most famous persons) of one special Countrie . . ." [215] In the text itself Lambarde listed the early kings of Kent and observed truly that history and topography had to be treated together:

> Now, although it might here seeme convenient, before I passed any
> further, to disclose such memorable things, as haue chanced during
> the reignes of all these forenamed Kings: yet for asmuch as my pur-
> pose specially is to write a topographie, or description of places, and

no chronographie, or story of time, (although I must now and then vse both, since the one can not fully bee performed without enter-lacing the other) and for that also I shall haue iust occasion hereafter in the particulars of this Shyre, to disclose many of the same, I will at this present, and that by way of digression onely, make report of one or two occurrents that happened vnder Ethelbert, and Eadric, two Kings of this countrey.[216]

Lambarde's scholarship was superior to that of most of the English legal antiquaries of his day, but he was far from being as subtle or learned as the French legal humanists. Lambarde believed in Geoffrey's British history, although he referred with respect to Polydore Vergil and Brian Twynne, both skeptics. At heart a lawyer, he failed to develop a strong awareness of historical process. He summed up his own scholarly methods in a sentence: "And to the end that the trueth may appeare by collation of the diuers reports, I will first shew, what the common opinion . . . is, and then afterward what these other men write concerning the same." [217] Within limits, it was a sound method, well enough suited to the descriptive survey; collation might help to detect a falsehood or confirm a fact, but it was not a method adapted to establishing historical contexts or dealing with complex problems of relevance. The limits of the descriptive survey were set by the nature of the questions asked; these remained, for the most part, fairly simple and straightforward.

The best and the best known descriptive survey was Camden's *Britannia*. The "Discovery of England" was going on apace by the time Camden wrote.[218] He had the benefit of Leland's manuscript notes and the encouragement and help of a number of British scholars—most importantly he had the support of Abraham Ortelius, the Flemish geographer. The *Britannia* was first published in Latin in 1586, and later much expanded; its success was immediate, its importance immense. It introduced English readers to some of the ideas of historical criticism found in continental, especially French, scholarship; and the *Britannia* re-established England's reputation in the European world of learning. In his last "Preface to the Reader" Camden described exactly what he had done and how he had set about doing it:

My enquiries into the etymology and first inhabitants of Britain were conducted with hesitation; and in such uncertainty I have

pronounced boldly on nothing, convinced that the origins of the nations of remote antiquity are necessarily obscure . . . I have investigated the antient divisions of Britain and given a brief account of
the orders and courts, and of the flourishing kingdoms of England,
Scotland, and Ireland. In the same brief manner I have described as
exactly as I could the bounds and qualities of the soil, the places
memorable in antiquity, the dukes, earls, barons, and the most antient and illustrious families; for it is impossible to mention them
all . . . I have omitted nothing that tended to discover truth in
matters of antiquity; to which purpose I have called in the assist-
ance of a smattering of the antient British [Welsh] and the Saxon
tongues. I have travelled over almost all England, and consulted the
most experienced and learned persons in each county. I have carefully read over our own writers, and those among the Greek and
Roman authors who made the least mention of Britain. I have consulted the public records, ecclesiastical registers, many libraries, the
archives of cities and churches, monuments, and old deeds, and
have made use of them as of irrefragable evidence, and when necessary quoted their very words however barbarous, that truth may
have its full weight.[219]

He went on to point out that his principal design was to "trace
out and rescue from obscurity" those places which had been mentioned by ancient Roman writers. Hence the rather curious organization of the work: the supposed British tribal locations were su-
perimposed on the actual county divisions, which in effect were
the true units of organization. Camden followed the ancient
Roman itineraries, making every effort to solve the problem of identifying Roman roads, sites, and place names. His purpose was in
part patriotic—to show that Britain, while an imperial province,
had shared in the common culture of the ancient world; and in
part scholarly—to acquaint European readers with British history,
antiquities, and places of interest.[220] The theory of imperial rights
vested in the English national monarchy may also have drawn his
attention to Roman remains.

Camden's success in solving many of the problems posed by the
Roman itineraries was a tribute to his scholarly originality and
skill, and to the help he received—Ralph Brook's criticism of Camden's integrity and scholarship was misplaced. In keeping with
the Roman (and humanistic) emphasis of the *Britannia* was the
ironic rejection of Geoffrey's arguments for the Trojan origin of the
British race and name. Camden knew that he risked making ene-

mies of those who preferred Trojans to Frenchmen as ancestors, and that he could not expect to write about antiquity without making errors: "For who is so skillfull as in this dark occan of antiquity to struggle with time without splitting on the rocks." [221] All nations, except those mentioned in Scripture, lay under a cloud of darkness, error, and ignorance about their origins—"nor indeed can it be otherwise, considering how deeply the truth must be sunk in the revolutions of so many ages." [222] Everyone was at liberty to hold that Brutus was the father and founder of the British nation, but Camden's irony was unmistakable when he wrote that he would "not go about to disprove it." [223] His refutation took the form of a conjecture, designed to show that the British must have been descended from Noah's son, Japhet, whose eldest son, Gomer, founded Gaul. All the evidence indicated that the British derived both their origin and their name from the Gauls:

> And this origin from Gomer and Gaul seems more interesting, antient, and better founded than that from Brutus and Troy. Nay, I think I could prove that it comes nearest to truth, and that our Britans are really derived from Gaul, from their name, situation, religion, manners, and language, in all which particulars there seems to have been such a correspondence between the oldest Gauls and Britans, as if they had been one people.[224]

Here was a contextual argument, based on the coherence of evidence in several fields; it was the distinguishing trait of the best French scholarship.[225] Moreover, in carrying out his plan for the *Britannia*, Camden paid particular attention to the coherence of the arguments in each section. He had, of course, the weight of the best authorities behind his rejection of Brutus; the myth was simply irrelevant to history. In his conjectures about Roman remains he was sometimes wrong but never silly; plausible conjectures would long remain necessary to historians who asked how, why, and to what end. Camden's contribution to the idea of exact, professional scholarship in England was immense. Unlike Stow, who was not a university man and not an internationally known scholar, Camden had the proper credentials; he could and did bring to English historical scholarship a new dignity and depth.

Camden reinterpreted the whole history of Roman Britain. This by itself deserved the approbation of his learned contemporaries and of posterity. In fact he did more than this: he bridged the gap between territorial description and territorial history. It was perfectly fitting that the man who knew most about England's green and pleasant land should have undertaken to write the history of Elizabeth's reign. The *Annals of Elizabeth* (1615) belong properly to the seventeenth century, and to Camden's maturity, but in the *Annals* he made use of the methods developed in the *Britannia*. The section on Cambridgeshire in the *Britannia* illustrates some of Camden's methods and interests. Under the general heading of "ICENI," Camden began his description of the shire by giving the derivation of the name, following this with a description of the principal landmarks, both historical and topographical; he noted some of the important families, gave a brief outline of the founding of Cambridge University and the dates of the founding of halls and colleges, proceeded on around the shire, making comments on the history of the Fen country and the Isle of Ely, and closed with a short paragraph on the earldom of Cambridge. Camden wrote about important landmarks and about well-known local families. This was appropriate to the scale of the work and to Camden's sense of the dignity of history.

It remained for Stow, in the *Survey of London* (first edition, 1598), to show what could be done with information about the generations of forgotten citizens who had done so much to make London great. Camden was more learned than Stow, but he recognized in the older man that spring of originality, and that same patient attention to detail, that marked his own historical scholarship.[226] Like Stow, Camden admitted his errors and pursued truth—good historians have seldom been content merely to play it safe. Camden accumulated many more notes than he could use; and some of these, the by-product of *Britannia*, he published simply as *Remaines of a Greater Work Concerning Britain*. In it Camden gathered some of the raw materials for social history, even though he tried to satisfy only an antiquarian curiosity. The chapters on epigrams, apparel, wise sayings, etc. were held together by no connective narrative, and Camden did not ask the questions that a modern social historian would ask, yet the book was in many ways original. Certainly it suggests why the antiquarian movement exerted such a strong influence on historiography. Antiquarian collecting habits and antiquarian scholarship, based largely on the use of nonliterary evidence, were essential to the expansion of history in Elizabethan England.[227]

In 1589 Richard Hakluyt published *The Principall Navigations, Voiages and Discoveries of the English Nation, made by Sea or over Land, to the most remote and farthest distant Quarters of the earth at any time within the compasse of these 1500 yeeres*. It was the first large installment of Hakluyt's lifelong labor "in the sweet studie of the historie of Cosmographie." [228] The history of the expansion of England had never before been written. Hakluyt's range and industry were formidable, and if his scholarship was less impressive than Camden's it was still sound, painstaking, and influential. Because the *Principall Navigations* has so often been referred to as a "great prose epic" it is necessary to insist that it was history, that it was called history by Hakluyt, and that later historians have pointed out that it must be read as economic history, not just as propaganda.[229] The work may have been basically an anthology of materials written by others, but it was also history made relevant to practical needs and national interests. Long before the younger Hakluyt began to publish the papers he had been collecting for years, he had made them available to interested merchants, explorers, and geographers. The patriotic, imperial chords in the *Voiages* struck a response in the hearts of contemporaries and later Englishmen alike—the Hakluyts were among the first modern imperialists. Richard Hakluyt gave to the prose of history epic and dramatic dimensions, even though the burden of constant compilation was wearisome. There is no better illustration of the importance of historical accumulation—the pattern of accretion—in Tudor historiography. In the Preface to the greatly expanded second edition of 1598 (completed in 1600), Hakluyt explained his purpose in writing, his trials, and what it was he had achieved. His words are worth a lengthy quotation:

> Having for the benefit and honour of my Countrey zealously bestowed so many yeres, so much travaile and cost, to bring Antiquities smothered and buried in darke silence, to light, and to preserve certaine memorable exploits of late yeeres by our English nation atchieved, from the greedy and devouring jawes of oblivion: to gather likewise, and as it were to incorporate in one body the torne and scattered limmes of our ancient and late Navigations by Sea, our voyages by land, and traffiques of merchandise by both: and having (so much as in me lieth) restored ech particular member, being before displaced, to their true joynts and ligaments; I meane, by the helpe of Geographie and Chronologie (which I may calle the Sunne

and the Moone, the right eye and the left of all history) referred ech particular relation to the due time and place: I do this second time . . . presume to offer unto thy view this first part of my threefold discourse. For the bringing of which into this homely and rough-hewn shape, which here thou seest; what restlesse nights, what painefull dayes, what heat, what cold have I endured; how many long & chargeable journeys I have travailed; how many famous libraries I have searched into; what varietie of ancient and moderne writers I have perused; what a number of old records, patents, privileges, letters, &c. I have reddemed from obscuritie and perishing . . .[230]

Here was the authentic voice of Elizabethan patriotism and scholarship.

More than most historical writers Hakluyt understood the close connection between history and other disciplines, especially geography; Elizabethan historians all profited from the discoveries of workers in other fields. By the time Hakluyt had reached the third volume of the Voiages in 1600, he had extended by one hundred years the period covered in the first edition and had more than tripled the amount of medieval material. Not only was the historical perspective longer but new information—based on a wider variety of original sources—revealed much more about economic history. Yet, even though the medieval sections were enlarged, the primary emphasis was on the expansion of Tudor England, on the achievements of his own contemporaries. Hakluyt was in many ways an abstract of his age: industrious in the pursuit of knowledge, traditional in belief, daring in reconnaissance, and articulate in love of country and history. Like so many of the Tudor historians he could not imagine that the statistics of voyaging, the cost of provisioning and outfitting ships, belonged properly in a history. Belief in the "dignity of history" encouraged historians to write about personalities rather than pounds, shillings, and pence. Still, all Hakluyt's faults as a historian (including his clumsiness in organization) weigh less than his virtues. He chronicled and admired the expansion of Elizabethan England, although he little understood how, in the long run, that expansion would transform his world.

There is no need to stretch out further on the rack of summary the body of Tudor historiography. The conclusions of this chapter are no more than the starting points for further interrogations. It would seem that a good case can be made for saying that historical consciousness preceded historical revolution, that modern professional scholarship developed on the foundation of a widespread interest in history. Specialization was impossible before general history was at least available in outline. Historiography responded to, influenced, and moved along with the other intellectual currents of the time. This did not mean that historiography progressed at the same rate as other disciplines: historians achieved rather more than most natural scientists, except for Gilbert, and a few mathematicians, naturalists, and astronomers in Tudor England. The basis for the comparison between history and science is to some extent arbitrary, yet the structure of scientific and historical revolutions can be compared, just as the timing of significant discoveries in each field can be fixed. The logical coherence and the aesthetically appealing explanations of the scientific revolution have perhaps diverted attention from the fact that natural science, even in the seventeenth century, was no more *immediately* revolutionary in its effects than history. Indeed it might be argued that the science of Harvey or Gilbert was less important in its direct utilitarian consequences than the historical scholarship of Foxe, Spelman, or Selden.

The development of broad-based humanistic scholarship in the sixteenth century made possible the breakthroughs in philology, geography, diplomatics, sigillography, and other fields that were so important for the whole subsequent development of historiography. The "capital" accumulated in the course of the seventeenth century (or from about 1580 to 1680) in the form of new methods, interpretations, and collections of information, served historians well until the nineteenth century. This concentration of intellectual capital for investment was made possible partly by the growth of historical interests and consciousness during the sixteenth century in England, France, and elsewhere in Europe, and partly by what might be called the "primitive" accumulation of historical capital in the form of methods. In nineteenth-century England a new series of interpretations of Tudor history, based on archival research and on newly printed documents, began to be published. The historical revolution of the nineteenth century bore many similarities to that of the sixteenth and seventeenth centuries, but there was this difference: the earlier revolution did not sustain its own momentum or develop its own party of professional historians and professional institutions. The nineteenth-century revolution did—and that is one important reason why historians in the twentieth century have been able to rewrite the whole history of Tudor England. Even the most radical revisions, however, depend not only on new techniques and new evidence in a particular area or period, but on discoveries in other areas and related periods. The debates about Tudor history in the twentieth century have been marked by geographical and chronological comparisons, by references to cultural, political, and religious traditions, and to the long-range consequences of particular events. In this sense at least it might be said that there can be no specialization without generalization. Tudor history is a part of European history, which is a part of world history. If the earlier sixteenth century saw the beginning of a new interest in social causation, which in the long run would transform chronicles into history, the twentieth century has seen a far greater expansion and development of conceptual and methodological tools. Perhaps we are now under the domination of what Henry Adams called the "law of acceleration" in history. According to Adams an American who lived into the year 2000 would think in complexities unimaginable to an earlier mind and would deal with problems altogether beyond the range of earlier society. That historians in Britain and America, and perhaps in every advanced industrial country, have acquired new perspectives along with a new technology is not to be doubted; that historians cannot afford to neglect the problem of transmitting historical and historiographical traditions, thereby establishing continuities with the past, is also not to be doubted. John Selden expressed the historian's dilemma: "Ay, or no never answered any Question. The not distinguishing where things should be distinguished, and the not confounding, where things should be confounded is the cause of all the mistakes in the World." [231] The historian's task has not always been understood to include such an undertaking to distinguish and to confound—to distinguish significant from insignificant change; to confound or bring together real common problems and important continuities. Tudor chroniclers and antiquaries lacked Selden's historical understanding; Selden, for all his greatness, knew less history than many lesser men today. The rate of historiographical progress has changed; the historians' problems, however, remain much the same. Understanding the Tudor past has been the work of many generations, and many historians. Learning has also been advanced by those who have collected, edited, and compiled, and by those who have listened and suggested changes. Knowledge of how history has been written is the precondition for progress in historiography. Significant changes derive from significant continuities. History includes the history of history.

NOTES

1. See A. L. Rowse, *The Expansion of Elizabethan England* (New York, 1955), p. vii; cf. J. H. Parry, *Europe and the Wider World 1415–1715* (London, 1949).
2. J. H. Parry, *The Age of Reconnaissance* (London, 1963), p. 14. See also pp. 34–37; see Boies Penrose, *Travel and Discovery in the Renaissance* (New York, 1962), p. 325.
3. Parry, *op. cit.*, p. 3.
4. *Ibid.*, p. 15.
5. See Carlo M. Cipolla, *Guns, Sails and Empires* (New York, 1965), pp. 18–19.
6. See A. L. Rowse, *The Elizabethans and America* (New York, 1959), esp. pp. x, 154, and *passim*.
7. Sir Thomas More, *Utopia* (London, 1910), p. 9.
8. See Wilcomb E. Washburn, "The Meaning of 'Discovery' in the Fifteenth and Sixteenth Centuries," *American Historical Review*, LXVIII, No. 1 (1962), 1–21. See also Elizabeth L. Eisenstein, "The Impact of Printing on Western Society and Thought," *Journal of Modern History*, XL, No. 1 (March 1968), 24–25.
9. J. R. Hale, "Gunpowder and the Renaissance," in *From the Renaissance to the Counter-Reformation: Essays in Honor of Garrett Mattingly*, ed. Charles H. Carter (London, 1965), p. 135.
10. Cf. Penry Williams, *Life in Tudor England* (London, 1964); and G. M. Trevelyan, *English Social History* (New York, 1943), pp. 162–163.
11. The spelling is modernized. See Philip Stubbes, *Anatomy of the Abuses in Shakespeare's Youth A.D. 1583*, ed. Frederick J. Furnivall (London, 1917–1919), pp. 116–117.
12. See Eisenstein, *op. cit.*, p. 25. See also H. S. Bennett, *English Books and Readers* (Cambridge, 1952, 1965), Vol. I, *1475–1557*; Vol. II, *1558–1603*.
13. Eisenstein, *op. cit.*, p. 7.
14. *Ibid.*, p. 9.
15. See S. B. Chrimes, *English Constitutional Ideas in the Fifteenth Century* (Cambridge, 1936), pp. 250–252, 207–212, and *passim* dealing with law and custom.
16. See Eisenstein, *op. cit.*, pp. 9–11, 14–16, 20–21, 24–29, 35–40, 43, 46, 48.
17. *Ibid.*, p. 19.
18. See William H. Dunham, Jr., "Magna Carta and British Constitutionalism," in *The Great Charter: Four Essays on Magna Carta and the History of Our Liberty* (New York, 1966), p. 36.
19. See Eisenstein, *op. cit.*, p. 25.
20. *Ibid.*, p. 28.
21. *Ibid.*, pp. 46–48.

22. The evidence for this generalization cannot be given in a footnote. An essay of considerable interest is that by the historian, Christopher Morris, "Shakespeare's Politics," *Historical Journal*, VIII, No. 3 (1965), 293–308.
23. This was especially true of the earlier variorum editions of, e.g., *Richard III* (1908) and *Henry IV, Part I* (1936) and *Part II* (1940).
24. For example, see A. P. Rossiter, *Angel with Horns* (New York, 1960), esp. the lecture "The Unity of *Richard III.*" Rossiter denies (p. 2) that the play is in any important sense "historical." Rossiter and Reese are reprinted in selections in the Globe Bantam Shakespeare—a series edited by Oscar James Campbell, Alfred Rothschild, and Stuart Vaughan. The series contains extracts from modern critical essays; there is also a series of *Twentieth Century Interpretations*, ed. Maynard Mack, with a volume of essays on *Henry V*, ed. Arnold Berman; see also Eugene M. Waith, *Shakespeare: The Histories* (Englewood Cliffs, 1965). The best editions of the history plays are those by J. Dover Wilson for "The New Shakespeare" and the revised volumes of "The Arden Shakespeare." The standard bibliographical guides to Shakespeare may be used to track down less familiar essays. The approaches of earlier scholars and critics may be sampled in Augustus Ralli, *A History of Shakespeare Criticism* (London, 1932). Perhaps the most useful *general* bibliography is to be found in the "Reports on Scholarship in the Renaissance" in the *Renaissance Quarterly*. See also A. L. Rowse, *William Shakespeare, A Biography* (New York, 1963).
25. See E. M. W. Tillyard, *Shakespeare's History Plays* (Middlesex, 1962), pp. 54–70, 98–126, 319–322. An essential work is T. W. Baldwin, *William Shakespere's Small Latine & Lesse Greeke* (Urbana, 1944); see II, 562–577.
26. See Harley Granville Barker, "From *Henry V* to *Hamlet*," in *Aspects of Shakespeare: Being British Academy Lectures* (Oxford, 1930), pp. 49–83.
27. George Pierce Baker, *The Development of Shakespeare as a Dramatist* (New York, 1916), pp. 178–180.
28. See R. H. Jones, *The Royal Policy of Richard II* (Oxford, 1968), p. 113.
29. *Henry V*; see Act IV, scene 1, lines 247–300.
30. Quoted in Tillyard, *op. cit.*, p. 100.
31. See John Bale, *King Johan*, ed. J. H. P. Palford, (London, 1931). Also Jesse W. Harris, *John Bale: A Study in the Minor Literature of the Reformation* (Urbana, 1940).
32. *As You Like It*, Act III, scene 2, lines 326–327.
33. This view differs from the sharp distinction between histories and tragedies advocated by Lily B. Campbell, *Shakespeare's Histories, Mirrors of Elizabethan Policy* (San Marino, 1958), pp. 16–17; cf. pp. 306–307.
34. See Frances W. Yates, *The Art of Memory* (London, 1966), esp. pp. 241–242, 277 ff., 342–367, and 362–364.
35. See Richard S. Sylvester, "Cavendish's *Life of Wolsey*: The Artistry of a Tudor Biographer," *Studies in Philology*, LVII (1960), 44–71, esp. 58–63 on history and tragedy.
36. See James Emerson Phillips, *Images of a Queen* (Berkeley, 1964), esp. pp. 6–7, 201–203.
37. Cf. *John Knox's History of the Reformation in Scotland*, ed. William Croft Dickinson (New York, 1950), II, 70. God punished Scotland because the queen was wicked, etc.
38. See Hardin Craig, *The Enchanted Glass* (Oxford, 1936). Also E. M. W. Tillyard, *The Elizabethan World Picture* (London, 1950), *passim*.
39. See Edwin Haviland Miller, *The Professional Writer in Elizabethan England* (Cambridge, Mass., 1959), pp. 27 ff.

40. See also R. C. Prasad, *Early English Travellers in India: A Study in Travel Literature of the Elizabethan and Jacobean Periods* (Delhi, 1965).

41. See Margaret T. Hodgen, *Early Anthropology in the Sixteenth and Seventeenth Centuries* (Philadelphia, 1964), esp. pp. 7–10, 386–430. On Sebastian Münster see Gerald Strauss, "A Sixteenth Century Encyclopedia: Sebastian Münster's *Cosmography* and Its Editions," in Carter, *op. cit.*, pp. 145–163.

42. See J. H. M. Salmon, *The French Religious Wars in English Political Thought* (Oxford, 1959), esp. pp. 15 ff.

43. Sir Walter Ralegh, *The History of the World*, ed. Oldys (London, 1736), Vol. I, Bk. II, Chap. 21, Sect. vi, p. 306.

44. Stephen Toulmin and June Goodfield, *The Discovery of Time* (London, 1965), p. 15. The important article by G. Wylie Sypher, "Similarities Between the Scientific and the Historical Revolution at the End of the Renaissance," *Journal of the History of Ideas*, XXVI, No. 3 (1965), 353–368, deals with Bacon and La Popelinière but suggests broader problems. See also Franklin L. Baumer, "Intellectual History and Its Problems," *Journal of Modern History*, XXI (September 1949), 191–203, esp. 196. The problem of what constitutes an adequate method for intellectual history is discussed by Rush Welter, "The History of Ideas in America: An Essay in Redefinition," *Journal of American History*, LI, No. 4 (March 1965), 599–614.

45. The classical background of historical thought is discussed by George H. Nadel, "Philosophy of History before Historicism," *History and Theory*, III, No. 3 (1964), 291–315. See also Beatrice Reynolds, "Shifting Currents in Historical Criticism," *Journal of the History of Ideas*, XIV (October 1953), 471–492; George Wylie Sypher, "La Popelinière's *Histoire de France*: A Case of Historical Objectivity and Religious Censorship," *Journal of the History of Ideas*, XXIV (January–March 1963), 41–54; and Julian H. Franklin, *Jean Bodin and the 16th Century Revolution in the Methodology of Law and History* (New York, 1963), esp. pp. 72 ff.

46. Myron P. Gilmore, "The Renaissance Conception of the Lessons of History," in *Facets of the Renaissance*, ed. William H. Werkmeister (New York, 1959), p. 73. An important article which opens up new lines of interpretation and suggests that history developed in a "progressivist" context is that by Arthur B. Ferguson, "Circumstances and the Sense of History in Tudor England: The Coming of the Historical Revolution," *Medieval and Renaissance Studies* (1968), pp. 170–205.

47. C. S. Lewis, *English Literature in the Sixteenth Century* (Oxford, 1954), p. 61; also T. D. Kendrick, *British Antiquity* (London, 1950); Helen C. White, *Tudor Books of Saints and Martyrs* (Madison, 1963), esp. the chapter on Foxe. On early Tudor historiography see J. R. Trimble, "Early Tudor Historiography 1485–1548," *Journal of the History of Ideas*, II (1950), 30–41.

48. See S. E. Lehmberg (ed.), *Sir Thomas Elyot, The Book Named the Governor*, (New York and London, 1962), pp. 228–229.

49. Baumer, *op. cit.*, p. 195.

50. Cf. J. G. A. Pocock, *The Ancient Constitution and the Feudal Law* (Cambridge, 1957), p. 20; also Christopher Hill, *Intellectual Origins of the English Revolution* (Oxford, 1965), Chap. 5; Holdsworth's volumes on the history of English law contain many examples (see, e.g., V, 480); and see also Conyers Read (ed.), *William Lambarde and Local Government* (Ithaca, 1962), for examples of the casual uses of history by a well-known commentator on the work of justices of the peace. See also R. J. Schoek, "Early Anglo-Saxon Studies and Legal Scholarship in the Renaissance," *Studies in the Renaissance*, V (1958).

51. See *The Reports of Sir Edward Coke, Knt., in English, in Thirteen Parts Complete,* rev. and trans. George Wilson (London, 1777), Vol. II, Report III, Preface, pp. xxi–xxii. In Coke's text this is not quite so pointed as it is in Brady, who took Coke to task. See Robert Brady, *Complete History of England* (London, 1685), I, 180–181; also 175 ff.

52. Brady, *op. cit.,* p. 180.

53. See William S. Holdsworth, *A History of English Law* (London, 1922–1926), V, 478–480, on Coke as a "historical lawyer."

54. For an illuminating discussion of Coke's ideas about law and reason, see Hill, *op. cit.,* Chap. 5. The passage was quoted by Brady, *op. cit.,* p. 180.

55. From the "Remonstrance against Tonnage and Poundage," printed in Samuel Rawson Gardiner (ed.), *The Constitutional Documents of the Puritan Revolution 1625–1660* (3rd ed.; Oxford, 1962), p. 71.

56. Hill, *op. cit.,* p. 258. There was a very widespread use of historical argument by legal writers. Holdsworth discusses many of the better known examples, and it should be emphasized that civil lawyers were, if anything, more history-minded than common lawyers. See Arthur B. Ferguson, "The Tudor Commonweal and the Sense of Change," *Journal of British Studies,* III, No. 1 (November 1963), 11–35, esp. 21.

57. B. G. G. Wormald, "The Historiography of the English Reformation," in *Historical Studies,* ed. T. Desmond Williams (London, 1958), p. 50.

58. The most recent full-length study of Foxe and his influence on English historiography is William Haller, *The Elect Nation: The Meaning and Relevance of Foxe's Book of Martyrs* (New York, 1964). Essential background is also provided in Margaret Aston, "Lollardry and the Reformation: Survival or Revival?" *History,* XLIX, No. 166 (June 1964), 149–170.

59. British Museum, Hargrave MS 311, fol. 80 v. This is a translation of parts of Sander's *De Origine ac Progressu Schismatis Anglicani.* See White, *op. cit.,* Chap. 7. Glanmor Williams, "Some Protestant Views of Early British Church History," *History,* XXXVIII, 219–233, contains valuable information on Protestant views. The fullest account of church historical controversy is still Pontien Polman, *L'Elément Historique dans la Controverse Religieuse du XVIe Siècle* (Gembloux, 1932), which, despite its theological commitment to Roman Catholicism, is useful as a guide to both Protestant and Catholic positions.

60. Haller, *op. cit.,* p. 73; see also pp. 57, 59, 75, 77, 95, 108, 120, 130, 132 ff., 138, and Chap. 5.

61. *Ibid.,* pp. 130–131.

62. Aston, *op. cit.,* p. 154.

63. *Ibid.,* p. 165. A. G. Dickens, *The English Reformation* (London, 1964), pp. 186 ff., esp. 187, points out that we cannot understand the doctrinal changes introduced by Cranmer if we ignore "the massive evidence concerning his independent study of the early Fathers and of later theologians."

64. W. H. Greenleaf, *Order, Empiricism, and Politics: Two Traditions of English Political Thought 1500–1700* (Oxford, 1964), provides a clear analysis of two quite different political traditions, both of which made use of historical facts and arguments. Latin historiography is discussed by Beatrice R. Reynolds, "Latin Historiography: A Survey 1400–1600," *Studies in the Renaissance,* II (1955), 7–66, esp. 58; the most evident change in historiography, as in other fields, especially after about 1550, was the increase of secularism: see Charles L. Kingsford, *English Historical Literature in the Fifteenth Century* (Oxford, 1931), pp. 253–274, esp. p. 266 on Stow. Cf. V. H. Galbraith, *Historical Research in Medieval England* (London, 1951), pp. 18, 29. See Mark H. Curtis, *Oxford and Cambridge in Transition, 1558–1642* (Oxford, 1959), p. 123.

65. See Thomas Hearne, *A Collection of Curious Discourses* (London, 1771), I, 289. Camden's comments on the Brute legend are discussed by Kendrick, *op. cit.*, pp. 105–109.

66. Galbraith, *op. cit.*, p. 12. For more detailed discussion of the Society of Antiquaries, and of the public records and libraries (and for more complete bibliographical references), see F. Smith Fussner, *The Historical Revolution* (London, 1962), Chaps. 3, 4, 5.

67. Quoted by Francis R. Johnson and Sanford V. Larkey, "Thomas Digges, the Copernican System, and the Idea of the Infinity of the Universe in 1576," *Huntington Library Bulletin*, No. 5 (April 1934), p. 111.

68. See Thomas S. Kuhn, *The Copernican Revolution: Planetary Astronomy in the Development of Western Thought* (New York, 1959), pp. 78–184; cf. I. Bernard Cohen, *The Birth of a New Physics* (New York, 1960).

69. Cf. Thomas Kuhn, *The Structure of Scientific Revolutions* (Chicago, 1962), pp. 16–17. Kuhn reserves the term "paradigm" for science (p. 15) and notes that ad hoc explanations were common in many scientific fields; he also argues that even today the social sciences are in a pre-paradigmatic stage (p. 159).

70. It might be argued that "antiquity" constituted a similar paradigm: cf. Richard Foster Jones, *Ancients and Moderns: A Study of the Background of the Battle of the Books* (St. Louis, 1936), pp. 10, 23, and *passim*. The importance of ancient usage may be studied in Sir Simonds D'Ewes, *The Journals of All the Parliaments during the Reign of Queen Elizabeth* (London, 1682). "Paradigmatic" explanations were rare in history, but the analogy with scientific paradigms appears to be illuminating.

71. William Lambarde, *Archeion: or A Discourse upon the High Courts of Justice in England*, ed. Charles H. McIlwain and Paul L. Ward (Cambridge, Mass., 1957), p. 133. On the doctrine of custom, see Pocock, *op. cit.*, Chap. 2; see also Conyers Read (ed.), *William Lambarde and Local Government* (Ithaca, 1962), pp. 103, 177, and *passim*. According to Coke, "Prescription is a title taking his substance of use and time allowed by the law . . ." See Sir Edward Coke, *The First Part of the Institutes . . . or A Commentary on Littleton* (London, 1639), p. 113, Sect. 170.

72. On Lambarde's revisions see *op. cit.*, pp. 153–176, *passim*. The development of the theory of feudalism by Spelman and others is discussed by Pocock, *op. cit.*

73. See Sir Robert Filmer, *Patriarchia*, ed. Peter Laslett (Oxford, 1949), pp. 106–107. Cf. Pocock, *op. cit.*, *passim*.

74. Only a very rash man would maintain that such a generalization fits *all* the known facts. The point is that it serves as a hypothesis, or heuristic device, in terms of which useful comparisons can be made. There is a good deal of information on London science and medicine in Christopher Hill, *op. cit.*, Chap. 2. The importance of Vesalius, whose methods eventually won due recognition, should be considered in the wider context of borrowing or adaptation. See C. D. O'Malley, *Andreas Vesalius of Brussels 1514–1564* (Berkeley, 1964). Greenleaf suggests that the empiricism of the "Baconians" may have had roots in medieval neo-Aristotelianism (*op. cit.*, p. 154, and cf. p. 228). Paracelsus wrote that it behooves the historiographer "to be well versed also in the history of heaven; to compare supernal and nether histories together." See D. Kurze, "Prophecy and History," *Journal of the Warburg and Courtauld Institutes*, XXI (1958), 76. At Oxford the importance of Vesalius was, it seems, quickly recognized: see *Oxford College Libraries in 1566: Guide to an Exhibition* (Oxford, 1956), p. 9.

75. See Nadel, *op. cit.*, *passim*. Borrowing by scholars from one another has received a good deal of attention from intellectual historians, but more is at issue here than exchanging books, manuscripts, and references. As Panofsky has pointed

out, the Renaissance introduced "transmission belts" not only between the manual and intellectual spheres but also between different fields: "we can observe the formation of groups and friendships conducive to cross-fertilization between all kinds of people, including the much-maligned humanists; on the other hand, we can observe a combination of many interests in one and the same person." See Erwin Panofsky, "Artist, Scientist, Genius: Notes on the Renaissance-Dämmerung," in *The Renaissance* (New York, 1962), p. 138. Borrowing in the sense specified by Panofsky did not, of course, begin in the Renaissance, but it was accelerated by changes in technology, and especially by the spread of print. There are suggestive comments in Walter I. Trattner, "God and Expansion in Elizabethan England: John Dee, 1527–1583," *Journal of the History of Ideas*, XXV, No. 1 (1964), 17–34.

76. [William Camden], *Remaines of a Greater Worke Concerning Britaine* (London, 1605), pp. 12–13; cf. Greenleaf, *op. cit.*, p. 228, on Bacon.

77. Panofsky, *op. cit.*, p. 140.

78. See A. G. Dickens, *Lollards and Protestants in the Diocese of York, 1509–1558* (Oxford, 1959), p. 6. See also Kenneth Charlton, *Education in Renaissance England* (London, 1965).

79. Glanmor Williams, "The Achievements of William of Salesbury," *Denbighshire Historical Society, Transactions*, XIV (1965), 91.

80. Information on the better known figures, and on many who are obscure, may be found in the *Dictionary of National Biography*. Unless otherwise noted, information about individuals is based on the *D.N.B.* The Catholic writers were, except during Mary's reign, forced to use secret presses or to publish on the continent. For bibliographical and other information, see A. C. Southern, *Elizabethan Recusant Prose 1559–1582* (London, 1950); also cf. J. B. Code, *Queen Elizabeth and the Catholic Historians* (1934).

81. Cf. *Elizabeth of England . . . by John Clapham*, ed. Evelyn Plummer Read and Conyers Read (Philadelphia, 1951), Introduction; A. G. Dickens, *Cromwell and the Reformation* (London, 1959), pp. 39–40.

82. The quotation is from the *D.N.B.* article on Sir Thomas Smith. The best biography is Mary Dewar, *Sir Thomas Smith, A Tudor Intellectual in Office* (London, 1964). The *De Republica Anglorum*, ed. L. A. Alston (Cambridge, 1906), reprints the 1583 edition with additional material from later texts. Smith's appeal to history is significant: He was a civilian who often invoked comparative history. See *De Republica*, pp. 12, 19, 28, 68, 105, 114–116, 125–126, 135, 142–143, for examples.

83. Hill, *op. cit.*, Chap. 2, discusses the medical profession; and there is much information on the Royal College members in Sir George Clark, *History of the Royal College of Physicians and Surgeons* (Oxford, 1964).

84. See John Caius, *A Boke or Counseill against the Disease Called the Sweate*, ed. Archibald Malloch (reprinted [New York], 1937). There are references to Thucydides (fol. 8 v.), to the chronicles (fol. 9 v.), and to various historical instances of this or similar diseases. His history of Cambridge University was of little value.

85. Hill, *op. cit.*, p. 69.

86. *D.N.B.* under Hakluyt, Richard; also Irwin R. Blacker (ed.), *Hakluyt's Voyages* (New York, 1965), which contains useful selections, and a short Introduction stressing this point.

87. Cf. Christopher Hill, *Economic Problems of the Church* (Oxford, 1956), Chap. 9. The differences between lay and clerical intellectuals doubtless should not be overstressed, but it is surely significant that not only was divinity "no profession for the upper classes" (*ibid.*, p. 208) but that, "as a profession com-

pared with other professions, the church did not hold out good prospects to the worldly-wise" (*ibid.*, p. 215).

88. This is the statement in the *D.N.B.*; but cf. Cyprian Blagden, *The Stationers Company* (Cambridge, Mass., 1960), Chap. 1 and pp. 295–296.

89. Grafton's influence may be traced in the products of his printing business. It is worth noting that he printed Caius's book on *The Sweate* (1552); *Actes of Parliament* (1552 and 1553); Patten's *Diary of the Expedition into Scotland;* Hardyding's *Chronicle;* Hall's *Chronicle,* and other works of history, especially in the 1560s.

90. H. T. Buckle, *History of Civilization* (New York, 1910), I, 267. Although a great deal of work has been accomplished that illuminates the relationships between history and science, much still remains to be done. Controversy about the importance of humanism in the development of science is but one example of the broad problem of relating science to the humanities and history. Hajo Holborn, "History and the Study of the Classics," *Journal of the History of Ideas,* XIV (1953), stresses the importance of the study of the classics for the development of many kinds of intellectual endeavor (p. 35); Charles Singer, *A Short History of Scientific Ideas* (Oxford, 1959), argues that the sixteenth century marks a frontier in science (p. 187) but urges that ". . . both the medieval heritage of Greek science and the Renaissance heritage of Greek literature proved barren by themselves. It was not until the one fertilized the other that there was vital growth" (p. 193). Thomas S. Kuhn in *The Copernican Revolution,* suggests that the excessive bitterness evoked by the Copernican controversy was owing to the fact that Copernicanism was "indirectly involved in the larger religious battle between the Protestant and Catholic Churches" (*op. cit.,* p. 196). Perhaps the most notable contribution to the study of the relationships between science and scholarship during the Renaissance is George Sarton, *Appreciation of Ancient and Medieval Science during the Renaissance* (New York, 1961), in which Sarton observes that "The main evil of Renaissance science was its love of words . . ." (p. 95). What is most suggestive is that the late sixteenth century was a period of rapid advance in so many intellectual fields.

91. J. G. A. Pocock, "The Origins of the Study of the Past: A Comparative Study," *Comparative Studies in Society and History,* IV, No. 2 (1963), 212.

92. Cf. Edward Shils, "The Intellectuals and the Powers: Some Perspectives for Comparative Analysis," *Comparative Studies in Society and History,* I (1958–1959), 5–22, esp. 11. It is perhaps worth noting again that Protestant political, ecclesiastical, and economic thought tended to justify the origins of authority by appealing to history, largely because Protestant churches were not *institutionally* legitimized by tradition or history in the sense that the Roman Catholic Church was. This point emerges from C. H. George and K. George, *The Protestant Mind of the English Reformation* (Princeton, 1961).

93. See *The English Works of Thomas Hobbes,* ed. Sir William Molesworth (London, 1840), IV, 16.

94. James Ussher, *A Body of Divinitie, or the Svmme and Svbstance of Christian Religion* (7th ed.; London, 1677), p. 4. For attribution of this work, see James Ussher, *The Whole Works of the Most Reverend James Ussher, D.D.,* ed. Charles Richard Elvington (Dublin, 1847), 248–250.

95. Ussher, *A Body of Divinitie,* pp. 5, 7, 8, 9.

96. The evidence for this and the preceding statements may be found throughout the literature of controversy. The starting place for information and bibliography is R. F. Jones, *op. cit.* Lawrence Stone, *The Crisis of the Aristocracy*

(Oxford, 1965), pp. 23–27, discusses some of the problems of pedigree hunt-ing; and Powell Mills Dawley, *John Whitgift and the Reformation* (London, 1955), is informative on church attitudes in general. Hooker's argument in favor of bishops in *The Laws of Ecclesiastical Polity* (London, 1907) was based partly on "antiquity," a preoccupation which Foxe and others shared, even though the conclusions of different writers varied; in Parliament the Arthur Hall case in 1580 turned on the point that Hall was accused of having written a "false and slanderous" discourse against "the Antiquity and Authority of the Commons House . . . wherein he hath falsely sought . . . to impugne, de-face, blemish and diminish the Power, Antiquity and Authority of this House, and the interest that it hath always, and in all ages had . . ." See D'Ewes, *op. cit.*, p. 296, col. 2, p. 298, col. 1. Clearly it is necessary to distinguish different types of argument and to attempt to understand why the argument from antiquity was first abandoned in science.

97. Quoted by Brady, *op. cit.*, p. 180.
98. Ussher, *A Body of Divinitie*, pp. 10, 13, 14. See John Jewel, *An Apology for the Church of England*, ed. J. E. Booty (Ithaca, 1963), pp. 83–84. Ussher's work on church history in 1613, *Gravissimae Questionis de Christianarum Ec-clesiarum*, was thought of as a continuation of Jewel. See Ussher, *Works*, I, 34.
99. Geoffrey Ingle Soden, *Godfrey Goodman, Bishop of Gloucester 1583–1656* (London, 1953), p. 87.
100. John Strype, *Life and Acts of Mathew Parker* (London, 1821), II, 517–519.
101. From an "Act of the Privy Council on the Position of the Communion Table at St. Gregory's," November 1633, in Gardiner, *op. cit.*, p. 104.
102. See R. Koebner, "The Imperial Crown of This Realm: Henry VIII, Con-stantine the Great, and Polydore Vergil," *Bulletin of the Institute of His-torical Research*, XXVI (1953), 29–52, esp. 41–42. Cf. J. E. Neale, "Sir Nicholas Throckmorton's Advice to Queen Elizabeth on Her Accession to the Throne," *English Historical Review*, LXV (1950), 91–98, esp. 94. See *Stat-utes of the Realm* (reprinted [London], 1963), esp. e.g., 2 & 3 Edw. VI, c. 36 (IV, Part 1, 78); 7 Edw. VI, c. 12 (IV, Part 5, 177); 1 Eliz. c. 1, c. 3, c. 11, etc. (IV, Part 1, 350, 358, 372, etc.), for examples of historical argument.
103. G. R. Elton, "Parliamentary Drafts, 1529–1549," *Bulletin of the Institute of Historical Research*, XXV (1952), 117. Cf. Elton's "The Evolution of a Reformation Statute," *English Historical Review*, LXIV (1949), 174–197, esp. 196.
104. *Statutes of the Realm*, 2 & 3, Edw. VI, c. 1, 1548 (IV, Part 1, 37).
105. *Statutes of the Realm*, 1 Eliz., c. 1, 1558–1559 (IV, Part 1, 350–351); 1 Mary 1553 (Sess. 2), c. 1 (IV, Part 1, 200–201). Both acts appeal to historical ex-perience under Henry VIII. See also 1 and 2 Philip and Mary, c. 8 (IV, Part 1, 246–247); and 5 Eliz., c. 1 (IV, Part 1, 402–403).
106. See *State Papers Henry VIII* (London, 1830–1852), IX, Part V, No. 744, 230–231; and 243–246, 265. The text of the declaration was printed both in Grafton's *A Chronicle at Large* (London, 1569), pp. 482 ff., and in Hall's *Chronicle*.
107. Medieval distinctions here are not at issue. See Wolfart Pannenberg, "Her-meneutics and Universal History," in Robert W. Frank (ed.) and Gerhard Ebeling (assoc.), *History and Hermeneutic* (New York, 1967), p. 123. Also the essay by Friedrich Gogarten, "Theology and History," in *ibid.*, pp. 35–81, esp. 72 ff.
108. Pannenberg, *op. cit.*, p. 126. See also E. G. Rupp in *The Church's Use of the Bible*, ed. D. E. Ninehan (London, 1963), pp. 82, 73–87 *passim*. Also

The Cambridge History of the Bible, esp. Vol. II, *The West from the Reformation to the Present Day*, ed. S. L. Greenslade; and the forthcoming *History of the Bible in English*, part of the Cambridge series.

109. See Alfred W. Pollard, *Records of the English Bible* (London, 1911), p. 283.
110. J. A. Froude, *The Reign of Henry VIII* (London, 1909), II, 229.
111. See E. G. Rupp, *Studies in the Making of the English Protestant Tradition* (Cambridge, 1966), p. 88 and *passim*.
112. Cf. John Donne: "We look upon God, in History, in matter of fact, upon things done, and set before our eyes; and so that Majesty, and that holy amazement, is more to us than ever it was to any other religion." Quoted by C. A. Patrides as Frontispiece to *The Phoenix and the Ladder* (Berkeley, 1964).
113. B. Cohen, "The Pasts of an Indian Village," *Comparative Studies in Society and History*, III (1960–1961), 249.
114. It is also true that the emergence of the early modern nation-state in France and England contributed to this development, and especially led to the political use of historical argument. By the beginning of the sixteenth century "What made the difference was at any rate in part the conviction in high places that apologists in the neo-Latin of the humanists, writing the history of a dynasty in a modern and convincing way, were as indispensable as neo-Latin writing diplomats and secretaries." See Denys Hay, "History and Historians in France and England," *Bulletin of the Institute of Historical Research*, XXXV (1962), 126. Cf. Greenleaf, *op. cit.*, pp. 114 ff.
115. This was not a complete text. See the Camden Society vols. for 1844 and 1846. These cover books I–VIII, and XXIII–XXV.
116. See Denys Hay, *Polydore Vergil, Renaissance Historian and Man of Letters* (Oxford, 1952), pp. 79–128.
117. *Polydore Vergil's English History*, Vol. I, Containing the First Eight Books, ed. Sir Henry Ellis (London, 1846), p. 26; also pp. 29–31, 107.
118. *Ibid.*, p. 32.
119. *Ibid.*, p. 33.
120. Cf. F. J. Levy, *Tudor Historical Thought* (San Marino, 1967), p. 58.
121. See Margaret T. Hodgen, "Ethnology in 1500: Polydore Vergil's Collection of Customs," *Isis*, LVII, No. 189, 315–324. This article rates Vergil's book very highly as an example of early anthropological thought.
122. *Polydore Vergil's English History*, ed. Ellis, p. 52.
123. See *The Anglica Historia of Polydore Vergil*, A.D. 1485–1537, ed. and trans. Denys Hay (Camden ser., Vol. LXXIV; London, 1950), pp. 121, 137, 163.
124. Sir Walter Ralegh, *op. cit.*, I, Preface, xxxi.
125. *The Anglica Historia of Polydore Vergil*, ed. Hay, p. 231; see also pp. 235, 286–287, 317, and *passim*.
126. See *ibid.*, *passim*.
127. *Ibid.*, p. xxxvii.
128. See Paul Murray Kendall, *Richard III, the Great Debate* (New York, 1965), pp. 496–514, for a discussion of the historiographical influence of More.
129. See *Grafton's Chronicle, or A Chronicle at Large, and Meere History of the Affayres of Englande and Kinges of the Same Deduced from the Creation of the Worlde, vnto the First Habitation of Thys Islande . . . A.D. 1569.* The edition of 1809 has been used; see pp. xiii–xvi, "Thomas N. to the Reader."
130. See Richard S. Sylvester, *The History of King Richard III*, Vol. II of *The Complete Works of St. Thomas More* (New Haven, 1963), pp. xcvii–xcviii.
131. *Ibid.*, p. 81.

132. *Ibid.*, p. 83; see also p. 86.
133. *Ibid.*, p. 86.
134. The debate on Richard III continues, but few historians are prepared to white-wash Richard. Walpole's "Historic Doubts" are reprinted in Paul Murray Kendall (ed.), *Richard III, the Great Debate* (New York, 1965).
135. See Lehmberg, *op. cit.*, p. vii.
136. *Ibid.*, p. 14.
137. *Ibid.*, p. 15.
138. *Ibid.*, pp. 34–37.
139. *Ibid.*, pp. 38–39.
140. *Ibid.*, pp. 40–51.
141. *Ibid.*, pp. 228–229.
142. *Ibid.*, p. 228; see also pp. 228–231. Roger Ascham's theory of history writing was in some ways similar to Elyot's. See Walter F. Staton, Jr., "Roger Ascham's Theory of History Writing," *Studies in Philology*, LVI, No. 1 (1959), 123–137.
143. See *Grafton's Chronicle*, 1569, p. 1.
144. See Fussner, *op. cit.*, Chap. 11, *passim*.
145. C. L. Kingsford, *English Historical Literature in the Fifteenth Century* (Oxford, 1913), p. 266.
146. *Ibid.*, p. 269.
147. *Ibid.*, p. 271.
148. *Ibid.*
149. Holinshed's *Chronicles*, 1587 edition [*The First and Second Volumes of Chronicles . . . First Collected and published by Raphaell Holinshed, William Harrison and others . . .*], hereafter referred to as Holinshed, I & II, or Holinshed III for the third volume. Quote from Holinshed I & II, "Harrison's Description," Epistle.
150. Holinshed I & II, "Description," p. 28, col. 1, sig. Div.
151. *Hamlet*, Act I, scene 1, lines 121–123.
152. Holinshed I & II, "Historie of England," p. 202, col. 1.
153. *Ibid.*, "To the Readers."
154. *Ibid.*, "To the Right Worthie and honourable gentleman Sir Walter Raleigh knight . . ." sig. Aii, r.
155. *Ibid.*, sig. Aii, v.
156. *Ibid.*, sig. Aii, v.
157. *Ibid.*, sig. Aiii, v.
158. Holinshed, III, 1268, sig. Ggggggiii, r. The Greek type face for "rho" (ρ) was different in the sixteenth century and has not been duplicated.
159. *Ibid.*, sig. Aiii, r to Aiii, v. "The Preface to the Reader."
160. *Ibid.*, sig. Aiii, v.
161. *Ibid.*, sig. Dooooooii, r. col. 1.
162. The Vespasiano *Memoirs* have been reprinted in the translation of William George and Emily Waters, with an Introduction by Myron Gilmore, in *Renaissance Princes, Popes and Prelates: The Vespasiano Memoirs* (New York, 1963).
163. Donald A. Stauffer maintained in his now dated work, *English Biography before 1700* (Cambridge, Mass., 1930), pp. 45–46, that John Hayward was the first to distinguish between history and biography in *The Life and Raigne of King Henrie the IIII* (1599). See also John A. Garraty, *The Nature of Biography* (New York, 1957).
164. *The Lives of the Noble Grecians and Romans Compared Together by That*

Grave, Learned Philosopher and Historiographer Plutarch . . . Translated out of the Greek into French by James Amyot and out of French into English by Thomas North (New York, 1941), I, xlv–xlvi. On the basic distinction see A. H. Burford, "History and Biography: The Renaissance Distinction," in *A Tribute to G. C. Taylor* (Chapel Hill, 1952).

165. See Maitland's essays in the *British Magazine* for 1837 and in "Notes on the Contributions of the Reverend George Townsend . . . to a New Edition of Foxe's Martyrology" (London, 1841–1842). The Cattley text remains the one most likely to be consulted in libraries.

166. Mozley was less disposed than Haller to praise Foxe as a historian, but recent scholarship has tended to vindicate many of Foxe's facts.

167. John Foxe, *The Acts and Monuments of John Foxe* (New York, 1965; a reprint of the Cattley-Townsend text), I, xvii, from Foxe's Preface "To the True and Faithful Congregation of Christ's Universal Church." See also I, xviii.

168. *Ibid.*, p. xix.

169. *Ibid.*, p. xx; see also IV, 250–253.

170. See *ibid.*, I, 87 ff.

171. This refers, of course, only to the 1563 and later editions. See *ibid.*, p. xxv, "The Utility of This Story."

172. *Ibid.*, p. xxvi; cf. pp. 88 ff.

173. Haller, *op. cit.*, p. 221.

174. See Foxe, *Acts and Monuments*, IV, 252–253; also III, 718–722.

175. See *ibid.*, I, xxxv. Also J. F. Mozley, *John Foxe and His Book* (New York, 1940), pp. 86–87.

176. Foxe, *Acts and Monuments*, VI, 658.

177. *Ibid.*, I, xxvii.

178. *Ibid.*, V, 397.

179. *Ibid.*, p. 401.

180. Haller, *op. cit.*, p. 132.

181. Foxe, *Acts and Monuments*, I, xxxvi.

182. See Jewel, *op. cit.*, p. xxxix.

183. *Ibid.*, p. xliii.

184. See *Correspondence of Matthew Parker*, ed. John Bruce (Cambridge, 1853), pp. 161, 219–220.

185. Jewel, *op. cit.*, p. 18.

186. *Ibid.*, p. 93.

187. There is a long, biased but useful introduction in Nicholas Sander, *The Rise and Growth of the Anglican Schism*, trans. and ed. David Lewis (London, 1877).

188. Sander, *op. cit.*, Preface, p. cxlvii.

189. *Ibid.*, p. 154.

190. *Ibid.*, p. 162

191. *Ibid.*, p. 221.

192. *Ibid.*, p. 233; see also pp. 334–335.

193. *John Knox's History of the Reformation in Scotland*, ed. William Croft Dickinson (New York, 1950), II, 3, "Prefatio."

194. *Ibid.*, II, 23; 4–5, and *passim*.

195. On this general topic see D. P. Walker, *The Decline of Hell* (Chicago, 1964).

196. See *The Execution of Justice in England by William Cecil*, [and] *A True, Sincere, and Modest Defense of English Catholics by William Allen*, ed. Robert M. Kingdon (Ithaca, 1965), p. 19; see also p. 38. The Introduction

is also valuable. Burghley was much concerned with Sander's history, as was Archbishop Parker. See *Correspondence of Matthew Parker*, pp. 409–413, 430–431.

197. Technically Cecil's pamphlet was published in January 1583—i.e., 1584 new style.

198. Kingdon, *op. cit.* Introduction, pp. xiii–xxxvii, *passim*.

199. *Ibid.*, p. 26.

200. *Ibid.*, p. 180

201. For these earlier controversies see esp. William Pierce, *An Historical Introduction to the Marprelate Tracts* (London, 1908), and two books by Donald J. McGinn, *The Admonition Controversy* (New Brunswick, 1947), and *John Penry and the Marprelate Controversy* (New Brunswick, 1966). V. J. K. Brook, *Whitgift and the English Church* (London, 1957), and Powell Mills Dawley, *op. cit.*, are valuable.

202. See Peter Munz, *The Place of Hooker in the History of Thought* (London, 1952), pp. 195–197 and *passim*. Cf. Fritz Levy, *Tudor Historical Thought* (San Marino, 1967), pp. 112–113.

203. Cf. Munz, *op. cit.*, pp. 196–197 for the argument about "induction." Munz does not elaborate on the "inductive" argument, but there is no doubt that Hooker is nonhistorical in most of the passages cited (Book I, Sect. VIII, par. 1–11).

204. Hooker, *op. cit.*, I, 425; also 331, 365, and *passim*.

205. See Munz, *op. cit.*, pp. 8, 14.

206. Hooker, *op. cit.*, I, 362.

207. *Ibid.*, p. 332.

208. *Ibid.*, pp. 256–268.

209. *Ibid.*, p. 269.

210. *Ibid.*, p. 214; see also G. G. Coulton, *Medieval Panorama* (New York, 1947), pp. 681–704, esp. 695–696.

211. Hooker, *op. cit.*, II, 7; cf. 486–490.

212. *Ibid.*, p. 471.

213. See "Two London Chronicles from the Collections of John Stow," ed. C. L. Kingsford, *Camden Miscellany* (3rd ser., Vol. XVIII; London, 1910).

214. *Ibid.*, pp. 45–47.

215. I have quoted from "William Lambarde's *A Perambulation of Kent*," ed. Frederick P. Hard (unpublished Ph.D. thesis, Indiana University, 1966). This contains the edition of 1596, with variant readings, and a valuable Introduction. This text, edited by Hard, will be forthcoming in the Folger Shakespeare Series. The quotation is from sig. A3r.

216. Lambarde, *Perambulation* (1596), sig. G5v.

217. *Ibid.*, sig. H3r.

218. See Robin Flower, "Laurence Nowell and the Discovery of England in Tudor Times," *Proceedings of the British Academy*, XXI (1935), 47–73, for the discovery theme; Fritz J. Levy, in "The Making of Camden's *Britannia*," *Bibliothèque D'Humanisme et Renaissance*, XXVI (Genève, 1964), 70–97, gives a full account of Camden's circle of friends and of the influences on Camden. G. E. Fussell, *The Exploration of England* (London, 1935), gives a select bibliography of works on travel and topography beginning in 1580—useful for later collections and books on topography.

219. See William Camden, *Britannia or a Chorographical Description of the Flourishing Kingdoms of England, Scotland, and Ireland*, trans. Richard Gough (London, 1789), Vol. I, "Mr. Camden's Preface to the Reader," sig. ar.

220. See Levy, *Tudor Historical Thought*, 152–153, and Chap. 4 *passim*; also his article, "The Making of Camden's *Britannia*"; also Gough's "Life" in his edition of *Britannia*.
221. Camden, *Britannia*, Vol. I, "Mr. Camden's Preface." Camden did make some surprising errors, one of the more interesting being his derivation of the English name of Sweinsey (i.e., Swansea in Glamorganshire) "so called by the English from the porpoises" (II, 495).
222. *Ibid.*, I, "Britain," iii.
223. *Ibid.*, p. vi; cf. II, 478, Camden's comment on Geoffrey of Monmouth.
224. *Ibid.*, I, "Britain," vii; also, on the name of Britain, xviii.
225. See, for example, *ibid.*, pp. xi–xii, xviii, and all three volumes, *passim*.
226. On Stow, see Fussner, *op. cit.*, Chap. 8.
227. Cf. A. D. Momigliano, *Studies in Historiography* (London, 1966), pp. 1–9.
228. See Richard Hakluyt, *The Principal Navigations, Voyages, Traffiques & Discoveries of the English Nation* (reprinted New York, 1965), I, xxi, from "The Epistle Dedicatorie in the First Volume of the Second Edition, 1598."
229. Hakluyt referred to "This historie" in his "Preface to the Reader" in the first edition. Irwin R. Blacker, in his edition of *Hakluyt's Voyages* (New York, 1965), pp. 2–3, makes the point about economic history.
230. Hakluyt, *op. cit.*, I, xxxix–xl.
231. John Selden, *Table Talk*, ed. S. W. Singer (London, 1856), p. 138.

Acknowledgments

THE AUTHOR WISHES to thank the following publishers and individuals for permission to reprint from their works. Aldine Publishing Co. and the University of Edinburgh Press, H. G. Richardson and G. O. Sayles, *The Governance of Medieval England from the Conquest to Magna Carta*; George Allen & Unwin Ltd., W. K. Jordan, *Philanthropy in England 1480–1660*; Edward Arnold Ltd., D. V. Glass and D. E. C. Eversley, eds., *Population in History: Essays in Historical Demography*; Associated Book Publishers Ltd. and Methuen & Co., Ltd., J. W. Allen, *A History of Political Thought in the Sixteenth Century* and G. R. Elton, *England under the Tudors*; Barnes & Noble, Inc., C. P. Gooch, *History and Historians in the Nineteenth Century*; Basic Books, Inc., Robert A. Nisbet, *The Sociological Tradition* and E. A. Wrigley, ed., *An Introduction to English Historical Demography: From the Sixteenth to the Nineteenth Century*; G. Bell & Sons, Ltd., H. Butterfield, *The Whig Interpretation of History*; A. C. Black, Ltd. and Barnes & Noble, Inc., E. Lipson, *Economic History of England*; the Bodley Head, B. G. G. Wormald, "The Historiography of the English Reformation," in T. Desmond Williams, ed., *Historical Studies*; Cambridge University Press, C. R. Cheney, *The Records of Medieval England, An Inaugural Lecture*; G. R. Elton, *The Tudor Constitution* and *The Tudor Revolution in Government*; David Knowles, *The Religious Orders in England*; Elizabeth Lamond, ed., *A Discourse of the Common Weal of This Realm of England* by Sir Thomas Smith; G. R. Potter, ed., *New Cambridge Modern History*, Vol. I, Sir George Clark, "General Introduction"; Joan Simon, *Education and Society in Tudor England*; and Joan Thirsk, ed., *The Agrarian History of England and Wales*, Vol. IV, *1500–1640*; Jonathan Cape Ltd., J. E. Neale, *Elizabeth I and Her Parliaments 1559–1581*, *Elizabeth I and Her Parliaments 1584–1601*, and *Essays in Elizabethan History*; Collins Publishers, Marie Boas, *The Scientific Renaissance*; Columbia University Press, W. Haller, *The Rise of Puritanism*; J. M. Dent & Sons Ltd., S. E. Lehmberg, ed., *The Governor* by Sir Thomas Elyot; Cornell University Press, John Jewel, *An Apology for the Church of England* (© 1963); C. H. McIlwain, *Constitutionalism: Ancient and Modern* (© 1947); and John U. Nef, *Industry and Government in France and England, 1540–1640*; Doubleday & Co., Reinhard Bendix, *Max Weber, An Intellectual Portrait*; Dover Publications, Andrew D. White, *A History of the Warfare of Science with Technology*; Duke University Press, Arthur B. Ferguson, *The Articulate Citizen and the English Renaissance*; E. P. Dutton & Co., S. E. Lehmberg, ed., *The Governor* by Sir Thomas Elyot, Everyman's Library; Encounter, H. R. Trevor-Roper, "Witches and Witchcraft"; William Haller, *Foxe's Book of Martyrs and the Elect Nation*; Hamish Hamilton Ltd., L. B. Namier, *Avenues of History*; Harcourt, Brace & World, Inc., J. M. Keynes, *A Treatise on Money*; Harper & Row, P. O. Kristeller, *Renaissance Thought* (© 1961) and G. H. Nadel, ed., *Studies in the Philosophy of History* (© 1965); Harvard University Press, E. C. Furber, *Changing Views of British History*; Earl Hamilton, *American Treasure and the Price Revolution in Spain*; Eugene Rice, Jr., *The Renaissance Idea of Wisdom*; and Michael Walzer, *The Revolution of the Saints*; Heinemann Educational Books Ltd., Lord Ernle, *English Farming Past and Present*; Holt, Rinehart and Winston, Inc., Denys Hays, ed., *The Renaissance Debate*; Houghton Mifflin Company, Wallace K. Ferguson, *The Renaissance in Historical Thought*; Joel Hurstfield, *The Queen's Wards: Wardship and Marriage under Elizabeth I*;

Hutchinson Publishing Group Ltd., Arthur Koestler, *The Sleepwalkers* and Stephen Toulmin and June Goodfield, *The Discovery of Time*; The John Hopkins Press, Leo Spitzer, *Classical and Christian Ideas of World Harmony*; Longmans Green and Co., Peter Burke, *The Renaissance*; J. H. Hexter, *Reappraisals in History*; A. F. Pollard, *The Evolution of Parliament* and *Henry VIII*; and Lawrence Stone, *Social Change and Revolution in England*; Lutterworth Press, Maurice Beresford, *The Lost Villages of England*; Manchester University Press, T. F. Tout, *Chapters in the Administrative History of Medieval England*; Oxford University Press, A. G. Dickens, *Lollards and Protestants in the Diocese of York 1509–1558*; Waldo Hilary Dunn, *James Anthony Froude, A Biography 1818–1856*; W. H. Greenleaf, *Order, Empiricism and Politics: Two Traditions of English Political Thought 1500–1700*; Christopher Hill, *Economic Problems of the Church* and *Intellectual Origins of the English Revolution*; F. M. Powicke, *The Reformation in England*; Lawrence Stone, *The Crisis of the Aristocracy 1558–1641*; Glanmor Williams, *Owen Glendower*; Penguin Books, R. H. Tawney, *Religion and the Rise of Capitalism*; Philosophical Library, William Croft Dickinson, ed., *John Knox's History of the Reformation in Scotland*; Prentice-Hall, Inc., Philip Rieff, "The Meaning of History and Religion in Freud's Thought," Bruce Mazlish, ed., *Psychoanalysis and History* (also *The Journal of Religion* and the University of Chicago Press); Princeton University Press, Hans Baron, *The Crisis of the Early Italian Renaissance: Civic Humanism and Republican Liberty in an Age of Classicism and Tyranny* (© 1966) and Charles H. and Catherine George, *The Protestant Mind of the English Reformation* (© 1961); G. P. Putnam's Sons, A. F. Pollard, *Thomas Cranmer and the English Reformation 1489–1556*; Random House, Alfred A. Knopf, Philippe Ariès, *Centuries of Childhood: A Social History of Family Life*, trans. by Robert Baldick; Routledge and Kegan Paul Ltd., Kenneth Charlton, *Education in Renaissance England* and John U. Nef, *The Rise of the British Coal Industry*; St. Martin's Press, Ronald Robinson and John Gallagher, *Africa and the Victorians*; Charles Scribner's, Max Weber, *The Protestant Ethic and the Spirit of Capitalism*, trans. by Talcott Parsons; Sheed & Ward Ltd., G. Constant, *The Reformation in England: The English Schism and Henry VIII 1509–1547*; Stanford University Press, John F. New, *Anglican and Puritan: The Basis of Their Opposition 1558–1640*; *The Times* for articles from *The Times Literary Supplement*; Frederick Ungar Publishing Co., Erich Fromm, *Marx's Concept of Man*; University of California Press, Patrick Collinson, *The Elizabethan Puritan Movement*; Peter Gay, *A Loss of Mastery: Puritan Historians in Colonial America*; and A. L. Kroeber and Clyde Kluckhohn, *Culture: A Critical Review of Concepts and Definitions*; University of Chicago Press, T. S. Kuhn, *The Structure of Scientific Revolutions*; Craig Thompson, trans., *Colloquies of Erasmus*; and Claude Lévi-Strauss, *The Savage Mind*; University of Michigan Press, Sylvia L. Thrupp, *The Merchant Class of Medieval London 1300–1500*; University of Southern California Press, William Werkmeister, ed., *Facets of the Renaissance*; University of Wisconsin Press, Marshall Clagett, *Critical Problems in the History of Science* and Tinsley Helton, ed., *The Renaissance: A Reconsideration of the Theories and Interpretations of the Middle Ages*; C. A. Watts & Co., T. B. Bottomore and M. Rubel, eds., *Karl Marx: Selected Writings*; Wiedenfeld & Nicolson, Arnaldo D. Momigliano, *Studies in Historiography* and J. H. Parry, *The Age of Reconnaissance*; Yale University Press, C. H. McIlwain, *The High Court of Parliament and Its Supremacy*; J. E. Neale, *The Elizabethan House of Commons*; and Richard S. Sylvester, *Complete Works of St. Thomas More*, Vol. 2, *The History of Richard III*.

Index

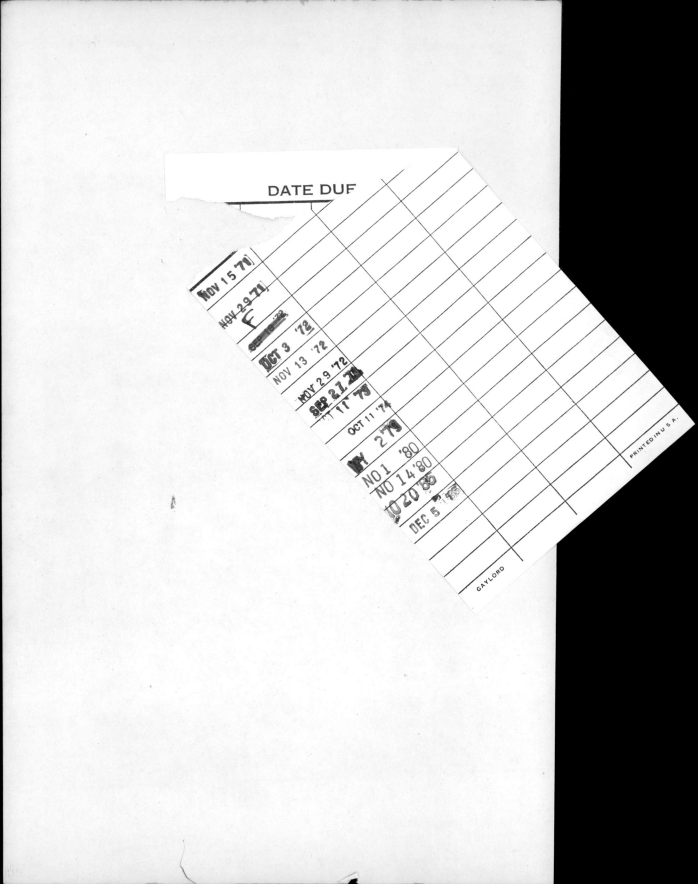

DATE DUE

NOV 15 70

NOV 29 71

F

OCT 3 '72

NOV 13 '72

NOV 29 '72

SEP 2 1 73

OCT 11 '74

NO 1 '80

NO 14 '80

DEC 5

PRINTED IN U.S.A.

GAYLORD